# Practical Spanish Grammar

Wiley Self-Teaching Guides teach practical skills from accounting to astronomy, management to mathematics. Look for them at your local bookstore.

## Languages

*French: A Self-Teaching Guide*, by Suzanne A. Hershfield

*German: A Self-Teaching Guide*, by Heimy Taylor

*Italian: A Self-Teaching Guide*, by Edoardo A. Lebano

*Advanced Spanish Grammar: A Self-Teaching Guide*, by Marcial Prado

## Business Skills

*Making Successful Presentations: A Self-Teaching Guide*, by Terry C. Smith

*Managing Assertively: A Self-Teaching Guide*, by Madelyn Burley-Allen

*Managing Behavior on the Job: A Self-Teaching Guide*, by Paul L. Brown

*Teleselling: A Self-Teaching Guide*, by James Porterfield

*Successful Time Management: A Self-Teaching Guide*, by Jack D. Ferner

## Science

*Astronomy: A Self-Teaching Guide*, by Dinah L. Moche

*Basic Physics: A Self-Teaching Guide*, by Karl F. Kuhn

*Chemistry: A Self-Teaching Guide*, by Clifford C. Houk and Richard Post

*Biology: A Self-Teaching Guide*, by Steven D. Garber

## Other Skills

*How Grammar Works: A Self-Teaching Guide*, by Patricia Osborn

*Listening: The Forgotten Skill, A Self-Teaching Guide*, by Madelyn Burley-Allen

*Quick Vocabulary Power: A Self-Teaching Guide*, by Jack S. Romine and Henry Ehrlich

*Study Skills: A Student's Guide for Survival, A Self-Teaching Guide*, by Robert A. Carman

# Practical Spanish Grammar

## A Self-Teaching Guide

### Third Edition

# Nelly Zamora-Breckenridge

JB JOSSEY-BASS™
A Wiley Brand

Published by John Wiley & Sons, Inc., Hoboken, New Jersey.
Published simultaneously in Canada.

The manufacturer's authorized representative according to the EU General Product Safety Regulation is Wiley-VCH GmbH, Boschstr. 12, 69469 Weinheim, Germany, e-mail: Product_Safety@wiley.com.

For general information on our other products and services or for technical support, please contact our Customer Care Department within the United States at (800) 762-2974, outside the United States at (317) 572-3993 or fax (317) 572-4002.

Wiley also publishes its books in a variety of electronic formats. Some content that appears in print may not be available in electronic formats. For more information about Wiley products, visit our web site at www.wiley.com.

*Library of Congress Cataloging-in-Publication Data*

Names: Zamora-Breckenridge, Nelly, author.
Title: Practical Spanish grammar : a self-teaching guide / Nelly
  Zamora-Breckenridge.
Description: Third edition. | Hoboken, New Jersey : John Wiley & Sons,
  2025. | Text in English and Spanish.
Identifiers: LCCN 2025021932 (print) | LCCN 2025021933 (ebook) | ISBN
  9781394280315 (paperback) | ISBN 9781394280339 (adobe pdf) | ISBN
  9781394280322 (epub)
Subjects: LCSH: Spanish language—Self-instruction. | Spanish
  language—Textbooks for foreign speakers—English. | Spanish
  language—Grammar. | Spanish language—Grammar—Problems, exercises,
  etc. | LCGFT: Textbooks.
Classification: LCC PC4112.5 .Z36 2025 (print) | LCC PC4112.5 (ebook) |
  DDC 468.2/421—dc23/eng/20250614
LC record available at https://lccn.loc.gov/2025021932
LC ebook record available at https://lccn.loc.gov/2025021933

Cover design: Paul McCarthy

# Contents

# Preface

It's been almost three decades since the second edition of *Practical Spanish Grammar: A Self-Teaching Guide* was published, the first two editions of which were written by the late Dr. Marcial Prado, Professor Emeritus at California State University, Fullerton. When the Wiley publishing group approached me to write the third edition of this grammar text, I was grateful to take on the task. In this third edition, significant changes and revisions have been made, incorporating entirely new dialogues with current topics and adding practical vocabulary to each chapter to provide a more relevant and effective learning experience for today's students. New examples have also been included, in line with the topics of each unit. It is important to mention that the original structure of the book, as developed by Professor Prado in the first two editions, has been respected and followed.

As this book is geared toward learning Spanish grammar, the goal of this third edition is to provide readers and students with a basic understanding of the most prevalent grammatical structures in Spanish through ongoing review and practice with supplementary exercises and activities in each lesson.

*Practical Spanish Grammar: A Self-Teaching Guide,* third edition aims to teach the essentials of the Spanish language at beginner level in a practical and structured way. This text is designed for your use as a self-teaching guide, and it allows you to progress at your own pace as you practice and master the points covered in each lesson. This new edition also includes new examples that reflect the advances and changes in technology and new forms of communication in a global society to ensure students are prepared for the demands of an ever-changing job market. We hope this third edition will help you explore the fascinating world of Spanish grammar as a multicultural language with greater enthusiasm and confidence.

This book uses a linguistic approach in treating grammatical structures. Concise and down-to-earth explanations are followed by completion exercises for testing and reinforcing comprehension of the grammar. As always, new words have to be learned in each lesson. To help you in this, a variety of exercises reinforces your learning and expands your vocabulary. Furthermore, the new words are used in the grammar sections, both in the examples and in the exercises.

## Features Contained in the 15 Lessons

■ A list of *palabras nuevas* (*new words*) with supplementary exercises for their gradual incorporation into learning Spanish. Also included in the list are terms that present some difficulty because they are considered false cognates or because they are English terms used incorrectly as Spanish words. In addition to the vocabulary, some frequently used expressions in Spanish have also been included.

■ Each chapter includes new dialogues with current topics and relevant vocabulary for today's students. Each dialogue is followed by exercises in comprehension and vocabulary.

■ Each chapter also has three grammar sections with respective supplementary exercises. Students will find answers to the exercises for self-correction at the end of Chapters 4, 8, 12, and 15.

■ There is a comprehensive vocabulary list for easy reference at the end of the book.

## What's New in This Third Edition?

Although Spanish grammar itself has not undergone major changes over the years, vocabulary and expressions constantly evolve to adapt to the needs of each generation and the constant changes of the society in which we live. Therefore, in this third edition the vocabulary for each lesson has been carefully revised and updated. It is worth clarifying that Spanish, like many other languages, presents countless regional and dialectal variations. The purpose of this third edition is to present a more standardized approach to the Spanish language and not to include all the lexical possibilities regarding regional usage. In some cases, lexical entries have been included regarding widely known word usages. Here are some of the changes that have been made to this edition.

1. Unlike the two previous editions, which opted not to include verb forms related to Peninsular Spanish, this edition includes both Peninsular Spanish verb forms and structures related to the conjugation of *vosotros*, and Latin American Spanish verb forms and structures related to its corresponding *ustedes*. At the same time, examples have been created that include both regional varieties.

2. *Dialogues.* The dialogues in each lesson are completely new and designed for students immersed in a global world where culture, technology, social media, and mobility are part of their understanding and identity.

3. *Grammar.* Three sections have been added to the grammar sections in this edition: one related to *diminutivos* (*diminutives*), another related to the *se accidental* (*se for unplanned occurrences*), and a section explaining the differences in use of *por and para*.

4. *Vocabulary*. This edition includes explanations of commonly used terms and expressions that may present some difficulty to students new to Spanish. Emphasis has been placed on English/Spanish cognates, whose use has influenced the understanding and correct use of some commonly used expressions and vocabulary. Supplementary activities and exercises have reinforced practice in the use of gender and number forms, which present constant challenges for Spanish learners.

5. An easy-to-reference vocabulary list is included at the end of the book. It includes just over 1,500 entries in the *Spanish–English* section and a similar number in the *English–Spanish* section. The vocabulary has been carefully selected based on the lessons studied in the book, while also incorporating commonly used terms in contemporary Spanish. The vocabulary includes words related to banking, finance, technology, real estate, and global communication, among other topics.

## Acknowledgments

I would like to thank the Wiley editorial team for their support and guidance throughout the process of revising and updating this third edition of the book, especially Ashante Thomas for her time and dedication and for the regular meetings monitoring the progress of the project. I also thank Rosemary Morlin for her valuable comments and suggestions, which have been essential and have contributed to improving the quality of the book. I want to thank Valparaiso University, where I worked as a Spanish professor for almost 30 years, allowing me to delve into the richness of Spanish as a language through teaching and research. I am greatly thankful to my husband John and to my daughter Sarita for their continuous love, support and encouragement in this process. And thank you also to Toby, our dog, for teaching me the importance of some short breaks too while working.

Nelly Zamora-Breckenridge

# Spanish Sounds

There are a few sounds in Spanish that do not exist in English, and vice versa. Some sounds are the same in both languages. An important fact to keep in mind is that in Spanish we run several words together to form what is called a "breath group"; in other words, we link together all the words between pauses. As a result, we omit one of two identical vowels or consonants, and we soften certain consonants (such as *b, d, g)* within the breath group.

EX:  **Ella va a ver a mi hijo.** (Pronounced as **éyabábéramíjo.**)

Guidelines on how to pronounce letters of the Spanish alphabet are given below using English words with corresponding sounds.

A.  **Vowels.** There are five vowels in Spanish: a, e, i, o, u. Whether stressed or unstressed, the sounds of these vowels are clear, tense, and short. The stress doesn't change a vowel in Spanish the way it does in English. For example, the three *a*'s of *Panamá* have the same sound.

1.  In Spanish the letter *A* is pronounced with the mouth open as in the *a* of English *far.*

    EXS: **mañana, banana, Canadá, habilidad, área**

2.  *E* is pronounced with the lips stretched and the tongue higher than when pronouncing *a*, as in the vowel sound of English *pet.*

    EXS:  **Europa, departamento, vez, perro, excelente**

3.  *I* and *Y* are pronounced with the lips very stretched and the tongue nearly touching the roof of the mouth, as in English *see*, but shorter. When *y* is by itself, it means *and*. *Y* may also appear at the end of a word after another vowel.

    EXS:  **ciudad, sí; Juan y María, soy, ideal**

4.  *O* is pronounced with the lips rounded as in the *o* of English *for.*

    EXS:  **profesor, tonto, solo, octavo, hotel, doctor**

5. *U* is pronounced in a very rounded way and its pronunciation formed in the back of the mouth, as in English *boot*, but shorter.

   EXS: tú, Cuba, luna, universidad, Raúl

6. Semivowels. Spanish semivowels *i*, *u*, are pronounced shorter than *i*, *u*, whenever they are unstressed and are directly preceded or followed by another vowel. They are the "weak" part of the two-vowel combination we call diphthong.

   EXS: aire [ai], viaje [ia], causa [au], agua [ua], veinte [ei], bien [ie], euro [eu], bueno [ue], boina [oi], violín [io], estadounidense [ou], cuota [uo], ciudad [iu], muy [ui]

B. Consonants. In general, Spanish consonants are pronounced with less strength and friction than English consonants, especially *b*, *d*, *g*. The following consonants are used in standard Latin American Spanish. There is an extra consonant sound in Spain, which we will mention at the end.

1. The letters *b* and *v* in Spanish are pronounced like the letter *b* in English when they occur at the beginning of a breath group, after a pause, or after a nasal sound. In other cases, they are pronounced softly, with a slight friction between the lower and upper lips. The sound of *v* in English does not exist in Spanish.

   EXS: labio, voz, nuevo, bebida, vida

2. The letter *c* + *a*, *o*, *u*, *l*, or *r* and the letter combination *qu* (with silent *u*) + *e* or *i* are pronounced like the English letter *k*, but they are never followed by the puff of air heard in the English initial *k*.

   EXS: casa, cosa, cuando, clase, crema; que, Quito, Quijote

   The spelling with *k* is used in a few foreign words such as **kilómetro, kiosko, kimono**; but even these words can be spelled with *qu.*

   The combination *ch* in Spanish is pronounced in the same way as the *ch* letter combination in English words like *church*. The Real Academia de la Lengua Española stopped considering the combination "ch" as a letter since 1994. It is placed under the letter "c" in any dictionary.

   EXS: muchacho, chico, mucho, chofer, Chile

3. The letter *d* is pronounced with the tip of the tongue against the upper teeth at the beginning of a breath group and after an *n*. Within the breath group, it is pronounced in the same way as the *th* letter combination in English, as in *father* and *there*, but with even less friction.

   EX: código, día, debate, doctora, Indiana

4. The letter *f* is pronounced in the same way as the letter *f* in English. Unlike English, however, this sound in Spanish is never written as *ph* or *ff*.

   EXS: teléfono, oficina, fax, fósforo, infeliz

5. The letter *g* + *a*, *o*, *u*, *r*, or *l* and the letter combination *gu* + *e* or *i* are pronounced like the g in *get* at the beginning of a breath group or after an *n*. Otherwise, they are pronounced in a similar way as the sound of *g* in *sugar*— softly, and with only a slight friction.

   EX:  **gato, globo; agua, guerra, guitarra**

   The *u* of *gu* is silent. When it is pronounced, it is written with a diaeresis (two dots), as the *gü* in *lingüística* and *vergüenza*.

6. The letter *h* in Spanish is never pronounced.

   EX:  **hablar [aßlár], prohibir [proißír], alcohol [alkól], hospital [ospitál]**

7. In Spanish the letter *j* + *a*, *e*, *i*, *o*, or *u* and the letter *g* + *e* or *i* are pronounced like the *h* in *hat,* but with more friction in the back of the mouth.

   EXS:  **Jalisco, lenguaje, garaje, videojuego; gente, gimnasio, biología**

   The *x* of *México* and *Texas* is pronounced in the same way as the *j* or *g*.

8. The letter *l* is pronounced like the *l* in English in words like *let*. The sound of the *l* at the end of a syllable or word in English is very soft, dark, and relaxed. The sound of the *l* in Spanish is always clear, high, and tense, with the tip of the tongue touching the roof of the mouth. This sound more than any other will readily betray an English accent.

   EXS:  **los, libro, hotel, mil, luz**

   The double *l (ll)* and the *y* are pronounced in the same way as the *y* in English, but usually with more friction, depending on the country. The Real Academia de la Lengua Española stopped considering "ll" as a letter since 1994. It is always found under the letter "l" in any dictionary.

   EXS:  **llamar, mayo, lluvia, calle, coyote, collar**

   In Argentina this sound has a lot of friction, similar to English *s* in words like *pleasure* and *lesion*.

9. The letter *m* is pronounced like the letter *m* in English. However, this sound in Spanish is never written as *mm*.

   EXS:  **madre, mesa, inmediato, permiso, comunicación**

10. The letter *n* is pronounced the same way as the letter *n* in English.

    EXS:  **nada, renta, negocio, corazón, nube**

11. The letter *ñ* in Spanish is pronounced in the same way as the letters *ny* and *ni* in English in words like *canyon* and *onion*.

    EXS:  **mañana, España, ñandú, año, cañón**

12. The letter *p* in Spanish is pronounced like the English *p* in *spy,* and it is never followed by the puff of air heard in the English initial *p* of *pie*. You would

have a strong English-language accent if you pronounced that puff of air in Spanish words with initial *p*.

EXS:   papa, Pedro, papel, persona, puerta

13. The *r* is pronounced like the *t* in English in words like *water* and *matter*. When the *r* is at the beginning of a word or after s or n, the sound is like the ***rolled r*** (double r).

EXS:   pero, para, árbol, comer, caro, Rosa, Israel, honra.

14. The double *r (rr)* has no comparable sound in many forms of English. The tip of the tongue moves quickly five to eight times against the gum ridge. It is a trilled sound.

EXS:   perro, arroz, carro, torre, carretera

The single *r* at the beginning of a word and after *n, l,* or *s* is pronounced in the same way as the double *r* in Spanish.

EXS:   rosa [rrosa], rojo [rrójo]; honra [ónrra], alrededor [alrreðeðór], Israel [Isrraél]

15. Four different letters in Spanish have the same sound as the s in English. They are: 1) the *s* in front of any vowel or final syllable *(soy, ojos, estoy)*. 2) in the Americas, the *z* in front of *a, o, u,* and at the end of a word *(zapato, feliz, vez)*. 3) in the Americas, the *c* and the letter combination *sc* in front of *e* or *i* *(felices, felicidades, ascensor)*. 4) the second half of the sound of the letter *x* *(examen [eksámen], sexto [séksto])*. Avoid the sound of the letter *z* in English in words like *zapato, visita, presidente.*

16. The letter *t* is pronounced with the tip of the tongue against the upper teeth, never followed by the puff of air heard in English initial *t*. There is no double *t (tt)* or *th* in Spanish orthography.

EXS:   tú, Tomás, torta, tamal, teléfono

17. In Spain there is a sound not heard in Spanish America. It is the sound of the letter *z* and the letter *c* in front of *e* or *i*. It is exactly like the sound for the *th* letter combination in English in words like *thought* and *thing*.

EXS:   zapato, feliz, cielo, Cecilia, corazón

## OTHER FACTS TO CONSIDER

1. There is no letter *w* in the Spanish alphabet except as it occurs in a few foreign words, such as **Washington, sandwich,** which is also spelled **sángüiche, sánduche.** Spanish has the same sound as the English *w* for the letter *u* preceded by *h* and followed by *e* or *i*.

EXS:   huevo [wéßo], hueso [wéso], huir [wír]

2. Identical vowels between two words are pronounced as just one vowel. The same is true for two identical consonants within the breath group.

   EXS:  va a casa [bákása], le encanta [lenkánta], el lado [eláðo]

## Summary

1. The five vowels *a, e, i, o, u,* are short, tense, and clear, with or without stress.

2. Avoid the English sound of *a* as in *Ann.* There is no such sound in Spanish, which uses instead the sound of *a* as in *far.*

3. Avoid the lengthening of final vowels as is done in English; for example, *no* is much shorter in Spanish than it is in English where the glide is added to the *o.*

4. A diphthong occurs whenever *i* or *u* is directly preceded or followed by another vowel: *aire, piano, causa, puerta.*

5. Consonants *b, d, g,* within a breath group are very soft in Spanish: **lado** [láðo].

6. Consonants *c, p, t,* at the beginning of words are never followed by the puff of air heard in English initial consonants *c, p, t.*

7. The *h* is always silent. The *u* is silent in *qu* and *gue, gui,* but not in *güe, güi.*

8. Strengthen the sound of *h* in English for the Spanish *j* and *g:* **Juan, gente, Gibraltar, Jiménez.**

9. Keep your tongue high to pronounce final *l,* or you will betray a strong English accent: *tal.*

10. In words written with the letter *z,* pronounce the *z* as if it were the English letter s.

11. Avoid the sound of the English *z* for the single s between vowels in words like *visita* and *presente.*

12. Link the words together within a breath group as if they were one long word.

13. Don't make the stressed syllable too long to avoid the *uh* sound of English in the unstressed syllable that follows the stressed vowel.

# 1 Saludos (*greetings*) y despedidas (*farewells*)

## EXPRESIONES BÁSICAS (*Basic Expressions*)

*Saludos formales*
Buenos días, señor Pérez.
Buenas tardes, señora López.
Buenas noches, señorita García.
¿Cómo está usted?
Muy bien, gracias. ¿Y usted?
Bastante bien, gracias.
Regular. No muy bien.

*Saludos informales*
¡Hola! ¿Qué tal?
¿Cómo estás?
¿Cómo vas? (¿Cómo andás?)
¿Qué hay de nuevo? (¿Qué onda?)

*Despedidas*
Adiós
Chao/chau
Hasta luego.
Hasta mañana.
Nos vemos más tarde.

*Formal Greetings*
Good morning, Mr. Pérez.
Good afternoon, Mrs. López.
Good evening, Miss García
How are you?
Very well, thank you. And you?
Fairly well, thank you.
So-so. Not too well.

*Informal Greetings*
Hi! How are things?
How are you?
How is it going?
What's up?

*Farewells*
Bye
Bye
So long.
See you tomorrow.
See you later.

| | |
|---|---|
| Hasta pronto | See you soon/So long. |
| ¡Que te vaya bien! | Good luck! |

| *Expresiones de cortesía* | *Courtesy Expressions* |
|---|---|
| Con permiso/disculpe. | Excuse me. |
| De nada/Por nada. | You're welcome. |
| Gracias. | Thank you/Thanks. |
| Lo siento. | I am sorry. |
| Por favor | Please |

| *Las presentaciones* | *Introductions* |
|---|---|
| *Formal* | *Formal* |
| ¿Cómo se llama usted? | What is your name? |
| Me llamo Carlos Zapata. | My name is Carlos Zapata. |
| Yo soy Carlos Zapata. | I am Carlos Zapata. |
| Mucho gusto | Pleased to meet you |
| El gusto es mío. | The pleasure is mine. |

| *Informal* | *Informal* |
|---|---|
| ¿Cómo te llamas? | What is your name? |
| Me llamo Sara. | My name is Sara. |
| Encantada(o) | Delighted/Pleased to meet you |

# PRACTIQUE LAS NUEVAS EXPRESIONES (*Practice the Basic Expressions*)

1. How do you greet your coworker at 8:00 A.M? _____.
2. If you see your best friend at the mall, how do you greet her/him?
   _____.
3. How do you ask your teacher how she/he is doing? _____.
4. If someone asks you, how are you? How do you respond? _____.
5. How do you say goodbye to your classmate, if you are planning to see him/her the following day? _____.
6. How do you say *please* in Spanish? _____.
7. If someone does a favor to you, how do you reply? _____
8. How do you say *I am sorry* in Spanish? _____.
9. *Good-bye* is _____ in Spanish, and *So long* is _____.
10. How do you say *you're welcome* in Spanish? _____.
11. How do you say *what's your name (formal)* in Spanish? _____.

# PALABRAS NUEVAS (*New Words*)

You will find these words in the grammar explanations and in exercises in this lesson, and also in later lessons. Try to memorize them, and pay attention to the spelling, including the written accents.

| | | | |
|---|---|---|---|
| el/la amigo(a) | friend | la mesa | table |
| el acta | minutes (meeting) | la mochila | backpack |
| el ave | bird | la mujer | woman |
| la biblioteca | library | la noche | night |
| el bolígrafo | pen | la oficina | office |
| el chico | boy | la palabra | word |
| la chica | girl | el papel | paper |
| la clase | class | la pluma | pen |
| el colegio | school | la práctica | practice |
| el color | color | el portátil | laptop |
| el/la compañero/ a de clase | classmate | el/la profesor(a) | professor (secondary/high school/university faculty) |
| el/la compañero/ a de trabajo | coworker | | |
| el/la computador(a) | computer | el programa | program |
| la comunicación | communication | la red | network |
| la comunidad | community | la tableta | tablet |
| la conexión | connection | la universidad | college/university |
| la conversación | conversation | la vez | time (in a series) |
| el correo electrónico | email | el wi fi | Wifi |
| el cuaderno | notebook | *Expresiones de periodos de tiempo durante el día* | *Expressions of periods of time during the day* |
| el día | day | | |
| el diagrama | diagram | | |
| el escritorio | desk | | |
| la escuela | school | por la mañana | in the morning |
| el/la estudiante | student | por la noche | at night |
| el hombre | man | por la tarde | in the afternoon |
| el instituto | institute/secondary or high school | | |
| el/la jefe | boss | *Verbos* | *Verbs* |
| el/la joven | young person | decir | to say |
| el lápiz | pencil | encontrar | to find |
| la lección | lesson | escribir | to write |
| la librería | bookstore | hacer | to do |
| el libro | book | practicar | to practice |
| el/la maestro(a) | teacher (primary/ elementary school) | preguntar | to ask a question |
| | | saludar | to greet someone |
| la mañana | morning | tener | to have |
| | | ver | to see |

## ALGUNOS COGNADOS (*Some Cognates*)

agenda, ángel, animal, artista, bus, cereal, chocolate, color, criminal, debate, decisión, doctor, exterior, garaje, hospital, hotel, idea, menú, papel, policía, porcentaje, reunión, televisión, taxi.

### NOTAS

1. Notice that nouns in Spanish, unlike English, have a gender: feminine or masculine, even though those that refer to nonliving things. Many nouns that refer to males are masculine, and the words often end in an "o". And nouns that refer to females are feminine, and the words often end in an "a". Keep in mind that there are always exceptions to this rule, and it would be important to memorize those words. Some examples: **el programa** (*program*), **el tema** (*theme*), **el día** (*day*). All end in "a" but are considered masculine.

2. You may have noticed that many words look alike in Spanish and English, some of them even have the very same spelling. These words are called *cognates*. Cognates may or may not have the same meaning in both languages. When they have different meanings, they are known as *unreliable cognates* or *false friends,* and they can be deceptive. You will find some unreliable cognates later in this book.

3. The word **policía** is singular in Spanish. **La policía** can mean a "police women" or it can mean "the police department" as whole. **El policía** means a "police man". **Los/las policías** with an "s" at the end is plural because it is referring to more than one person. Unlike English, the word **la gente** (*people*) is singular. EX: "**En general**, *la gente es* **muy amable**." (*In general people are very friendly*)

## PRACTIQUE LAS PALABRAS NUEVAS (*Practice the New Words*)

A. Write the Spanish cognate for each of the following words.

1. agenda _____
2. bus _____
3. chocolate _____
4. communication _____
5. conversation _____
6. decision _____
7. garage _____
8. hotel _____
9. institute _____
10. menu _____
11. police _____
12. percentage _____
13. reunion _____
14. television _____
15. taxi _____

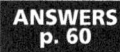
**ANSWERS
p. 60**

B. Did you memorize the new words? Can you write the Spanish equivalent for each of the following words?

1. bookstore _____
2. library _____
3. classmate (male) _____
4. coworker (female) _____
5. friend (female) _____
6. school (elementary) _____
7. college/university _____
8. email _____

9. network _____
10. program _____
11. word _____
12. man _____
13. woman _____
14. young person _____
15. student _____

**ANSWERS
p. 60**

C. Complete the sentences with the right word in *Spanish* from the list of *palabras nuevas*.

1. If I need to buy a book, I will go to _____ (*bookstore*), but if I just need to borrow a book for my class, I can go to _____ (*library*).

2. Martha has three classes, one at 8:00 A.M., another at 9:30 A.M. and the last one at 11:00 A.M. Martha has all her classes _____ (*in the morning*). Pedro has all his classes _____ (*in the afternoon*). Susana does not have classes, but she works _____ (*at night*).

3. The most common way of communication among employees at work is _____ (*email*).

4. Many students need to bring _____ (*laptop*) to their classes every day.

5. My best friend Juan Carlos is studying Civil Engineering at _____ (*college/university*).

6. Many people like to live in a _____ (*city*) like Vancouver although it is very expensive.

7. In Indiana there is a lot of farmland. Many people prefer to live in _____ (*countryside*) because it is peaceful and less polluted than the city.

# GRAMMAR I   ARTÍCULOS INDEFINIDOS (*Indefinite Articles*) • GÉNERO (*Gender of Nouns*)

A. Articles are words that modify nouns by indicating if the noun is specific or general.

Spanish has indefinite and definite articles. We will start by studying indefinite articles in this book.

There are two indefinite articles in English: *a* and *an*, as in *a book, an animal*. In Spanish the indefinite articles are **un**, which is masculine, and **una**, which is feminine, as in *un* señor, *una* señora. The terms *masculine* and *feminine* are used in a grammatical meaning and they are not related to biological gender.

B. Nouns referring to males are masculine, and nouns referring to females are feminine, as in *un* hombre, *una* mujer, *un* estudiante, *una* estudiante. The article tells a male from a female when the noun has the same spelling for males and females.

   EX: *un* joven (*a young male person*); *una* joven (*a young female person*)

C. Nouns referring to *things* are neuter in English (= *it*). In Spanish, they are either masculine or feminine, and they take either *un* or *una*. In this case, the gender of the noun—that is, whether it is masculine or feminine—has nothing to do with the idea of males or females; remember grammatical gender is merely a characteristic of all nouns in Spanish.

   EX: *una* mesa, *un* cuaderno, *un* bolígrafo, *una* palabra

D. The only way to predict the gender of an inanimate noun in Spanish is by looking at the final letter(s) of the word.

   1. Nouns ending in *l, o, n, e, r,* and *s* (*L-O-N-E-R-S*) are almost always masculine.

   2. Nouns ending in *d, ión, z,* and *a* (*D-IÓN-Z-A*) are almost always feminine.

      EXS: *un* papel, *un* libro, *un* color, *un* garaje, *un* portátil, *una* comunidad, *una* lección, *una* conversación, *una* mochila

E. There are important exceptions to these two rules, and they should be memorized when you learn new words.

   1. Some nouns ending in *-ma* are masculine rather than feminine.

      EXS: *un* proble*ma*, *un* te*ma*, *un* progra*ma*, *un* diagra*ma*, *un* poe*ma*

   2. The following nouns are other important exceptions.

| | | |
|---|---|---|
| una calle (*a street*) | una muerte (*a death*) | un avión |
| una clase | una noche | un camión (*a truck*) |
| una llave (*a key*) | una suerte (*a destiny*) | un día |
| una mano | una tarde | un lápiz |

# PRACTIQUE LOS ARTÍCULOS INDEFINIDOS (*Practice the Indefinite Articles*)

**ANSWERS p. 60**

1. The two indefinite articles in Spanish are _____ and _____. Their English translation is _____ or _____.

2. The difference between *un* and *una* is what we call gender: *un* is _____, whereas *una* is _____.

3. All the nouns referring to males are _____, and all the nouns referring to females are _____.

4. We can say that there are three genders in the English pronoun system: a) masculine (males: *he/him*); b) feminine (females: *she/her*); and c) neuter: (*it*), which refers to _____—that is, inanimate nouns, such as *book, email, laptop*.

5. In Spanish we don't have neuter nouns: they are either _____ or _____ —that is, they take *un* or *una*.

6. Is there any significance to the gender of nouns referring to things? _____. Actually, the only way to tell whether the noun referring to a thing is masculine or feminine is by the last _____ of the noun.

7. The article may serve to distinguish a male from a _____ when the same word is used for both of them. For example, *un* **joven** means _____, and *una* **joven** means _____.

8. You can predict the gender of an inanimate noun by the last _____ of the word. A word ending in *-o* is masculine and a word ending in *-a* is _____.

9. How about the other final letters that predict the gender of a noun? Most nouns ending in _____ are masculine, and most nouns ending in _____ are feminine.

10. Therefore, you can predict that the word *corazón* (*heart*) is _____, a word like *mes* (*month*) is _____, and a word like *universidad* (*university*) is _____.

11. About 10 percent of the nouns ending in *-e* are feminine and 90 percent are _____. For example, _____ **tarde** (*an afternoon*), _____ **noche** (*a night*).

12. An important exception to these rules is nouns ending in *-ma* that are _____ rather than feminine—for example, _____ **problema** (*a problem*).

13. Other exceptions are *mano* and *día:* we say _____ **mano** (*a hand*) and _____ **día** (*a day*). For the same reason, you did not learn **Buenos días** but _____ for *good morning*.

14. Do we say **una lápiz** or **un lápiz**? _____ Una tarde or un tarde? _____.

# PRÁCTICA

ANSWERS
p. 61

Write *un* or *una* in the space before the noun.

| | | |
|---|---|---|
| 1. _____ ave | 8. _____ oficina | 15. _____ avión |
| 2. _____ palabra | 9. _____ colegio | 16. _____ noche |
| 3. _____ programa | 10. _____ tarde | 17. _____ problema |
| 4. _____ artista (*women*) | 11. _____ mañana | 18. _____ papel |
| 5. _____ policía (*man*) | 12. _____ decisión | 19. _____ lección |
| 6. _____ mano | 13. _____ universidad | 20. _____ día |
| 7. _____ portátil | 14. _____ vez | |

# GRAMMAR II ARTÍCULOS DEFINIDOS Y CONTRACCIONES
## (Definite Articles and Contractions)

A. In English there is only one definite article: *the*. In Spanish there are four: **el/la** (*masculine, feminine singular*) and **los/las** (*masculine, feminine plural*). These articles agree in gender and number with the nouns they precede.

B. We use *el/los* with masculine nouns and *la/las* with feminine nouns. Remember that nouns referring to males are always masculine and nouns referring to females are always feminine. Things are either masculine or feminine, according to the last letter(s) of the word.

   1. Nouns ending in *l, o, n, e, r,* and *s* (*L-O-N-E-R-S*) are generally *masculine*.

   2. Nouns ending in *d, ión, z,* and *a* (*D-IÓN-Z-A*) are generally *feminine*.

      EXS:  *el* tren, *el* nombre, *el* papel, *el* lunes
            *la* lección, *la* luz, *la* verdad

C. Remember that there are important exceptions to these rules. Review them:

   1. Nouns ending in *-ma* are masculine rather than feminine: **el problema, el tema**.

   2. Nouns like *la* mano, *el* día, *la* clase, *la* noche, *la* tarde, *el* lápiz, *el* avión, and *el* camión are other exceptions.

D. The article *la* precedes feminine nouns, but if the feminine noun begins with a stressed *a, el* is used instead of *la*. Actually, the noun may begin with *a* or *ha* because the *h* is silent in Spanish.

   EXS:  *el* agua, *el* acta, *el* ave PLURAL: *las* aguas, *las* actas, *las* aves
         *el* hambre (pronounced [elámbre]). PLURAL: *las* hambres

   But we say *la* internauta, *la* americana, because the initial **a** of each word is unstressed.

E. This same rule applies to the indefinite article *una*, which precedes all feminine nouns, except the ones beginning with stressed *a*.

   EXS:  *un* ave rather than *una* ave, *un* acta rather than *una* acta

   But *una* astronauta, *una* americana, because the initial *a* of each word is unstressed.

F. We have only two contractions in Spanish—that is, two words combine into one. The prepositions *de* (*of, from*) and *a* (*to*) are combined with the article *el*.

   1. de + el becomes **del** (*of the*)

   2. a + el becomes **al** (*to the*)

      EXS:  el árbol *del* patio (*the tree in the yard*), la luz *del* día (*the light of the day*)
            **Voy al** patio. (*I am going to the yard.*) BUT **Voy a la** casa. (*I am going to the house.*)

# PRACTIQUE LOS ARTÍCULOS DEFINIDOS (*Practice the Definite Articles*)

**ANSWERS p. 61**

1. The definite article *the* has four possible translations in Spanish: _____.

2. Inanimate nouns (things) are usually masculine in Spanish when they end in _____, and they are feminine when they end in _____.

3. According to these rules, you can predict the gender of most nouns; for example, *paz* is_____, *sol* is _____, *crayón* is _____.

4. There are exceptions to these rules; for example, nouns ending in *-ma* are _____, such as _____ **problema** (*the problem*), and _____ **programa** (*the program*).

5. A few nouns ending in *-z* are masculine rather than _____, such as _____ **lápiz** (*the pencil*); but _____**luz** (*the light*), _____ **vez** (*the time*) and _____ **paz** are femenine.

6. The preposition *de* (*of*) followed by the article *el* becomes one word: _____. The preposition *a* (*to*) followed by the article *el* becomes one word: _____.

7. Not every feminine noun takes the feminine article *la* or *una;* the masculine article *el* or *un* is used instead if the noun begins with a _____*a* [á], such as _____ **ave** (*bird*), and _____ **agua** (*water*). The plural forms require *las:* **las aves, las aguas**.

8. Which letter is always silent in Spanish? _____. This means that if a feminine noun starts with *ha* [á], it will take the definite article _____rather than _____. For example, _____ **hambre** ([*the*] *hunger*).

9. Is it correct Spanish to say **el americana?** _____. Here we don't use *el* because the first *a* is not _____: phonetically, [amerikána].

10. We say *la casa* _____ **presidente**, because *de + el* contracts into _____.

11. Is *la casa de la señora* correct? _____. There is no contraction formed with *de* and the feminine article _____. There are no contractions formed with the plural articles either: **a los, de los, a las, de las**.

# PRÁCTICA

**ANSWERS p. 61**

Write *el* or *la* in the space before the noun.

| | | |
|---|---|---|
| 1. _____ agua | 8. _____ red | 15. _____ hotel |
| 2. _____ acta | 9. _____ lápiz | 16. _____ comunidad |
| 3. _____ biblioteca | 10. _____ hambre | 17. _____ mesa |
| 4. _____ turista (*male*) | 11. _____ mujer | 18. _____ chico |
| 5. _____ joven (*female*) | 12. _____ conversación | 19. _____ diagrama |
| 6. _____ clase | 13. _____ librería | 20. _____ correo |
| 7. _____ computador | 14. _____ luz | electrónico |

# GRAMMAR III   PRONOMBRES de sujeto (*Subject Pronouns*)

A.  Memorize the subject pronouns in the chart.

| Singular | (English) | Plural | (English) |
|---|---|---|---|
| yo<br>tú<br>usted (Ud.)<br>él/ella | I<br>you (*familiar*)<br>you (*formal*)<br>he/she | nosotros(as)<br>vosotros(as)<br>ustedes (Uds.)<br>ellos/ellas | we<br>you [all] (*Spain*)<br>you [all] (*Latin America*)<br>they (*males/females*) |

Note that:

1. *I* is always capitalized, *yo* is not. Each refers to the speaker in the sentence.

2. *Nosotros* becomes *nosotras* if the speakers in the sentence are all females. If the speakers are males and females, the masculine *nosotros* is used instead.

3. *Tú* is the familiar form for singular *you*; it is used among friends and within the family. Its frequency of usage as compared to the formal *usted* may vary from country to country.

4. *Vosotros(as)* is the plural of *tú*; it is used mainly in Spain. In Latin America the plural of *tú* is *ustedes*.

5. The American *voseo* is a historical, regional and grammatical variation of the use of *tú*. Although its use alternates with the use of the form *tú*, many Latin American regions are differentiated by its wide use. *Voseo* is understood as the use of **vos** instead of the second person singular *tú*. Its use affects and modifies verbal conjugations with their respective regional variations. The countries with the most widespread use of the **vos** form are Argentina, Chile, Uruguay, Paraguay, and Central American countries such as Guatemala and Nicaragua. We also find it in some regions of Colombia.

    EX:  *Vos **tenés** un **computador nuevo**/tú **tienes** un **computador nuevo**. (you have a new computer).*

    *Vos **hablás** muy **rápido**/tú **hablas** muy rápido. (you speak very fast)*

    *Vos **vivís** cerca de la universidad/tú **vives** cerca de la universidad. (you live near the university)*

    For the purpose of this book, we will study the forms corresponding to the pronoun *tú* and not the pronoun *vos* because the latter is strictly regional in its use.

6. *Usted* and the plural *ustedes* are more formal than *tú*; they are used with persons we don't know well. In Latin America *ustedes* is the plural both of *tú* and of *usted*, since *vosotros(as)* is not used.

7. *Ellas* refers only to females, whereas *ellos* may refer only to males or to combinations of males and females.

8. There are two pronouns with a written accent (*acento escrito*): tú and él.

9. In some circumstances subject pronouns are not used in Spanish since the ending of the verb indicates the person.

> EX: *¿Vamos a estudiar a la biblioteca? (Shall we study in the library?).*
> *(vamos=nosotros form in present).*

B. There is *no subject pronoun* for the English neuter *it*. The subject pronoun is usually omitted with inanimate nouns (things) in Spanish.

> EXS: ¿*La mujer* es americana? —Sí, *ella* es americana. (*Yes, <u>she</u> is American.*)
> ¿*La mesa* es americana? —Sí, es americana. (*Yes, it is American.*)

The same rule applies in the plural: *ellos* and *ellas* refer to persons or animals, never to things.

**NOTAS**

1. *Usted* is abbreviated into *Ud.* or *Vd.* and *ustedes* into *Uds.* or *Vds.* The reason for the *V* in *Vd.* and in *Vds.* is that historically the origin of *usted* is *vuestra merced* (*your grace*).

# PRACTIQUE LOS PRONOMBRES DE SUJETO (*Practice the Subject Pronouns*)

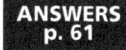

1. Which pronoun is always capitalized in English but not in Spanish? _____ = _____.

2. The pronoun *we* has two possible words in Spanish: _____/_____.

3. *Vosotros* is the plural of _____ in Spain, but it is not used in Latin America. In its place, Latin Americans use _____.

4. Which one is more familiar, *tú* or *usted* ? _____.

5. *Nosotras* is used when two or more _____ are speaking, but *nosotros* can be all males or a combination of males and _____.

6. If Mr. Pérez is talking for himself and his wife, which pronoun is he going to use? _____

7. In Spanish *you* can be either *tú* or *usted* depending on the relationship with the speaker. *Usted* shows respect, whereas *tú* is more intimate. A Spanish-speaking student would address his teacher as _____, and the teacher would reply with _____. The same principle applies to parents and children.

8. The mark (´) on a vowel in Spanish is called **acento,** and later you will learn the rules for its use. Which are the two pronouns with **acento**? _____ and _____.

9. *He* always refers to a person (or an animal—especially a pet) as subject of a sentence. The Spanish word for *he* is _____, for *she* is _____, and for *it* is _____.

10. If we talk to Mary and Jane, we refer to them as *they*; the Spanish pronoun is _____. If we talk to Mary and Joe, we refer to them as *they*; the pronoun is _____.

11. If we talk about the *tables*, we refer to them as *they* as the subject of a sentence; the Spanish equivalent for *they* in this case is _____.

12. How do you know when to use *tú* and when to use *usted?* When you call a person by his or her first name (John, Mary, and so on), you use *tú*. When you use last names (Mr. Martínez, Miss García), you use _____.

13. *Usted* is abbreviated in two ways: _____ and _____; and *ustedes* is abbreviated in two ways, too: _____ and _____.

# PRÁCTICA

Write the Spanish pronouns.

1. we (*all females*) _____.
2. you (*familiar singular*) _____.
3. you (*male and female, familiar plural, Spain*) _____.
4. they (*all females*) _____.
5. they (*things, inanimate nouns*) _____.
6. you (*formal singular*) _____.
7. they (*all males*) _____.
8. we (*males and females*) _____.
9. they (*males and females*) _____.
10. you (*formal plural-Latin America*) _____.
11. he/she/it _____/_____/_____.
12. I _____.
13. You and me (*male and female*) _____.
14. Marcos and Javier _____.
15. You and your friend (*Latin America*) _____.

# 2 Nuevas generaciones
## (*New Generations*)

## PALABRAS NUEVAS (*New Words*)

You will find these words in the grammar explanations and in exercises in this lesson, and also in later lessons. Try to memorize them, and pay attention to the spelling, including the written accents.

| | | | |
|---|---|---|---|
| el anillo | ring | las escaleras | stairs |
| el año | year | la generación | generation |
| los apuntes | notes (taken in a class/meeting) | el gimnasio | gym |
| | | la hierba | grass |
| el borrador | eraser | la iglesia | church |
| el café | coffee (drink) | el Instagram | Instagram |
| el café/la cafetería | coffee shop (place) | el/la internet | Internet |
| la canción | song | la luz | light |
| la característica | characteristic | el mensaje de texto | text message |
| el celular/móvil (Spain) | celular | el mes | month |
| | | la nota/la calificación | grade |
| la cena | dinner | la oficina de admisiones | admissions office |
| la cerveza | beer | | |
| el/la comprador(a) | buyer | el oro | gold |
| el/la consumidor(a) | consumer | los padres/los papás | parents |
| el coro | choir | el periódico | newspaper |
| el ejercicio | exercise/activity | el problema | problem |

| | | | |
|---|---|---|---|
| el proyecto | project | *Verbos* | *Verbs* |
| las redes sociales | social networks/ media | abrir | to open |
| | | aprender | to learn |
| robótica | robotics | asignar | to assign |
| la semana | week | asistir | to attend (a class/ meeting) |
| la tarea | homework | | |
| el/la taxista | taxi driver | atender | to attend (to someone) |
| el té | tea | | |
| la tecnología | technology | beber | to drink |
| el tema | topic/theme | borrar | to erase |
| el tiempo | time | cenar | to have dinner |
| la tienda | store | comer | to eat |
| el TikTok | TikTok | comprender | to understand |
| el traductor de Google | Google Translator | conversar | to chat (to converse) |
| el/la turista | tourist | corresponder | to correspond |
| la ventana | window | creer | to think/to believe |
| el vino | wine | depender de | to depend on |
| | | encantar | to like/to love something |
| *Adjetivos* | *Adjectives* | | |
| actual | current | estar | to be |
| amable | nice/friendly/kind | estudiar | to study |
| brillante | bright/brilliant | ganar | to win/to earn |
| buen(o)(a) | good | gustar | to like |
| centenial (generación Z) | centennial (Generation Z) | hablar | to speak/to talk |
| | | leer | to read |
| compulsivo(a) | compulsive | mirar | to watch |
| difícil | difficult | nacer | to be born |
| divertido(a) | fun | pasar tiempo | to spend time |
| exigente | demanding | pensar | to think |
| importante | important | poder | to be able, can |
| inteligente | intelligent | preferir | to prefer |
| interesante | interesting | querer | to want |
| nuevo(a) | new | recibir | to receive |
| obsesionado(a) | obsessed | saber | to know |
| preocupado(a) | worried/ preoccupied | salir de | to leave a place |
| | | ser | to be |
| último(a) | last | subir | to go up |
| | | tomar (apuntes/ clases) | to take (notes/ classes) |
| *Adverbios* | *Adverbs* | | |
| Además | besides/moreover | tomar (bebidas) | to drink |
| como | like/as | usar | to use |
| mucho | a lot | visitar | to visit |
| poco | little | vivir | to live |
| también | also/too | | |
| tampoco | neither/either | *Otras expresiones* | *Other Expressions* |
| | | en casa | at home |
| | | todos los días | every day |

## DIÁLOGO   En un café

*Valentina y María Fernanda conversan en un café sobre las diferentes características
de su generación.*

VALENTINA: Hola María Fernanda. ¿Cómo estás?

MARÍA FERNANDA: Muy bien. Y tú ¿qué tal?

VALENTINA: Yo estoy más o menos. Estoy un poco preocupada. Tengo un
proyecto para mi clase de comunicación sobre las características
de mi generación.

MARÍA FERNANDA: Muy interesante. Sabes que yo soy de la generación Z o centenial.

VALENTINA: ¿Sí? ¿de qué año eres?

MARÍA FERNANDA: Yo soy del año 2002.

VALENTINA: ¡Ah! Nosotras somos de la misma generación. Yo soy del año
2001. La generación Z corresponde a los años 1995 a 2010
aproximadamente.

MARÍA FERNANDA: Una característica de nuestra generación es que nos gusta mucho
la tecnología. Nos encanta el celular o móvil, como dicen en
España, y siempre nos gusta mirar las redes sociales.

VALENTINA: ¡Es verdad! Yo no puedo estar sin mi celular y también paso
mucho tiempo en las redes sociales, especialmente en Instagram
y en TikTok. Además, me gusta comprar todo por internet. Mis
padres dicen que yo soy una compradora exigente.

MARÍA FERNANDA: ¡Qué gracioso! Es verdad que somos parte de la generación Z.
Mis padres dicen que yo soy una chica muy independiente y una
consumidora compulsiva.

## DIALOGUE   *In a Coffee Shop*

*Valentina and María Fernanda talk in a coffee shop about the different characteristics
of their generation.*

VALENTINA: *Hello María Fernanda. How are you?*

MARÍA FERNANDA: *Very good. And how are you?*

VALENTINA: *I am more or less. I'm a little worried. I have a project for my
communication class about the characteristics of my generation.*

MARÍA FERNANDA: *Very interesting. You know that I am from generation Z or
Centennial.*

VALENTINA: *Yes? When were you born?*

MARÍA FERNANDA: *I was born in 2002.*

VALENTINA: *Oh! We are from the same generation. I was born in 2001.
Generation Z corresponds to the years 1995 to 2010 approximately.*

MARÍA FERNANDA:    *A characteristic of our generation is that we really like technology. We love cell phones or mobile phones, as they say in Spain, and we always like to look at social networks.*

VALENTINA:    *It's true! I can't be without my cell phone and I also spend a lot of time on social media, especially on Instagram and TikTok. Also, I like to buy everything online. My parents say that I am a demanding shopper.*

MARÍA FERNANDA:    *How funny! It is true that we are part of generation Z. My parents say that I am a very independent girl and a compulsive consumer.*

# PRÁCTICA

ANSWERS
p. 62

A. *Palabras nuevas.* Complete the sentences using the information from the dialogue.

1. Valentina y María Fernanda son de la _____ Z o centenial.
2. Ellas conversan en una _____.
3. Valentina tiene un _____ para su clase de comunicación.
4. María Fernanda nació (*was born*) en el _____ 2002.
5. Una _____ de la generación Z es que a los jóvenes les gusta mucho la _____.
6. Valentina no puede estar sin (*without*) su _____. Ella lo usa siempre.
7. Instagram y TikTok son dos _____ muy populares entre (*among*) los jóvenes.
8. María Fernanda es una _____ compulsiva.
9. A Valentina le gusta comprar todo por _____.
10. Los padres de Valentina piensan que ella es una _____ exigente.

ANSWERS
p. 62

B. **Underline the word that makes sense.**

1. Valentina hace sus compras en (la generación, el correo electrónico, el internet, las redes sociales).
2. Valentina y María Fernanda conversan en una (biblioteca, cafetería, casa, librería).
3. Valentina tiene un proyecto para su clase de (historia, ciencias, tecnología, comunicación).
4. María Fernanda es una consumidora (inteligente, brillante, compulsiva, exigente).
5. Valentina no puede estar sin su (celular, café, libro, portátil).

# PRACTIQUE LAS PALABRAS NUEVAS

**ANSWERS p. 62**

**A. Complete the sentence with the right word in Spanish.**

1. A los estudiantes les gusta tomar un buen café en la _____ (*coffee shop*) de la universidad.

2. El colegio de mi ciudad ganó (*won*) en una competencia de _____ (*robotics*).

3. Muchos _____ (*tourists*) visitan la ciudad de Barcelona en España.

4. El _____ (*project*) para la clase de ciencias es muy difícil.

5. La sociedad _____ (*current*) depende mucho de la _____ (*technology*).

6. Los jóvenes de esta generación están obsesionados con _____ (*social networks*) como Instagram, Snapchat y TikTok.

7. Los estudiantes tienen exámenes la última _____ (*week*) de clases.

8. Los _____ (*parents*) quieren un buen futuro para sus hijos.

9. Los chicos de la _____ (*generation*) Z o centenial no pueden vivir sin (*without*) su celular.

10. Un _____ (*problem*) de la educación actual es que los estudiantes usan mucho el celular en las _____ (*classes*).

11. Yo escribo muchos _____ (*text messages*) para mi trabajo.

12. El _____ (*choir*) del colegio es excelente.

13. Los estudiantes prefieren tomar _____ (*notes*) para sus clases en sus computadores.

14. Fanny tiene buenas _____ (*grades*) en sus clases.

15. Hoy mi hija Sofía quiere cenar _____ (*at home*).

**ANSWERS p. 62**

**B. Did you memorize the new words? Can you write the English equivalent for each of the following words?**

1. año _____
2. mes _____
3. día _____
4. clase _____
5. problema _____
6. ventana _____
7. mesa _____
8. compradora _____
9. consumidor _____
10. borrador _____
11. proyecto _____
12. tecnología _____
13. tema _____
14. generación _____
15. práctica _____

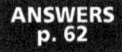

C. Vocabulary. Complete the sentences with the right word in *Spanish* from the list of *palabras nuevas*.

1. To erase a mistake, we can use a _____.
2. Many professors prefer to assign a _____ instead of an exam for the end of the semester.
3. The _____ that is in the dining room is made of wood.
4. The _____ is very important for our society.
5. My classroom has only one _____ to see outside.

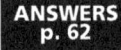

D. Match the columns by writing the appropriate letter.

| | | | |
|---|---|---|---|
| 1. _____ ventana | | A. | bright/brilliant |
| 2. _____ borrador | | B. | also/too |
| 3. _____ día | | C. | social networks |
| 4. _____ comprador | | D. | current |
| 5. _____ proyecto | | E. | demanding |
| 6. _____ tema | | F. | coffee shop |
| 7. _____ año | | G. | time |
| 8. _____ consumidora | | H. | buyer |
| 9. _____ tiempo | | I. | consumer |
| 10. _____ redes sociales | | J. | year |
| 11. _____ cafetería | | K. | day |
| 12. _____ actual | | L. | theme |
| 13. _____ exigente | | M. | eraser |
| 14. _____ brillante | | N. | window |
| 15. _____ también | | O. | project |

# GRAMMAR I   Las tres conjugaciones, presente indicativo de los verbos regulares que terminan en *ar*
## (*The Three Conjugations • Present Indicative of Regular -ar Verbs*)

A. The three conjugations

There are three kinds of verbs in Spanish, each classified according to the ending of the infinitive. The form of the verb listed in dictionaries is the infinitive. Its equivalent in English is the form that starts with *to: to speak*. The three kinds of verbs are said to be of the first, second, or third conjugation.

1. FIRST CONJUGATION: Verbs ending in **-ar**, such as **hablar** (*to speak*)

2. SECOND CONJUGATION: Verbs ending in **-er**, such as **comer** (*to eat*)

3. THIRD CONJUGATION: Verbs ending in **-ir**, such as **vivir** (*to live*)

   Every verb form is divided into two parts: *stem + ending*. The stem carries the meaning, and it is the same in all persons and tenses. The *ending* is the part that changes to signal the different persons (like *I, you, he, she*) and tenses (past, present, future).

EXS: **habl + ar.** The stem is **habl-** (*speak*), the ending is **-ar** (infinitive).
**habl + as.** The stem is **habl-** (*speak*), the ending is **-as** (*you (informal)*, present indicative).

**B.** Present indicative of regular *-ar* verbs

Look at the present indicative of *hablar* (*to speak*), given in the chart that follows.

| | *Habl ar* | | | *To Speak* |
|---|---|---|---|---|
| yo | habl o | | I | speak, am speaking, do speak |
| tú | habl as | | You (informal) | speak, are speaking, do speak |
| él/ella ⎱ | habl a | | ⎰ he / she | speaks, is speaking, does speak |
| Ud. ⎰ | | | ⎱ you (formal) | speak, are speaking, do speak |
| nosotros(as) | habl amos | | we | speak, are speaking, do speak |
| ellos/ellas/ | habl an | | they / you | speak, are speaking, do speak |
| Uds. | | | (*Latin America*) | |
| vosotros/as | habl áis | | You all (*Spain*) | speak, are speaking, do speak |

Note that:

1. The stem **habl-** is the same for all the persons, and it doesn't change for the different tenses. This is why we call *hablar* a regular verb.

2. The endings identify the persons and tense: **-o** means *yo* (*I*); **-amos** means *nosotros(as)* (*we*); **áis** means **vosotros/as**; **-as** means *tú* (familiar *you*); **-a** means *él, ella, usted,* (*he, she, you*) and **-an** means *ellos, ellas, ustedes,* (*they, you*). These endings are not the same in all the tenses.

3. Since the subject pronoun information is given by the verb ending, we omit the subject pronouns unless we want to add emphasis to the subject. For example, *Tú hablas español* means <u>You</u> speak Spanish (giving emphasis by raising the voice on *you*).

**C.** Uses of the present indicative

1. The present indicative is used to indicate *an action in progress* at the time of speaking. Notice that the progressive form is *mandatory* in English in this case.

   EX: *Hablo* español ahora. (<u>*I am speaking*</u> *Spanish now.*)

2. The present indicative is used to show a *habit*, something we continue doing. In this case, to show a *habit* or *custom*, we use the simple present in English.

   EX: *Hablo* español siempre. (<u>*I speak*</u> *Spanish all the time.*)

3. The present indicative can be used for *an action in the future*, but an adverb or a context to differentiate it from the present is needed. This use is very common in Spanish.

   EX: **Mañana** *hablo* con usted. (<u>*I will speak*</u> *with you tomorrow.*)

4. The present indicative also translates the emphatic *I do speak* by raising the voice on the verb or by adding an adverb such as *sí* (*indeed*), **ciertamente** (*certainly*), and so on.

EX:  **Elena sí** *habla* **inglés.** (*Helen <u>does speak</u> English.*)

# PRACTIQUE EL PRESENTE DE INDICATIVO

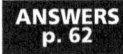

1. The three kinds of Spanish verbs are identified by the endings of the _____. The first conjugation ends in _____; the second, in _____; and the third in _____. Actually, we can say that the vowels **a, e, i,** identify these verbs, just as the *r* identifies the infinitives and *to* precedes all the infinitives in English.

2. The *stem* of a verb carries the basic _____, and it is repeated in all the persons and tenses. What is the stem of *hablar*? _____ And the stem of *vivir*? _____ And the stem of *comer*? _____.

3. The ending **-amos** gives the subject pronoun information for _____. The ending **-as** signals the subject _____, and the ending **-o** repeats the subject _____.

4. Any noun takes the same third-person verb ending as *él, ella, ellos,* or *ellas.* Now complete the sentence **Roberto** _____ **mucho.** (*Robert <u>talks</u> a lot.*)

5. *We* is a combination of *somebody else* and *I*; therefore, to say in Spanish *She and I speak Spanish*, you would say **Ella y yo** _____ **español.**

6. Notice that the stem of *estudiar* ends in an *i* after you drop the ending **-ar.** This means that we must keep that *i* in all the persons, moods, and tenses. Write how you would say *We study.* _____.

7. Since the verb endings repeat the information carried by the subject pronouns, we don't use the subject pronouns unless we want to add _____ to the subject.

8. The present indicative is used for an action in _____ at the time of speaking. For example, *She is studying now* is translated as **Ella** _____ **ahora.**

9. The verb *usar* has a short stem: _____. Write how you would say *We are using the book.* _____. Write how you would say *They are using the book.* _____.

10. A *habit* is an action we repeat many times. How would you say *I speak Spanish at home all the time?* **Siempre** _____ **español en casa.**

11. We can use the present indicative for a future action with the help of an adverb or a context. How would you say *I will study the lesson tomorrow?* _____ **la lección mañana.**

12. In Spanish we don't have an emphatic auxiliary like *do* in the sentence *You do speak well*. We use the ordinary present tense form **hablas;** and we either emphasize it with the voice, or we add an adverb like *sí* (*indeed, sure*) in front of it. Using this last method, write how you would say *Mary does study a lot*. **Maria _____ mucho.**

# PRÁCTICA

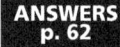
**ANSWERS
p. 62**

Complete the sentence with the correct form of the verb in parentheses.

1. Nosotros _____ (estudiar) en la biblioteca por la noche.
2. Yo _____ (preparar) pasta para la cena.
3. Sara _____ (necesitar) usar el traductor de Google para la tarea.
4. Inés _____ (tomar) té por las tardes.
5. María y yo _____ (cantar) en el coro de la iglesia.
6. Usted _____ (comprar) sus libros en el internet.
7. Tú _____ (amar) a tus padres.
8. Los profesores _____ (enseñar) clases todos los días.
9. Enrique Iglesias _____ (cantar) canciones (*songs*) en inglés y en español.
10. Los atletas _____ (practicar) en el gimnasio por las tardes.
11. Ustedes _____ (trabajar) en la oficina de admisiones de la universidad.
12. Yo _____ (regresar) a casa a las 5:30 P.M. todas las tardes.
13. Daniela _____ (montar) su bicicleta (*bike*) para ir (*to go*) a sus clases.
14. Los estudiantes de la clase de honores _____ (sacar) muy buenas notas en las pruebas.
15. Los niños (*children*) _____ (mirar) muchos videojuegos en sus tabletas.
16. Tú _____ (llegar) a la oficina a las 8:00 A.M. todos los días.
17. Luis _____ (tomar) apuntes en su clase de psicología.
18. Vosotras _____ (hablar) por teléfono por las mañanas.
19. Alejandro y tú _____ (practicar) pickleball por las tardes.
20. Las tiendas _____ (mandar) mensajes de texto a sus clientes.

# GRAMMAR II Verbos regulares que terminan en *er* y en *ir*
## (*Regular Verbs Ending in -er and -ir*)

A.  The present indicative of *comer* and *vivir*

The regular verb **comer** (*to eat*) is a second conjugation verb, ending in **-er** in the infinitive. The regular verb **vivir** (*to live*) is a third conjugation verb ending in **-ir**. These two kinds of verbs share the same endings in almost all the tenses. Memorize their present indicatives.

|  | *Com er*<br>(*to eat*) | *Vi ir*<br>(*to live*) |
|---|---|---|
| yo | com o | viv o |
| tú | com es | viv es |
| él / ella / Ud. | com e | viv e |
| nosotros(as) | com emos | viv imos |
| ellos / ellas / Uds. | com en | viv en |
| vosotros/as | com éis | viv ís |

Note that:

1.  The stem of *comer* is **com-**, and the stem of *vivir* is **viv-**. The stem carries the meaning of the verb. Both stems stay the same in all the persons and tenses: present, past, future.

2.  The endings are very similar to those of the first conjugation: **-o** means *yo;* **-emos** and **-imos** mean *nosotros/as;* **-es** means *tú;* **-éis** and **ís** mean *vosotros/as;* **-e** means *él / ella / Ud.;* and **-en** means *ellos / ellas / Uds.*

3.  The endings of *comer* and *vivir* are the same in all the persons except the first- and second-person plural: **com emos** *vs.* **viv imos; com éis** *vs.* **viv ís.** The difference is the same as in the infinitive: **e** *vs.* **i.**

B.  Uses of the present indicative

The uses of the present indicative are the same for second- (**comer**) and third-conjugation (**vivir**) verbs as they are for first-conjugation (**hablar**) ones. In fact, they are the same for all the verbs in the language, including the ones that are just being coined, like **faxear** (*to fax*). Let's review these uses:

1.  An action *in progress.*

    EX:  *Ella come* **ahora mismo.** (*She's eating* right now.)

2.  An action as a *habit.*

    EX:  *Ella* **siempre** *come* **mucho.** (*She always eats a lot.*)

3.  An action in the future.

    EX:  **¿Dónde** *comes* **mañana?** (*Where will you eat tomorrow?*)

4. The present indicative translates the English emphatic form *do* + (verb) by raising the voice on the verb or by adding an adverb such as *sí* (*sure, indeed*), *ciertamente* (*certainly*), and so on.

   EX:  *Ud. sí come* **muchas verduras.** (<u>*You do eat*</u> *lots of vegetables.*)

# PRACTIQUE EL PRESENTE DE INDICATIVO

**ANSWERS**
p. 63

1. The second kind of verb is characterized by the _____ ending of the infinitive, and the third kind by the _____ ending

2. The stem carries the _____ of the verb. What is the stem of *escribir?* _____ And the stem of *leer?* _____

3. The subject pronouns are usually omitted in Spanish because the _____ of the verb carries the same *information*. For example, the ending -o means _____.

4. You may have noticed that the difference between *habl amos* and *com emos* is the ending -amos *vs.* -emos, or better yet, the vowels a and e. What is the **nosotros** form of **vivir?** _____. You can see the vowel i in contrast with the vowels **a** and **e.**

5. *Comer* and *vivir* have the same endings in all the persons of the present indicative except in the _____ and _____. Note that it is the same vowels that differentiate the second from the third conjugation: -er *vs.* -ir.

6. The present indicative of any verb is used for an action *in progress*. For example, *Where are you living now?* is translated as **¿Dónde** _____ **Ud. ahora?**

7. A *habit* is an action we repeat many times. If the habit still exists now, we express that action in the _____. For example, *You drink water all the time* is translated as **Usted siempre** _____ **agua.** (*beber*)

8. The present tense is often used instead of the *future* tense for an action still to come. For example, **Mañana (yo)** _____ **la novela** *La casa de los espíritus* de Isabel Allende. (*leer*)

9. *Escribir* means *to write.* Can you write in English the four meanings of *escribimos?*

   a) An action in progress: _____.

   b) An action as a habit: _____.

   c) An action in the future: _____.

   d) An action with emphasis: _____.

# PRÁCTICA

Complete each sentence with the correct form(s) of the verb(s). (Remember that the pronouns can be omitted but that they are given in parentheses as clues for the persons you have to use in your answers.)

1. (Nosotros) _____ español en este libro. (*aprender*)
2. El Dr. Zapata _____ el periódico por las mañanas. (*leer*)
3. (Tú) _____ la lección. (*comprender*)
4. La tienda _____ a las 9:30 A.M. todos los días. (*abrir*)
5. Los alemanes (*Germans*) _____ mucha cerveza durante la celebración de Oktoberfest. (*beber*)
6. Antonio y yo _____ las escaleras para ir a nuestra oficina. (*subir*)
7. El avión no _____ muy tarde de Madrid. (*salir*)
8. Ellas _____ en un restaurante elegante. (*comer*)
9. Ustedes no _____ la verdad. (*creer*)
10. Yo _____ muchos correos electrónicos en mi trabajo. (*escribir*)
11. Vosotros _____ las escaleras todos los días. (*subir*)
12. Mi familia _____ en Sevilla, España. (*vivir*)
13. El niño _____ el libro para su clase de historia. (*recibir*)
14. Los jóvenes _____ a una conferencia sobre Robótica. (*asistir*)
15. La profesora _____ a sus estudiantes durante sus horas de oficina. (*atender*)

# GRAMMAR III   Formas y usos de los verbos ser y estar
## (*Forms and Usage of ser and estar = to be*)

**A.** *Ser* and *estar* (*to be*) in the present indicative

|  | **S er**<br>(*To be*) | **Est ar**<br>(*To be*) |  |
|---|---|---|---|
| yo | s oy | est oy | I am |
| tú<br>él/ella }<br>Ud. | er es<br><br>es | est ás<br><br>est á | you are<br>he/she/it is<br>you are |
| nosotros (as) | s omos | est amos | we are |
| ellos/ellas/Uds. | s on | est án | they/you (all) are (*Latin America*) |
| vosotros/as | s ois | est áis | you (all) are (*Spain*) |

Note that:

1. These two verbs are irregular because they don't follow the conjugations of regular -ar, -er, and -ir verbs. They have changes in the stems and in the endings.

2. Like *to be, ser* and *estar* are irregular in more ways than other verbs are. However, you will learn all these irregular forms easily, because you will use them often.

3. The first person ending for both verbs is -oy instead of -o as in **hablo, vivo, leo.**

4. *Estar* has four forms with a written accent: **estás, está, estáis, están.**

   (NOTE: If you pay attention to the words with written accents as you go along, you will find it easier to learn the rules about the accent when you study them later.)

B. Uses of *ser* and *estar*

   1. *Ser* is used to identify a person, an animal, a concept, a thing, or any noun.

      EX:   Esto *es* una tableta. (*This is a tablet.*)

   2. *Ser* is used to express profession or occupation.

      EX:   El señor Soto *es* maestro. (*Mr. Soto is a teacher.*)

   3. *Estar* is used to show the location of a person, animal, or thing. (Compare this use of *estar* with *to stay* in English.)

      EXS:   **El cuaderno** *está* **aquí.** (*The notebook is here.*)

      **Esteban** *está* **en Australia.** (*Esteban is in Australia.*)

   4. *Ser* is used with an adjective to show that a characteristic is the *norm* for the noun. For example, it is the norm for snow to be white, soft, cold, and so on.

      EXS:   **La nieve** *es* **blanca.** (*Snow is white.*)

   5. *Ser* is used to express origin or nationality.

      **Salma Hayek** *es* **mexicana.** (*Salma Hayek is Mexican.*)

   6. *Estar* is used with an adjective to show that the characteristic is a *change* or a *condition.*

      EXS:   **Esta nieve** *está* **roja.** (*This snow is red* [because of red paint or blood].)
      **Esta hierba** *está* **verde.** (*This grass is green* [because of fertilizers or watering].)

   7. *Ser* is used to express time. **Son las 10:00 de la mañana/am.** (*It is 10:00 A.M.*).

   8. *Ser* is used with the preposition **de** to indicate:

      a) ORIGIN: **Este vino** *es* **de España.** (*This wine is from Spain.*)

      b) MATERIAL: **La mesa** *es* **de plástico.** (*The table is made of plastic.*)

      c) POSSESSION: **La mochila** *es* **de mi amigo.** (*The backpack belongs to my friend.*)

# PRACTIQUE *SER* Y *ESTAR*

ANSWERS
p. 63

1. There are two verbs in Spanish for English *to be:* _____.

2. *Ser* is an -er verb and *estar* is an -ar verb, but they don't follow the patterns of *comer* and *hablar*. For this reason, we say that they are _____ verbs.

3. The first persons of *hablar* and *comer* end with the vowel o; the first persons of *ser* and *estar* don't end with *o* but with _____.

4. *Estar* has three forms, each with a written accent (*acento escrito*): _____.

5. Which verb is used to show the *place* where a person, an animal, or a thing *is*, *ser* or *estar*? _____ For example, **Marcos** _____ **en el gimnasio.**

6. Which verb is used to *identify* something, *ser* or *estar*? _____. For example, **Madrid** _____ **la capital de España.**

7. When Shakespeare wrote *to be or not to be,* perhaps he was thinking that a person should identify himself or herself the way he or she is. How would you translate that saying in Spanish? _____.

8. An adjective shows a characteristic of a noun: *red, big, good, roomy,* and so on. If that characteristic is a *norm* for the noun, we use the verb _____ in Spanish. If that characteristic is a *change* for the noun, we use _____.

9. Grass is usually green; that seems to be the *norm* for grass. In Spanish you say **La hierba** _____ **verde.**

10. It is a *norm* for coffee to be brown when roasted, but not to be hot or cold. You heat it to make it hot. That's a *change:* **El café** _____ **caliente.**

11. To indicate the *origin* of a person, a product, and so on, we use the verb _____ in Spanish. For example, **El taxista** _____ **de Córdoba.** After all, giving the origin of a person or product is a way of identifying that person or product.

12. To indicate the *material* something is made of, we use the verb _____. For example, **El anillo** _____ **de oro.** It's another way of identifying something.

13. To show *possession* in Spanish, we use the verb _____. For example, **El celular** _____ **de Roberto.**

# PRÁCTICA

ANSWERS
p. 63

Complete each sentence with the correct form of *ser* and/or *estar*.

1. Yo _____ de España. ¿De dónde _____ ustedes?

2. Ella _____ americana, pero esta semana _____ en Barcelona.

3. Muchas personas piensan que el mejor café _____ de Colombia.

4. Los estudiantes _____ en la clase de bioquímica.

5. ¿Quién (*who*) _____ la nueva presidente de México ahora?

6. Vosotras _____ en el gimnasio.

7. Pepe y yo no _____ uruguayos sino (*but*) argentinos.

8. ¿Cómo _____ usted hoy? —(Yo) _____ muy bien, gracias.

9. La temperatura _____ muy fría hoy (*cold*).

10. La nieve _____ blanca; la hierba (*grass*) _____ verde.

11. La sopa _____ caliente (*hot/temperature*) y la salsa _____ picante (*hot/spicy*) hoy.

12. Mi hermana _____ ingeniera química.

13. Nosotros _____ en el aeropuerto porque vamos a viajar a Perú.

14. El agua _____ buena para la salud (*health*).

15. La clase de comunicación _____ a las 9:30 A.M.

# EXPRESIONES CON EL VERBO *ESTAR*

| | |
|---|---|
| estar aburrido(a) | to be bored |
| estar alegre/feliz (contento(a)) | to be happy/content |
| estar avergonzado(a) (apenado/apenada) | to be embarrassed |
| estar bien | to be okay/well |
| estar cansado(a) | to be tired |
| estar enamorado(a) de | to be in love with |
| estar enfermo(a) | to be sick |
| estar enojado(a) | to be angry |
| estar equivocado(a) | to be wrong |
| estar listo(a) (para) | to be ready to do something |
| estar mal(a) | to be bad (to feel bad/sick) |
| estar ocupado(a) | to be busy |
| estar seguro(a) de (que) | to be sure |
| estar triste | to be sad |

# EXPRESIONES CON EL VERBO *SER*

| | |
|---|---|
| ser aburrido(a) | to be boring |
| ser listo(a) | to be smart |
| ser malo(a) | to be bad (as a quality) |

# PRÁCTICA

ANSWERS
p. 63
Write the following sentences in Spanish using the expressions of the verbs *ser* and *estar*.

1. You are wrong! _____

2. Mireya is ready to take the exam. _____

3. Francisco is in love with Janet. _____

4. I am sure the library opens at 9:00 A.M. _____

5. La Señora López is very busy today. _____

6. Methodology class is boring. _____

7. The children are bored at home. _____

8. The boss is bad with the employees. _____

9. Martha is very smart. _____

10. Nancy is very tired today. _____

# 3 Vidas ocupadas
## (*Busy Lives*)

## PALABRAS NUEVAS

| | | | |
|---|---|---|---|
| administración | management/business administration | fecha | date (calendar) |
| | | fiesta | party |
| aló (bueno) | hello (when answering a phone call) | fin de semana | weekend |
| | | forma | way |
| audio | audio | fraternidad | fraternity |
| bolso | purse | funcionar bien/ mal | to work well/bad (referring to electronics) |
| buena suerte | good luck | | |
| cámara | camera | | |
| cantante | singer | ingeniero (a) | engineer |
| carrera | career/major | kiubo (qué hubo) | What's up? |
| chao | bye (informal) | lenguas/idiomas | languages |
| cita | date (romantic date)/ appointment | madre/mamá | mother |
| | | maestría | master's degree |
| clases virtuales | online classes | mayoría | most/majority |
| compañía | company (place to work) | mercadotecnia | marketing |
| conferencia | | Navidad | Christmas |
| contaduría | conference accounting | novela | novel |
| | | padre/papá | father |
| estar seguro (a) | to be sure | país | country |
| éxito | success | película | movie |
| familia | family | ¿Por qué? | why |

| | | | |
|---|---|---|---|
| porque | because | dar | to give |
| propina | tip | decir | to say/to tell |
| razón/motivo | reason/purpose | describir | to describe |
| requisito | requirement | desear | to wish/to want |
| reunión de trabajo | work meeting | empezar | to start/to begin |
| | | enseñar | to teach |
| rubí | ruby | entender | to understand |
| salario | salary | funcionar | to work/to function |
| tener razón | to be right | imagine | to imagine |
| trabajo | job/work | ir | to go |
| viaje | trip | pronunciar | to pronounce |
| vida | life | recordar | to remember |
| video conferencia | video conference | tener que | to have to |
| | | tener razón | to be right |
| Zoom | Zoom | trabajar | to work |

| *Adjetivos* | *Adjectives* |
|---|---|
| algunos (as) | some/few |
| anual | yearly |
| caro (a) | expensive |
| festivo | holiday |
| internacional | international |
| mensual | monthly |
| ocupado (a) | busy/occupied |
| preparado (a) | prepared/ready |
| próximo (a) | next |
| remoto (a) | remotely/remote |
| semanal | weekly |
| solo (a) | alone |

| *Los días de la semana* | *The Days of the Week* |
|---|---|
| el/los lunes | Monday/s |
| el/los martes | Tuesday/s |
| el/los miércoles | Wednesday/s |
| el/los jueves | Thursday/s |
| el/los viernes | Friday/s |
| el/los sábado/s | Saturday/s |
| el/los domingo/s | Sunday/s |

| *Adverbios* | *Adverbs* |
|---|---|
| ahora | now |
| allá | there/over there |
| muy/súper | very/extremely |
| sólo/solamente | only |
| ya | already |

| *Los meses del año* | *The Months of the Year* |
|---|---|
| enero | January |
| febrero | February |
| marzo | March |
| abril | April |
| mayo | May |
| junio | June |
| julio | July |
| agosto | August |
| septiembre | September |
| octubre | October |
| noviembre | November |
| diciembre | December |

| *Verbos* | *Verbs* |
|---|---|
| celebrar | to celebrate |
| considerar | to consider |
| costar | to cost |

Note that. . .

1.  Many Hispanic countries use different words to describe the same thing. For example: "**aló**" is an expression to answer a phone call. It is used in Colombia. "**Bueno**" is used in México. Both are the equivalent of "hello".

2.  In English, it is the norm to use the preposition "on" when referring to the days of the week: *I have a meeting* **on** *Monday,* or *I have three classes* **on** *Mondays.* In Spanish, the norm is to use the definitive masculine article (singular or plural) instead of the preposition: *Tengo una reunión* **el lunes***, o Tengo tres clases* **los lunes***.*

3.  Days of the week and months of the year do not use capital letters like in English. Days of the week are masculine in Spanish and therefore use the masculine article *(el lunes/los lunes).*

4.  The word *date* has different meanings in Spanish. ¿**Cuál es la** <u>fecha</u> **de hoy?** (*What is today's date?*). **Tengo** <u>una cita</u> **romántica y estoy muy feliz.** (*I have a date and I am very happy*). Attention: cita also means *appointment*: "**Tengo** <u>una cita</u> **con el dentista**" means *I have a dentist's* **appointment***.*

# PRACTIQUE LAS PALABRAS NUEVAS

**ANSWERS p. 63**

**A.** Write the article *el* or *la* before each noun. Remember that *el* is used before nouns ending in *L-O-N-E-R-S* and *la* before those ending in *D-IÓN-Z-A.*

1.  _____ trabajo
2.  _____ videoconferencia
3.  _____ razón
4.  _____ viaje
5.  _____ maestría
6.  _____ cámara
7.  _____ compañía
8.  _____ audio
9.  _____ vida
10. _____ forma

**ANSWERS p. 64**

**B.** Los meses del año. Complete the sentences with words from the chapter vocabulary.

1.  La navidad (*Christmas*) se celebra en este mes _____.
2.  El primer mes del año es _____.
3.  En Estados Unidos y otros países se celebra San Valentín en _____.
4.  La fiesta de la Independencia de los Estados Unidos se celebra en este mes _____.
5.  La fiesta de acción de gracias (*Thanksgiving*) se celebra en el mes de _____.
6.  En el mes de _____ la mayoría de los colegios de Estados Unidos empiezan su año académico.
7.  En el mes de _____ se celebra en varios países el día de la madre.
8.  En el mes de _____ se celebra en algunos países el día del padre.

9. El primer lunes de este mes _____ se celebra el día del trabajo (*Labor Day*) en los Estados Unidos.

10. Halloween es una celebración que se celebra el 31 de este mes _____.

**ANSWERS p. 64**

C. **Los días de la semana. Fill in the correct word.**

1. El cuarto (*fourth*) _____ de noviembre se celebra el Día de Acción de Gracias en Estados Unidos.

2. El día _____ muchas personas asisten a la misa (*mass*) o servicios religiosos. Es un día de descanso.

3. El _____ 13 es un día que está en muchas películas de horror.

4. El _____ y el _____ se consideran días de fin de semana (*weekend*).

5. El primer _____ de septiembre se celebra el Día del Trabajo (*Labor Day*) en los Estados Unidos.

# DIÁLOGO Una semana muy ocupada

*Javier y Ernesto están conversando sobre su semana muy ocupada.*

JAVIER: ¿Aló? ¿Con quién hablo?

ERNESTO: Kiubo Javier, soy Ernesto, ¿Cómo vas?

JAVIER: Hola Ernesto, ¿Qué hay de nuevo?

ERNESTO: Te cuento que esta semana va a estar de locos.

JAVIER: ¿Por qué dices eso? ¿Mucho trabajo?

ERNESTO: Voy a estar super ocupado toda la semana y además tengo que viajar por razones de trabajo.

JAVIER: Sí, te entiendo. Yo también voy a estar ocupado. Como sabes estoy estudiando una maestría en mercadotecnia y tengo clases virtuales tres días a la semana. Tengo clase por la tarde todos los lunes, miércoles y viernes de 5:00 P.M. a 7:00 P.M. Como te puedes imaginar, con la familia, el trabajo y ahora la maestría estoy muy ocupado.

ERNESTO: Tienes razón. Tenemos vidas muy ocupadas. Yo tengo que viajar a la ciudad de México para una reunión de trabajo la próxima semana. Voy a estar algunos días allá y voy a trabajar para la compañía de forma remota. Necesito estar seguro de que mi computador, mi audio y mi cámara funcionen bien. Tengo tres videoconferencias en mi agenda y necesito estar muy bien preparado.

JAVIER: Pues, te deseo muy buena suerte en tu viaje y en tu trabajo. Tal vez, si tienes tiempo por la noche el viernes podemos conversar por Zoom. ¿Te parece bien?

ERNESTO: Me encanta la idea. Muchos éxitos en tus clases para la maestría. Nos hablamos por Zoom el viernes próximo.

JAVIER: Hasta el viernes. Chao.

# DIALOGUE   *A Busy Week*

*Javier and Ernesto are having a phone conversation about their busy week.*

JAVIER:        Hello? Who am I talking to?

ERNESTO:    What's up Javier, I'm Ernesto, how are you doing?

JAVIER:        Hello Ernesto, What's new?

ERNESTO:    Let me tell you that this week is going to be crazy.

JAVIER:        Why do you say that? a lot of work?

ERNESTO:    I'm going to be super busy all week and I also have to travel for work.

JAVIER:        Yes, I understand. I'm going to be busy too. As you know, I am studying a master's degree in marketing and I have virtual classes three days a week. I have afternoon classes every Monday, Wednesday, and Friday from 5:00 P.M. to 7:00 P.M. As you can imagine, with family, work and now my master's degree, I am very busy.

ERNESTO:    You're right. We have very busy lives. I have to travel to Mexico City for a work meeting next week. I'm going to be there for a few days and I'm going to work for the company remotely. I need to make sure my computer, audio, and camera will work well. I have three video conferences on my agenda and I need to be very well prepared.

JAVIER:        Well, I wish you good luck on your trip and in your work. Maybe if you have time on Friday night we can chat on Zoom. Is that okay with you?

ERNESTO:    I love the idea. Good luck in your classes for your master. We'll talk via Zoom next Friday.

JAVIER:        Until Friday. Bye.

# PRÁCTICA

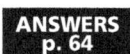

**A.** Complete the story using the information from the dialogue.

Javier y Ernesto tienen una semana muy (1) _____. Javier está estudiando una (2) _____ en Mercadotecnia. Él toma clases (3) _____ tres veces por (4) _____. Ernesto tiene que viajar a la (5) _____ de México porque tiene una (6) _____ de trabajo y también tiene tres (7) _____ durante la semana. Javier y Ernesto van a conversar por (8) _____ el viernes por la noche.

**B. Match the two columns.**

| | | | |
|---|---|---|---|
| 1. \_\_\_\_ algunos | | A. | yearly |
| 2. \_\_\_\_ maestría | | B. | success |
| 3. \_\_\_\_ mensual | | C. | way |
| 4. \_\_\_\_ ahora | | D. | monthly |
| 5. \_\_\_\_ éxito | | E. | marketing |
| 6. \_\_\_\_ viaje | | F. | few |
| 7. \_\_\_\_ forma | | G. | weekly |
| 8. \_\_\_\_ semanal | | H. | remotely |
| 9. \_\_\_\_ mercadotecnia | | I. | busy |
| 10. \_\_\_\_ remoto | | J. | prepared |
| 11. \_\_\_\_ ocupado | | K. | now |
| 12. \_\_\_\_ preparado | | L. | trip |
| 13. \_\_\_\_ anual | | M. | Master's degree |

# GRAMMAR I   Los adjetivos (*Adjective-Noun Agreement • Plural of Nouns and Adjectives*)

A.  An adjective describes a noun with such characteristics as color, shape, size, quality, nationality, and so on. The adjective agrees with its noun in *gender* (masculine/feminine) and *number* (singular/plural) in Spanish. In English adjectives never change; there is no agreement.

> EXS:  **un trabajo bueno** (*a good job*): masculine singular
> **una semana ocupada** (*a busy week*): feminine singular
> **unos trabajos buenos** (*some good jobs*): masculine plural
> **unas semanas ocupadas** (*some busy weeks*): feminine plural

B.  Adjectives ending in *o* change to *a* in the feminine: **bueno/buena.** If the adjective ends in any other letter, the feminine is the same as the masculine (there is no gender change).

> EXS:  **trabajo interesante/compañía/excelente, mejor trabajo/mejor maestría**

C.  Adjectives ending in *L-N-R-S* (part of *L-O-N-E-R-S*) and *referring to nationalities* add an *a* to the last consonant to form the feminine. They are also used as nouns.

> EXS:  **un profesor español/una profesora española, un español/una española**
> **un ingeniero inglés/una ingeniera inglesa, un inglés/una inglesa**
> **un instituto alemán/una universidad alemana, un alemán/una alemana**

D. *Plural* means two or more. Nouns and adjectives follow the same rules to form the plural.

1. If a word ends in a vowel, we add an *s:* **trabajo bueno/trabajos buenos.**

2. If a word ends in a consonant, we add *es:* **reunión virtual** (*virtual meeting*)**/reuniones virtuales.**

3. If a word ends in a *z,* we change *z* to *c* and add *es:* **vez/veces.**

4. If a word ends in an *s,* there are two rules for the plural.

   a) If the *s* is preceded by a *stressed vowel,* we add *es:* **inglés/ingleses.**

   b) If the *s* is preceded by an *unstressed vowel,* there is no change.

   EXS:  *un* **lunes/***dos* **lunes,** *una* **crisis/***dos* **crisis**

5. There are a few words ending in *stressed í* or *stressed ú,* that have two plural forms, one in *es* and the other in *s.*

   a) The *es* plural form is traditional, formal usage now: **rubí/rubíes, hindú/ hindúes** (*Hindu*)**, champú/champúes.**

   b) The *s* plural form is colloquial and very common today: **rubí/rubís, hindú/ hindús, champú/champús.**

E. The position of the adjective is often different in Spanish than in English. **In Spanish, descriptive adjectives** <u>usually follow the noun</u>. Adjectives of quantity, however, precede the noun, as in English.

   EX:  <u>una</u> conferencia *importante***/**<u>muchas</u> conferencias *importantes*

# PRACTIQUE LOS ADJETIVOS

**ANSWERS p. 64**

1. An adjective describes a _____. In Spanish the adjective changes with the noun for gender and _____.

2. Remember that nouns ending in *L-O-N-E-R-S* are _____. This means that these six endings will match adjectives ending in the letter _____.

3. Nouns ending in *D-IÓN-Z-A* are _____. These endings will match adjectives ending in the letter _____.

4. Do adjectives that end in *e* change from masculine to feminine? _____ For example, **libro interesante, conferencia** _____.

5. Which is correct, **trabajo bueno** or **trabajo buena**? _____.

6. Which is correct, **viaje largo** or **viaje larga**? _____.

7. Remember that nouns ending in *ma* are *not* feminine. Would you say **programa americano** or **programa americana**? _____.

8. Which is correct, **luz rojo** or **luz roja**? _____.

9. Would an adjective ending in *e*, such as **grande**, change from masculine to feminine? _____.

    EXS: **un colegio grande, una universidad** _____

10. The plural of *bueno* is _____. We add an *s* because the last letter is a _____.

11. The plural of *razón* is _____. We add *es* because the last letter is a _____.

12. The plural of *vez* is _____. We add *es* because the last letter is a consonant, but we change the *z* to _____ because in Spanish there is rarely a *z* before an *e* or an *i*.

13. The plural of *martes* is _____. The last letter is an *s*, and the preceding vowel, *e*, carries no _____; so there is no change.

14. The plural of *inglés* is _____. The last letter is an *s*, but it is preceded by a _____ vowel, *é*. Therefore we add *es*.

15. There are two plurals for words ending in stressed *í* or *ú*: *s* and _____. The traditional plural of the precious stone **rubí** is _____, whereas the modern plural is _____.

# PRÁCTICA

ANSWERS
p. 64

A. **Write the plural form.**

1. una lección interesante _____

2. un ejercicio difícil _____

3. un programa aburrido _____

4. una clase grande _____

5. la profesora americana _____

6. el jefe español _____

7. la mejor universidad _____

8. un trabajo importante _____

9. la reunión virtual _____

10. una conferencia internacional _____

11. el rubí caro (*traditional form*) _____

12. la luz roja _____

13. el champú americano (*modern form*) _____

14. un lunes festivo _____

15. un martes ocupado _____

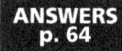

**ANSWERS**
**p. 64**

B. Underline the adjective that agrees with the noun. Two answers are possible in two cases. (Remember the rules for masculine/feminine gender.)

1. programa (bueno, buena, buenos, buenas)
2. universidad (americano, americanos, americana, americanas)
3. lunes (festivo, festiva, festivos, festivas)
4. profesoras (ocupado, ocupada, ocupados, ocupadas)
5. jóvenes (inteligente, inteligentes, inteligentas, inteligentos)
6. clase (grande, granda, grandes, grandas)
7. luz (roja, rojo, rojas, rojos)
8. viernes (pasado, pasada, pasados, pasadas)
9. librería (hispano, hispana, hispanos, hispanas)
10. rubís (caro, cara, caros, caras)

# GRAMMAR II    Presente del indicativo of *ir, dar, ver, saber* y *decir* (*Present Indicative of To Go, To Give, To See, To Know, and To Say*)

Memorize the present indicative of the verbs in the chart.

|  | *Ir* (to go) | *D ar* (to give) | *V er* (to see) | *Sab er* (to know) | *Dec ir* (to say) |
|---|---|---|---|---|---|
| yo | v oy | d oy | ve o | sé | dig o |
| tú | v as | d as | v es | sab es | dic es |
| él/ella/Ud. | v a | d a | v e | sab e | dic e |
| nosotros(as) | v amos | d amos | v emos | sab emos | dec imos |
| ellos/ellas/Uds. | v an | d an | v en | sab en | dic en |
| vosotros/as | v ais | d ais | v eis | sab éis | dec ís |

Note that:

1. *Ir* and *dar* are irregular because they add *y* to the *o* in the first person singular, just like *ser* (*soy*) and *estar* (*estoy*).

2. *Ver* is irregular in the first person singular because it adds an *e* to the stem *v:* (yo) **veo**.

3. *Saber* is very irregular in the first person singular. The *yo* form is *sé*.

4. *Decir* is the most irregular verb in this group. As a stem-changing verb, it changes *e* to *i* in *digo, dices, dice, dicen*. It also changes *c* to *g* in *digo*.

5. The person and number correspondence between the ending of a verb and its subject is the same for all these verbs.

-o (-oy) → yo, -mos → nosotros, -s → tú, -n → ellos/ellas/ustedes

The only exception is the -*é* of *sé*.

**NOTA**

Quite frequently we use *ir* + *a* + (infinitive) to indicate an action in the future, parallel to the English *to be* + *going* + (infinitive). In this case *ir* is used in the present indicative.

EX: Ellos *van a trabajar* mañana. (*They are going to work tomorrow.*)

# PRACTIQUE LOS VERBOS

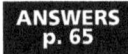

1. The basic meaning of a verb is carried by the _____ of the verb. For example, the part of *saber* with the meaning *to know* is _____.
2. *Dar* is an -**ar** verb; its stem is very short: _____. *Ver* is an -**er** verb, and its stem is also very short: _____. Remember that the stem is the part of the verb that is repeated in all the tenses if the verb is regular. If the verb is irregular, the stem changes.
3. The letter that is repeated in all present indicative forms of the verb *ir* is

   _____.

4. Most verbs have an -*o* for **yo** in the present indicative, but a few have -*oy* instead. For example, from *ir* get yo _____, and from *dar,* yo _____.
5. For *saber* we don't say yo **sabo**, but yo _____. For *decir* we don't say yo **deco**, but yo _____.
6. For *ver* (*v er*) we don't say **yo vo**, but yo _____. Notice the difference in spelling between *van* and *ven*: *van* means *they* _____; *ven* means *they*

   _____.

7. The person and number correspondence between the ending of a verb and its subject is the same for all verbs: -**mos** means _____; -**s** means _____, and -**n** means _____.
8. We can use the simple present indicative for an action in the future, for example, **Voy a clase mañana** (*I will go to class tomorrow*). We can also use the verb *ir* followed by the preposition *a* and the main verb: **Voy a verte mañana.** (*I am going to see you tomorrow*). How would you say *He is going to eat?* _____
9. The present tense can be used for an action that is a habit. How would you say *I always tell the truth* in Spanish? **Yo siempre** _____.

# PRÁCTICA

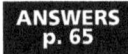

Complete each sentence with the correct present indicative form of the verb in parentheses.

1. Vosotros _____ a la universidad todos los días. (*to go*)
2. Los estudiantes *ya no* (*no longer*) _____ televisión. (*to watch*)
3. Tú siempre _____ la verdad. (*to say*)

4. Valentina _____ todas las respuestas. (*to know*)

5. Nosotras _____ la propina. (*to give*)

6. Yo no _____ a la fiesta sola. (*to go*)

7. Santiago y tú _____ muchos videos de TikTok. (*to see*)

8. Camila y Naty _____ hablar español *y* francés. (*to know [how]*)

9. El jefe _____ muchas instrucciones siempre. (*to give*)

10. Usted nunca _____ nada. (*to say*)

11. Yo _____ usar el programa de Excel. (*to know [how]*)

12. Tú _____ muchos videos en YouTube. (*to see*)

13. Nosotros no _____ usar el programa de inteligencia artificial. (*to know [how]*)

14. Emilia _____ a estudiar conmigo en la biblioteca. (*to be going to go*)

15. Los voluntarios les _____ agua a los atletas. (*to give*)

# GRAMMAR III   Palabras interrogativas y números en español
## (*Question Words • Numbers in Spanish*)

### PALABRAS INTERROGATIVAS (*Question Words*)

**A.** Memorize the following question words. Notice that all of them have a written accent (**acento**).

| | |
|---|---|
| **¿Adónde?** *Where to?* | **¿Dónde?** *Where?* |
| **¿Cómo?** *How?* | **¿De dónde?** *From where?* |
| **¿Cuál?/cuáles?** *Which?/Which ones?* | **¿Qué?** *What?* |
| **¿Cuándo?** *When?* | **¿Quién (es)?** *Who?(plural)* |
| **¿Cuánto(a)?** *How much?* | **¿Para qué?** *What for?* |
| **¿Cuántos(as)?** *How many?* | **¿Por qué?** *Why?* |
| **¿De quién?** *Whose?* | |

*¿Adónde?* can be spelled as two words: *¿A dónde?*

Notice the inverted question mark (¿) at the beginning of a question.

EX:   ¿A dónde piensas ir después del trabajo? (*Where are you planning to go after work?*)

In questions beginning with question words, the subject (**ustedes** in this case) *follows* the verb rather than preceding it.

EX:   **¿Cuándo tienen ustedes la conferencia?** (*When do you have the conference?*)

B. **¿Por qué?** *(why)* is with two words with a written accent and **porque** *(because)* it is just one word and it doesn't carry a written accent. The expression *Because of. . .* in Spanish could be translated as *debido a. . ., a causa de. . .* or *por.*

> EX:   ¿**Por qué** estás triste? **Porque** tengo una crisis de amor. (*Why are you sad? Because I have a love crisis).*
> **A causa de** (*por/debido a*) la lluvia la competencia se canceló. *(Due [because of. . .] to the rain the competition was canceled).*

C. Question words carry a written accent (') when used in *direct* questions as well as in *indirect* ones.

> EX:   **Deseo saber** *cómo* estás. (*I want to know <u>how</u> you are.*)

D. To ask about time, use the expression ¿**Qué hora es?** (*What time is it?).* To answer use always the definitive feminine article (singular or plural) with the time. Hours in Spanish are always feminine.

> EX:   **Es <u>la una</u> de la tarde.** (*It is 1:00 P.M.*) or **Son <u>las ocho</u> de la mañana.** (*It is 8:00 A.M.*)

E. To ask at what time is an event or an activity, use the preposition "**a**" before the question word. EX: ¿<u>A qué</u> **hora es el concierto de Shakira?** (*At what time is Shakira's concert?).* To answer use the preposition "**a**" before the time. **El concierto es <u>a</u> las 9:00 P.M.** (*The concert is at 9:00 P.M.*). Remember that the singular article is used with the hour 1, the other hours use the plural article.

> EX:   **la 1:20 P.M., las 3:25 A.M., las 6:30 P.M.**

F. To ask about the current date (day/month/year) use the expression ¿**Qué fecha es?** or ¿**Cuál es la fecha de hoy?** or ¿**A qué fecha estamos?** (*What is the date?/What date is today?).* To answer: **Hoy es el 5 de septiembre.** (*Today is September 5th*).

G. ¿**Qué?** or ¿**Cuál?** (*What?/Which?).* Use ¿**qué?** + **ser** when you want to ask for a definition or explanation.

> EX:   ¿**Qué es** el tango? (*What is the tango?). El tango es un baile típico de Argentina.*

Use ¿**cuál?** + **ser** when you want to ask about a specific choice among a set of options.

> EX:   ¿**Cuál es** tu canción de tango favorita? (*Which one is your favorite tango song?*)

Note that if there is not the verb *ser* after ¿**qué?** or ¿**cuál?** when you ask for a specific choice, either of the two can be used. See in the examples that ¿**qué?** and ¿**cuál?** are followed by a **noun** and not by the verb **ser.**

> EX:   ¿**Qué** *música* prefieres? ¿**Cuál** *música* prefieres? (*What music do you prefer?*)

## LOS NÚMEROS (Numbers in Spanish)

| | | | | | |
|---|---|---|---|---|---|
| 0 | cero | 17 | diecisiete | 60 | sesenta |
| 1 | un/uno/una | 18 | dieciocho | 70 | setenta |
| 2 | dos | 19 | diecinueve | 80 | ochenta |
| 3 | tres | 20 | veinte | 90 | noventa |
| 4 | cuatro | 21 | veintiuno(a) | 100 | cien, ciento |
| 5 | cinco | 22 | veintidós | 101 | ciento uno (un, una) |
| 6 | seis | 23 | veintitrés | 200 | doscientos(as) |
| 7 | siete | 24 | veinticuatro | 300 | trescientos(as) |
| 8 | ocho | 25 | veinticinco | 400 | cuatrocientos(as) |
| 9 | nueve | 26 | veintiséis | 500 | quinientos(as) |
| 10 | diez | 27 | veintisiete | 600 | seiscientos(as) |
| 11 | once | 28 | veintiocho | 700 | setecientos(as) |
| 12 | doce | 29 | veintinueve | 800 | ochocientos(as) |
| 13 | trece | 30 | treinta | 900 | novecientos(as) |
| 14 | catorce | 31 | treinta y uno | 1.000 | mil |
| 15 | quince | 40 | cuarenta | 2.000 | dos mil |
| 16 | dieciséis | 50 | cincuenta | 1.000.000 | un millón |

**D.** Notice the following facts about numbers.

1. The numbers from 16 to 29 are written as only one word and pronounced with only one phonetic stress. (In English compound numbers carry two stresses.)

   EXS: **dieciséis** (*síxtéen*), **veintidós, veintitrés, veintiséis.**

2. For *one* we use **un** before a masculine noun, **una** before a feminine noun, **uno** when the masculine noun is omitted, and **una** when the feminine noun is omitted.

   EXS: **un** libro, **una** novela. ¿Lee usted **un** libro? —Sí, leo **uno.**

   This same rule applies to compounds: **veintiún** libros, **veintiuna** mesas.

3. **Cien** is used before nouns and for the number 100. **Ciento** is used when counting after 100 and before 200 (101, 120, 140, 199 and so on); 130 = **ciento treinta,** and in compound numbers. 255 = **doscientos cincuenta y cinco.**

   The expression *one hundred percent* is **cien por ciento, cien por cien,** or **ciento por ciento,** according to the country and region.

4. In the hundreds (**doscientos, trescientos, cuatrocientos**), we use *doscientas, trescientas, cuatrocientas* when we talk about feminine nouns, as in **quinientas mesas.**

5. *Mil* doesn't change: mil, **dos mil, tres mil,** and so on. Notice that we don't say **un mil** for *one thousand;* simply **mil.** We use the plural **miles** to refer to a large but inexact amount. English uses *hundreds* or *tons* in this case.

   EX: **Tengo *miles* de amigos.** (*I have <u>hundreds [tons] of friends</u>*).

6. Notice the spelling of *million:* **millón** (not -**llion**). The plural is ***millones,*** and like ***millón,*** it is always followed by *de* before the noun we are counting.

    EX:  **un millón de dólares** (*a million dollars*)

7. To express the years in Spanish, you use the number the way it is. Unlike English, Spanish does not separate the numbers.

    EX:  *2025 (twenty, twenty-five): English*
    EX:  *2025* (**dos mil veinticinco**): **Spanish**

### NOTA

In Latin America the use of periods and commas in numbers varies. In countries like Mexico, Honduras and other Central American and Caribbean countries, periods are use for decimals and commas for thousands, as in the United States. In several South American and Southern Cone countries, periods are used for thousands and commas for decimals.

# PRACTIQUE LAS PALABRAS INTERROGATIVAS (*Question Words*)

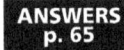
**ANSWERS p. 65**

1. ¿_____ vives? Vivo en La Paz, Bolivia.
2. ¿_____ cuesta (*cost*) un boleto de avión para ir a Cochabamba? Cuesta $900.00 dólares.
3. ¿_____ es la película (*movie*)? La película es a las 6:30 P.M.
4. ¿_____ hora es? Son las 12:45 P.M.
5. ¿_____ es la fiesta de la fraternidad? La fiesta de la fraternidad es el viernes por la noche.
6. ¿_____ estudias (tú) español? (Yo) Estudio español porque quiero vivir en Perú.
7. ¿_____ enseña tu clase de español? La profesora Ramírez enseña mi clase de español.
8. ¿_____ es tu profesora? Ella es inteligente y divertida.
9. ¿_____ estás hoy? Yo estoy muy cansado.
10. ¿_____ carrera estudias en la universidad? Yo estudio negocios y mercadeo.
11. ¿_____ te gusta hacer los fines de semana? Los fines de semana me gusta ir al cine (*go to the movies*).
12. ¿_____ es tu red social favorita? Mi red social favorita es Instagram.
13. ¿_____ clases tomas este semestre? Este semestre tomo contaduría, administración y español.

14.  ¿_____ es tu clase más difícil?

   La clase de contaduría es muy difícil.

15.  ¿_____ música te gusta?

   Me gusta la salsa.

16.  ¿_____ es tu cantante favorito?

   Marc Anthony es uno de mis cantantes favoritos.

# PRACTIQUE LOS NÚMEROS

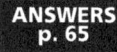

1.  In Spanish, *zero* is not spelled with a *z* but a _____. Notice that *diez* (10) has a *z*, but *dieziséis* is incorrect; it **should be** _____. **Remember that this same change** occurs in the plural of nouns and adjectives ending in *z*: **lápiz/lápices.**

2.  How many stresses does a compound number have in Spanish? _____. For example, **veinticinco** has the stress in the second number: _____.

3.  There are two words for 100 in Spanish: _____. and _____. Before a noun such as **pesos**, we say _____ **pesos.**

4.  Do we use *cien* or *ciento* in numbers over one hundred? _____ For example, on a Spanish bank bill 105 pesos is spelled like this: _____.

5.  The indefinite article **un/una** is exactly like the number *one* in Spanish: **un** is used before a _____ noun, and **una** before a _____ noun.

6.  *Uno* is used when a _____ noun is omitted, that is, when it's alone. For example, **¿Desea Ud. un lápiz? —Sí, deseo** _____.

7.  *Dos cientos* (200) is not correct; it should be _____. All multiples of one hundred change from *masculine* to *feminine* just like any other adjective. How do you say *three hundred people?* _____ **personas.**

8.  How do you say *one thousand* in Spanish? _____ (Notice that we don't translate *one!*) How do you say *two thousand?* _____.

9.  *Millión* is not correct in Spanish; it should be _____ The plural of *millón* is _____ (no written accent! You'll understand why later).

10.  We use the preposition _____ between **millón** or **millones** and the noun being counted. For example, *two million dollars* is **dos** _____ **dólares.**

11.  To indicate **mil** and **millón** in Spanish, do we use a comma or a period? _____. How do we indicate decimals, with a comma or a period? _____.

12.  Write how this figure would appear in Spanish: *2,200,300.50:* _____.

# PRÁCTICA

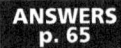
ANSWERS
p. 65

Palabras interrogativas. Complete sentences 1 to 9 with the translation of the word in parentheses.

1. ¿_____ vas a Cabo San Lucas? (*when*)
2. ¿_____ es tu libro favorito? (*which one*)
3. ¿_____ ves Snapchat todo el tiempo? (*why*)
4. ¿_____ maletas puedes llevar para el viaje? (*how many*)
5. ¿_____ clase de vino prefieres tomar? (*what/which one*)
6. Yo no sé _____ vive mi compañera Andrea. (*where*)
7. La profesora de administración de negocios va a decir _____ es el mejor de todos los estudiantes. (*which one*)
8. ¿_____ va usted después de clase? (*where to*)
9. ¿_____ café desea usted, señora? (*how much*)

# PRÁCTICA

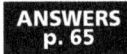
ANSWERS
p. 65

### Los Números

**Complete sentences 10 to 20 by writing out the number(s) in parentheses in Spanish).**

1. Elena sabe _____ lenguas (*languages*); yo sólo sé _____. (*3, 1*)
2. Jorge necesita tomar _____ requisito de humanidades, y yo también necesito _____. (*1, 1*)
3. Mañana es el día _____ de junio (*June*). (*16*)
4. ¿Tú vas a cumplir _____ años? ¡Es imposible! (*22*)
5. Necesito _____ dólares para comprar unas cosas. (*55*)
6. Este bolso cuesta _____ dólares. ¡No lo puedo creer! (*500*)
7. Esta cuenta del gas es de _____ pesos. (*110*)
8. ¿Quién va a pagar los _____ dólares? (*2.000,00*)
9. Aquí trabajan todos los días _____ personas. (*240*)
10. El salario para un profesional en Latinoamérica puede ser de _____ de pesos mensuales. ¡muy bajo! (*2.000.000,00*)
11. Tienes razón _____. (*100 percent*)

# PRACTIQUEMOS MÁS LOS NÚMEROS

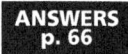

Write the number in Spanish.

*Modelo*: 100 = cien

1. 7 _____
2. 11 _____
3. 18 _____
4. 22 _____
5. 30 _____
6. 39 _____
7. 46 _____
8. 55 _____
9. 61 _____
10. 76 _____
11. 83 _____
12. 99 _____
13. 114 _____
14. 202 _____
15. 313 _____
16. 676 _____
17. 1000 _____
18. 1010 _____
19. 2025 _____
20. 4.000.000 _____

# ALGUNAS FECHAS IMPORTANTES EN LA HISTORIA
## (*Some Important Dates in History*)

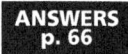

Write the year in letters in Spanish.

1. Independencia de los Estados Unidos (1776): _____
2. La llegada del hombre a la luna (1969): _____
3. Atentados del 11 de septiembre (2001): _____
4. El descubrimiento de América (1492): _____
5. La caída del muro de Berlín (1989): _____

# 4 Una familia unida y activa
## (*A Close and an Active Family*)

| | | | |
|---|---|---|---|
| el/la abuelo(a) | grandfather grandmother | el/la hermano (a) | brother/sister |
| los abuelos | grandparents | el/la hermanastro (a) | stepbrother/stepsister |
| la ayuda | help | el/la hijo (a) | son/daughter |
| el/la bisabuelo(a) | great-grandfather great-grandmother | el/la hijastro(a) | stepson/stepdaughter |
| la celebración | celebration | la hora | time (hour) |
| la cena | dinner | los juegos | games |
| el clima | weather | el laboratorio | laboratory |
| el cumpleaños | birthday | la madrastra | stepmother |
| el/la cuñado (a) | brother-in-law sister-in-law | la madre/la mamá | mother/mom |
| la dirección | address | la maqueta | project model |
| el/la esposo (a) | husband/wife/ (spouse) | la media hermana | half-sister |
| la fecha | date (regarding calendar) | el medio hermano | half-brother |
| | | el/la mellizo (a) | fraternal brother/ sister |
| flamenco | flamenco | la memoria | memory |
| el/la gato(a) | cat | el merengue | merengue dance |
| el/la gemelo(a) | twin brother/sister | el/la nieto (a) | grandson granddaughter |
| | | el/la novio (a) | boyfriend/girlfriend |

| la nuera | daughter-in-law |
| la ocasión | occasion |
| el padre/el papá | father/dad |
| los padres | parents |
| los parientes | relatives |
| el/la perro (a) | dog |
| el ponqué/la torta/ el pastel | cake |
| el/la primo (a) | cousin |
| el/la prometido (a) | fiancé |
| la radio/el radio | radio station/radio |
| la salsa | salsa dance |
| el/la sobrino (a) | nephew/niece |
| el suegro | father-in-law |
| la suegra | mother-in law |
| el/la tío (a) | uncle/aunt |
| la vejez | old age |
| el/la viudo (a) | widower/widow |
| el yerno | son-in-law |

| *Adjetivos* | *Adjectives* |
| bonito (a) | pretty/beautiful |
| casado (a) | married |
| complicado (a) | complicated |
| divorciado (a) | divorced |
| enamorad (a) | in love |
| enviudado (a) | widowed |
| espectacular | espectacular |
| extendida | extended |
| feliz/alegre | happy |
| feo (a) | ugly |
| guapo (a) | handsome |
| inmediata | immediate |
| lindo (a) | pretty/beautiful |
| mayor | older |

| menor | younger |
| paterno | paternal |
| pobre | poor |
| pública | public |
| rico (a) | rich |
| separado (a) | separated |
| soltero (a) | single |
| triste | sad/unhappy |
| viejo (a) | old |

| *Verbos* | *Verbs* |
| bailar | to dance |
| concluir | to conclude |
| conducir | to drive |
| construir | to build |
| cumplir años | to celebrate his/her birthday |
| dormir | to sleep |
| escuchar | to listen |
| estar enamorado (a) de | to be in love with |
| huir | to flee |
| invitar | to invite |
| jugar | to play |
| morir | to die |
| ofrecer | to offer |
| oír | to hear |
| parecer | to seem/to look like |
| preparar | to prepare |
| producir | to produce |
| reconocer | to recognize |
| tocar instrumento | to play an instrument |
| traducir | to translate |
| traer | to bring |
| venir | to come |

## Note That . . .

1. *Abuelos* has two different meanings, according to the context: *grandfathers* or *grandparents* [grandmothers and grandfathers]). The same thing happens with all the pairs in family words, such as **hermanos, hijos, padres,** and so on.

   EXS: **hermanos** (*brothers/brother*[*s*] *and sister*[*s*])
   **tíos** (*uncles/aunt*[*s*] *and uncle*[*s*]).

2. *Soltero (a)* means *single* and it is used when the person is not married. It is not used to indicate that a person does not have a boyfriend/girlfriend. Remember that *single* referring to a one-way (*trip*) is **sencillo**.

3. *Mayor* is used in a polite way to indicate that someone is old instead of viejo (a).

   EX: **Don Jorge es un hombre mayor.** (*Don Jorge is an old man*). When *old* is used to describe the age of an object, it is normal to use **viejo (a)**. **Esa casa es vieja.** (*That is an old house*)

4. *Novio (a)* is the equivalent of boyfriend/girlfriend. In Chile, they use the expression **pololo (a)** for boyfriend/girlfriend.

5. *Prometido (a)* (*fiancé*) is used when someone is engaged and he or she is getting married.

6. *Separado (a)* is used when a married couple or a couple in a relationship decide to split and go different ways breaking off their relationship without going through formal divorce proceedings.

7. **To be in love with** is "estar enamorado (a) de. . ." **To fall in love with** is "enamorarse de. . .". Note that the preposition in Spanish is "de" referring to a person. Julieta **está enamorada de** Romeo. Romeo **se enamoró de** Julieta.

8. *Conducir* means *to drive* in Spain, *to conduct* in all the other countries. In Latin America *to drive* is **manejar.**

9. *Oír* can mean both *to hear* and *to listen*, just like **ver** can mean *to see* and *to watch*. The verb *escuchar* also means *to listen*, but it is used less frequently than *oír*.

# PRACTIQUE LAS PALABRAS NUEVAS

**A.** Write *el* or *la* in front of the noun.

| | | | |
|---|---|---|---|
| 1. ____ abuelo | 5. ____ madre | 9. ____ prima | 13. ____ novio |
| 2. ____ pariente | 6. ____ hermano | 10. ____ papá | 14. ____ tía |
| 3. ____ cuñado | 7. ____ padrastro | 11. ____ bisabuelo | 15. ____ nieta |
| 4. ____ media hermana | 8. ____ prometida | 12. ____ yerno | 16. ____ nuera |

**B.** Complete the following sentences about the family.

1. La madre de mi mamá es mi _____.

2. El hermano de mi padre es mi _____.

3. Las hijas de mi hermana son mis _____.

4. Los hijos de mi hija son mis _____.

5. La hija de mi tío es mi _____.

6. Las hermanas de mi papá son mis _____.

7. Mis abuelos paternos son los padres de mi _____.

8. La esposa de mi hermano es mi _____.

9. El padre de mi esposa es mi _____.

10. La hija de mi padrastro es mi _____.

11. La mamá de mi esposo es mi _____.

12. Yo soy la _____ de mi abuela.

**ANSWERS p. 66**

C. Match the two columns.

1. _____ cuñado                    A. hija de mi tía
2. _____ nieto                     B. mamá de mi esposo
3. _____ sobrina                   C. mamá de mi abuela
4. _____ prima                     D. parientes
5. _____ suegro                    E. mis padres
6. _____ bisabuela                 F. hermana de mi papá
7. _____ mi papa y mi mamá         G. hija de mi hermana
8. _____ tíos, primos, abuelos     H. hijo del hijo de mi abuelo
9. _____ tía                       I. papá de mi esposa
10. _____ suegra                   J. esposo de mi hermana

# DIÁLOGO   Una celebración familiar en casa de Lorena

*Lorena es una joven profesional colombiana que tiene una familia extendida muy unida y quiere invitar a sus familiares para celebrarle el cumpleaños a su mamá. Lorena habla con su tía Nora por teléfono.*

LORENA:     ¡Hola tiíta! ¿Cómo estás?

TÍA NORA:   ¡Hola Lorenita! ¡Qué alegría escucharte! ¿Cómo va todo?

LORENA:     Muy bien tiíta. Aunque estoy un poco ocupada en el trabajo. Te llamo porque quiero hacerle una celebración especial a mi mami para el día de su cumpleaños. Como sabes ella cumple el 22 de marzo. ¡Cumple 60 años!

TÍA NORA:   Sí Lorenita, lo sé. Siempre recuerdo el cumpleaños de mi hermana Licita. Esta es una fecha muy importante. ¿Qué piensas hacer?

LORENA:     Me gustaría hacer una celebración familiar con una cena especial y me gustaría que tú, tío Adolfo y mis primos Diego y Esteban vengan a la cena. También quiero invitar a mi tío Alberto y a su esposa Amalia. Por supuesto, mi hermano Fernando y mi padrastro Manuel van a venir también.

TÍA NORA:   Me parece excelente idea. ¿Necesitas ayuda? ¿Quieres que traiga el ponqué o la torta de cumpleaños?

LORENA: Sí tiíta, muchas gracias. Tú sabes cuál torta le gusta a mi mamá. Yo voy a preparar algunas actividades y juegos divertidos para la ocasión.

TÍA NORA: ¿A qué hora es la celebración?

LORENA: Yo creo que a las 5:00 P.M. está bien. ¿Recuerdas la casa donde vivo ahora? Está muy cerca de la casa de mi abuelita Susana. La mamá de mi papá.

TÍA NORA: Claro que sí. Sé donde está la casa de tu abuelita. A propósito, ¿cómo está tu abuelita? ¿Cuántos años tiene ahora?

LORENA: Tiene ochenta y nueve años. Ya está muy viejita. Tiene problemas con su memoria y muchas veces se le olvidan las cosas.

TÍA NORA: Sí Lorenita, la vejez es dura. Los años no pasan solos.

LORENA: Bueno. . .tiíta, los espero el día 22 para la celebración. Me encantó conversar contigo.

TÍA NORA: Gracias Lorenita por la invitación. Estoy muy contenta de poder reunirnos para celebrarle el cumpleaños a mi hermanita. Nos vemos pronto.

## DIALOGUE *A Family Celebration at Laura's House*

*Lorena is a young Colombian professional who has a very close-knit extended family and wants to invite her relatives to celebrate her mother's birthday. Lorena talks to her Aunt Nora on the phone.*

LORENA: *Hello dear aunt! How are you?*

AUNT NORA: *Hello Lorenita! What a joy to hear from you! How is everything going?*

LORENA: *Very good aunt. Although I'm a little busy at work. I'm calling you because I want to throw a special celebration for my mom on her birthday. As you know, her birthday is March 22. She turns 60!*

AUNT NORA: *Yes Lorenita, I know. I always remember my sister Licita's birthday. This is a very important date. What are your plans?*

LORENA: *I would like to have a family celebration with a special dinner and I would like you, Uncle Adolfo and my cousins Diego and Esteban to come to dinner. I also want to invite my uncle Alberto and his wife Amalia. Of course, my brother Fernando and my stepfather Manuel are coming too.*

AUNT NORA: *I think it's an excellent idea. Do you need help? Do you want me to bring the birthday cake?*

LORENA: *Yes, auntie, thank you very much. You know which cake my mom likes. I am going to prepare some fun activities and games for the occasion.*

AUNT NORA:      *At what time is the celebration?*

LORENA:      *I think 5:00 P.M. is fine. Do you remember the house where I live now? It is very close to my grandmother Susana's house. My dad's mom.*

AUNT NORA:      *Of course. I know where your grandmother's house is. By the way, how is your grandmother? How old is she now?*

LORENA:      *She is eighty-nine years old. She is very old. She has problems with her memory and often forgets things.*

AUNT NORA:      *Yes Lorenita, aging is hard. The years do not pass alone, as we said in Colombia.*

LORENA:      *Well. . . dear aunt, I'll wait for you on the 22nd for the celebration. I loved talking to you.*

AUNT NORA:      *Thank you Lorenita for the invitation. I am very happy to be able to get together to celebrate my little sister's birthday. See you soon.*

# PRÁCTICA

**ANSWERS
p. 66**

**A.** *La familia de Lorena.* Complete the story using the information from the dialogue.

Lorena es una (1) _____ profesional colombiana que tiene una (2) _____ muy unida. La (3) _____ de Lorena se llama Liz, pero cariñosamente sus hermanos le dicen "Licita". Lorena quiere hacerle una celebración a su mamá porque es su (4) _____. Su mamá cumple (5) _____ años. Nora es la (6) _____ de Lorena y la (7) _____ de Liz. Lorena quiere invitar también a su (8) _____ Adolfo y sus (9) _____ Diego y Esteban. Fernando, el (10) _____ de Lorena, también va a venir a la celebración. Lorena tiene un (11) _____. Él se llama Manuel. Manuel es el nuevo (12) _____ de Licita. Lorena vive cerca de la casa de su (13) _____ Susana. Susana tiene problemas de (14) _____. Ella tiene (15) _____ años. Norita está muy feliz de celebrarle el cumpleaños a su hermana.

**ANSWERS
p. 67**

**B.** Match the two columns.

1. _____ Lorena es la . . . de la señora Susana.
2. _____ Fernando y Diego son . . .
3. _____ Licita es la . . . de Nora.
4. _____ Manuel es el . . . de Licita.
5. _____ Esteban es el . . . de Nora.
6. _____ Adolfo es el . . . de Licita.
7. _____ La señora Susana es la . . . de Lorena.
8. _____ Manuel es el . . . de Lorena.
9. _____ Diego es el . . . de Lorena.
10. _____ Fernando y Lorena son . . .

A. esposo
B. hijo
C. abuelita
D. primo
E. hermanos
F. hermana
G. padrastro
H. nieta
I. cuñado
J. primos

# GRAMMAR I    Presente del indicativo de los verbos oír, traer, conocer y huir (*Present Indicative of to hear, to bring, to know, and to flee*) • Diferencias entre saber y conocer (*Contrasting saber and conocer*)

A. Memorize the present indicative of the verbs in the chart.

|  | *o ir*<br>(*to hear*) | *tra er*<br>(*to bring*) | *conoc er*<br>(*to know*) | *hu ir*<br>(*to flee*) |
|---|---|---|---|---|
| yo | oig o | traig o | conozc o | huy o |
| tú | oy es | tra es | conoc es | huy es |
| él/ella/Ud. | oy e | tra e | conoc e | huy e |
| nosotros(as) | o imos | tra emos | conoc emos | hu imos |
| ellos/ellas/Uds. | oy en | tra en | conoc en | huy en |
| vosotros/as | o ís | tra éis | conoc éis | hu ís |

Note that:

1. *Oír* has a short stem: o-. It expands to **oig-** for the first-person singular, and to **oy-** for all the other persons except **oímos**, which is regular.

2. The stem of *traer* is **tra-**, and it is expanded to **traig-** in *traigo*. The other persons are regular: **traes, trae,** and so on.

3. *Conocer* has the stem **conoc-**. In the first-person singular the final *c* changes to *z* and adds the letter *c* with the [k] sound: **conozco.** Remember that *c* followed by *e* or *i* is pronounced *s* in Latin America and in some parts of Andalucia in southern Spain.

4. *Huir* has the stem **hu-**, which is expanded to **huy-** in all the forms except **huimos,** which is regular.

B. Verbs conjugated like *conocer* and *huir*

Most verbs ending in -cer and -cir add *c* in the yo form, like *conocer.* Verbs ending in -uir add *y* in all the forms except **nosotros,** just like *huir.*

| *-cer* | *-cir* | *-uir* |
|---|---|---|
| **aparecer** to appear | **conducir** to drive | **concluir** to conclude |
| **nacer** to be born | **producir** to produce | **construir** to build |
| **ofrecer** to offer | **reducir** to reduce | **destruir** to destroy |
| **parecer** to seem, look like | **traducir** to translate | **huir** to flee, escape |
| **reconocer** to recognize |  | **instruir** to instruct |

C. Differences between *saber* and *conocer*

1. *Conocer* is *to be acquainted with, to meet people.*

2. *Conocer* is *to know places, countries,* and *people,* in the sense of being familiar with them or have visited those places.

   EXS:  **¿Conoces a mi tío?** (*Are you <u>acquainted with</u> my uncle?*)

   **¿Conoces (a) Colombia?** (*Do you <u>know</u> Colombia? Have you been to Colombia? Are you familiar with the place/country?*)

   Some regions use the preposition **a** before cities and countries following *conocer*. Other regions omit it.

   EX:  **Conozco Bogotá./Conozco a Bogotá.** (*I <u>know</u> Bogotá. [I have visited Bogotá]*)

3. *Saber* is *to know facts, information.*

   EX:  **Sé donde vive tu abuelita.** (*I <u>know</u> where your grandmother lives.*)

4. *Saber* is *to know by heart,* like numbers.

   EX:  **¿Sabes mi teléfono?** (*Do you <u>know</u> my telephone number?*)

5. *Saber* is *to know how (skills),* but we don't translate the word *how.*

   EX:  **Laura *sabe* diseñar videos para promocionar productos.** (*Laura <u>knows</u> <u>how</u> to design videos to promote products.*)

# PRACTIQUE LOS VERBOS

**ANSWERS p. 67**

1. *Oír* has three different stems in the present: _____, _____, _____. The only regular form is (**nosotros**) _____ (with a written accent!).

2. *Traer* and *caer* are irregular in the first person only: _____/_____. Both add these two letters to the stem: _____.

3. *Conocer* changes to yo _____. The *c* has changed to *z* because of a spelling rule, but it has added the sound [k], which is the letter _____.

4. Most of the verbs ending in -**cer** and -**cir** are irregular like *conocer*. For example, from *ofrecer,* yo _____; and from *conducir,* yo _____.

5. The stem of *huir* is **hu-**, but it adds the letter _____ in **huyo, huyes,** and so on. The only regular form is (**nosotros**) _____.

6. All the verbs ending in -**uir** add the *y* to the stem like *huir.*

   EXS:  **construir,** yo _____; **concluir,** ellos _____.

7. *Nacer* is a passive verb in English, *to be born.* We use this verb in the past more often than in the present: *I was born in . . .* But it is possible to say *I am born,* at least in poetry. The translation in Spanish is _____.

8. *Saber* and *conocer* mean *to know.* Which one do you use for *to know* or *meet people?* _____ And *to know facts?* _____.

9. *To know how* implies knowledge, skills, and practice. Do you use *saber* or *conocer?* _____. Do you translate *how* in *to know how?* _____.

10. If you *know a city* or *a state, meaning that you have been there,* do you use *saber* or *conocer?* _____. For example, **Nosotros** _____ **Bogotá.**

11. If you *know* my telephone number and my address, it means that you have memorized numbers and names. How would you say *I know your telephone number?* _____ **tu número de teléfono.**

12. How do you say *I know how to dance salsa?* _____.

# PRACTIQUE LOS VERBOS *SABER* Y *CONOCER* (*to know*)

ANSWERS p. 67

Complete con la forma correcta de los verbos *saber* y/o *conocer*

1. Yo _____ dónde está la biblioteca pública. Está en la calle Michigan.

2. Mi amiga _____ bailar flamenco muy bien.

3. Nosotros no _____ a los padres de mi amigo Pedro.

4. Tú _____ tocar el violín muy bien.

5. Los jóvenes _____ jugar muchos videojuegos.

6. Mi tío no _____ jugar al golf.

7. Yo _____ Hawaii y me parece (*I think*) que es espectacular.

8. Mi amiga y yo no _____ Costa Rica, pero _____ que su clima es muy agradable.

9. Tú _____ hablar español, pero no _____ hablar francés.

10. Yo _____ muy bien a mis estudiantes; _____ que tengo 23 estudiantes en la clase.

11. Muchas personas de Colombia no _____ el departamento del Amazonas al sur del país.

12. Mi amiga Elsa _____ la dirección de mi casa.

13. Yo _____ que este ejercicio es un poco difícil.

14. El próximo mes Erica y sus amigas van a _____ la ciudad de Paris en Francia. Van a ir por primera vez.

15. La situación de nuestra amiga es un poco complicada. Nosotras no _____ cómo ayudarla (*help her*).

# PRÁCTICA

ANSWERS p. 67

Complete each sentence with the correct form(s) of the verb(s) in parentheses.

1. Colombia _____ muy buen café. (*to produce*)

2. Juan Miguel no _____ todavía porque sólo tiene 14 años. (*to drive*)

3. Mi esposo _____ ruidos (*noises*) por la noche. (*to hear*)

4. Los gatos de Francisco _____ por la ventana. (*to flee, go away*)

5. Tú no _____ mucho porque tienes mucho trabajo. (*to sleep*)

6. Mi primo Daniel _____ una maqueta de un laboratorio para su clase de genética. (*to build*)

7. Muchos niños _____ de hambre (*hunger, starvation*) todos los días. (*to die*)

8. (Yo) _____ el carro a la universidad todos los días. (*to bring*)

9. Tu novia _____ que es muy simpática. (*to seem*)

10. Mi suegra no _____ sus errores. (*to recognize*)

11. Mi abuela _____ a todos sus parientes. (*to remember*)

12. Mi cuñada _____ los mensajes de texto del español al alemán porque trabaja en una compañía multinacional alemana. (*to translate*)

13. Lucrecia _____ bien la ciudad de Nueva York. Ha visitado (*have visited*) la ciudad muchas veces. (*to know*)

14. (Nosotros) _____ bailar salsa y merengue muy bien. (*to know how*)

15. La familia le _____ una fiesta de compromiso a los novios. (*to offer, give*)

# GRAMMAR II   Los diminutivos (*Diminutives*)

**A.** Diminutives are words, adjectives or names, that indicate small size and are used to express affection, youth, or also to downplay the importance of a subject or something.

**B.** The most common ending of words with diminutives forms in the Hispanic world are *ito, ita, itos, itas*. Also, in some countries they use *illo, illa, ico, ica* and the corresponding plural forms. Words such as abuelita, Laurita, casita, etc., are some few examples of diminutives.

**C.** The following rules apply when you form the diminutives.

1. Diminutives can be used with three different types of words: nouns, adjectives, and adverbs. For example: casa = *casita* (nombre); pequeño= *pequeñito* (adjetivo); rápido = *rapidito* (adverbio).

2. If the words end in a non-stressed vowel (without accent), the final vowel is eliminated and the ending *ito* is added if it is masculine or *ita* if it is feminine. For example: mesa = mes = mesita; Laura = Laur = Laurita; hermano = herman= hermanito; tía=ti =tiíta

3. If the final vowel of the word is *e*, the diminutive is formed with the ending *ecito o ecita*. Por ejemplo: jefe = jef= jefecito; calle = call = callecita; fuerte = fuert=fuertecito/a

4. If the words have only one syllable (monosyllable), the diminutive is formed with the ending *ecito/ecita*. For example: tren = trencito; sol=solecito; pan=panecito

If the monosyllable ends in *z*, the *z* changes to *c* when forming the monosyllable. For example: luz = lucecita; pez= pececito; voz = vocecita

5. If the words have more than one syllable and end in a consonant, to form the diminutive the ending *cito* or *cita* is added. For example: color = colorcito; mujer =mujercita; joven = jovencito/a

D. A few exceptions can be given as follows: Oscar = Osquitar; Marcos=Marquitos. In these cases, to maintain the pronunciation of the sound [k] in words like Oscar [oskar] and Marcos [markos], to form the diminutive the consonant *c* is changed to *qu* because c+i has the sound [s] and not [k]. Osquitar [oskitar]; Markitos [markitos]

E. On some occasions, the ending *ito/a* and ico/a can be used interchangeably. In the case of the word foto (fotografía). Both *fotito* and *fotico* forms can be used. Another example: fiesta = *fiestita/fiestica*.

# PRACTIQUE LOS DIMINUTIVOS

ANSWERS
p. 67

Completa con la forma correcta del diminutivo.

1. Mi tía Inés tiene un _____ (perro) muy gracioso. Se llama Toby.
2. El carro de Lina es _____ (pequeño).
3. Mi tío Manuel vive en una _____ (casa) muy linda cerca a un lago.
4. La tía _____ (Elsa) es muy cariñosa y amable.
5. La _____ (hija) de Oscar practica la gimnasia.
6. La _____ (bebé) de mi prima tiene 3 meses.
7. Javier es un _____ (joven) muy guapo.
8. El _____ (papel) está en la mesa.
9. Mis _____ (primos) viven en Medellín.
10. La _____ (abuela) de Francisco está enferma.

# PRÁCTICA

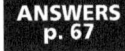
ANSWERS
p. 67

Escriba el diminutivo de cada palabra.

1. lápiz _____
2. cuaderno _____
3. abuela _____
4. doctor _____
5. mujer _____
6. sobrina _____
7. animal _____
8. escuela _____

9. ángel _____
10. hombre _____
11. tiempo _____
12. borrador _____
13. hijo _____
14. viaje _____
15. bus _____
16. noche _____
17. joven _____
18. papel _____
19. vez _____
20. trabajo _____

# GRAMMAR III    Formas negativas (*Negative Forms*)

**A.** Memorize the following negative and affirmative words.

**jamás/siempre** never/always
**nada/algo** nothing/something
**nadie/alguien** nobody/somebody
**ninguno/alguno** no one, none/some

**no/sí** no/yes
**nunca/siempre** never/always
**sin/con** without/with
**tampoco/también** neither, either/also

**B.** Notice the following rules about the words in the list above.

1. *Jamás* and *nunca* mean *never, but jamás* is more emphatic. Actually the two words can be used in the same sentence to make the negation even stronger.

    EX:  **Carlos *nunca jamás* estudia.** (*Charles <u>never never</u> studies.*)

2. *Nadie* and *alguien* refer to people only, whereas *nada* and *algo* refer to things.

    EXS:  **¿*Alguien* sabe esta palabra?** (*Does <u>anybody</u> know this word?*) **Nadie** dice eso. (<u>*Nobody*</u> *says that.*)

3. *Alguno* and *ninguno* refer to people or things. They change to *alguna/ninguna* for the feminine. *Algunos(as)* is the plural of *alguno(a), but ninguno(a)* has no plural. *Alguno* and *ninguno* become *algún/ningún* in front of a masculine noun: *algún* **libro**.

    EX:  **¿Conoces a *algún* francés en París? —No, no conozco a *ninguno*.** (*Do you know <u>any</u> French people in Paris? —No, I don't know <u>any</u>.*)

4. *Alguno* is used only before a noun, or as a pronoun when the noun has already been mentioned, whereas *alguien* is always used without a noun. The same rule applies to *ninguno* versus *nadie*.

    EXS:  **¿Cuántos niños vienen? —No viene *ninguno*.** (*How many boys are coming? —<u>None</u> are coming.*)

¿Conoces esos libros? —Sí, conozco *algunos.*
(*Do you know those books? —Yes, I know <u>some</u>.*)

C. **Double negative in Spanish**
If a sentence starts with a negative word, an affirmative word cannot be used after the verb. Another negative word must be used. For example, it's incorrect to say **No viene alguien;** it must be **No viene nadie.** The double negative is summarized in the following chart. Notice that it is possible to have a triple negative.

| Negative word | + | Verb | + | Negative word | + | Negative word |
|---|---|---|---|---|---|---|
| (Ella) No | | dice | | nada | | nunca |

EXS: Juan *no* habla español *tampoco.* (*John <u>doesn't</u> speak Spanish <u>either</u>.*)
Juan *no* fuma *nada nunca.* (*John <u>doesn't</u> smoke <u>anything ever</u>.*)

D. **Simple negative and double negative**
A simple or double negative can often be used to carry the same message. The double negative is more emphatic.

EXS: *Nadie* habla español aquí. = *No* habla *nadie* español aquí. (*<u>Nobody</u> speaks Spanish here.*)
Ella *tampoco* habla español. = Ella *no* habla español *tampoco.* (*She <u>doesn't</u> speak Spanish <u>either</u>.*)

# PRACTIQUE LAS PALABRAS NEGATIVAS

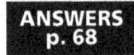
**ANSWERS p. 68**

1. Lo contrario de (*the opposite of*) *alguno* es _____, y lo contrario de *algo* es _____.

2. Lo contrario de *también* es _____, y lo contrario de *con* es _____.

3. Which is more emphatic, **Nadie habla** or **No habla nadie?** _____.

4. ¿Cuál es correcto, **Él es no bueno** or **Él no es bueno?** _____.

5. ¿Cuál es correcto, **Él está no aquí** or **Él no está aquí?** _____.

6. *Alguno/ninguno* become _____/_____ in front of a masculine noun.

7. When we say **nadie** in Spanish, we mean **ninguna** _____, and when we say **nada**, we mean **ninguna** _____.

8. **Tú no sabes inglés también** is incorrect; it should be: **Tú no sabes inglés** _____.

9. Lo contrario de (*the opposite of*) *nadie* es _____.

10. Lo contrario de *tampoco* es _____.

11. Lo contrario de *siempre* es _____.

12. Lo contrario de *sin* es _____.

13. Lo contrario de **ningún** es _____.

14. ¿Cómo traduce usted *I know nothing?* _____.

15. ¿Cómo traduce usted *I don't know anything?* _____.

16. **No digo algo** es incorrecto. Debe ser _____.

17. **No habla alguien** es incorrecto. Debe ser _____.

18. **Nunca digo algo** es incorrecto. Debe ser _____.

19. **No trabaja también** es incorrecto. Debe ser _____.

20. **No tengo algún** libro es incorrecto. Debe ser _____.

21. **Ella es no peruana** es incorrecto. Debe ser _____.

22. **Ella está no bien** es incorrecto. Debe ser _____.

23. There are two words for *anything* in Spanish: _____.

24. There are two words for *also* in Spanish: _____.

25. There are two words in Spanish for *never*: _____.

# PRÁCTICA

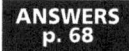

Change the following sentences to the negative forms.

1. Hay algo interesante en la programación de eventos para hoy. _____

2. Neflix tiene algunas películas bolivianas. _____

3. El profesor de historia enseña geografía también. _____

4. Tú siempre estudias en la biblioteca de la universidad. _____

5. El jefe prepara algo especial para los empleados. _____

6. Me gusta leer todo. _____

7. Hay algunos estudiantes excelentes en mi clase de contaduría. _____

8. Oigo noticias en la radio siempre. _____

9. Siempre estamos cansados. _____

# ANSWERS LESSONS 1–4

## Lesson 1

### Practique las nuevas expresiones

1. Buenos días
2. ¡Hola! ¿Qué tal?
3. ¿Cómo está usted?
4. Varias opciones: muy bien/bien/más o menos/regular/mal
5. Hasta mañana/hasta luego
6. Por favor
7. Muchas gracias
8. Lo siento
9. Adiós/Hasta luego
10. De nada
11. ¿Cómo se llama usted?

### Practique las palabras nuevas (*Practice the new words*)

A.
1. agenda
2. autobús/bus
3. chocolate
4. comunicación
5. conversación
6. decisión
7. garaje
8. hotel
9. instituto
10. menú
11. policía
12. porcentaje
13. reunión
14. televisión
15. taxi

B.
1. librería
2. biblioteca
3. compañero (de clase)
4. compañera (de trabajo)
5. amiga
6. escuela/colegio de primaria
7. universidad
8. correo electrónico
9. red
10. programa
11. palabra
12. hombre
13. mujer
14. joven
15. estudiante

C. Vocabulario
1. librería. . .biblioteca
2. por la mañana. . .por la tarde. . .por la noche
3. correo electrónico
4. el portátil (el computador portátil)
5. la universidad
6. ciudad
7. el campo

### Practique los artículos (*Practice the articles*)

1. un/una/a/an
2. masculine/feminine
3. masculine/feminine
4. things
5. masculine/feminine
6. No/letter(s)
7. female/a young man/a young woman
8. letter(s)/feminine
9. *L-O-N-E-R-S/D-IÓN-Z-A*
10. masculine/masculine/ feminine
11. masculine/una/una
12. masculine/un
13. una/un/Buenos días
14. un lápiz/una tarde

## Práctica

| | | | | |
|---|---|---|---|---|
| 1. un | 5. un | 9. un | 13. una | 17. un |
| 2. una | 6. una | 10. una | 14. una | 18. un |
| 3. un | 7. un | 11. una | 15. un | 19. una |
| 4. una | 8. una | 12. una | 16. una | 20. un |

## Practique los artículos definidos (*Practice the definite articles*)

1. el/la, los/las
2. *L-O-N-E-R-S/D-IÓN-Z-A*
3. feminine/masculine/masculine
4. masculine/el/el
5. feminine/el/la/la/la
6. del/al
7. stressed/el/el
8. h/el/la/el
9. No/stressed
10. del/del
11. Yes/la

## Práctica

| | | | | | | |
|---|---|---|---|---|---|---|
| 1. el | 4. el | 7. el | 10. el | 13. la | 16. la | 19. el |
| 2. el | 5. la | 8. la | 11. la | 14. la | 17. la | 20. el |
| 3. la | 6. la | 9. el | 12. la | 15. el | 18. el | |

## Practique los pronombres de sujeto (*Practice the subject pronouns*)

1. I/yo
2. nosotros/nosotras
3. tú/ustedes
4. tú
5. females/females
6. nosotros
7. usted/tú
8. tú/él
9. él/ella/nothing
10. ellas/ellos
11. nothing
12. usted
13. Ud./Vd., Uds./Vds.

## Práctica

| | | | |
|---|---|---|---|
| 1. nosotras | 5. nothing | 9. ellos | 13. nosotros |
| 2. tú | 6. usted | 10. ustedes | 14. ellos |
| 3. vosotros | 7. ellos | 11. él/ella/nothing | 15. ustedes |
| 4. ellas | 8. nosotros | 12. yo | |

# Lesson 2

## Práctica

A. 1. generación
   2. cafetería
   3. proyecto
   4. año

   5. característica. . .tecnología
   6. celular/móvil
   7. redes sociales

   8. consumidora
   9. internet
   10. compradora

B. 1. el internet
   2. cafetería

   3. comunicación
   4. compulsiva

   5. celular

## Practique las palabras nuevas

A. 1. cafetería
   2. robótica
   3. turistas
   4. proyecto
   5. actual. . .tecnología

   6. redes sociales
   7. semana
   8. padres
   9. generación
   10. problema . . .clases

   11. mensajes de texto
   12. coro
   13. apuntes
   14. notas
   15. en casa

B. 1. year
   2. month
   3. day
   4. class

   5. problem
   6. window
   7. table
   8. buyer (female)

   9. consumer (male)
   10. eraser
   11. project
   12. technology

   13. theme/topic
   14. generation
   15. practice

C. 1. borrador
   2. proyecto
   3. mesa
   4. tecnología
   5. ventana

D. 1. N
   2. M
   3. K

   4. H
   5. O
   6. L

   7. J
   8. I
   9. G

   10. C
   11. F
   12. D

   13. E
   14. A
   15. B

## Practique el presente de indicativo

1. infinitive/ar/er/ir
2. meaning/habl-/viv-/com-
3. nosotros/tú/yo
4. habla

5. hablamos
6. estudiamos
7. emphasis
8. progress/estudia

9. us-/usamos/usan
10. hablo
11. estudio
12. sí estudia

## Práctica el presente del indicativo—verbos AR

1. estudiamos
2. preparo
3. necesita
4. toma
5. cantamos

6. compra
7. amas
8. enseñan
9. canta
10. practican

11. trabajan
12. regreso
13. monta
14. sacan
15. miran

16. llegas
17. toma
18. habláis
19. practican
20. mandan

### Practique el presente del indicativo

1. -er/-ir
2. meaning/escrib-/le-
3. ending/yo
4. vivimos
5. first and second person plural
6. vive
7. present indicative/bebe
8. leo
9. We are writing/We write/We will write/We do write

### Práctica el presente del indicativo verbos *er/ir*

1. aprendemos
2. lee
3. comprendes
4. abre
5. beben
6. subimos
7. sale
8. comen
9. creen
10. escribo
11. subís
12. vive
13. recibe
14. asisten
15. atiende

### Practique *ser* y *estar*

1. ser/estar
2. irregular
3. oy
4. estás/está/están
5. estar/está
6. ser/es
7. Ser/o no ser
8. ser/estar
9. es
10. está
11. ser/es
12. ser/es
13. ser/es

### Práctica

1. soy/son
2. es/está
3. es
4. están
5. es
6. estáis
7. somos
8. está . . . estoy
9. está
10. es/es
11. está. . .está
12. es
13. estamos
14. es
15. es

### Práctica

1. ¡Estás equivocado(a)!
2. Mireya está lista para tomar el examen.
3. Francisco está enamorado de Janet.
4. Estoy seguro/a que la biblioteca abre a las 9:00 A.M.
5. La señora López está muy ocupada hoy.
6. La clase de metodología es aburrida.
7. Los niños están aburridos en casa.
8. El jefe es malo con los empleados.
9. Martha es muy lista (inteligente).
10. Nancy está muy cansada hoy.

# Lesson 3

### Practique las palabras nuevas

A. 
1. el
2. la
3. la
4. el
5. la
6. la
7. la
8. el
9. la
10. la

B. Los meses del año.

| | | | | |
|---|---|---|---|---|
| 1. diciembre | 3. febrero | 5. noviembre | 7. mayo | 9. septiembre |
| 2. enero | 4. julio | 6. agosto | 8. junio | 10. octubre |

C. Los días de la semana.

1. jueves    2. domingo    3. viernes    4. sábado. . .domingo    5. lunes

## Práctica

A. 1. ocupada    3. virtuales    5. ciudad    7. videoconferencias
   2. maestría    4. semana    6. reunión    8. Zoom

B. 1. F    3. D    5. B    7. C    9. E    11. I    13. A
   2. M    4. K    6. L    8. G    10. H    12. J

## Practique la gramática

1. noun/number
2. masculine/o
3. feminine/a
4. no/interesante
5. trabajo bueno
6. viaje largo
7. programa americano
8. luz roja
9. No/grande
10. buenos/vowel
11. razones/consonant
12. veces/c
13. martes/stress
14. ingleses/stressed
15. es/rubíes/rubís

## Practique la forma plural

A. 1. unas lecciones interesantes
   2. unos ejercicios difíciles
   3. unos programas aburridos
   4. unas clases grandes
   5. las profesoras americanas
   6. los jefes españoles
   7. las mejores universidades
   8. unos trabajos importantes
   9. las reuniones virtuales
   10. unas conferencias internacionales
   11. los rubíes caros
   12. las luces rojas
   13. los champús americanos
   14. unos lunes festivos
   15. unos martes ocupados

B. 1. bueno
   2. americana
   3. festivo/festivos
   4. ocupadas
   5. inteligentes
   6. grande
   7. roja
   8. pasado/pasados
   9. hispana
   10. caros

## Practique los verbos

1. stem/sab-
2. d-/v-
3. v
4. voy/doy
5. sé/digo
6. veo/go/see
7. nosotros/tú/ellos, ellas, ustedes
8. (Él) va a comer
9. digo la verdad

## Práctica verbos *ir, ver, saber, dar, decir*

1. vais
2. ven
3. dices
4. sabe
5. damos
6. voy
7. ven/veis
8. saben
9. da
10. dice
11. sé
12. ves
13. sabemos
14. va a ir
15. dan

## Practique las palabras interrogativas

1. dónde
2. cuánto
3. a qué hora
4. qué
5. cuándo
6. por qué
7. quién
8. cómo
9. cómo
10. qué/cuál
11. qué
12. cuál
13. qué/cuáles
14. cuál
15. qué/cuál
16. cuál/quién

## Practique los números

1. c (cero). . . dieciséis
2. one. . . cin
3. cien...ciento/cien
4. ciento. . . ciento cinco pesos
5. masculine. . . femenine
6. masculine. . . uno
7. doscientos. . . trescientas
8. mil. . . dos mil
9. millón. . . millones
10. de. . . millones de
11. period. . . comma
12. 2.000.200.300, 50

## Practique las palabras interrogativas

1. cuándo
2. cuál
3. por qué
4. cuántas
5. qué/cuál
6. dónde
7. cuál
8. a dónde
9. cuánto

## Práctica

1. tres. . . una
2. un. . . uno
3. dieciséis
4. veintidós
5. cincuenta y cinco
6. quinientos
7. ciento diez
8. dos mil
9. doscientas cuarenta
10. dos millones
11. cien por ciento

## Practiquemos más los números

1. siete
2. once
3. dieciocho
4. veintidós
5. treinta
6. treinta y nueve
7. cuarenta y seis
8. cincuenta y cinco
9. sesenta y uno
10. setenta y seis
11. ochenta y tres
12. noventa y nueve
13. ciento catorce
14. doscientos dos
15. trescientos trece
16. seiscientos setenta y seis
17. mil
18. mil diez
19. dos mil veinticinco
20. cuatro millones

## Algunas Fechas Importantes De La Historia

1. mil setecientos setenta y seis
2. mil novecientos sesenta y nueve
3. dos mil uno
4. mil cuatrocientos noventa y dos
5. mil novecientos ochenta y nueve

# Lesson 4

## Practique las palabras nuevas

A.
1. el
2. el/la
3. el
4. la
5. la
6. el
7. el
8. la
9. la
10. el
11. el
12. el
13. el
14. la
15. la
16. la

B.
1. abuela
2. tío
3. sobrinas
4. nietos
5. prima
6. tías
7. papá/padre
8. cuñada
9. suegro
10. hermanastra
11. suegra
12. nieta

C.
1. J
2. H
3. G
4. A
5. I
6. C
7. E
8. D
9. F
10. B

## Práctica

A.
1. joven
2. familia
3. mamá/madre
4. cumpleaños
5. 60
6. tía
7. hermana
8. tío
9. primos
10. hermano
11. padrastro
12. esposo
13. abuelita/abuela
14. memoria
15. 89

B. 1. H   3. F   5. B   7. C   9. D
2. J   4. A   6. I   8. G   10. E

## Practique los verbos

1. o-/oig-/oy-/oímos
2. traigo/caigo/ig
3. conozco/c
4. ofrezco/conduzco
5. y/huimos
6. construyo/concluyen
7. nazco
8. conocer/saber
9. saber/no
10. conocer/conocemos
11. sé
12. sé bailar salsa

## Practique los verbos *saber y conocer*

1. sé
2. sabe
3. conocemos
4. sabes
5. saben
6. sabe
7. conozco
8. conocemos. . .sabemos
9. sabes. . .sabes
10. conozco. . .sé
11. conocen
12. sabe
13. sé
14. conocer
15. sabemos

## Practique los verbos

1. produce
2. conduce
3. oye
4. huyen
5. duermes
6. construye
7. mueren
8. traigo
9. parece
10. reconoce
11. recuerda
12. traduce
13. conoce
14. sabemos
15. da

## Practique los diminutivos

1. perrito
2. pequeñito
3. casita
4. Elsita
5. hijita
6. bebecita
7. jovencito
8. papelito
9. primitos
10. abuelita

## Practique los diminutivos

1. lapicito
2. cuadernito
3. abuelita
4. doctorcito
5. mujercita
6. sobrinita
7. animalito
8. escuelita
9. angelito
10. hombrecito
11. tiempito
12. borradorcito
13. hijito
14. viajecito
15. busecito
16. nochecita
17. jovencito/a
18. papelito
19. vecesita
20. trabajito

## Practique las palabras negativas

1. ninguno. . .nada
2. tampoco. . .sin
3. no habla nadie
4. Él no es bueno
5. Él no está aquí
6. algún. . .ningún
7. persona. . .cosa
8. tampoco
9. alguien
10. también
11. nunca (jamás)
12. con
13. algún
14. no sé nada
15. no sé nada
16. no digo nada
17. no habla nadie
18. nunca digo nada
19. no trabaja tampoco
20. no tengo ningún libro
21. ella no es peruana
22. ella no está bien
23. algo/nada
24. también/tampoco
25. nunca/jamás

## Practique las formas negativas

1. No hay nada interesante en la programación de eventos para hoy.

2. Netflix no tiene ninguna película boliviana.

3. El profesor de historia no enseña geografía tampoco/el profesor de historia tampoco enseña geografía.

4. Tú nunca estudias en la biblioteca de la universidad/tú no estudias nunca en la biblioteca de la universidad.

5. El jefe no prepara nada especial para los empleados.

6. No me gusta leer nada.

7. No hay ningún estudiante excelente en mi clase de contaduría.

8. No oigo noticias en la radio nunca./Nunca oigo noticias en la radio.

9. Nunca estamos cansados./No estamos cansados nunca.

# 5 En el aeropuerto internacional Adolfo Suárez Madrid–Barajas

## (*At Adolfo Suárez Madrid–Barajas International Airport*)

## PALABRAS NUEVAS

| | | | |
|---|---|---|---|
| la aduana | customs | clase económica | economy class |
| la aerolínea[1] | airline | clase ejecutiva | business class |
| el aeropuerto | airport | el compartimiento | overhead |
| el/la agente | agent | superior | compartment |
| el asiento | seat | el despegue | takeoff |
| el aterrizaje | landing | el destino | destination |
| el avión | airplane | la disponibilidad | availability |
| el/la auxiliar de | stewardess/flight | el/la empleado(a) | employee |
| vuelo[2] | attendant | el equipaje | luggage/baggage |
| el billete/boleto/ | airplane ticket | el equipaje de mano | carry-on baggage |
| pasaje de avión | | la escala | stop/stopover |
| la cabina del avión | airplane cabin | la hora | hour |
| el cinturón de | seat belt | la llegada | arrival |
| seguridad[3] | | | |

| | | | |
|---|---|---|---|
| la maleta | suitcase | facturar | to check in |
| el maletín | briefcase | inspeccionar | to inspect |
| el mostrador de la aerolínea | airline counter | llegar | to arrive |
| | | mostrar (ue)[5] | to show |
| el/la pasajero(a) | passenger | pedir (i) | to ask for |
| el pasaporte | passport | poder (ue) | to be able to |
| el pase de abordar/ pasabordo/ la tarjeta de embarque | boarding pass | poner | to put |
| | | querer (ie) | to wish, want |
| | | salir | to leave |
| | | seguir (i) | to follow |
| el pasillo | aisle | sentarse (ie) | to sit down |
| el personal de administración de seguridad | security administration agents | servir (i) | to serve, help |
| | | subir | to go up, climb |
| | | viajar | to travel |
| primera clase | first class | volar (ue) | to fly |
| el/la piloto | pilot | volver (ue) | to come back |
| la puerta de embarque | door, boarding gate | | |
| | | *Adjetivos* | *Adjectives* |
| la reservación | reservation | alto(a) | high, tall |
| la sala de embarque | departure lounge | atrasado(a) | delayed/late |
| la salida | departure, exit | bajo(a) | low, short |
| el/la terminal | terminal | corto(a) | short |
| la ventana | window | estupendo(a) | terrific |
| la ventanilla[4] | small window | híbrido | hybrid |
| el viaje | travel, trip | largo(a) | long |
| el vuelo | flight | medio(a) | half |
| la zona para recoger el equipaje o las maletas/reclamación de equipajes | baggage claim | rápido(a) | fast, quick |
| | | sencillo(a)[7] | single (*room*), one way (*ticket*) |
| | | simpático(a) | nice, pleasant |
| *Verbos* | *Verbs* | *Expresiones* | *Expressions* |
| abordar | to board | antes (de) | beforehand, before |
| abrochar(se) | to fasten | a tiempo | on time |
| aterrizar | to land | después (de) | after, afterwards |
| ayudar | to help | en punto | sharp (exact time) |
| bajar (de) | to get off, go down | ida y vuelta | round-trip |
| | | más o menos | more or less |
| comprar | to buy | o | or |
| desembarcar | to disembark | tener que + (**infinitivo**) | to have to + (infinitive) |
| deshacer | to undo, melt | | |
| despegar | to take off | salir de + (**lugar**) | to leave (a place) |
| detener | to stop, detain (people) | | |

### NOTAS

1. **Aerolínea** is synonymous with **línea aérea**.

2. *Auxiliar de vuelo* is used in some countries for *stewardess*; other countries use *azafata/o, aeromoza/o*. The word *sobrecargo* is also used for both men and women working on the airplane.

3. *Cinturón de seguridad* (*safety belt, seat belt*), or simply **cinturón**, is used for the belt people wear in airplanes or cars. The belt people wear as part of clothing is called **cinturón**; *cinta* is *ribbon*.

4. *Ventanilla* means *small window;* and it is used to refer to the *teller's window* in the bank and to the *small window* in an airplane, a car, at the post office, and so on.

5. The letters in parentheses following some verbs — (*i*), (*ie*), (*ue*) — are for **stem-changing verbs**. Those verbs undergo a vowel change in all forms of the present tense except the nosotros/as and vosotros/as forms. They will be studied in this unit.

6. *Pensar (ie)* + (infinitive) means *to plan, to intend to do something* + (verb).

   EX:  **Pienso ir a México** = <u>*I plan to go*</u> *to Mexico*.

7. *Sencillo (a)* means *simple* referring to people, problems, and so on. It means *single* or *one way* when talking about hotel room reservations or transportation tickets. The opposite is *ida y vuelta*, that is, *round trip*. However, in Mexico **viaje redondo** is used for *round trip*.

8. *Antes* and *después* require *de* when a noun or an infinitive follows.

   EXS:  **Voy *antes* de comer.** (*I'll go <u>before</u> eating.*)
   **Voy *después* de la comida.** (*I'll go <u>after</u> dinner.*)

# PRACTIQUE LAS PALABRAS NUEVAS

**ANSWERS p. 135**

A. Write the article *el* or *la* before the noun. Remember that *avión* and *camión* (**truck**) are masculine. All other *-IÓN* nouns are feminine.

| | | |
|---|---|---|
| 1. _____ avión | 5. _____ reservación | 9. _____ ventanilla |
| 2. _____ auxiliar de vuelo | 6. _____ equipaje | 10. _____ pasaporte |
| 3. _____ clase ejecutiva | 7. _____ cinturón de seguridad | 11. _____ piloto |
| 4. _____ vuelo | 8. _____ pasaje | 12. _____ maleta |

**ANSWERS p. 135**

B. Underline the word that makes sense in each group.

1. El pasajero llega (al pasaje, a la llegada, al pasillo, al aeropuerto) para tomar su vuelo.

2. La auxiliar de vuelo les sirve (los cinturones de seguridad, las bebidas, la maleta, el pasaporte) a los pasajeros en el avión.

3. En el aeropuerto facturamos (la habitación, el pasaje, el pasaporte, el equipaje).

4. En el avión nos abrochamos (la maleta, el cinturón de seguridad, la puerta, el pasaje).

5. Los vuelos de la aerolínea United salen por (el pasillo, el aeropuerto, la terminal, la maleta) # 1 del aeropuerto de Chicago.

6. Yo siempre prefiero un asiento en (el pasillo, el baño, la sala de espera, la recepción) del avión.

7. Mis amigos y yo esperamos en (la zona de seguridad, el restaurante, la cabina, la sala de embarque) antes de abordar el avión.

8. Decimos adiós a los amigos antes de (subir, servir, deshacer, comprar) al avión.

9. Pensamos hacer (un asiento, una salida, un viaje, una aduana) a Las Vegas en enero.

10. Salimos por la puerta de (aerolínea, aduana, equipaje, salida).

11. Vamos a comer después de (llegar, poder, poner, seguir) a nuestro destino.

12. El personal de administración de seguridad inspecciona el equipaje en (el pasaje, la aduana, la maleta, el pasaporte).

13. El avión sale (a tiempo, a la ventanilla, al asiento, al empleado).

14. Necesito un pasaje (corto, de ida y vuelta, más o menos, a tiempo).

15. Señor Martínez, ¿en qué puedo (comprarle, seguirle, servirle, deshacerle)?

**ANSWERS p. 135**

C. **Match the two columns.**

| | |
|---|---|
| 1. _____ abrocharse | A. avión para ir a recoger las maletas |
| 2. _____ llegar | B. al avión por la puerta de embarque |
| 3. _____ facturar | C. el pasaporte para viajar a España |
| 4. _____ subir | D. de ida y vuelta |
| 5. _____ mostrar | E. volver |
| 6. _____ sentarse | F. las bebidas en el avión |
| 7. _____ servir | G. hacer un viaje al norte de España |
| 8. _____ comprar un pasaje | H. el cinturón de seguridad |
| 9. _____ salir del | I. en la aduana de Madrid |
| 10. _____ pensar en | J. el equipaje/las maletas |
| 11. _____ inspeccionar la maleta | K. en el asiento del pasillo |
| 12. _____ ir y (*the opposite*) | L. a tiempo al destino |

## DIÁLOGO   En el aeropuerto internacional Adolfo Suárez Madrid–Barajas

*Esteban llega al mostrador de la aerolínea Iberia en el aeropuerto internacional Adolfo Suárez Madrid–Barajas y habla con un agente de Iberia para cambiar su asiento en el avión.*

AGENTE:   Buenos días, señor. ¿En qué puedo servirle?

ESTEBAN:   Buenos días. Me gustaría saber si es posible cambiar mi asiento de la clase económica a la clase ejecutiva o a primera clase para mi vuelo a Lima, Perú.

AGENTE:   Espere un momento y miro si hay disponibilidad en su vuelo.

ESTEBAN:   Muchas gracias.

AGENTE:   ¿Cuál es su código de reserva?

ESTEBAN:   Mi código de reserva es IB24RES.

AGENTE:   ¿Cuál es su nombre completo?

ESTEBAN:   Esteban Zambrano.

AGENTE:   Señor Zambrano, creo que si hay disponibilidad en primera clase ¿Prefiere un asiento en la ventanilla o en el pasillo?

ESTEBAN:   Me gustaría un asiento en la ventanilla, por favor. ¿Qué costo adicional tiene el cambio de asiento?

AGENTE:   El costo adicional sería (*would be*) de 300 euros. Su nuevo asiento es el número 6A, con ventanilla.

ESTEBAN:   ¡Estupendo! Muchas gracias. Aquí tiene mi pasaporte y mi tarjeta de crédito.

AGENTE:   Gracias. Aquí tiene su pasaporte, su pasabordo y su recibo. Su puerta de embarque es la número 7 y necesita estar allá 45 minutos antes de la salida de su vuelo ¿Qué equipaje desea facturar?

ESTEBAN:   Quiero facturar esta maleta.

AGENTE:   Muy bien. Recuerde que puede llevar el equipaje de mano con Ud. en el avión.

ESTEBAN:   Muchas gracias por su ayuda.

AGENTE:   ¡Buen viaje!

## DIALOGUE   *At Adolfo Suárez Madrid–Barajas International Airport*

*Esteban arrives at the Iberia airline counter at Adolfo Suárez Madrid–Barajas airport and speaks to an Iberia agent to change his seat on the plane.*

AGENT:   *Good morning, sir. How can I help you?*

ESTEBAN:   *Good morning. I would like to know if it is possible to change my seat from economy class to business class or first class for my flight to Lima, Peru.*

| | |
|---|---|
| AGENT: | *Please wait a moment and I will see if there is availability on your flight.* |
| ESTEBAN: | *Thank you very much.* |
| AGENT: | *What is your reservation code?* |
| ESTEBAN: | *My reservation code is IB24RES.* |
| AGENT: | *What is your full name?* |
| ESTEBAN: | *Esteban Zambrano.* |
| AGENT: | *Mr. Zambrano, I believe there is availability in first class. Would you prefer a window or aisle seat?* |
| ESTEBAN: | *I would like a window seat, please. What is the additional cost for changing seats?* |
| ESTEBAN: | *The additional cost would be 300 euros. Your new seat is number 6A, with a window.* |
| ESTEBAN: | *Great! Thank you very much. Here is my passport and credit card.* |
| AGENT: | *Thank you. Here is your passport, your boarding pass and your receipt. Your boarding gate is number 7 and you need to be there 45 minutes before your flight departs. What luggage do you want to check in?* |
| ESTEBAN: | *I want to check this bag.* |
| AGENT: | *Very well. Remember that you can take your carry-on luggage with you on the plane.* |
| ESTEBAN: | *Thank you very much for your help.* |
| AGENT: | *Have a good trip!* |

# PRÁCTICA

**A. En el aeropuerto internacional Adolfo Suárez Madrid–Barajas. Complete the story using the information from the dialogue.**

Esteban llega al (1) _____ de la aerolínea Iberia en el (2) _____ Adolfo Suárez Madrid–Barajas y habla con un (3) _____ de la aerolínea. Esteban quiere cambiar su asiento de la clase (4) _____ a la clase (5) _____ o a primera clase. El agente le dice que si hay disponibilidad y le asigna un asiento en la (6) _____. Esteban necesita pagar (7) _____ euros adicionales por el cambio. Él paga con su (8) _____. Esteban factura una (9) _____. El agente le da a Esteban su pasaporte, su recibo y su (10) _____. Esteban necesita estar en la sala de embarque 45 minutos antes de la (11) _____ de su vuelo.

**B. Match the two columns.**

| | | | |
|---|---|---|---|
| 1. _____ | El código de reserva es. . . | A. | en la ventanilla |
| 2. _____ | Esteban prefiere viajar en . . . | B. | aeropuerto en Madrid, España |
| 3. _____ | Esteban puede llevar . . . | C. | un pasaporte |
| 4. _____ | El agente le asigna a Esteban un asiento. . . | D. | un pase de abordar para subir al avión |

5. _____ Para viajar de España a Perú, Esteban necesita tener. . .

    E.  su equipaje de mano con él en el avión

6. _____ El agente le entrega a Esteban . . .

    F.  mostrador de la aerolínea para hablar con el agente

7. _____ El cambio de asiento tiene un costo de. . .

    G.  IB24RES

8. _____ Adolfo Suárez-Barajas es el nombre del . . .

    H.  la puerta de embarque para el vuelo a Lima

9. _____ Esteban llega al. . .

    I.  clase ejecutiva o primera clase

10. _____ 7 es el número de . . .

    J.  300 euros

---

## GRAMMAR I Presente del indicativo de los verbos irregulares tener, poner, salir y hacer (*Present Indicative of Irregular Verbs To Have, To Come, To Put, To leave, and To Do*)

A. Memorize the present indicative of the verbs in the chart.

| | Ten er (*to have*) | Ven ir (*to come*) | Pon er (*to put*) | Sal ir (*to leave*) | Hac er (*to do*) |
|---|---|---|---|---|---|
| yo | teng o | veng o | pong o | salg o | hag o |
| tú | tien es | vien es | pon es | sal es | hac es |
| él/ella/Ud. | tien e | vien e | pon e | sal e | hac e |
| nosotros(as) | ten emos | ven imos | pon emos | sal imos | hac emos |
| ellos/ellas/Uds. | tien en | vien en | pon en | sal en | hac en |
| vosotros/as | ten éis | ven ís | pon éis | sal ís | hac éis |

Note that:

1. These five verbs add a *g* to the stem in the first-person singular. Actually, *hacer* changes *c* to *g: hac-* changes to *hag-* in *yo hago*.

2. *Poner, salir,* and *hacer* are regular in all forms except the subject **yo**. All persons except **yo** have the same stem as the infinitive: **pon-, sal-,** and **hac-**.

3. *Tener* and *venir* change *e* to *ie* in the second and third persons: **tienes, tiene, tienen.** They belong to a large group of stem-changing verbs.

4. There are many compounds of these five verbs. The compounds have the same changes as the original verbs. There are two of them in this lesson: **detener** (**de + tener**) meaning to *stop, arrest* and **deshacer** (**des + hacer**) meaning to *undo, unpack, melt.*

    EXS: **Ella *se detiene* en la luz roja.** (*She <u>stops</u> at the red light.*)

          **Yo *deshago* la maleta.** (*I <u>am unpacking</u> the suitcase.*)

B. Common uses of *tener*:

1. *Tener* means to have, possess.

   EX:  **Tengo un carro híbrido.** (*I have a hybrid car*.)

2. *Tener que* + *(infinitive)* indicates obligation; it is equivalent to the English to have to + (verb).

   EX:  **¿Cuándo tienes que ir a Lima?** (*When do you have to go to Lima?*)

C. Common expressions with the verb *tener*:

1. *Tener . . .años* (*to be . . .years old*).

   EX:  **Andrea tiene 12 años.** (*Andrea is 12 years old.*)

2. *Tener (mucho) calor/frío* (*to be (very) hot/cold*).

   EX:  **Tú tienes mucho frío.** (*You are very cold*).

3. *Tener (mucho) cuidado* (*to be (very) careful*).

   EX:  Luis tiene mucho cuidado cuando maneja. (*Luis is very careful when he drives.*)

4. *Tener (mucha) hambre/sed* (*to be (very) hungry/thirsty*).

   EX:  **Yo tengo mucha sed.** (*I am very thirsty.*)

5. *Tener (mucho) miedo de* (*to be (very) afraid/scared of*).

   EX:  **Nosotros tenemos miedo de las arañas.** (*We are afraid of the spiders.*)

6. *Tener (mucha) prisa* (*to be in a (big) hurry*).

   EX:  **Paula tiene mucha prisa.** (*Paula is in a big hurry.*)

7. *Tener (la) razón* (*to be right*).

   EX:  **Tienes razón. Hoy es martes.** (*You are right. Today is Tuesday.*)

8. No *tener (la) razón* (*to be wrong*).

   EX:  **Esteban no tiene la razón. El vuelo sale a las 3:00 P.M. y no a la 1:00 P.M.** (*Esteban is wrong. The flight leaves at 3:00 P.M. instead of 1:00 P.M.*)

9. *Tener (mucho) sueño* (*to be sleepy*).

   EX:  **Los estudiantes tienen sueño en clase.** (*Students are sleepy in class*.)

10. *Tener (mucha) suerte* (*to be lucky*).

   EX:  **Amanda tiene mucha suerte en los negocios.** (*Amanda is very lucky in business.*)

D. Here are some uses of *salir, venir,* and *hacer*.

1. *Salir para (a) means* to go to a place. *Indicates* someone's destination.

   EX:  Esteban sale para Lima a las 3:00 P.M. (*Esteban leaves for Lima at 3:00 P.M.*)

2. *Salir* means *to go away, leave;* and it requires *de* when the point of departure is mentioned in the sentence. *To leave* is followed by the place *without* a preposition.

   EX: **Esteban *sale de* Madrid en avión.** (*Esteban leaves Madrid by plane.*)

3. **Salir** with the preposition **con** means *to go out with.*

   EX: **Martha *sale con* sus amigos los sábados por la tarde.** (*Martha goes out with her friends on Saturday afternoon.*)

4. *Venir* means *to come,* and it is the opposite of *ir. Venir* is to move from anywhere to where the speaker is, and *ir* is to move from the speaker to somewhere else. Note that both *ir* and **venir** can mean *to come,* depending on the context.

   EX: **¿Cuándo *vienes* a verme? —Voy mañana.** (*When are you coming to see me? —I am coming tomorrow.*)

5. *Hacer* is used in expressions related to weather, such as, *"Hace calor"* (*It is hot*), *"Hace frío"* (*It is cold.*), *"hace (mucho) viento"* (*It is (very) windy.*)

6. *Hacer ejercicio* means *to exercise.*

   EX: **Tú *haces ejercicio* todos los días.** (*You exercise everyday.*)

# PRACTIQUE LAS EXPRESIONES CON EL VERBO *TENER*

**ANSWERS p. 136**

Traduce las siguientes frases al español.

1. Rodrigo is very hungry today:

   _____

2. Carolina is afraid of the darkness (*oscuridad*):

   _____

3. I am very hot today:

   _____

4. My friends are lucky when they go to the casino:

   _____

5. Mr. Zapata is in a hurry. He has a meeting (*reunión*):

   _____

6. You are very sleepy:

   _____

7. Gloria is right. The movie (*película*) is at 5:30 P.M:

   _____

8. We are very thirsty:

   _____

9. Mónica is 15 years old:

_____

10. You and Pablo are not right. The party is on Saturday:

_____

11. I have to study today:

_____

12. Julio and Sandra are very cold:

_____

13. Students have to buy the airplane tickets:

_____

14. Marisol has to travel to Spain:

_____

15. You are 50 years old:

_____

# PRÁCTICA

A. **Complete with the right answer.**

1. *Tener* has three different stem changes in the present: _____, _____, _____, and all three share the same basic meaning of possession; in English, *tener* means _____.

2. *Vengo, tengo, pongo,* and *salgo* are irregular because they add the letter _____ to their stems: **ven-, ten-, pon-, sal-.** *Hacer* changes the *c* to _____ in yo _____.

3. *Vienes* and *tienes* change the original *e* from **ven-** and **ten-** to _____. Are *venimos* and *tenemos* irregular? _____.

4. In order to translate the idea of obligation involved in *to have to* + (verb), Spanish adds _____ to *tener.* How do you say *I have to leave?* _____.

5. *Salir* means *to leave.* If we mention the place we are leaving, we need the preposition _____ before the place.

6. *Venir* means _____. In English *to come* can mean to move toward the speaker or away from the speaker, whereas in Spanish *venir* only means to move from somewhere to where the _____ is.

7. A child who replies *I'm coming, Mom* is moving toward her. How would you say in Spanish *I'm coming now, Mom?* **Ahora** _____, **mamá.**

8. Compound verbs follow the same changes as the original verbs. If *deshacer* is *to undo, unpack,* how would you say *I am unpacking my suitcase?* **Yo** _____ **mi maleta.**

9. If *detener* is *to stop, detain (people),* how do you say: *They are stopping at the light?* **Ellos se** _____ **en el semáforo (luz).**

**ANSWERS**
**p. 136**

B. Complete each sentence with the correct form of the verb in the present indicative. (Before starting this exercise, review the new verbs in the vocabulary at the beginning of this lesson.)

1. Este avión _____ de Madrid. (*to come*)

2. Mañana (yo) _____ comprar un pasaje para viajar a Los Ángeles. (*to have to*)

3. La asistente de vuelo _____ a los pasajeros. (*to help*)

4. ¿Cuándo _____ tú para Argentina? (*to leave*)

5. Los pasajeros se _____ el cinturón de seguridad en el avión. (*to fasten*)

6. ¿_____ usted su pasaporte para viajar? (*to have*)

7. (Yo) _____ la mochila en el compartimiento superior del avión. (*to put*)

8. ¿Cuándo _____ el vuelo IB 321 de Barcelona? (*to arrive*)

9. Francisco _____ dos maletas. (*to check*)

10. Los pasajeros _____ del avión. (*to get off*)

C. Complete with the right verb in present tense. ¿poner, tener, venir, salir, hacer?

1. Yo siempre _____ mi maleta de mano en el compartimiento superior del avión.

2. Nosotros _____ para Chicago mañana.

3. Tú _____ escala en Atlanta antes de llegar a Chicago.

4. Vosotros _____ a nuestra casa para visitarnos.

5. Elizabeth _____ con sus amigos los viernes por la noche.

6. Ustedes _____ su vuelo para París a las 10:00 A.M.

7. Yo _____ ejercicio en el gimnasio tres veces por semana.

8. Camilo _____ 17 años.

9. Tú _____ un carro híbrido. Funciona (*works*) con gas y electricidad.

10. Mis amigos _____ hoy a mi casa a visitarme.

---

# GRAMMAR II  ¿Qué hora es? (*What time is it?*)

A. Memorize the following expressions for telling the time.

| | | | |
|---|---|---|---|
| 1. | *Exact time:* | Es la una. | (*It's one o'clock.*), |
| | (**Hora exacta**) | Son las dos. | (*It's twelve o'clock.*) |
| | | Son las diez. | (*It's ten o'clock.*) |
| 2. | *After the hour:* | Es la una y diez. | (*It's 1:10.*) |
| | (+) = **y** | Son las dos y cuarto. | (*It's 2:15.*) |
| | | Son las dos y quince. | (*It's 2:15.*) |
| | | Son las dos y media. | (*It's 2:30.*) |
| | | Son las dos y treinta. | (*It's 2:30.*) |

3. *Before the hour:*    Es la una *menos* diez.       (*It's 12:50.*)
   (-) = **menos**        Son las dos *menos* cuarto.   (*It's 1:45.*)
                          Son las dos *menos* quince.   (*It's 1:45.*)
                          Son las dos *menos* veinte.   (*It's 1:40.*)

B. *De la mañana/de la tarde/de la noche:* A.M. and P.M.

1. **A.M.** = **de la mañana** (from midnight to noon)

2. **P.M.** = **de la tarde** (from noon to sunset—officially, 6:00 P.M.)

   = **de la noche** (from sunset to midnight—officially, 6:00 P.M. to midnight)

C. Notice that we say **Es la una** (*hora*); the word *hora* is understood. The verb **es** (**ser**) changes to the plural **son** from two to twelve: the hours are more than *one*.

D. To express *sharp* when referring to time, we say **en punto** or **exactamente**. To express *about,* we can say **más o menos** (*more or less*) and **como**. To say *at,* we use the preposition **a** followed by the article **la** or **las**.

   EXS: **Son las dos *más o menos*.** (*It's __about__ two o'clock.*)
   **Son *como* las dos.** (*It's __about__ two o'clock.*)
   **Llegamos *a la* una.** (*We arrive __at__ one o'clock.*)

E. *De la tarde/de la noche* will change with the season of the year, just like the greetings **Buenas tardes/Buenas noches**. On programs, schedules, and so on, after 6:00 P.M. is considered evening.

F. To ask for the time use **¿Qué hora es?** In Mexico they use the plural form **¿Qué horas son?**

G. To ask *at* what time is an event (or some activity), use the preposition *a* in Spanish at the beginning of the question.

   EX: **¿A qué hora es la reunión?** (*At what time is the meeting?*) **La reunión es *a las* 9:00 A.M.** (*The meeting is at 9:00 A.M.*)

H. Official time expressed in newscasts, newspapers, plane and train schedules, TV programs, and so on, uses the 24-hour clock and the words *hora* or *horas*. Expressions such as *de la mañana, de la tarde,* are omitted. For example, **El accidente ocurrió *a las 14* (*catorce*) *horas*** in colloquial Spanish would be **El accidente ocurrió *a las dos de la tarde*.** (*The accident occurred at 2:00 P.M.*)

# PRACTIQUE LA HORA

**ANSWERS p. 136**

1. *Son* and *es* are forms of the verb *ser;* the verb used for identification. To tell the time we use the singular form **es** with the number _____, and the plural **son** with the numbers _____.

2. In telling the time, *fifteen minutes* has two possible words in Spanish: _____ and _____.

3. In telling the time, *thirty minutes* also has two possible words in Spanish:
   _____ and _____.

4. To tell the minutes *after* the hour, we add the minutes with the conjunction
   _____. To subtract minutes *before* the next hour, we use the word
   _____.

5. How do you translate *sharp* when talking about time? _____.
   How do you say *about* when talking about time? _____ or
   _____.

6. There is only one translation for AM: _____.

7. There are two translations for PM: _____ and _____.

8. Is it correct to say **Salgo a una** (*I'm leaving at one o'clock*)? _____
   The article _____ is missing before **una.**

9. When telling time, we say **a las dos, a la una,** with the articles **la** and **las** because
   the feminine word _____ is understood.

10. To ask at what time is an event, it is necessary to use the preposition
    _____ at the beginning of the question.

11. In newscasts, newspapers, plane schedules, TV programs, and so on, the
    _____-hour clock is used. The word _____ precedes the
    number *one;* the word _____ precedes the numbers *two* to *twenty-
    four.* The words _____ and _____ are always used in
    time expressions with the 24-hour clock. The expressions **de la mañana** and **de la
    tarde** are omitted.

# PRÁCTICA

**ANSWERS
p. 137**

Translate the following time expressions.

1. It's 3:10 P.M. _____

2. It's 2:15 A.M. _____

3. It's 1:30 P.M. _____

4. It's 5:50 A.M. _____

5. It's 11:00 P.M. _____

6. It's 11:20 A.M. _____

7. It's 12:45 P.M. _____

8. It's 1:05 A.M. _____

9. El avión sale _____. (*at 2:00 P.M. sharp*)

10. En mi casa cenamos todos los días _____. (*at 5:30 P.M.*)

# GRAMMAR III  Presente del indicativo de los verbos que cambian de raíz (*Present Indicative of Stem-Changing Verbs*)

A. Memorize the present indicative of the verbs in the chart.

| | pens ar *(to think)* | volv er *(to return)* | ped ir *(to ask for)* | segu ir *(to follow)* |
|---|---|---|---|---|
| yo | piens o | vuelv o | pid o | sig o |
| tú | piens as | vuelv es | pid es | sigu es |
| él/ella/Ud. | piens a | vuelv e | pid e | sigu e |
| nosotros(as) | pens amos | volv emos | ped imos | segu imos |
| ellos/ellas/Uds. | piens an | vuelv en | pid en | sigu en |
| vosotros/as | pens áis | volv éis | ped ís | segu ís |

Note that:

1. All these verbs are called stem-changing verbs because they change a vowel in the stem.

2. The stem of *pensar* is **pens-**, but the *e* changes to *ie* in all the persons except **pensamos** and **pensáis**, which is regular.

3. *Volver* changes *o* to *ue* in all the persons except **volvemos** and **volvéis**.

4. *Pedir* and *seguir* have the same stem change: *e* changes to *i* in all the persons except the first and second person plural: **pedimos, pedís** and **seguimos, seguís**.

5. *Seguir* has the stem **segu-**, with a silent *u*, when it is followed by *i* or *e*: **seguir, sigues, sigue, seguimos, seguís, siguen**. However, the *u* is dropped in front of *o*: **sigo**.

B. Here is a partial list of stem-changing verbs. Notice that on vocabulary lists and, in most dictionaries, (*ie*), (*ue*), or (*i*) appears after certain verbs. This is to remind you that it's a stem-changing verb. These are the stem-changing verbs you have encountered so far:

| e → ie | o → ue | e → i |
|---|---|---|
| empezar to begin | mostrar to show | pedir to ask for |
| pensar to think, plan | encontrar to find | repetir to repeat |
| querer to wish; to love | poder to be able to, can | seguir to follow |
| sentarse to sit down | volar to fly | servir to serve |
| tener to have, possess | volver to return | decir to say, tell |

C. Following are uses of *pedir, querer*, and *volver*.

1. *Pedir* means *to ask for*. Notice that *for* is not translated in Spanish.

   EX: **Voy a pedir café.** (*I'm going <u>to ask for</u> coffee.*)

2. To *ask a question* is *preguntar* or *hacer una pregunta*.

3. *Querer* means *to wish, want,* when used with things and actions; but it means *to love* when referring to people, and it is used with the preposition *a* linking the verb with the noun.

    EXS:  *Quiero* una casa grande. (*I* <u>want</u> *a big house.*)
    ¿*Quieres a* tu mamá? (*Do you* <u>love</u> *your mother?*)

4. *Volver* means *to return, come back.* *Volver a* + (infinitive) means that an action is being repeated. It means *to do again.*

    EXS:  ¿**Cuándo vuelves a clase?** (*When* <u>are</u> *you* <u>returning</u> *to class?*)
    **Ella vuelve a viajar a Chile.** (*She* <u>is traveling again</u> *to Chile.*)

# PRACTIQUE LOS VERBOS

1. The stem of *querer* is _____, and the stem of *quieres* is _____. This means that the vowel e in the infinitive has changed to _____.

2. The stem of *decir* is _____, and the stem of *dices* is _____. This means that the vowel e in the infinitive has changed to _____.

3. The stem of *poder* is _____, and the stem of *puedo* is _____. In this case, the vowel o has changed to _____.

4. Is the stem of *pedimos* the same as the stem of *pedir*? _____. Then *pedimos* is regular because the stem doesn't change.

5. *Querer* means *to wish, want* when it's used with things, but it means *to love* when it's used with _____; for example, José _____ a su esposa.

6. In the expression *to ask for,* the word _____ is not translated in Spanish. How do you say *we ask for?* _____. And *they ask for?* _____.

7. *Servir* (*i*) is a stem-changing verb like *pedir.* How do you say *I'm serving dinner?* _____ la comida. And *they are serving?* _____.

8. *Volar* (*ue*) is a stem-changing verb, like *volver.* How do you complete this sentence? **El avión** _____ **de San Francisco a Chicago.**

9. *Mostrar* is a stem-changing verb, like *volver.* Remember that we can use the present with future meaning. How do you say *I'll show it to you?* **Yo te lo** _____.

10. The stem of *seguir* is _____, and the stem of *sigues* is _____; but the letter _____ is silent, and it is dropped before an **o.** How do you say *I follow you?* (**Yo**) **te** _____.

11. *Volver* is *to return,* but *volver a* + (infinitive) means *to do* _____. For example, **Volvemos a viajar** means _____.

# PRÁCTICA

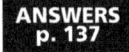
ANSWERS
p. 137

Complete each sentence with the correct form of the verb in parentheses.

1. Ninguna persona (*no one*) _____ fumar en un avión. (*can*)

2. Sí, ellas _____ mañana de Madrid a Nueva York. (*to fly*)

3. ¿Cuándo _____ ustedes de sus vacaciones? (*to return*)

4. Nosotros _____ hacer un viaje a Argentina. (*to plan*)

5. ¿Por qué _____ (tú) ser asistente de vuelo? (*to want*)

6. Los pasajeros _____ las instrucciones de los asistentes de vuelo. (*to follow*)

7. Esteban le _____ un café a la azafata. (*to ask for*)

8. (Yo) me _____ a la ventanilla derecha. (*to sit*)

9. El turista le _____ el pasaporte al inspector de aduana. (*to show*)

10. Las asistentes de vuelo _____ la comida en el avión. (*to serve*)

11. Diana le _____ al agente de la aerolínea si puede llevar la maleta de mano en el compartimiento del avión. (*to ask a question*)

12. Sí, yo sí _____ estudiar español en Costa Rica. (*to plan*)

13. El avión _____ muy alto en el cielo (*sky*). (*to fly*)

14. No, yo no _____ ir el lunes a clase. (*to be able to*)

15. ¿Señor Zambrano, usted _____ su pasaje de ida y vuelta? (*to have*)

# 6 Vamos de vacaciones
## (*Let's Go on Vacation*)

## PALABRAS NUEVAS

| | | | |
|---|---|---|---|
| la agencia de viajes | travel agency | la escalera | staircase/ladder |
| el alojamiento | lodging | la estación | season (winter, fall, etc.) |
| los alrededores | surroundings | | |
| el ascensor[1] | elevator | la estación de buses | bus station |
| la averiguación | inquiry | la estación del tren | train station |
| el botón[2] | button | el estacionamiento | parking |
| el botones | bellboy | la excursión | excursion |
| la cama | bed | la fecha | date |
| la cama doble | double bed | el hotel | hotel |
| la cama sencilla | single/twin bed | el/la huésped | guest |
| el/la ciudadano(a) | citizen | el itinerario | itinerary |
| el clima | weather/climate | la llave/la tarjeta | key/key card |
| el cuarto | room | la lluvia | rain |
|    la habitación | | el lugar/sitio | place |
|    recámara | | la moneda del país | currency of the country |
| el desayuno | breakfast | | |
| el dinero | money | la nieve | snow |
| la divisa | foreign money/ currency | la nube | cloud |
| | | la opción | option/choice |
| la época | season, epoch | el paisaje | landscape/scenery |
| | | el parque | park |
| | | el peso[3] | peso |

85

| la piscina/la alberca | pool |
| el piso | floor, story |
| el plan turístico | plan for the tour |
| la playa | beach |
| la plaza | square |
| el precio | price |
| el promedio | average |
| la propina | tip |
| la recepción | front desk |
| la/el recepcionista | receptionist |
| el recorrido | tour/itinerary |
| el complejo turístico/resort | resort |
| las ruinas | ruins |
| el seguro de viajes | travel insurance |
| el servicio a los cuartos | room service |
| la temperatura | temperature |
| la temporada alta/ baja | high season/low season |
| el tiempo compartido | timeshare |
| el/la turista | tourist |
| las vacaciones | vacation |
| la visa | visa |
| la vista | sight, view |

| *Verbos* | *Verbs* |
| abrir | to open |
| broncearse | to tan (to get a tan) |
| cambiar | to change |
| cerrar (ie) | to close |
| chatear | to chat |
| cobrar | to charge, get paid |
| confirmar | to confirm |
| conversar | to chat, to converse |
| decidir | to decide |
| diseñar | to design |
| divertirse (ie) | to have fun |
| empacar | to pack |
| encargarse | to be in charge |
| estacionar, parquear | to park |
| firmar | to sign |
| incluir (y) | to include |
| interesar | to interest |

| llover (ue) | to rain |
| nadar | to swim |
| nevar (ie) | to snow |
| permitir | to allow |
| preferir (ie) | to prefer |
| quedarse | to stay |
| recorrer | to tour |
| registrarse[4] | to register |
| reservar | to reserve |
| revisar | to review |
| subir | to go up |
| tomar el sol | to sunbathe |
| tratar de[5] | to try to |
| visitar | to visit |

| *Adjetivos* | *Adjectives* |
| agradable | pleasant |
| animado(a) | lively |
| antiguo(a) | ancient, former |
| bastante | enough |
| bronceado(a) | tanned |
| correspondiente | corresponding |
| costoso(a) | expensive |
| disponible | available |
| nublado(a) | cloudy |
| nuevo(a) | new |
| próximo(a) | next |
| razonable | reasonable |
| turístico(a) | touristic |
| vigente | current |

| *Algunos adverbios de lugar* | *Some Adverbs of Place* |
| abajo | down there |
| acá/aquí | here |
| adentro | inside |
| afuera | outside |
| ahí/allí | there |
| allá | over there |
| arriba | up there |
| cerca | near/close |
| lejos | far/far away |

| *Expresiones* | *Expressions* |
| ¿A cómo está...?/¿Cuánto cuesta? | What's the price of. . .?/How much does it cost? |

| | | | |
|---|---|---|---|
| Aquí tiene la llave. | Here is the key/key card. | porque | because |
| ¿En qué puedo servirle? | How can I help you? | por tal razón | for that reason |
| | | ¡Que tenga un buen día! | Have a nice day! |
| enseguida, en seguida | right away | una temperatura promedio | an average temperature |

**"hacer" con expresiones del tiempo/clima**

| | | | |
|---|---|---|---|
| en un par de días | in a couple of days | ¿Qué tiempo hace?/¿Qué clima hace?/ ¿Cómo es el clima? | What's the weather like? |
| es decir | that is to say | | |
| hacer las maletas | to pack (to pack the suitcases) | | |
| ir de vacaciones | to go on vacation | hacer buen tiempo | to have good weather |
| la temporada de vacaciones | vacation season | hacer bueno | |
| | | hacer mal tiempo | to have bad weather |
| las vacaciones de primavera | spring break | hacer malo | |
| Patrimonio Histórico de la Humanidad | World Heritage Site | | |

hacer (mucho) { calor / fresco / frío / sol / viento }  to be (very) { hot / cool / cold / sunny / windy }

| | | | |
|---|---|---|---|
| ¿Podría ayudarnos? | Could you help us? | | |
| por día | per day | | |
| por eso | because of that | | |

tener { ansias de / ganas de }  to feel like, want

## NOTAS

1. *Ascensor* is used in Spain and some Latin American countries for *elevator*. *Elevador* is also used in some other countries in Latin America and this word is as old as the first elevator installed in Latin American hotels.

2. Notice that the plural of **botón** is **botones** (*buttons*), but this plural form becomes singular to designate the name of a person "with many buttons": *a bellboy*. We say **un botones, dos botones** (*one bellboy, two bellboys*).

3. *Peso* is the currency of Argentina, Chile, Colombia, Cuba, Mexico, and Uruguay. *Euro* is the currency of Spain.

4. *Registrarse* is used to register at a hotel, at city hall, and to register a car at the motor vehicle bureau. These places have a *registro*. We use **matricular** or **inscribir** for *to register* a student in a school.

5. *Tratar de* + (infinitive) is translated as *to try to* + (infinitive).

   EX: **Juan trata de terminar su carrera para graduarse.** (*John is trying to finish his career to graduate.*)

# PRACTIQUE LAS PALABRAS NUEVAS

**ANSWERS**
**p. 138**

**A.** Write *el, la, los,* or *las* before each noun.

1. ____ ascensor
2. ____ hotel
3. ____ botones
4. ____ agencia
5. ____ itinerario
6. ____ recepción
7. ____ estación
8. ____ dinero
9. ____ divisas
10. ____ paisaje
11. ____ turistas
12. ____ temporada
13. ____ lluvia
14. ____ viaje
15. ____ llaves

**ANSWERS**
**p. 138**

**B.** *Palabras nuevas.* ¿Qué palabra corresponde en español a la descripción?

1. La oficina que visitamos si queremos preguntar por un viaje a Europa: _____

2. Lo que (*what*) necesitamos tomar si no podemos usar las escaleras para subir a un piso superior: _____

3. Tiene arena (*sand*) muy suave (*smooth*) para caminar cerca al mar (*sea*): _____

4. Cuando llegamos al hotel para registrarnos es el primer lugar que visitamos: _____

5. Muchas universidades tienen estas vacaciones durante los meses de marzo y abril: _____

6. Australia siempre requiere una _____ para que las personas puedan entrar como turistas al país.

7. La agencia de viajes diseña un plan turístico con un _____ con fechas y horas específicas.

8. Cuando viajamos siempre nos gusta saber si hace calor o frío, es decir, queremos saber cómo es el: _____

9. Si queremos viajar durante las vacaciones de verano debemos hacer las _____ en el hotel con mucho tiempo antes.

10. Una persona que visita diferentes lugares o países por placer es un/una: _____

**ANSWERS**
**p. 138**

**C.** Let's remember the verbs in Spanish.

1. to park _____
2. to sunbathe _____
3. to rain _____
4. to go up _____
5. to reserve _____
6. to register _____
7. to tour _____
8. to travel _____
9. to chat _____
10. to stay _____
11. to pack _____
12. to prefer _____

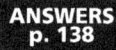
p. 138

**D. Write the expression in Spanish to complete each sentence.**

1. Estamos en Sevilla en agosto y la temperatura es de 110°F (43C). _____. (*It is very hot.*)

2. Estoy en Chicago en febrero y la temperatura es 25°F. _____. (*It is very cold.*)

3. Antonio está en Michigan en enero y todo está muy blanco (*white*). Hay mucha _____ (*snow*).

4. El agua que cae cuando llueve es la _____ (*rain*).

5. Una pareja (*couple*) duerme mejor en _____ (*queen-size bed*).

6. En Zaragoza en el mes de marzo _____. (*It is very windy.*)

7. Todas las ciudades antiguas de España y Latinoamérica tienen una _____ central en el centro de la ciudad (*square*).

8. Mi casa no está cerca de aquí; al contrario, está _____ (*far away*).

9. En Puerto Rico en el mes de diciembre _____. (*It is very sunny.*)

10. La persona del hotel que lleva las maletas es el _____. (*bellboy*)

11. Para abrir la habitación de nuestro hotel se necesita una _____ (*key card*).

12. En Viña del Mar, Chile, el clima es excelente casi todo el año. _____. (*The weather is good.*)

13. Cuando _____, me pongo botas (*boots*) y abrigo (*coat*). (*It is cold*)

14. Cuando _____, tomo agua fría o una Coca-Cola. (*It is hot.*)

15. En el sur de España en invierno _____. (*It is cool.*)

ANSWERS
p. 138

**E. Match the two columns.**

1. _____ Nadamos en            **A.** dólares a euros en el aeropuerto
2. _____ Firmamos...           **B.** practicar español en Madrid
3. _____ Abrimos...            **C.** lugares históricos importantes
4. _____ Subimos...            **D.** la propina en el precio
5. _____ Tomamos el sol...     **E.** el nombre en el registro del hotel
6. _____ Estacionamos...       **F.** en el recorrido a las ruinas
7. _____ Cambiamos...          **G.** la piscina del hotel
8. _____ Tratamos de...        **H.** el coche (carro) en el estacionamiento del hotel
9. _____ Nos divertimos...     **I.** las maletas en el ascensor
10. _____ Visitamos...         **J.** la puerta de la habitación con la llave
11. _____ Incluimos...         **K.** en la playa

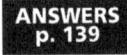

F. Practice the new verbs by filling in the present indicative forms of the verbs given. (The verb is the core of the Spanish language. Once you master the verb system, you master the language. Notice the irregular verbs in Lesson 5, indicated with [ie], [ue], [y]).

1. En Lima, Perú, por lo general, _____ muy poco. (*to rain*)

2. En Búfalo, estado de Nueva York, _____ mucho todos los años. (*to snow*)

3. Cuando voy de vacaciones, siempre me _____. (*to have fun*)

4. Todos los años mi esposa y yo _____ Vancouver. (*to visit*)

5. ¿ _____ ustedes una habitación con vista a la piscina o al patio interior? (*to prefer*)

6. El inspector o agente de la aduana _____ las maletas. (*to open*)

7. Las puertas del hotel se _____ a las 12:00 P.M. (*to close*)

8. Nosotros _____ dólares por euros en la recepción del hotel a un buen precio (*to change*)

9. El precio del hotel _____ el desayuno. (*to include*)

10. ¿Por qué no _____ Ud. _____ hablar siempre español? (*to try to*)

# DIÁLOGO   Vamos de vacaciones

*La familia López piensa viajar a Guatemala para las vacaciones de primavera y por tal razón están haciendo las averiguaciones necesarias. El señor López chatea por internet con Mariela Hurtado, una representante de una agencia de viajes de Guatemala.*

| | |
|---|---|
| Señor López: | Hola. Buenas tardes. |
| Mariela H: | ¿En qué puedo servirle señor López? |
| Señor López: | Mi familia y yo pensamos viajar a Guatemala para las vacaciones de primavera y nos gustaría saber qué opciones tenemos de alojamiento y planes turísticos para visitar los mejores lugares del país. |
| Mariela H: | Con mucho gusto. Nuestra agencia de viajes puede ayudarles a diseñar un recorrido por los mejores lugares de Guatemala. ¿Cuántos días piensan quedarse en Guatemala? |
| Señor López: | Pensamos quedarnos una semana. Queremos viajar de sábado a sábado. ¿Sabe usted si necesitamos visa para viajar a Guatemala? Nosotros somos estadounidenses. |
| Mariela H: | Una semana me parece estupendo para visitar Guatemala. Déjeme decirle que los ciudadanos de Estados Unidos no necesitan visa para entrar a Guatemala. |

| Señor López: | ¡Qué bien! ¿En una semana qué lugares usted nos recomienda visitar? |
|---|---|
| Mariela H: | Creo que los sitios más bonitos para visitar son: la ciudad colonial de Antigua, Patrimonio Histórico de la Humanidad; el Lago Atitlán y sus alrededores y las ruinas mayas del Parque Nacional de Tikal. |
| Señor López: | ¿Cómo es el clima en Guatemala durante el mes de marzo? |
| Mariela H: | Guatemala tiene un clima muy agradable con temperaturas cercanas a los 80 Fahrenheit. Además, tiene pocos días de lluvia. Es una excelente temporada para visitarnos. |
| Señor López: | ¿Entonces usted podría ayudarnos con las reservaciones? Creo que mi familia y yo preferimos un hotel de tres o cuatro estrellas en lugar de un Airbnb para nuestro viaje. También nos gustaría dos habitaciones, una habitación con cama doble y otra habitación con dos camas sencillas para nuestros hijos. |
| Mariela H: | Muy bien señor López. Yo me encargo de organizar todo y hacer las reservaciones correspondientes. En un par de días les voy a mandar el itinerario correspondiente para que ustedes los revisen. |
| Señor López: | Muchas gracias, señorita Mariela. Entonces nos estamos comunicando. |
| Mariela H: | Muchas gracias, señor López por usar los servicios de nuestra agencia de viajes. |

# DIALOGUE  *Let's Go on Vacation*

*The López family plans to travel to Guatemala for spring break and for this reason they are making the necessary inquiries. Mr. López chats online with Mariela Hurtado, a representative of a Guatemalan travel agency.*

| Mr. López: | *Hi! Good afternoon.* |
|---|---|
| Mariela H: | *How can I help you, Mr. López?* |
| Mr. López: | *My family and I are planning to travel to Guatemala for spring break and we would like to know what accommodation options we have and tourist plans to visit the best places in the country.* |
| Mariela H: | *Of course! We can help you. Our travel agency can help you design a tour of the best places in Guatemala. How many days do you plan to stay in Guatemala?* |
| Mr. López: | *We plan to stay a week. We want to travel from Saturday to Saturday. Do you know if we need a visa to travel to Guatemala? We are Americans.* |
| Mariela H: | *A week seems great to visit Guatemala. Let me tell you that United States citizens do not need a visa to enter Guatemala.* |

| | |
|---|---|
| MR. LÓPEZ: | *Wonderful! In a week what places do you recommend we visit?* |
| MARIELA H: | *I think the most beautiful places to visit are: the colonial city of Antigua, a World Heritage Site, Lake Atitlan and its surroundings and the Mayan ruins of the Tikal National Park.* |
| MR. LÓPEZ: | *What is the weather like in Guatemala during the month of March?* |
| MARIELA H: | *Guatemala has a very pleasant climate with temperatures close to 80 Fahrenheit. It also has few rainy days. It is an excellent season to visit us.* |
| MR. LÓPEZ: | *So, could you help us with reservations? I think my family and I prefer a three- or four-star hotel instead of an Airbnb for our trip. We would also like two rooms, one room with a double bed and another room with two single beds for our children.* |
| MARIELA H: | *Very good Mr. López. I am in charge of organizing everything and making the corresponding reservations. In a couple of days, I will send you the corresponding itinerary for you to review.* |
| MR. LÓPEZ: | *Thank you very much Miss Mariela. So, we'll stay in touch.* |
| MARIELA H: | *Thank you very much Mr. López for using the services of our travel agency.* |

## NOTE

Hotels in Hispanic countries are classified in five categories. In some countries they use the word *estrella* (*star*) instead of *clase*. The hotel with five stars is the most elegant and expensive. Notice that in Mexico they use the word *recámara* instead of *habitación* (*room*).

# PRÁCTICA

**ANSWERS p. 139**

**A. Complete the story using the vocabulary.**

La familia López piensa viajar a Guatemala para las (1) _____. La señorita Mariela Hurtado trabaja para una (2) _____ y ella puede ayudarles a organizar una (3) _____ para visitar los mejores lugares de Guatemala. La familia López piensa estar una (4) _____ visitando el país. La señorita Hurtado les recomienda visitar Antigua, una ciudad colonial que es (5) _____ por su importancia histórica. El clima en Guatemala es muy (6) _____ durante el mes de marzo con una (7) _____ promedio de (8) _____ Fahrenheit (26C). Además, hay pocos días de (9) _____. La familia López prefiere un (10) _____ de tres o cuatro estrellas. También prefieren dos (11) _____, una con cama doble y la otra habitación con dos camas (12) _____ para los hijos. En un par de días la señorita Hurtado les va a enviar el (13) _____ con toda la información para el (14) _____.

**ANSWERS**
**p. 139**

B. Underline the correct answer.

1. Subimos a nuestra habitación por el ascensor o por (la plaza, el parque, la escalera, la piscina).

2. En la ciudad de Búfalo en el estado de Nueva York (hace fresco, nieva, hace calor, llueve) mucho en invierno.

3. Para pedir comida o bebida en mi habitación pido (servicio, registro, fecha, botones) al cuarto.

4. Esta ventana tiene una (vista, temperatura, paisaje, alrededores) bonita a la plaza central.

5. El precio de la habitación es (doble, razonable, disponible, estrecho).

6. Para cambiar (recorridos, divisas, cuartos, itinerarios) vamos a un banco.

7. Cuando hablamos de habitación con cama (sencilla, pequeña, doble, nueva) pensamos en una pareja (*couple*).

8. Cuando firmamos, escribimos nuestro(a) (*our*) (visa, nombre, precio, reservación).

9. Vamos a la piscina para (caminar, nadar, subir, dormir).

10. La agente de la agencia de viajes ayuda a organizar (un servicio, un itinerario, una divisa, una vista) con actividades y horas específicas para visitar Guatemala.

# GRAMMAR I  Expresiones idiomáticas con hacer y tener
## (*Idiomatic Expressions with hacer and tener*)

A. **¿Qué tiempo hace?** (*How's the weather?*) To talk about the weather in Spanish, the verb **hacer** (*to make*) is used with nouns such as **calor** (*heat*), **sol** (*sun*), and **viento** (*wind*). Note that these are idiomatic expressions and different from English. Memorize the following expressions.

B. The adjectives **mucho** (*much*) and **poco** (*little*) are used with nouns to express that it is, for example, *very hot* or *not very sunny*. As adjectives, **mucho** and **poco** must agree with the noun.

EX: **Hoy hace *mucho viento* y *poco sol*.** (*Today it's <u>very windy</u> and <u>not very sunny</u>.*)

1. Note that **nublado** is an exception.

EX: **Está nublado.** (*It is cloudy.*)

C. Let's remember some expressions with *tener* that we studied in Unit 5. To say that you are *feeling* hot, cold, hungry, thirsty, and so on, there are idiomatic expressions with the verb *tener*. In these expressions, the verb *tener* (*to have*) is used with nouns such as **calor** (*heat*), **frío** (*cold*), **hambre** (*hunger*), **sed** (*thirst*), and so on.

Memorize the following expressions.

| | |
|---|---|
| **Tengo frío.** *I'm cold.* | **Tengo suerte.** *I'm lucky.* |
| **Tengo calor.** *I'm hot.* | **Tengo sueño.** *I'm sleepy.* |
| **Tengo hambre.** *I'm hungry.* | **Tengo cuidado.** *I'm careful.* |
| **Tengo sed.** *I'm thirsty.* | **Tengo éxito.** *I'm successful.* |
| **Tengo razón.** *I'm right.* | **No tengo razón.** *I'm wrong.* |

D. Adjectives such as **mucho** (*much*) and **poco** (*little*) are used with the nouns and must agree with them.

EXS: **Tengo** *poca hambre.* (*I am <u>not very hungry.</u>*)
**Ella tiene** *mucho sueño.* (*She is <u>very sleepy.</u>*)

E. The verb *tener* is also used in two other idiomatic expressions that are different from English.

1. To express age, *tener* + (**años** [*years*]) is used.

EXS: **Ella tiene trece años.** (*She is thirteen years old.*)
**Los abuelos tienen muchos años.** (*The grandparents are very old.*)

2. To express desire or inclination, *tener* + (**ganas de**) or *tener* + (**ansias de**) are used.

EX: ¿*Tienes ganas de* **tomar una cerveza?** (*Do you want a beer?*)
*No tenemos ganas (ansias) de* **ir a clase.** (*We don't feel like going to class.*)

Note that *tener ganas* and *tener ansias* both require the preposition *de*.

F. Remember that the above expressions are used in the contexts mentioned. The verbs *estar* and *ser* are used with nouns and adjectives. *Estar* is used with qualities that could possibly change.

EX: **El agua no** *está* **fría;** *está* **caliente.** (*The water is not cold; it is hot.*)

(Water can be cold or hot. This indicates a change in the state of the water.)

*Ser* is used with adjectives that describe the norm for the particular noun. These qualities are unlikely to change—the size, shape, texture, or color of an object, for example, or such things as personal characteristics when referring to people.

EX: **La nieve** *es* **blanca; no** *es* **azul ni verde.** (*The snow is white; it is not blue nor green.*)

# PRACTIQUE LAS EXPRESIONES

**ANSWERS**
**p. 139**

1. In the expression *hace frío,* is *frío* an adjective or a noun? _____.

2. To say *It is very hot* we use the expression *hace* _____.

3. *Hace muy sol* is not correct. It should be _____.

4. In Spanish people and animals "have" hunger or cold; whereas in English they "are" hungry or cold. How would you say *I'm hungry* in Spanish? _____.

5. *Tenemos muy hambre* is not correct because *hambre* is a noun. *Mucho hambre* is not correct either because *hambre* is feminine. It must be *Tenemos* _____.

6. *To be wrong* is the opposite of *to be right.* In Spanish the opposite of *tener razón* is _____.

7. How would you translate literally *tengo sed?* _____.

8. *Tener ganas* (or *ansias*) always needs the preposition _____ before the noun or the infinitive. How would you say *I feel like sleeping?* **Tengo** _____.

9. Remember that *ser* identifies a noun with a characteristic that is the _____ for that noun. For example, **la escalera** _____ **estrecha** (*is*).

10. *Estar* indicates the result of a _____; it doesn't indicate the norm for a noun. For example, *this room is very cold* translates into **Esta habitación** _____ **muy fría.**

# PRÁCTICA

**ANSWERS**
**p. 139**

Complete each sentence with the correct form of *ser, estar, hacer,* or *tener.*

1. Alaska _____ un estado de los Estados Unidos.

2. En Andalucía, España, _____ mucho calor en verano.

3. Creo que el botones del hotel _____ menos de 50 años.

4. La recepcionista _____ ocupada ayudando a otras personas en la recepción.

5. El agua de la piscina _____ muy fría hoy.

6. Vamos a comer algo porque (yo) _____ mucha hambre.

7. ¿Es verdad que en Chicago siempre _____ mucho viento?

8. El café _____ una bebida muy popular.

9. Voy a dormir porque _____. (*I'm sleepy*)

10. La ciudad de Antigua está en Guatemala. Usted _____. (*You're right.*)

# GRAMMAR II  Adjetivos y pronombres demostrativos (*Demonstrative Adjectives and Pronouns*)

**A.** The demonstrative adjectives and pronouns are words that are used to point out and identify people and things. They precede the noun they modify.

**B.** Memorize the demonstrative adjectives and pronouns in the chart.

| Distance | Masculine | Feminine | (English) | |
|---|---|---|---|---|
| Near speaker | este (cuarto) estos (cuartos) | esta (cama) estas (camas) | this (room, bed) these (rooms, beds) | |
| Near listener | ese (cuarto) esos (cuartos) | esa (cama) esas (camas) | that (room, bed) those (rooms, beds) | (near you, the listener) |
| Far both from speaker and listener | aquel (sitio) aquellos (sitios) | aquella (playa) aquellas (playas) | that (place, beach) those (places, beaches) | ([way] over there) |

Note that:

1. Demonstrative adjectives show the *distance* a noun is from the speaker, the listener, or from both of them. When the speaker talks about something nearby, she will use *este/estos, esta/estas.*

   EXS: *este* **cuarto**, *esta* **cama** (<u>this</u> room, <u>this</u> bed)

2. When the speaker is talking about something *near the listener,* he will use *ese/esos, esa/esas.*

   EX: **¿Cómo** *se* **llama ese agente?** (*What is the name of <u>that</u> agent?*)

3. When the speaker refers to something *far both from her and the listener,* she will use **aquel/aquellos, aquella/aquellas.**

   EX: **¿Quién es** *aquel* **niño** *allá lejos?* (*Who is <u>that</u> boy <u>over there</u>?*)

**C.** The neuter forms *esto/eso/aquello* are used to refer to something when we don't specify what we're talking about. There are no neuter nouns in Spanish. We use *esto/eso/aquello* to refer to a statement, a speech, or an idea.

   EXS: **¿Qué es** *eso* **que tienes en la mano?** (*What's <u>that</u> you have in your hand?*)
   **¿Quieres tener éxito? Para** *eso* **tienes que estudiar mucho.**
   (*Do you want to be successful? For <u>that</u> you have to study a lot.*)

**D.** Demonstratives can be used in two ways: (1) as adjectives in front of a noun, as in the examples under B above; (2) as pronouns, that is, when something is omitted because it is understood.

   In 2010, La Real Academia de La Lengua Española (RAE) ruled that the written accent on demonstrative pronouns did not comply with accentuation rules and therefore it shouldn't be used.

EXS: ¿Quieres *este* libro? —No, quiero *ese*. (*Do you want <u>this</u> book? —No, I want <u>that</u> one.*)

¿Vas a comprar *ese* carro? —No, voy a comprar *aquel*. (*Are you going to buy <u>that</u> car? —No, I'm going to buy <u>that</u> one over there.*)

Notice that in English you add *one* to *this* and *that* when the noun is omitted.

# PRACTIQUE LOS DEMOSTRATIVOS

**ANSWERS p. 140**

1. If I'm talking about things or people *near me,* I use any of these four demonstratives: _____.

2. If I'm talking about things or people *near you* (the listener), I use any of these four demonstratives: _____.

3. Demonstrative adjectives must agree with the noun in gender (masculine/feminine) and _____, just like other adjectives or articles.

4. Notice that in English *that* and *those* are used for something near the listener or far from the listener; you would have to add *over there* to specify that something is far from both the listener and the speaker. In Spanish we have two different demonstratives for *that* and *those:* **ese** *vs.* _____, **esos** *vs.* _____, **esa** *vs.* _____, and **esas** *vs.* _____.

5. Which word don't we translate in the expression *this one?* _____.

6. The neuter demonstratives **esto, eso,** and **aquello** are never used in front of a _____. In other words, they are like pronouns; they replace statements, speeches, or ideas. Do they take an accent? _____.

7. Have you noticed that the *masculine* form of the demonstratives doesn't end in *o* like that of many other adjectives? Actually, it ends in the vowel _____, except for **aquel**.

8. The difference in distance between **ese** and **aquel** (what is *near* or *far* from the listener) is relative. The tendency today is to use **ese** more than **aquel**; the same is true for their neuter counterparts: _____.

# PRÁCTICA

**ANSWERS p. 140**

Complete each sentence with the correct demonstrative. Pay attention to number and gender.

1. ¿Conoces a _____ señora que está allí en la recepción? (*that*)

2. El agua de _____ (*this*) piscina tiene la temperatura muy agradable; pero _____ (*that*) piscina tiene el agua más fría.

3. ¿Qué es _____ que llevas en la maleta? (*that*)

4. _____ llave de la habitación es de mi amigo José. (*this*)

5. _____ (*this*) hotel es más costoso que _____ (*that one*) en el que tú estás.

6. ¿Qué es _____ que se ve cerca de la playa? (*that*)

7. Puedes secarte (*dry*) con _____ toalla. (*this*)

8. No quiero _____ (*this*) vista; prefiero _____. (*that one*)

9. No puedo aceptar _____ precio. (*that*)

10. _____ restaurante es muy bueno. (*this*)

# GRAMMAR III   Adjetivos y pronombres posesivos (*Possessive Adjectives and Pronouns*)

**A.** *Possessive adjectives and possessive **pronouns** express ownership or possession.*

**B.** Memorize the possessive adjectives and pronouns in the chart.

| Persons | Weak Forms | Strong Forms | | (English) | |
|---|---|---|---|---|---|
| | Adjectives Masc. & Fem. | Pronouns Masculine | Pronouns Feminine | Adjectives | Pronouns |
| First | mi/mis | mío/míos | mía/mías | my | mine |
| Second | tu/tus | tuyo/tuyos | tuya/tuyas | your | yours |
| Third | su/sus | suyo/suyos | suya/suyas | his/hers/its their | his/hers/its theirs |
| First plural | nuestro/a/s | nuestro/nuestros | nuestra/nuestras | Our | Ours |
| Second plural (Spain) | vuestro/a/s | vuestro/vuestros | vuestra/vuestras | your | yours |

Note that:

1. Possessive adjectives are placed before the noun they modify. *Tu cuarto* tiene cama sencilla. *Nuestra habitación* tiene cama doble.

2. Possessive pronouns are used to replace a noun. *Las reservaciones suyas. Las suyas.* (*Your reservations*)

3. The short forms are used only before nouns and agree in number with those nouns: mi libro/mis libros.

4. *Nuestro/nuestros, nuestra/nuestras, vuestro/vuestros, vuestra/vuestras,* do not have short forms. They always agree with the nouns they modify in gender and number: *nuestro carro/nuestra maleta/vuestras llaves.*

5. Usually, the short forms such as mi/tu/su are unstressed. They are pronounced as if they belonged to the next word, just like the articles el/los, la/las.

C. The long forms are used after the noun or alone as pronouns. They carry stress, and we can emphasize them in our intonation. Notice that in English the pronouns have different forms than the adjectives: *my* vs. *mine*, *your* vs. *yours*, **and so on. In** Spanish they are the same.

EX: **El libro *mío* está aquí; el *tuyo* está en casa.** (*My book is here; yours is at home.*)

D. English pronouns *mine, yours,* and so on never take an article, whereas Spanish *mío /tuyo,* and so on always need the article when they are pronouns, except after *ser.*

EX: **Este libro *es mío;* ¿dónde *está el tuyo?*** (*This book is* mine; *where's* yours?)

We use *el mío/el tuyo* with *ser* if the noun is being differentiated from other nouns:

EX: **¿Los libros? No sé cuál es *el tuyo,* pero éste es *el mío.*** (*The books? I don't know which one is* yours, *but this one is* mine.)

E. In English the third person has more forms than others, because there are three different subjects to refer to: *he → his, she → her, it → its,* and the plural *they → their.* In Spanish there is only one form for all of them: **su/sus.** This means that *su/sus* can be very ambiguous. To make the meaning clear, the preposition *de* plus the pronoun (**de + él, de + ella, de + usted,** and so on) is sometimes used after the noun (instead of *su/sus* before the noun).

EXS: **Conozco a tus abuelos; *su casa* (*la casa de ellos*) es grande.** (*I know your grandparents;* their house *is large.*)
**Aquí están Carlos y María; *el carro de él* es este.** (*Here are Carlos and Maria;* his *car is this one.*)

F. With parts of the body and clothes we are wearing, we use definite articles (**el/los, la/las**) in Spanish, since ownership is obvious. In English we use possessive adjectives instead.

EX: **Lávese *las* manos.** (*Wash* your *hands.*)

# PRACTIQUE LOS POSESIVOS

**ANSWERS**
**p. 140**

1. There are three short forms of the possessives in the singular: _____, _____, _____, and three in the plural: _____, _____, _____.

2. Do you usually stress *mi/tu/su?* _____.

3. *Su* can be translated five different ways in English, including the possessive referring to *Ud./Uds.* Possible translations are: _____.

4. *Tu hijos* is incorrect because *hijos* is plural; it should be _____.

5. Are the long forms **mío/tuyo/suyo** used before or after the noun?

_____.

6. *Mine/yours*, and so on stand alone (without a noun). Which forms stand alone in Spanish, **mi/tu/su or mío/tuyo/suyo?** _____.

7. The plural of *mi* is _____, and the plural of *tu* is

_____.

8. Remember that *tu* has two different meanings, depending on whether it's spelled with an accent (**acento**) or without it. **Tú** (with an accent) means _____, and **tu** (without an accent) means _____.

9. *Yo uso mi libro y tú usas tuyo* is incorrect. What's missing before *tuyo?*

_____.

10. If we want to talk about *Mary's house* we can say **su casa** in Spanish, without repeating **María.** However, **su casa** can be confusing; we can clarify it by saying

_____.

11. Spanish possessives agree with the _____ that follows in gender and number.

12. Which form is correct, **nuestra cuarto** or **nuestro cuarto?** _____.

# PRÁCTICA

**ANSWERS p. 140**

Translate the possessives in parentheses.

1. _____ habitación está en el tercer piso y la _____ está en el último piso. *(my/yours)*

2. _____ maletas están en la recepción del hotel. *(our)*

3. Esta llave es _____; la _____ está en la mesa. *(mine/yours)*

4. Julio y Martha tienen un apartamento de tiempo compartido en Arizona. _____ apartamento es grande y con vista a un lago muy hermoso. *(their)*

5. Tengo _____ toalla de la playa en el cuarto. Mi hermana me va dar la _____. *(my/hers)*

6. Este hotel es de cinco estrellas; pero _____ precios son razonables. *(its)*

7. Debemos bajar por la escalera del hotel. _____ ascensor no funciona *(it is broken/it is not working)* *(its).*

8. El hotel Las Américas tiene más de cien habitaciones. *(our)* _____ habitación es una suite ejecutiva muy elegante.

9. _____ amigos de la universidad viven en Antigua, Guatemala. _____ casa es de estilo colonial. *(my/their)*

10. *(our)* _____ guía para el tour por la ciudad de Guatemala es muy joven e inteligente y se llama Susana.

# 7 Una cena deliciosa
## (*A Delicious Dinner*)

---

## PALABRAS NUEVAS

| *Las comidas* | *Meals* |
|---|---|
| el almuerzo | lunch |
| la cena | dinner |
| la comida | food/dinner/meal |
| el desayuno | breakfast |
| la entrada/los entremeses/ aperitivos | appetizers |
| el plato principal | main dish |

| *Las bebidas* | *Drinks/Beverages* |
|---|---|
| el agua | water |
| el agua mineral | mineral water |
| la bebida energizante | energy drink |
| el café | coffee |
| la cerveza | beer |
| el jugo | juice |
| la leche | milk |
| la leche de almendras | almond milk |
| la leche de soya | soy milk |

| | |
|---|---|
| la leche descremada | skimmed milk |
| la leche deslactosada | lactose free milk |
| el refresco | soft drink |
| la soda/gaseosa | soda/soft drink |
| el té | tea |
| el té helado | iced tea |
| el vino | wine |
| el vino tinto | red wine |
| el zumo (*Spain*) | *juice* |

| *Las carnes y comida de mar* | *Meat and Seafood* |
|---|---|
| el atún | tuna |
| el bistec | steak |
| los camarones | shrimp |
| la carne | meat |
| la carne de res | beef |
| el cerdo | pork |
| la chuleta de cerdo | (pork) chop |
| el cordero | lamb |

| | | | |
|---|---|---|---|
| la hamburguesa | hamburger | las papas/patatas (*Spain*) | potatoes |
| el jamón | ham | | |
| la langosta | lobster | las papas fritas | French fries |
| los mariscos | shellfish | el pepino cohombro | cucumber |
| el pavo | turkey | | |
| el perro caliente | hotdog | el pimentón | pepper |
| el pescado | fish | el tomate | tomato |
| el pollo | chicken | las verduras | vegetables |
| el pollo asado | roast chicken | la zanahoria | carrots |
| la salchicha | sausage | | |
| el salmón | salmon | *Otras comidas* | *Other Food* |
| | | el aceite | oil |
| *Las frutas* | | el aceite de oliva | olive oil |
| el aguacate/la palta(*Argentina*) | avocado | las aceitunas | olives |
| | | el aderezo | dressing |
| las bananas/los bananos | banana | el ajo | garlic |
| | | el arroz | rice |
| el durazno/ melocotón (*Spain*) | peach | el azúcar | sugar |
| | | el cereal | cereal |
| | | los condimentos | condiments |
| el limón | lemon | las galletas | cookies |
| la mandarina | mandarin, tangerine | los huevos | eggs |
| el mango | mango | los huevos revueltos | scrambled eggs |
| la manzana | apple | | |
| el melón | melon | los macarrones con queso | macaroni cheese |
| la naranja | orange | | |
| la papaya | papaya | la mantequilla | butter |
| la pera | pear | la margarina | margarine |
| la piña | pineapple | la mayonesa | mayonnaise |
| las uvas | grapes | el pan | bread |
| | | la pasta | pasta |
| *Las verduras y legumbres* | *Vegetables and legumes* | el pastel | pie, cake |
| | | la pimienta | black pepper |
| las arvejas/los guisantes | green peas | el queso | cheese |
| | | la sal | salt |
| el brócoli | broccoli | el sándwich/ emparedado/ bocadillo (*Spain*) | sandwich |
| el calabacín | zucchini | | |
| la cebolla | onion | | |
| la cebolla larga | scallion | la sopa | soup |
| el champiñón/ el hongo/la seta (*Spain*) | mushroom | la torta/el ponqué | cake |
| | | el vinagre | vinegar |
| los espárragos | asparagus | *Adjetivos* | *Adjectives* |
| los frijoles | beans | caliente | hot (temperature) |
| los garbanzos | chickpeas | condimentado(a) | seasoned |
| la lechuga | lettuce | delicioso(a) | delicious |
| el maíz | corn | dulce | sweet |

| | | | |
|---|---|---|---|
| **exquisite(a)** | exquisite | **freír/fritar** | to fry |
| **fresco(a)** | fresh | **hervir** | to boil |
| **frío(a)** | cold | **hornear** | to bake |
| **grasoso(a)** | greasy/fat | **preparar** | to prepare |
| **picante** | hot (spicy) | **probar** | to try |
| **rico(a)** | tasty/delicious | **saber (a algo)** | to taste like |
| **sabroso(a)** | delicious/tasty | | something |
| **salado(a)** | salty | **servir** | to serve |

| | | | |
|---|---|---|---|
| *Verbos* | *Verbs* | *Algunas* | *Some Conjunctions* |
| **adobar** | to marinate | *conjunciones* | |
| **almorzar** | to have lunch | **aunque** | *although/even* |
| **asar** | to roast | | *though* |
| **calentar** | to heat | **luego** | *then* |
| **cenar** | to eat dinner | **mientras** | *while* |
| **cocinar** | to cook | **pero** | *but* |
| **comer** | to eat | **o** | *or* |
| **condimentar** | to season | **y** | *and* |
| **desayunar** | to eat breakfast | | |

## NOTAS

1. *Banana* is one of the many words used for banana in Spanish. In Spain it is called **plátano**. Other common words are **banano, guineo**. In some Latin American countries *plátano* is a plantain that is cooked in many different ways.

2. *Frijol* is one of many words for bean. In some countries it is called **fréjol, poroto,** and **alubia**.

3. *Zumo* is *juice* in Spain. In Latin America, juice is called *jugo*.

4. *Pavo* is called **guajolote** in Mexico and **chompipe** in Central America.

5. *Cerdo* in general refers to the animal. *Puerco* is also another word for pig. Other words are **marrano, chancho, and cochino**.

6. Notice that *té* is written with **acento** to differentiate it from the pronoun **te** (*you*).

# PRACTIQUE LAS PALABRAS NUEVAS

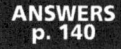
ANSWERS
p. 140

A. Write *el* or *la* before each noun.

1. _____ tomate
2. _____ arvejas
3. _____ aceite
4. _____ calabacín
5. _____ maíz

6. _____ leche
7. _____ mantequilla
8. _____ té
9. _____ pescado
10. _____ jugo

11. _____ azúcar
12. _____ sal
13. _____ pimienta
14. _____ salchicha
15. _____ pan

**ANSWERS**
**p. 141**

B. Palabras nuevas. Write the answer by using the following categories *verduras y legumbres/carnes y comida de mar/bebidas/frutas* to which the following food in the list belong.

1. café: _____
2. camarones: _____
3. manzana: _____
4. arvejas: _____
5. vino tinto: _____

6. cerdo: _____
7. uvas: _____
8. maíz: _____
9. calabacín: _____
10. soda: _____

**ANSWERS**
**p. 141**

C. ¿Desayuno, almuerzo o cena?

1. huevos revueltos _____.
2. salmón _____.
3. emparedado _____.
4. vino _____.
5. cereal _____.

**ANSWERS**
**p. 141**

D. *Let's remember these verbs.* Write the verb in Spanish.

1. To eat breakfast _____
2. To eat lunch _____
3. To eat dinner _____
4. To boil _____
5. To serve _____
6. To bake _____
7. To prepare _____
8. To eat _____

9. To taste like _____
10. To season _____
11. To roast _____
12. To heat _____
13. To cook _____
14. To fry _____
15. To marinate _____

**ANSWERS**
**p. 141**

E. Fill the blanks with a present indicative form of one of the verbs that follow.

| comer | beber | preparar | desayunar | cenar |
|-------|-------|----------|-----------|-------|
| asar | almorzar (ue) | hornear | hervir (ie) | calentar |

1. Mi madre _____ los huevos para el desayuno.
2. La cocinera (*cook*) _____ el bistec para la cena.
3. Sandra _____ un café todas las mañanas.
4. Alicia siempre _____ a las 12:30 P.M.
5. Nosotros _____ en familia todos los días a las 6:00 P.M.
6. Sofía _____ galletas con sus amigas.
7. Mi hija no _____ por las mañanas. Dice que prefiere almorzar temprano.
8. Yo no _____ comida frita (*fried*) porque no es buena para mi salud (*health*).

9. Los americanos _____ muchas hamburguesas para el día de la Independencia.

10. Tú siempre_____ la comida en el microondas (*microwave*).

# DIÁLOGO   Una cena deliciosa

*Amelia y Mateo son novios y van a casarse muy pronto. Amelia y Mateo invitaron a una cena especial a sus respectivas familias y la cena fue todo un éxito. Amelia le cuenta a su amiga Constanza sobre su cena especial.*

AMELIA:      Hola querida amiga Constanza, ¿cómo estás?

CONSTANZA:  Muy bien Amelia. ¡Qué bueno conversar contigo! Supe que tú y Mateo invitaron a sus familias a una cena el fin de semana pasado. ¿Cómo les fue?

AMELIA:      Sí Constanza. Tuvimos una cena especial, aunque fue un poco estresante por toda la preparación. Pero todo salió muy bien. Tú sabes que a Mateo le gusta el pollo para la cena así que preparamos pollo con verduras, ensalada y un pastel de manzanas. Todo quedó muy sabroso.

CONSTANZA:  El menú para la cena fue estupendo. ¿Con qué vegetales prepararon el pollo?

AMELIA:      Mateo compró unas pechugas de pollo y las adobó con ajo, pimienta y otros condimentos especiales. Además, preparamos unas papas al horno muy deliciosas.

CONSTANZA:  Y para la ensalada, ¿qué ingredientes usaron?

AMELIA:      Hicimos una ensalada con zanahorias, pepinos cohombros, lechuga, cebollas, aceitunas y ajo. Y le pusimos aceite de oliva como aderezo.

CONSTANZA:  ¡Qué delicia! ¿y quién horneó el pastel de manzanas?

AMELIA:      Querida amiga, tú sabes que a Mateo le encanta hornear. El horneó el pastel de manzanas y fue todo un éxito. La familia se lo comió todo.

CONSTANZA:  ¿Me guardaste un pedazo para mí?

AMELIA:      Por supuesto que sí. Y para la cena tomamos un vino tinto muy bueno. Es de Argentina. Fue muy apropiado para la cena.

CONSTANZA:  Me alegra mucho que la cena estuvo deliciosa y fue todo un éxito. ¿Qué dijeron los invitados

AMELIA:      Déjame decirte que todos estuvieron muy contentos y disfrutaron de la cena. Ninguno tenía restricciones alimenticias así que comieron todo sin problema. Mateo estaba muy feliz.

CONSTANZA:  Gracias por ponerme al día. Tenemos que seguir nuestra conversación otro día. Ahora tengo que ir al supermercado a comprar unas frutas que no tengo. Nos hablamos luego.

AMELIA:      Hasta pronto.

# DIALOGUE *A Delicious Dinner*

*Amelia and Mateo are dating and are going to get married very soon. Amelia and Mateo invited their respective families to a special dinner and the dinner was a success. Amelia tells her friend Constanza about her special dinner.*

AMELIA: Hello dear Constanza, how are you?

CONSTANZA: Very good Amelia. It's great talking to you! I heard that you and Mateo invited your families to dinner last weekend. How did it go?

AMELIA: Yes, Constanza. We had a special dinner although it was a little stressful because of all the preparation. But everything went very well. You know that Mateo likes chicken for dinner, so we prepared chicken with vegetables, salad, and an apple pie. Everything was very tasty.

CONSTANZA: The dinner menu looked great. What vegetables did you use with the chicken?

AMELIA: Mateo bought some chicken breasts and marinated them with garlic, pepper and other special seasonings. Plus, we made some delicious baked potatoes.

CONSTANZA: And for the salad, what ingredients did you use?

AMELIA: We made a salad with carrots, cucumbers, lettuce, onions, olives and garlic. And we added olive oil as a dressing.

CONSTANZA: What a delight! And who baked the apple pie?

AMELIA: My friend, you know that Mateo loves to bake. He baked the apple pie and it was a success. The family ate everything.

CONSTANZA: Did you save a piece for me?

AMELIA: Of course, I did. And for dinner we had a very good red wine. It was from Argentina. It was very appropriate for dinner.

CONSTANZA: I am very happy that dinner was delicious and a success. What did the guests say?

AMELIA: Let me tell you, everyone was very happy and enjoyed the dinner. None of them had any dietary restrictions so they ate everything without a problem. Mateo was very happy.

CONSTANZA: Thanks for updating me. We have to continue our conversation another day. Now I have to go to the supermarket to buy some fruits that I don't have. I will talk to you later.

AMELIA: See you soon.

# PRÁCTICA

ANSWERS
p. 141

**A. Complete the story using the information from the dialogue.**

Amelia y Constanza conversan sobre la cena que Amelia y su novio Mateo prepararon para sus familiares. Para la cena, ellos prepararon _____ (1) con _____ (2). A Constanza el _____ (3) para la cena le pareció estupendo. Mateo y Amelia acompañaron la cena con un _____ (4) de manzanas. A Mateo le encanta _____ (5). Y por eso él fue quien horneó el pastel. Algunos de los ingredientes que usaron para la _____ (6) fueron zanahorias, cebollas, lechuga, aceitunas, pepinos y _____ (7). El aderezo que usaron fue _____ (8). Para la cena bebieron un _____ (9) de la Argentina. La familia estuvo muy _____ (10) con la invitación a cenar.

ANSWERS
p. 141

**B. Práctica de vocabulario. Underline the correct answer.**

1. _____ son bebidas que no tienen alcohol, pero contienen mucha cafeína y mucha azúcar. (las bebidas energizantes, los jugos, las aguas minerales)

2. Muchas personas toman leche _____ porque tienen problemas con la lactosa. (con crema, natural, de almendras)

3. _____ (el té, la cerveza, el vino) es una bebida con alcohol que usa las uvas para su preparación.

4. _____ (los plátanos fritos, los burritos asados, las papas fritas) con las hamburguesas son muy populares para el almuerzo en los Estados Unidos.

5. Los ingleses tienen la costumbre de beber mucho (café, té, jugo), especialmente en las horas de la tarde.

6. En Centroamérica y en México se comen muchas tortillas de (papa, calabacín, maíz).

7. En Estados Unidos (las uvas, las naranjas, las piñas) se cultivan (*grow*) principalmente en Hawaii.

8. Es muy tradicional comer (pavo, cerdo, pollo) para el Día de Acción de Gracias en Estados Unidos.

9. Uno de los siguientes alimentos NO es una verdura (cebolla, pimentón, arroz).

10. El salmón es un tipo de (carne, pescado, verdura).

C. Match the two columns.

| | | | |
|---|---|---|---|
| 1. _____ beer. | | **A.** leche |
| 2. _____ lettuce | | **B.** zanahoria |
| 3. _____ orange | | **C.** naranja |
| 4. _____ carrot. | | **D.** pavo |
| 5. _____ fish | | **E.** lechuga |
| 6. _____ turkey | | **F.** maíz |
| 7. _____ black pepper | | **G.** cerveza |
| 8. _____ corn | | **H.** aceite |
| 9. _____ oil | | **I.** pimienta |
| 10. _____ milk | | **J.** pescado |

# GRAMMAR I   Nombres y pronombres de objeto directo • A personal (*Direct Object Nouns and Pronouns • Personal a*)

A. Direct objects respond to the question *what?* or *whom?* in relation with the verb.

¿Qué hornea Mateo? Mateo hornea el pastel.

El pastel is the direct object.

¿A quién invita Amelia? Amelia invita a Mateo.

In this example, Mateo is the direct object.

B. The direct object is the noun or pronoun that completes the meaning of a transitive verb. For example, *to buy* makes no sense without someone (the subject of the sentence) buying something. In the sentence **Compramos el arroz;** *arroz* is the direct object.

C. In Spanish, if the direct object is a person or a pet rather than a thing, the preposition *a* precedes it. This is called "*The personal a.*" This distinction is not made in English.

EXS: **Veo** *la leche.* (I see <u>the milk</u>.)
     **Veo** *a la niña.* (I see <u>the girl</u>.)

If the person is indefinite, *a* is omitted, and the person becomes "depersonalized," as if he or she were a thing.

EXS: **Veo** *al\** **cocinero.** (*I see the cook.*)
     **Necesito un cocinero.** (*I need a cook.*)

\*Remember the contraction *a + el = al.*

EX: Amelia llama **al** cocinero.

**D.** Memorize the direct object pronouns in the chart.

| Subject Pronoun | Direct Object Pronoun | (English) |
|---|---|---|
| yo | me | me |
| tú | te | you (*familiar*) |
| él | lo/le (*Spain*) | him, it/him |
| ella | la | her, it |
| ellos | los/les (*Spain*) | them |
| ellas | las | them |
| usted | lo/le (*Spain*)/la | you (*formal*) |
| ustedes | los/les (*Spain*)/las | you (*formal plural*) |
| nosotros(as) | nos | us |
| vosotros (as) | os | you (***Spain familiar plural***) |

Note that:

1. *Lo/los* are used in Latin America to refer to masculine nouns, either people or things. In Spain *le/les* is used if the direct object is a person and *lo/los* if it is a thing.

   EXS: SPAIN: ¿Ve usted *a Juan?* —Sí, *le* veo.
   LATIN AMERICA: ¿Ve usted *a Juan?* — Sí, *lo* veo.
   (*Do you see* John? — *Yes, I see* him.)

2. The direct object pronouns are unstressed in Spanish, and we pronounce them as if they were part of the verb; they cannot be emphasized phonetically. In English they are usually stressed.

3. In affirmative sentences in Spanish, the direct object pronoun precedes the conjugated verb. In English it always follows the verb. In negative sentences, the pronoun is placed between the word *no* and the verb.

   EX: Usted *me* entiende. (*You understand me.*)
   Usted no *me* entiende. (*You don't understand me.*)

4. If the direct object pronoun is the object of an infinitive, it may either precede the conjugated verb or follow the infinitive. When it follows the infinitive, it is attached to it, forming one word. The meaning is the same in both cases.

   EX: Quiero verte = *Te* quiero ver. (*I want to see* you.)

   The direct object pronoun may also be attached to an affirmative command.

   EX: ¡Dígame! (*Tell* me!)

# PRACTIQUE LOS PRONOMBRES DE OBJETO DIRECTO

ANSWERS
p. 142

1. *Yo conozco Amelia* is incorrect because *Amelia* is a person. It should be **Yo** conozco _____. For this reason, this preposition is called the "personal _____."

2. Remember that *nadie* is the negative of *alguien*, and that both refer to persons. Is it correct to say **Conozco alguien aquí.** _____. The preposition _____ is required in front of _____.

3. The direct object pronouns in Spanish never carry phonetic _____. That's why they are always pronounced as if they were part of the _____.

4. The third-person direct object pronouns are four in Latin America: _____.

5. In Spain people would say **¿Juan? No le veo**, whereas in Latin America they would say **¿Juan? No** _____. The same is true in the plural: *les* becomes _____.

6. Do the direct object pronouns precede or follow the conjugated verb in the indicative? _____. Do the same pronouns precede or follow the infinitive? _____.

7. An infinitive usually follows a verb form in the indicative. In this case the pronoun may follow the _____ or precedes the _____.

8. Which sentence is correct **Quiero ayudarte** or **Te quiero ayudar?** _____.

9. If the person who is the direct object is indefinite, we treat him or her as a "thing" by omitting the preposition _____. For example, *we need waitresses* would be in Spanish **Necesitamos** _____.

# PRACTICA

ANSWERS
p. 142

A. **Answer the questions by replacing the direct object noun with the pronoun. Pay attention to the verb. This is a good review of verbs you have learned in previous lessons.**

1. ¿Compras *las frutas?* — Sí, _____ compro.

2. ¿Escuchas a *tu amiga?* — Sí, _____ escucho.

3. ¿Preparas *el desayuno?* — Sí, _____ preparo.

4. ¿Lavas *las verduras?* — Sí, _____ lavo.

5. ¿Tomas *bebidas energizantes?* — No, no _____ tomo.

6. ¿Fríes *el pollo?* — No, no _____ frito.

7. ¿Comes *mucho salmón?* — No, no _____ como.

8. ¿Bebes *leche descremada?* — No, no _____ bebo.

9. ¿Adobas *el pescado?* — Sí, _____ adobo.

10. ¿Usas *los ajos* para adobar? — Sí, _____ uso.

**ANSWERS p. 142**

**B. Fill in the blank with the "personal *a*" if required. Remember the contraction *a* + *el* = *al*.**

1. ¿Por qué no invitas _____ hermano de Amelia a la cena?

2. No pienso invitar _____ nadie.

3. Josefina es vegetariana y no come _____ carne.

4. Mateo siempre escucha _____ Amelia.

5. Voy a llamar _____ camarero porque quiero pagar la cuenta.

**ANSWERS p. 142**

**C. Answer the questions with direct object pronouns *me/te/la/las/lo/los/nos*.**

**Modelo:** ¿Bebes **leche** por la mañana? No, no **la** bebo/Sí **la** bebo.

1. ¿Tomas *el café* todos los días?

_____

2. ¿Comes *los huevos* por las mañanas?

_____

3. ¿Calientas *el té* en el microondas?

_____

4. ¿Preparas *un sándwich* para el almuerzo?

_____

5. ¿Bebes *cerveza* los fines de semana?

_____

6. ¿Quién te llama? ¿Constanza? — Sí, Constanza _____ llama. (*she calls **me***)

7. ¿Quién escucha a Mateo? ¿Amelia? — Sí, Amelia _____ escucha. (*she listens **to him***)

8. ¿Quién me llama todos los días? — Mi madre _____ llama. (*My mom calls **me***)

9. ¿Quiénes nos ayudan a preparar la cena? — Sus amigos _____ ayudan. (*they help **us***)

10. ¿Vas a verme mañana? — Sí, _____ veo mañana. (*I see **you** tomorrow*)

# GRAMMAR II Pretérito de los verbos regulares (*Preterite of Regular Verbs*)

A. *The preterite* is a verbal tense that is used in Spanish to describe actions and states that were completed at a definite time in the past.

B. Memorize the preterite of regular verbs in the chart.

|  | *Habl ar* (to talk) | *Com er* (to eat) | *Viv ir* (to live) | (English) |
|---|---|---|---|---|
| yo | habl é | com í | viv í | I lived; I did live |
| tú | habl aste | com iste | viv iste | you lived; you did live |
| él/ella/Ud. | habl ó | com ió | viv ió | he/she/you lived, he/she/you did live |
| nosotros(as) | habl amos | com imos | viv imos | we lived; we did live. |
| vosotros(as) | habl asteis | com isteis | viv isteis | you all lived (Spain) |
| ellos/ellas/Uds. | habl aron | com ieron | viv ieron | they/you lived, they/you did live |

Note that:

1. The stems **habl-, com-, viv-,** are the same as in the present. They carry the dictionary meaning: *to talk, to eat, to live.*

2. The most important difference between the present and the preterite is the stress on the last syllable in the first- and third-person singular, along with new vowels. Compare *yo hablo* with *yo hablé, él come* with *él comió,* and so on.

3. The ending -mos for *nosotros/as* is the same as in the present, whereas for *tú* it is -aste and -iste, for *vosotros/as* is asteis and isteis, and for *ellos* it is -aron, and -ieron. Notice that -er and -ir verbs have the same endings in the preterite.

4. *Hablamos* (-ar verb) and *vivimos* (-ir verb) are the same in the present and the preterite. An adverb or context tells us how to interpret the meaning of these forms.

   EXS: *Hablamos con el niño ahora.* (We <u>are talking</u> to the boy <u>now.</u>)
   *Hablamos con el niño ayer.* (We <u>talked</u> to the boy <u>yesterday.</u>)

C. *Preterite* means *past.* There is another tense for a past action that we will study in another lesson "*the imperfect.*" For the time being, try to associate the Spanish preterite with the simple past in English: *lived, spoke, heard,* and so on. To translate the emphatic *did* as in *I did live in Quito,* we use an adverb such as **sí ciertamente: Yo sí viví en Quito** OR **Ciertamente yo viví en Quito.**

D. Spelling changes. Study the rules for spelling changes that follow.

   1. The preterite of verbs that end in -gar, -zar and -car change the spelling in the "yo" form:

   *Pagar, llegar,* and any verb with a *g* before the -ar ending add a *u* after the *g* before the ending -é. This *u* is not pronounced.

EX: pagar → (yo) pa**gu**é BUT (ella) pa**g**ó

*Comenzar, especializar,* and any verb with a *z* before the **-ar** ending change the *z* to *c* before the ending **-é**, just as *feliz* changes to *felices* and *felicidad.*

EX: comenzar → **(yo)** comen**c**é BUT (él) comen**z**ó, (ellas) comen**z**aron, and so on.

*Tocar, practicar,* and any verb with a *c* before the **-ar** ending change *c* to *qu* before the ending **-é**. The *u* of *qu* is always silent in Spanish.

EX: practicar → (yo) practi**qu**é BUT (Carlos) practi**c**ó

2. *Leer, caer, oír,* and any other verb with two consecutive vowels change the vowel *i* of the third person forms (plural and singular) to *y* whenever it appears between two other vowels.

EXS: leer → usted le**y**ó → ustedes le**y**eron BUT yo leí, tú leíste, nosotros leímos
oír → ella o**y**ó → ellas o**y**eron BUT yo oí, tú oíste, nosotros oímos

### NOTE

From *ver* we get **yo vi** (*I saw*), **él vio** (*he saw*). The *accent* is not needed because these forms have only one syllable; however, a compound verb such as **prever** (*to foresee*) will need **acento: yo preví** (*I foresaw*), **él previó** (*he foresaw*).

## PRACTIQUE EL PRETÉRITO

**ANSWERS**
**p. 142**

1. The stem of a verb carries the basic _____ of the verb. The stem of *comer* is _____, and the stem of *ver* is _____.

2. The personal ending **-mos** is for _____, the endings **-aste** and **-iste** are for _____, and the endings **-é** and **-í** for _____.

3. *Hablar* has two forms with an accent (**acento**) in the preterite: _____/
_____.

4. *Vivir* has two forms with an accent: _____/_____.

5. *Hablamos* and *vivimos* (and all the verbs ending in **-ar** and **-ir**) are the same in two tenses of the indicative: _____/_____.

6. From *apagar* we don't say **apagé** in the preterite. It should be _____, because **g** changes to _____ in front of the vowels **e** and **i**.

7. The word *preterite* means _____. In Spanish we call it **pretérito** rather than **pasado,** the word for *past.* How would you usually translate *pagué*? _____.

8. From *creer* we don't write **creió** but _____. The reason is that the *i* between two vowels (in this case **e** and **ó**) becomes _____.

9. From *tocar* we don't write **tocé**, but _____. The reason is that the *c* changes to _____ in front of the vowels **e** and **i**.

10. From *comenzar* we don't write **comenzé**, but _____. The reason is that we change *z* to _____ in front of *e* and *i*.

11. We don't write **leieron** but _____, because the *i* is between two vowels.

12. *Ud. vio* carries no accent because this verb has _____ syllable, whereas *Ud. previó* (*you foresaw*) needs _____ because it has two syllables, and the stress is on the last syllable ending in a vowel.

# PRÁCTICA

ANSWERS p. 142

A. **Fill in the blanks with the correct form of the preterite.**

1. Amelia y Mateo _____ una cena especial para los familiares. (*preparar*)

2. La cena _____ muy bien. (*salir*)

3. Constanza _____ con Amelia sobre (*about*) la cena. (*hablar*)

4. Los invitados _____ vino tinto de Argentina. (*beber*)

5. Mateo _____ un pastel de manzanas (*hornear*)

6. Yo _____ el pollo con pimienta, ajo y otros condimentos. (*adobar*)

7. Mateo y Amelia _____ las verduras en el supermercado. (*comprar*)

8. Yo _____ $120 dólares por los ingredientes para la cena. (*pagar*)

9. Mateo y yo _____ la casa muy bien. (*limpiar*)

10. Yo no _____ mucho. (*comer*)

ANSWERS p. 142

B. **Una invitación especial. Complete con la forma correcta de los verbos en pretérito:**

La semana pasada mi amigo Julio _____ (1 decidir) invitar a unos amigos a cenar a su casa. El jueves pasado, yo _____ (2 acompañar) a Julio al supermercado para comprar todos los ingredientes para preparar un arroz con pollo. El viernes, Julio y yo _____ (3 volver) a la casa después de clase y yo lo _____ (4 ayudar) a limpiarla. Luego, Julio _____ (5 preparar) el arroz con pollo y juntos, nosotros _____ (6 hornear) las galletas. A las siete en punto, nuestros amigos _____ (7 llegar). Ellos nos _____ (8 comprar) unas flores muy bonitas. Después de la cena, algunos amigos _____ (9 beber) vino y otros _____ (10 tomar) café. Nuestros amigos se fueron muy contentos a las 11:00 P.M.

ANSWERS
p. 143

C. Practice the direct object pronouns in the preterite. Answer the questions by replacing the noun with the corresponding pronoun.

> EX: ¿Te comiste *las galletas?* — Sí, me *las* comí. (Did you eat <u>the cookies</u>? — Yes, I ate <u>them</u>.)

1. ¿Ya cocinaste *la pasta*? —Sí, ya _____.

2. ¿Quién se bebió *el refresco*? —Lola se _____.

3. ¿Invitaste *a tus primos*? —No, no _____.

4. ¿Cocinaste bien *el pollo*? —Sí, _____.

5. ¿Quién lavó *las verduras*? —Roberto _____.

# GRAMMAR III   El acento (*The Written Accent*)

A. Spanish words carry *one* and *only one* phonetic stress. This stress is marked with a written accent ( ' ) according to the following fixed rules. For these rules to be effective, you should be able to "hear" the stress, and the other way around: these rules will help you to place the stress when you read if you don't know the word.

B. The following three rules show you when to add an accent mark.

1. Words with stress on the *last syllable* need an accent if the last letter is a vowel or the consonant **n** or **s**. Also, the word must have two or more syllables: **estás, está, están, aquí, menú, café, calabacín, pimentón, veintidós** (but **dos**), **también** (but **bien**).

2. Words with stress on the *next-to-last syllable* need an accent if the last letter is any consonant *except* **n** or **s**: **estándar, azúcar, fácil** (*easy*).

3. Words with stress *two syllables before the last* need an accent. Here the last letter has nothing to do with the accent: **número(s), fantástico(s), fríjoles, plátano, éxito.**

C. The exceptions to these three rules are for reasons other than the stress. There are two additional rules:

1. We write an accent on the vowel **i** or **ú** to break a diphthong—that is, when the *í* or the *ú* carries the stress and is before or after any of the other three vowels: **a, e, o.**

   EXS: **oír, día, tío, rubíes, hindúes, María, maíz** (*corn*)

2. One-syllable words do not have an accent unless they are homophonic words with the same spelling but different meanings and the only way to tell them apart is the accent on one of them. Try to memorize them.

   **dé** (*give*)/**de** (*of*)        **mí** (*me*)/**mi** (*my*)        **té** (*tea*)/**te** (*you-reflexive*)
   **él** (*he*)/**el** (*the*)        **sé** (*I know*)/**se** (*himself-reflexive*)  **tú** (*you*)/**tu** (*your*)
   **más** (*more*)/**mas** (*but*)    **sí** (*yes*)/**si** (*if*)

D. Remember that question words always have an accent, even though the above rules may not apply. This is also true for question words used in indirect questions.

EX: *¿Cuándo* quieres ir al supermercado? (*When do you want to go to the supermarket?*)

María sabe *cuándo* vamos a llegar. (*Mary knows <u>when</u> we're going to arrive.*)

No spelling rules, including rules for the accent, are as good as a "visual memory." Try to pay attention to the spelling of words as you learn them. *Be a good word-watcher!*

# PRACTIQUE EL ACENTO

ANSWERS
p. 143

1. How many stresses does a Spanish word carry? _____. For example, compound words such as *diecinueve* lose the stress of the first word. *Diecinueve* has no stress on *diec-* but on _____.

2. *Café* has an accent because the stress is on _____ syllable, and the last letter is a _____, as in **menú, está, preparó.**

3. *Pimentón* and *menús* need an accent because the stress is on the _____ syllable, and the last letters are the consonants _____ and _____.

4. *Principal, cenar,* and *arroz* don't carry an accent because the stress is on the _____ syllable, but the last letter is neither a _____ nor the consonants _____ or _____.

5. *Lápiz* and *árbol* carry an accent because the stress is one syllable before the last and the last letter is a _____ but not *n* or *s*.

6. *Espárragos, plátano,* and *brócoli* carry an accent because the stress is _____ syllables before the last. The _____ letter doesn't matter at all.

7. A diphthong is formed with two vowels in one syllable, one of which is either *i* or *u*. Both *María* and *oír* carry an accent for the same reason: to mark the break in the _____ between the í and the vowels _____ and _____.

8. In English *lead* can mean two different things (*an action* or a *mineral*), although the spelling is the same. In Spanish we indicate such differences with an accent. For example, *él* means _____, whereas *el* means _____.

9. The word *tú* means _____, whereas *tu* means _____.

10. The word *sí* means _____, whereas *si* means _____.

11. The word *más* means _____, whereas **mas** means _____.

12. Words with just one syllable don't need an accent: **dos, va, ve, tres, son,** and so on. However, if these words appear in compound words, they will need one; for example, *él prevé* (*he foresees*). How do you spell twenty-two in Spanish? _____.

# PRÁCTICA

**ANSWERS p. 143**

*Be a good word-watcher and a good listener!* All the following words have featured in previous lessons. Write the accent when needed.

1. agua
2. cafe
3. azucar
4. comer
5. dificil
6. pastel
7. adobar
8. maiz
9. tu (*you*)
10. pan
11. horneo
12. mi (*my*)
13. estan
14. feliz
15. mineral
16. tomates
17. menu
18. el (*he*)
19. atun
20. cena
21. exito
22. preparo
23. dia
24. novio
25. platano
26. practique
27. desayuno
28. simpatico
29. comida
30. el (*the*)
31. se (*I know*)

# 8 Las tradiciones y las fiestas
## (*Traditions and Celebrations*)

---

## PALABRAS NUEVAS

| *Las fiestas* | *Celebrations* | La Pascua | Easter |
|---|---|---|---|
| El Día de Acción de Gracias | Thanksgiving Day | La Semana Santa | Holy Week |
| El Día de las Brujas | Halloween | *Otras palabras* | *Other Words* |
| | | la alegría | joy/happiness |
| El Día de los Enamorados/ Día del Amor y la Amistad | Valentine's Day | el árbol de navidad | Christmas tree |
| | | la boda | wedding |
| | | el carnaval | Carnival (Shrove Tuesday) |
| El Día de la Independencia | Independence Day | la celebración | celebration |
| | | el festival | festival |
| El Día de la Madre | Mother's Day | la fiesta | party |
| El Día de los Muertos | Day of the Dead | la fiesta de cumpleaños | birthday party |
| El Día del Padre | Father's Day | los fuegos artificiales | fireworks |
| El Día del Trabajo | Labor Day | | |
| El día festivo/ feriado | Holiday | la llegada | arrival |
| | | las luces | lights |
| | | el Niño Dios | Baby Jesus |
| La Nochebuena | Christmas Eve | el Papá Noel | Santa Claus |
| La Navidad | Christmas Day | el pesebre | nativity set, crib |
| La Nochevieja | New Year's Eve | el regalo | gift |
| El Año Nuevo | New Year's Day | el reloj inteligente | smart watch |

118

| *Verbos* | *Verbs* | | |
|---|---|---|---|
| bailar | to dance | entretenido(a) | amusing |
| brindar | to toast | festivo(a) | festive |
| cantar | to sing | lleno(a) | full |
| cantar villancicos | to sing Christmas carols | religioso(a) | religious |
| | | sobrio(a) | sober |
| celebrar | to celebrate | sorprendido(a) | surprised |
| conmemorar | commemorate | triste | sad |
| dar regalos | to give gifts | único(a) | unique |
| disfrazarse | to dress up/disguise as | vacío(a) | empty |
| disfrutar | to enjoy | | |
| divertirse | to have fun | *expresiones de tiempo con el pretérito* | *expressions with preterite* |
| festejar | to feast/celebrate | | |
| jugar | to play (games) | anoche | last night |
| pasarlo/la bien | to have a good time | ayer | yesterday |
| | | anteayer | day before yesterday |
| tocar un instrumento | to play an instrument | la semana pasada | last week |
| | | el mes pasado | last month |
| | | el año pasado | last year |
| *Adjetivos* | *Adjectives* | el verano pasado | last summer |
| aburrido(a) | boring | el viernes pasado | last Friday |
| ateo(a) | atheist | hace una hora | an hour ago |
| borracho(a) | drunk | hace dos días | two days ago |
| contento(a) | happy | hace un año | a year ago |
| disfrazado(a) | disguised | hace un mes | a month ago |
| divertido(a) | fun | hace una semana | a week ago |

# PRACTIQUE LAS PALABRAS NUEVAS

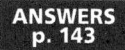
**ANSWERS p. 143**

**A. Write *el* or *la* before each noun.**

1. _____ celebración
2. _____ carnaval
3. _____ Año Nuevo
4. _____ Pascua
5. _____ boda
6. _____ festival
7. _____ luz
8. _____ fiesta
9. _____ regalo
10. _____ pesebre
11. _____ Nochebuena
12. _____ día
13. _____ alegría
14. _____ Navidad
15. _____ Semana Santa

**ANSWERS p. 143**

**B. Fiestas y celebraciones. Fill in the blanks with the following words.**

| | | | |
|---|---|---|---|
| El Día de los Muertos | La Pascua | El Día de Acción de Gracias | El Año Nuevo |
| El Día de la Independencia | La Nochebuena | El Día de la Madre | |
| La Navidad | El Día de las Brujas | | |
| | El Día de los Enamorados | | |

1. El primero de enero se celebra: _____.

2. En muchos países _____ se celebra el segundo domingo de mayo.

3. En México _____ es una celebración muy importante que se realiza el 2 de noviembre todos los años.

4. _____ se celebra en Estados Unidos el último jueves del mes de noviembre.

5. _____ se celebra en muchos países del mundo el 25 de diciembre.

6. _____ se celebra la noche del 24 de diciembre.

7. _____ se considera la celebración más importante del cristianismo.

8. _____ se celebra el 31 de octubre en muchos países de América.

9. Estados Unidos celebra _____ el día 4 de julio.

10. El 14 de febrero se celebra en Estados Unidos y en muchos otros países _____.

**ANSWERS p. 144**

C. Write the opposite of the following adjectives.

1. aburrido/a: _____.

2. alegre: _____.

3. lleno/a: _____.

4. religioso/a: _____.

5. sobrio/a: _____.

**ANSWERS p. 144**

D. Fill the blanks with the right verb in its preterite form.

| bailar | brindar | pasarlo bien | tocar | comer |
|--------|---------|--------------|-------|-------|
| celebrar | disfrutar | jugar | disfrazarse | tomar |

1. Valentina _____ de princesa Elsa para el Día de las Brujas.

2. Daniel y Susana _____ con champaña la llegada del Año Nuevo

3. Yo _____ la guitarra para la celebración del Día del Padre en mi colegio.

4. Tú _____ cartas (*cards*) con tus amigos el fin de semana pasado.

5. Nosotros _____ (*had a good time*) en casa de los abuelos para la celebración del Día de Acción de Gracias.

6. Camila _____ la fiesta de Navidad con la familia de su esposo.

7. Para celebrar el Día de Acción de Gracias nosotros _____ un pavo delicioso que preparó mi mamá.

8. ¡Tú _____ muchas cervezas el 4 de julio!

9. Andrea y Germán _____ tango para la celebración del Día de la Madre en el colegio.

10. Mi novia y yo _____ de una linda cena romántica para el Día de San Valentín.

# DIÁLOGO   Las celebraciones y festividades en el mundo hispano

*Isabel, Ana y Diego conversan sobre los días festivos en sus respectivos países. Los tres comparten sus opiniones. Isabel es chilena, Ana es estadounidense y Diego es peruano.*

ISABEL:   Me parece muy interesante el tema para nuestra conversación de hoy en clase. Ana, creo que en Estados Unidos ustedes no tienen muchos días festivos en general. ¿Tú qué piensas?

ANA:   Sí, estoy totalmente de acuerdo. Aquí en Los Estados Unidos son muy pocos los días festivos que se celebran en todo el país. Entre ellos están El Día de la Independencia, El Día de Acción de Gracias, La Navidad y El Año Nuevo. Sé que en Latinoamérica es muy diferente porque tienen muchos días festivos todo el año. ¿Es verdad?

DIEGO:   Tienes razón. En Latinoamérica hay países como Argentina, Chile y Colombia que tienen entre 18 y 20 días festivos al año. Muchos de los días festivos están relacionados con celebraciones religiosas católicas.

ISABEL:   Es verdad. Por ejemplo, en Chile tenemos como feriados de carácter general, El Viernes Santo y El Sábado Santo y creo que también es así en muchos países de Latinoamérica.

ANA:   En Estados Unidos por ser un país tan diverso culturalmente, La Semana Santa no hace parte de los días festivos. Aunque algunos colegios y universidades cristianas no tienen clases esos días. Esto depende de cada institución y de cada estado también.

DIEGO:   Es muy interesante. Nosotros en Perú, además de los feriados religiosos, tenemos muchos días festivos relacionados con batallas relacionadas con la independencia del Perú. Un ejemplo es la Batalla de Ayacucho que se celebra el 9 de diciembre y que ayudó a la consolidación de la independencia del Perú.

ISABEL: Diego, en Chile tenemos un día festivo que está relacionado con tu país, Perú. Es la celebración del Día de Las Glorias Navales. En donde se llevó a cabo la batalla entre Chile y Perú y la celebramos el día 21 de mayo.

ANA: Estoy aprendiendo mucho sobre los días festivos de Latinoamérica con nuestra conversación. Creo que mi día festivo favorito en Estados Unidos es El Día de Acción de Gracias porque representa unión, amistad y agradecimiento. Es muy especial para mí.

DIEGO: Para mí la celebración de Las Fiestas Patrias es mi favorita porque tenemos dos días de vacaciones, el 28 y 29 de julio. Y esos días tenemos muchas actividades y mucha comida para celebrar.

ISABEL: ¡Qué interesante! En Chile también tenemos dos días para celebrar la independencia, el 18 y 19 de septiembre. Pero creo que, para mí, mi celebración favorita es La Navidad porque me gusta decorar con muchas luces y me gusta reunirme con mi familia para celebrar y compartir.

ANA: Creo que se nos acabó el tiempo. Nos vemos mañana en clase para otra conversación interesante.

# DIALOGUE *Celebrations and Festivities in the Hispanic World*

*Isabel, Ana and Diego talk about the holidays in their respective countries. The three share their opinions. Isabel is Chilean, Ana is American, and Diego is Peruvian.*

ISABEL: *I find the topic for our conversation today in class very interesting. Ana, I think that in the United States you don't have many holidays in general. What do you think?*

ANA: *Yes, I totally agree. Here in the United States, there are very few holidays that are celebrated throughout the country. Among them are Independence Day, Thanksgiving Day, Christmas and New Year's Day. I know that in Latin America it is very different because they have many holidays all year round. It's true?*

DIEGO: *You're right. In Latin America there are countries like Argentina, Chile, and Colombia that have between 18 and 20 holidays a year. Many of the holidays are related to Catholic religious celebrations.*

ISABEL: *It's true. For example, in Chile we have general holidays, Good Friday and Holy Saturday and I think this is also the case in many Latin American countries.*

ANA: *In the United States, because it is such a culturally diverse country, Holy Week is not a holiday, although some Christian colleges and universities do not have classes on those days. This depends on each institution and each state as well.*

DIEGO:  *It's very interesting. We in Peru, in addition to religious holidays, have many holidays related to battles related to the independence of Peru. An example is the Battle of Ayacucho that is celebrated on December 9. This battle helped to consolidate the independence of Peru.*

ISABEL:  *Diego, in Chile we have a holiday that is related to your country, Peru. It is the celebration of the Day of Naval Glories. It is related to the battle between Chile and Peru. It is celebrated on May 21 every year.*

ANA:  *I'm learning a lot about Latin American holidays from our conversation. I think my favorite holiday in the United States is Thanksgiving because it represents togetherness, friendship, and gratitude. It's very special for me.*

DIEGO:  *For me, the celebration of independence is my favorite because we have a two-day holiday, July 28 and 29. And on those days we have many activities and a lot of food to celebrate.*

ISABEL:  *How interesting! In Chile we also have two days to celebrate independence, September 18 and 19. But I think that, for me, my favorite celebration is Christmas because I like to decorate my home with a lot of lights and I like to get together with my family to celebrate and share.*

ANA:  *I think we're out of time. See you tomorrow in class for another interesting conversation.*

# PRÁCTICA

**A.** Complete the story using the information from the dialogue.

Isabel, Ana y Diego conversan en su clase de comunicación sobre (1) _____ en sus respectivos países. (2) _____ es de Chile, (3) _____ es de Los Estados Unidos y (4) _____ es de Perú. Isabel piensa que Estados Unidos no tiene muchos días festivos. Ana está de acuerdo y dice que los festivos oficiales reconocidos en todo el país son (5) _____, (6) _____, La Navidad y El Año Nuevo. Diego les comenta a sus amigas que en países como (7) _____, (8) _____ y Colombia hay entre 18 y 20 días festivos al año. Diego dice también que muchos de estos días festivos están relacionados con fiestas (9) _____. Isabel les comenta que en Chile (10) _____ y el Sábado Santo son días festivos. Diego cuenta que en Perú hay varios días festivos relacionados con (11) _____. Un ejemplo es (12) _____ que se celebra el 9 de diciembre. Un festivo importante en Chile es (13) _____ que conmemora la batalla entre

Chile y Perú. Para Ana su día festivo favorito es (14) _____ porque representa unión, amistad y agradecimiento. Para Isabel su día festivo favorito es (15) _____ porque es una celebración en familia muy especial donde todos comparten.

**ANSWERS p. 144**

B. Underline the word that best completes the sentence.

1. Es un día festivo importante en Chile (La Batalla de Ayacucho, El Día de las Glorias Navales, El Día de Acción de Gracias).

2. Esta celebración se celebra principalmente en Estados Unidos (El Día de Acción de Gracias, El Día de Los Enamorados, El Día de La Madre).

3. Diego dice que esta celebración es muy importante en Perú (El Día del Padre, El Día de las Glorias Navales, La Batalla de Ayacucho).

4. Para esta celebración a muchas personas les gusta disfrazarse (El Día de los Enamorados, El Día de la Independencia, El Día de Las Brujas).

5. En México esta celebración del mes de noviembre es muy importante (El Día de los Muertos, El Día de Acción de Gracias, La Pascua).

# GRAMMAR I  Pretérito de verbos que cambian la raíz (*Preterite of Ste-Changing Verbs*)

A. Memorize the preterite forms of *dormir (to sleep)*, *pedir (to ask for/to order)*, and *sentir(se) (to feel)*.

| Subject | *Dorm ir* | *Ped ir* | *Sent ir(se)* | (English) |
|---|---|---|---|---|
| yo | dorm í | ped í | sent í | I slept, I did sleep/(asked/felt) |
| tú | dorm iste | ped iste | sent iste | you slept, you did sleep |
| él/ella/Ud. | d**u**rm ió | p**i**d ió | s**i**nt ió | he/she/you slept, he/she/you did sleep |
| nosotros/as | dorm imos | ped imos | sent imos | we slept, we did sleep |
| vosotros/as | dorm isteis | ped isteis | sent isteis | you (all) slept (Spain) |
| ellos/ellas/Uds | d**u**rm ieron | p**i**d ieron | s**i**nt ieron | they/you slept, they/you did sleep. |

Note that:

1. The preterite of *dormir* changes o to u only in the third-person singular and plural. *Morir (to die)* shows the same change in the stem: **murió → murieron**.

2. *Pedir* and *sentir* change e to i in the third-person singular and plural. Remember that *pedir* has this change in the present: **pido, pides, pide, piden,** BUT **pedimos.** Similarly, *Sentir* changes e to ie in the present: **siento, sientes, siente, sienten,** BUT **sentimos.**

B. Look at some more stem-changing verbs and review their meaning. Notice that they are all -ir verbs. Remember that the vowels in parentheses remind you of the change.

**divertir (ie, i)** to have fun
**preferir (ie, i)** to prefer
**sentir (ie, i)** to feel, sense
**repetir (i)** to repeat

**pedir (i)** to ask for/to order
**seguir (i)** to follow
**servir (i)** to serve
**vestir(se) (i)** to get dressed

1. The verbs marked with (ie, i) change *e* to *ie* in the present and *e* to *i* in the preterite.

   EX: **sentir** → **siente** (*he/she feels*), **sintió** (*he/she felt*)

2. The verbs marked with (i) change *e* to *i* in the present and also in the preterite.

   EX: **pedir** → **pide** (*he/she asks for*), **pidió** (*he/she asked for*)

3. The stem-changing verbs ending in -ar and -er change the stem in the present but not in the preterite:

   EX: **volver** → **vuelve** (*he/she returns*), BUT **volvió** (*he/she returned*)

# PRACTIQUE EL PRETÉRITO

**ANSWERS p. 144**

1. The stem of *dormir* is _____, and the stem of *durmió* _____. There has been a change in the stem from *o* to _____.

2. *Pedir* has the stem _____, and the stem of *pidieron* is _____. The *e* has changed to _____. How do you say *he asked for?* (Remember that you don't translate *for!*) _____.

3. *Morir* is a stem-changing verb like _____. How do you say *he died?* _____. How do you say *they died?* _____.

4. *Sentir* (*ie, i*) is also a stem-changing verb. In the present it changes *e* to _____; for example, yo _____. In the preterite it changes *e* to _____ in the third-person singular and plural; for example, él _____ (*he felt*).

5. Stem-changing verbs with changes both in the present and the preterite belong to the _____ conjugation—in other words, they end in -ir. Verbs ending in -ar and -er change the stem in the present but not in the _____.

6. *Volver* changes *o* to *ue* in the present; for example, yo _____ and ella _____. However, there is no change in the preterite: él _____.

7. *Dormir* (*ue, u*) has a double change in the stem. In the present it changes *o* to _____; for example, **ella** _____ (*sleeps*). In the preterite it changes *o* to _____; for example, **ella** _____ and **ellas** _____.

# PRÁCTICA

ANSWERS
p. 144

A. Complete each sentence with the correct preterite form of the verb in parentheses.

1. Mi mamá se _____ muy feliz de ver a todos sus hijos para La Navidad, y yo me _____ muy contenta de compartir con toda la familia. (*sentirse*)

2. ¿Cuándo _____ tu abuelita en Chile? (*morir*)

3. Diego _____ la champaña para el brindis de Año Nuevo. (*servir*)

4. Isabel _____ un celular último modelo para La Navidad, y Camila y yo _____ un reloj inteligente. (*pedir*)

5. Cecilia no _____ mucho el 31 de diciembre. (*dormir*)

6. Carmen se _____ en una hora, pero yo me _____ en diez minutos. (*vestirse*)

7. En la Batalla de Ayacucho en Perú muchas personas _____. (*morir*)

8. Carlitos _____ pavo para El Día de Acción de Gracias y tú _____ cacerola de habichuelas y pan de maíz porque eres vegetariana. (*preferir*)

9. Pedro _____ la canción de Feliz Navidad muchas veces. Yo no la _____. (*repetir*)

10. Todos mis amigos se _____ en la fiesta. (*divertirse*)

ANSWERS
p. 144

B. Write the preterite of the verb in parentheses.

1. Yo practico mi baile de tango en casa, pero *la semana pasada* yo lo _____ en la sala de baile de la universidad. (*practicar*)

2. Mi amiga Diana se disfraza todos los años para El Día de Las Brujas, pero *el año pasado* ella no se _____ porque estaba enferma. (*disfrazarse*)

3. Nancy sale del trabajo a las 5:00 P.M., pero *el viernes pasado* _____ a las 8:00 P.M. porque tenía una reunión muy importante. (*salir*)

4. Tú siempre pones buena música para las fiestas. Pero para la fiesta de Año Nuevo tú _____ música excelente. (*poner*)

5. Mis padres me visitan todos los meses. Pero *el mes pasado* ellos no me _____ porque estaban viajando. (visitar)

6. Juan y Felipe siempre compran los postres para la cena de Navidad, pero para este año ellos _____ el vino. (*comprar*)

7. Dany siempre se despierta antes de las 7:00 A.M., pero *ayer* no se _____ porque estaba muy cansado. (*despertarse*)

8. Mi esposo y yo siempre nos _____ durante las vacaciones, pero *el verano pasado* él no se _____ porque estuvo enfermo. (*divertirse*)

9. Yo no pido mucho para La Navidad, pero este año yo _____ un computador nuevo. (*pedir*)

10. Esteban vuelve todos los años para la celebrar La Pascua con su familia, pero este año él no _____ porque consiguió (*got*) un trabajo. (*volver*)

# GRAMMAR II  Pretérito de los verbos irregulares (*Preterite of Irregular Verbs*)

A. Memorize the preterite forms of *ser (to be)/ir (to go)*, *dar (to give)*, *venir (to come)*, *decir (to say)*, and *estar (to be)*.

| Subject | Ser/ir | D ar | Ven ir | Dec ir | Estar |
|---------|--------|------|--------|--------|-------|
| yo | fu i | d i | vin e | dij e | estuv e |
| tú | fu iste | d iste | vin iste | dij iste | estuv iste |
| él/ella/Ud. | fu e | d io | vin o | dij o | estuv o |
| nosotros/as | fu imos | d imos | vin imos | dij imos | estuv imos |
| vosotros/as | fu isteis | d isteis | vin isteis | dij isteis | estuv isteis |
| ellos/ellas/Uds. | fu eron | d ieron | vin ieron | dij eron | estuv ieron |

Note that:

1. *Ser* and *ir* have identical forms in the preterite. We need a context to distinguish between them.

    EXS: **El año pasado *fui* a Colombia.** (*I went to Colombia last year.*)
    **Fui instructor de Zumba en Bogotá.** (*I was a zumba instructor in Bogotá.*)

2. *Dar* is irregular because it doesn't take the endings of the -**ar** verbs, but resembles more the -**er** verbs. This is the only cross-conjugation in the Spanish verb system.

3. Notice that **fui, fue/di, dio** don't take an accent because they have only one syllable. The same rule applies to **vi, vio** (*I saw/he saw*).

4. *Venir, decir,* and *estar* are irregular for two reasons:

    a) They have changes in the stem: ven-/vin-, dec-/dij-, est-/estuv-.

    b) They have special endings in the first- and third-person singular: *e* instead of *í* and *o* instead of *ió*.

5. *Decir* takes the ending *-eron* rather than *-ieron*. This same change occurs with the verbs for which the stem of the preterite ends in *j,* such as **traer: traje, trajeron.**

B. The following verbs are irregular in the preterite, with the same kinds of change in the endings as **venir, decir,** and **estar.** Pay attention to the changes in the stems. These verbs do not take an accent in the preterite. Remember the meaning of these verbs in English: **andar** *(to walk),* **conducir** *(to drive),* **deshacer** *(to undo),* **detener** *(to stop),* **haber** *(there is/there are),* **hacer** *(to do/to make),* **poder** *(can/to be able to),* **poner** *(to put/to place),* **ponerse** *(to put on),* **producir** *(to produce),* **querer** *(to want/to love),* **saber** *(to know facts, information, skills [in present]/to find out [in preterite]),* **tener** *(to have),* **traer** *(to bring),* **estar** *(to be)*

andar → anduve, anduvo      poner → puse, puso
conducir → conduje, condujo      producir → produje, produjo
deshacer → deshice, deshizo      querer → quise, quiso
detener → detuve, detuvo      saber → supe, supo
haber → hube, hubo      tener → tuve, tuvo
hacer → hice, hizo      traer → traje, trajo
poder → pude, pudo      estar → estuve, estuvo

1. *Hacer* has the stem **hic-** in the preterite, and the *c* changes to *z* in *hizo.* This is a spelling change similar to that of *comenzar → comencé.*

2. The verb *querer* in the preterite followed by an infinitive normally means *to try (but fail)* to do something.

   EX: *Quise* **preparar más postres, pero no tuve tiempo.** *(I tried to prepare more desserts but I did not have enough time.)*

3. Most of the verbs above have compound forms that share the same changes of the simple verbs.

   EXS: **poner → puse/componer → compuse/imponer → impuse**

4. *Poder* in preterite normally means *to manage to do something.*

   EX: **Finalmente** *pude* **ver la película.** *(Finally, I managed to see the movie.)*

5. *Saber* in preterite means *to find out.*

   **Supe** que Mario y Carlota se casaron en Las Bahamas. *(I found out that Mario and Carlota got married in the Bahamas.)*

6. All verbs ending in *-ducir,* like *producir* and *conducir,* change the **c** to **j** in the preterite; and the ending **-ieron** shortens to **-eron.**

   EX: con*ducir,* condu*je,* condu*je*ron

# PRACTIQUE EL PRETÉRITO

1. *Dijo* is a preterite form, and it means *he/she said; digo* is a _____ indicative form, and it means _____.

2. From *saber* we say **yo sé** *(I know)* in the present. How would you say *I knew* in the preterite? _____.

3. *Hacer* has a triple stem: **hac-** in the infinitive, _____ and _____ in the preterite.

4. *Dijeron* has an irregular ending because the *j* "swallows up" the vowel _____. So instead of **-ieron**, the ending is _____.

5. All the verbs ending in **-ducir** change the *c* to _____ in the preterite. How would you say *they drove* (from *conducir*)? _____.

6. *Ponió* (from *poner*) is incorrect. It should be _____.

7. *Trajieron* is not correct. It should be _____ because of the *j*.

8. *Vino* (*he/she came*) and *vino* (*wine*) have the same spelling and sound. How can you tell one from another in a conversation or writing? _____.

9. *Yo andé por el parque* sounds like good Spanish, and some native speakers of Spanish would say it; but the correct form should be **Yo** _____ **por el parque**.

10. *Detener* is a compound of _____. How would you say in Spanish *the police stopped the criminal?* **La policía** _____ **al criminal**.

11. *Fue* means two things because it belongs to two verbs: _____ / _____. The reason is that *ser* and _____ share the same forms in the preterite.

12. *Dar* is irregular in the preterite because it follows the conjugation of -er verbs rather than _____ verbs. For example, we don't say **ellos daron** like **hablaron** but **ellos** _____.

13. *Dió* and *fué* are misspelled because of the _____. They must be spelled _____ and _____ because they have only one syllable.

# PRÁCTICA

**ANSWERS**
**p. 145**

A. **Fill in the blanks with the correct forms of the preterite.**

*El jueves pasado mi familia y yo celebramos el Día de Acción de Gracias en la casa de mis abuelos...*

1. Toda la familia _____ (ir) a la casa de los abuelos para la celebración del Día de Acción de Gracias.

2. Mis padres y yo _____ (traer) la ensalada y los postres.

3. Mis tíos y primos _____ (venir) también a celebrar con nosotros.

4. Los niños _____ (querer) jugar videojuegos, pero no _____ (poder) porque los tíos estaban viendo fútbol americano.

5. Tú _____ (tener) que ayudar a preparar la comida.

6. _____ (haber) suficiente comida para todos.

7. Mi abuelita _____ (saber) que Ana se comprometió con su novio.

8. A la 1:00 P.M. el pavo _____ (estar) listo.

9. Después de comer, mi abuelo _____ (hacer) una siesta.

10. Al día siguiente mi mamá _____ (decir) que la celebración fue excelente.

**ANSWERS p. 145**

B. **Change the verbs from present to preterite.**

Margarita no (1) *anda* al trabajo esta mañana, sino que (*but*) (2) *conduce* su carro nuevo. Hoy no (3) *está* en su oficina a las ocho en punto como de costumbre, porque (4) *tiene* que prepararle el desayuno a su hijo. Después que (5) *llega*, (6) *deja* las cosas en la mesa y (7) *se pone* a trabajar. Sus amigas (8) *hacen* café y le (9) *traen* una taza. Ella les (10) *dice* mil gracias.

1. _____       5. _____       9. _____

2. _____       6. _____       10. _____

3. _____       7. _____

4. _____       8. _____

# GRAMMAR III   Pronombres de objeto indirecto (*Indirect Object Pronouns*)

A. Indirect object nouns and pronouns indicate to whom or for whom an action is done. They tell who is affected by an action.

Indirect object pronouns:

1. Singular:

   **me** (to/for me)
   **te** (to/for you) (familiar)
   **le** (to/for you) (formal)
   (to/for him/her)

2. Plural:

   **nos** (to/for us)
   **os** (to/for you [all]) Spain
   **les** (to/for you [all]) Latin America
   (to/for them)

EX: **Mi esposo *me* regaló unas flores *(a mí).* (*My husband gave **me** some flowers.*)**
*Flowers* is the object of the action and ***me** (to me)* is the person for whom the action is done.
**Ana *nos* preparó una comida deliciosa. *(a nosotros).* (*Ana prepared us a delicious meal.*)**

When you give flowers to a friend, *friend* functions as the indirect object (IO) and *flowers* as the direct object (DO). In Spanish when a noun functions as the indirect object, it always takes the preposition *a:* **Usted le dio flores** *a* **su amiga.**

B. The forms of indirect object pronouns are the first- and second-person (plural and singular) are the same as the direct object pronouns: **me, te** (singular) and **nos, os** (plural).

C. Indirect object pronouns agree in number with the nouns but not in gender.

> EX: **Diego** *les* **preparó la comida** *a sus amigos*. *(Diego prepared food for his friends.)* **les = a sus amigos**
> **Los amigos** *le* **hicieron una fiesta** *a Isabel*. (*The friends threw a party for Isabel*) **le = Isabel**

D. Unlike the English language, indirect object pronouns are generally placed before the verb.

> EX: **Mi amiga** *me* **dio un regalo.** (My friend *gave* me a gift).

If the sentence is negative, the indirect object pronoun is placed after the negative **no** and before the conjugated verb.

> EX: **Mi papá no** *me* **envió el dinero.** (My father *did not send* me the money.).

When a conjugated verb in a sentence is followed by an infinitive, the indirect object pronoun can be placed or before the conjugated verb or after attached to the infinitive.

> EX:

1. **Andrea** *le* **quiere preparar una cena especial a su esposo para su cumpleaños.**

2. **Andrea quiere preparar***le* **una cena especial a su esposo para su cumpleaños.**

> *(Andrea wants to prepare a special dinner for her husband for his birthday.)*

E. In this chart we see the direct object, indirect object, reflexive, and object-of-preposition pronouns.

| Subject | Direct Object | Indirect Object | Reflexive | Object of Preposition |
|---|---|---|---|---|
| yo | me | me | me | mí |
| tú | te | te | te | ti |
| nosotros/as | nos | nos | nos | nosotros/as |
| vosotros/as | os | os | os | vosotros/as |
| Él/Ud. | lo | le (se) | se | él/Ud. |
| Ella/Ud. | la | le (se) | se | ella/Ud. |
| Ellos/Uds. | los | les (se) | se | ellos/Uds. |
| Ellas/Uds. | las | les (se) | se | ellas/Uds. |

Note that:

1. The first and second persons have the same pronouns for the direct object, the indirect object, and the reflexive: **me, te, nos, os.**

2. The third person has different pronouns: **lo, la, los,** and **las** for the direct object; **le (se)** and **les (se)** for the indirect object; and **se** for the reflexive.

3. The direct object, indirect object, and reflexive pronouns are always unstressed; whereas the object-of-preposition pronouns are always stressed.

F.   **Dar** is a verb that most of the time requires an indirect object pronoun. **Dar** *(to give)* has a different meaning than **regalar** *(to give a gift).*

EX:   La mamá *le dio* un beso *a su hija (The mother gave a kiss to her daughter.)*
Los papás *le regalaron* una consola de videojuegos *a Victor. (The parents gave (as a gift) Victor a videogame console.)*

G.   Some examples of verbs that are generally used with indirect object pronouns are: **dar** *(to give),* **decir** *(to say), enviar/mandar (to send),* **escribir** *(to write),* **explicar** *(to explain),* **mostrar** *(to show),* **prestar** *(to lend),* **regalar** *(to give as a gift),* **vender** *(to sell).*

H.   When direct object and indirect object pronouns are in the same sentence:

1. If both the direct object and the indirect object nouns become pronouns, they precede the verb in the indicative, and they follow the verb in the infinitive.

EXS:   **Ella** *me* **dio el libro** *a mí.* → **Ella** *me lo* **dio.** *(She gave it to me.)*
**Ella va a darme el libro** *a mí.* → **Ella va a dármelo.** *(She is going to give it to me.)*

2. The indirect object pronoun precedes the direct object, either with the indicative or the infinitive.

EX:   **Ella va a dár***melo.* → **Ella** *me lo* **va a dar.** *(She will give it to me.)*

3. If both the direct object and the indirect object are third person, the indirect object pronouns *le, les* become *se* as shown in parentheses in the chart. The indirect object pronoun precedes the direct object.

EX:   **Juan le dio flores a su amiga.** → **Juan** *le las* **dio.** → **Juan** *se las* **dio.**

I.   The pronouns used as object of prepositions can be added to the direct object and indirect object to add emphasis: **Ud. me vio a mí** is more emphatic than **Ud. me vio.**

*Ud. vio a mi* is incorrect. It needs *me* before the verb: **Ud me vio a mí.** This means that we cannot use the object-of-preposition pronouns for direct object and indirect object without the matching unstressed pronoun: **me, te, le, lo, la,** and so on.

J.   Indirect object pronouns should be used even when the indirect object noun is stated explicitly.

EX:   **Tú** *le* **regalaste una tableta** *a tu hijo. (You gave your son a tablet.)*

# PRACTIQUE LOS PRONOMBRES DE OBJETO

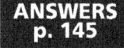

1. The pronouns *me, te, nos* are the same for the reflexive, the direct object, and the _____.

2. The pronouns *lo/la, los/las,* are third-person direct object pronouns; _____ are indirect object pronouns, and *se* is the _____ pronoun for the third person.

3. Do the direct object pronouns precede or follow the indirect object pronouns? _____. The two pronouns stay together before the verb in the _____ tenses, such as present, preterite, future, and so on.

4. If the infinitive follows the indicative in the same sentence, the direct object, indirect object, and reflexive pronouns may precede the _____ or follow the _____.

5. The indirect object pronouns *le, les,* become _____ when they are in front of any of the four direct object pronouns *lo/la, los/las.* Therefore, **Le lo regalo a ella** is wrong. The correct version is _____ a ella. (*I'm giving it to her [as a gift].*)

6. **Yo invité a ella** is not correct. We have to add _____ in front of *invité.*

# PRÁCTICA

**ANSWERS p. 145**

A. Complete each sentence with the indirect object pronoun.

1. Elena _____ envió un correo electrónico *a su jefe*.

2. ¿Por qué tú no _____ dijiste la verdad *a mí*?

3. Martín _____ explicó el problema *a sus amigos*.

4. Creo que mi hijo no _____ dijo toda la verdad *a nosotros*.

5. El banco _____ prestó el dinero *a la señora Morales*.

6. Mi novio _____ compró chocolates (*a mí*) para el Día de los Enamorados.

7. Alexandra _____ vendió un computador usado *a su amigo Javier*.

8. Yo _____ compré (*a vosotros*) los boletos para el concierto de música clásica.

9. Mauricio _____ escribió (*a ti*) un mensaje en WhatsApp y tú no _____ respondiste (*a él*).

**ANSWERS
p. 145**

**B.** Translate the following sentences. Pay attention to the placement of the indirect object pronoun and the preterite form of the verbs.

**1.** I bought my father a gift.

_____

**2.** My mother sent me a book.

_____

**3.** Your best friend told you the truth *(la verdad)*.

_____

**4.** Samuel gave you his telephone number *(el número de teléfono)*.

_____

**5.** Daniel gave his girlfriend a bouquet *(un ramo de flores)*.

_____

**6.** The students sent Professor Ramos an email *(correo electrónico)*.

_____

**7.** Camila gave me an idea.

_____

**8.** The teacher read a book to her students yesterday.

_____

**9.** Professor Soto asked me a question in class yesterday.

_____

**10.** They lent us $200.00.

_____

**ANSWERS
p. 146**

**C.** Answer the questions by changing the direct and indirect object nouns to pronouns. Pay attention to the verbs in preterite.

EX: ¿Cuándo **me** enviaste *el correo electrónico*? —Yo **te** *lo* envié anoche. (*When did you send **me** <u>the email</u>?) I sent <u>it</u> **to you** last night.*

**1.** ¿Cuándo *(tú)* le enviaste *el informe* a tu jefe?

(Yo) _____ _____ envié ayer.

**2.** ¿Quién **les** preparó *la cena* a los invitados?

Olivia _____ _____ preparó.

**3.** ¿Quién **les** explicó *la lección* a los estudiantes?

La profesora _____ _____ explicó.

**4.** ¿Quién **te** regaló *(a ti) ese reloj inteligente*?

Mis padres _____ _____ regalaron.

**5.** ¿Quién **le** trajo *esas flores* a mi mamá?

Mi hermano _____ _____ trajo.

# ANSWERS   LESSONS 5–8

## Lesson 5

### Practique las palabras nuevas

A.
| | | | |
|---|---|---|---|
| 1. el | 4. el | 7. el | 10. el |
| 2. el/la | 5. la | 8. el | 11. el/la |
| 3. la | 6. el | 9. la | 12. la |

B.
1. al aeropuerto
2. las bebidas
3. el equipaje
4. el cinturón de seguridad
5. la terminal
6. el pasillo
7. la sala de embarque
8. subir
9. un viaje
10. salida
11. llegar
12. la aduana
13. a tiempo
14. de ida y vuelta
15. servirle

C.
1. H (el cinturón de seguridad)
2. L (a tiempo al destino)
3. J (el equipaje: las maletas)
4. B (al avión por la puerta de embarque)
5. C (el pasaporte para viajar a España)
6. K (en el asiento del pasillo)
7. F (las bebidas en el avión)
8. D (de ida y vuelta)
9. A (avión para ir a recoger las maletas)
10. G (hacer un viaje al norte de España)
11. I (en la aduana de Madrid)
12. E (volver)

### Práctica

A. **En el aeropuerto internacional Adolfo Suárez Madrid–Barajas.**
1. mostrador
2. aeropuerto
3. agente
4. económica
5. ejecutiva
6. ventanilla
7. 300
8. tarjeta de crédito
9. maleta
10. pasabordo
11. salida

B. **Match the two columns.**
| | |
|---|---|
| 1. G | 6. D |
| 2. I | 7. J |
| 3. E | 8. B |
| 4. A | 9. F |
| 5. C | 10. H |

## Practique las expresiones con el verbo *tener*

1. Rodrigo tiene mucha hambre hoy.
2. Carolina tiene miedo de la oscuridad.
3. Yo tengo mucho calor hoy.
4. Mis amigos tienen suerte cuando van al casino.
5. El señor Zapata tiene prisa (afán). Él tiene una reunión.
6. Tú tienes mucho sueño.
7. Gloria tiene razón. La película es a las 5:30 P.M.
8. Nosotros tenemos mucha sed.
9. Mónica tiene 15 años.
10. Tú y Pablo no tienen razón. La fiesta es el sábado.
11. Tengo que estudiar hoy.
12. Julio y Sandra tienen mucho frío.
13. Los estudiantes tienen que comprar los pasajes de avión.
14. Marisol tiene que viajar a España.
15. Tú tienes 50 años.

## Práctica

A.
1. **teng/tien/ten/to have**
2. g/g/hago
3. ie/no
4. que/tengo que salir
5. de
6. to come/speaker
7. voy
8. deshago
9. detienen

B.
1. viene
2. tengo que
3. ayuda
4. sales
5. abrochan
6. tiene
7. pongo
8. llega
9. factura
10. se bajan

C.
1. pongo
2. salimos
3. haces
4. venís
5. sale
6. tienen
7. hago
8. tiene
9. tienes
10. vienen

## Practique la hora

1. 1 (una): singular/2–12: plural
2. quince/cuarto
3. treinta/media
4. y/menos

5. en punto/más o menos/como
6. de la mañana
7. de la tarde/de la noche
8. no/la
9. hora
10. a
11. 24/la/las/hora/horas

## Práctica

Translate the following expressions.

1. Son las tres y diez de la tarde.
2. Son las diez y quince de la mañana/Son las diez y cuarto de la mañana.
3. Es la una y treinta de la tarde/Es la una y media de la tarde.
4. Son las seis menos diez de la mañana.
5. Son las once de la noche en punto.
6. Son las once y veinte de la mañana.
7. Es la una menos cuarto de la tarde/Es la una menos quince de la tarde.
8. Es la una y cinco de la mañana.
9. a las dos en punto de la tarde.
10. a las cinco y media de la tarde/a las cinco y treinta de la tarde.

## Practique los verbos

1. quer-/quier-/ie
2. dec-/dic-/i
3. pod-/pued-/ue
4. yes
5. people/quiere
6. for/pedimos/piden
7. sirvo/sirven
8. vuela
9. muestro
10. segu-/sigu-/u/sigo
11. again/we are traveling again

## Práctica

1. puede
2. vuelan
3. vuelven
4. pensamos
5. quieres
6. siguen
7. pide
8. siento
9. muestra
10. sirven
11. pregunta/hace una pregunta
12. pienso
13. vuela
14. puedo
15. tiene

# Lesson 6

## Practique las palabras nuevas

**A.** 1. el      4. la      7. la      10. el       13. la
    2. el      5. el      8. el      11. los/las   14. el
    3. el/los  6. la      9. las     12. la        15. las

**B.** Palabras nuevas

1. la agencia de viajes          6. visa
2. el ascensor                   7. itinerario
3. la playa                      8. clima/tiempo
4. la recepción                  9. reservaciones
5. las vacaciones de primavera  10. turista

**C.** 1. estacionar/parquear    5. reservar        9. chatear
    2. tomar el sol              6. registrarse    10. quedarse
    3. llover                    7. recorrer       11. empacar
    4. subir                     8. viajar         12. preferir

**D.** 1. hace mucho calor       6. hace mucho viento   11. llave/tarjeta
    2. hace mucho frío          7. plaza               12. hace buen tiempo
    3. nieve                    8. lejos               13. hace frío
    4. lluvia                   9. hace mucho sol      14. hace calor
    5. una cama doble          10. botones             15. hace fresco

**E.** 1. G: la piscina del hotel
    2. E: el nombre en el registro del hotel
    3. J: la puerta de la habitación con la llave
    4. I: las maletas en el ascensor
    5. K: en la playa
    6. H: el coche en el estacionamiento del hotel
    7. A: dólares a euros en el aeropuerto
    8. B: practicar español en Madrid
    9. F: en el tour a las ruinas
    10. C: lugares históricos importantes
    11. D: la propina en el precio

F.  1. llueve
    2. nieva
    3. divierto
    4. visitamos
    5. Prefieren
    6. abre
    7. cierran
    8. cambiamos
    9. incluye
    10. trata/de

## Práctica

A.  1. vacaciones de primavera
    2. agencia de viajes
    3. excursión
    4. semana
    5. Patrimonio Histórico de la Humanidad
    6. agradable
    7. temperatura
    8. 80
    9. lluvia
    10. hotel
    11. habitaciones
    12. sencillas
    13. itinerario
    14. viaje

B.  1. la escalera
    2. nieva
    3. servicio
    4. vista
    5. razonable
    6. divisas
    7. doble
    8. nombre
    9. nadar
    10. itinerario

## Practique las expresiones

1. noun
2. mucho calor
3. mucho sol
4. tengo hambre
5. mucha hambre
6. no tener razón
7. "I have thirst," but the correct way is I am thirsty.
8. de/ganas de dormir
9. norm/es
10. change/está

## Práctica

1. es
2. hace
3. tiene
4. está
5. está
6. tengo
7. hace
8. es
9. tengo sueño
10. tiene razón

## Practique los demostrativos

1. este/estos, esta/estas
2. ese/esos, esa/esas
3. number
4. aquel/aquellos/aquella/aquellas
5. one
6. noun/no
7. e
8. eso/aquello

## Práctica

1. esa
2. esta ...esa
3. eso
4. Esta
5. Este...ese
6. eso
7. esta
8. esta/esa
9. ese
10. Este

## Practique los posesivos

1. mi, tu, su/mis, tus, sus
2. no
3. his, her, its, their, your
4. tus hijos
5. after
6. mío, tuyo, suyo
7. mis/tus
8. you/your
9. el tuyo
10. la casa de ella
11. noun
12. nuestro cuarto

## Práctica

1. mi/tuya
2. nuestras
3. mía/tuya
4. su
5. mi/suya
6. sus
7. Su
8. nuestra
9. mis/Su
10. Nuestra

# Lesson 7

## Practique las palabras nuevas

A. 1. el
2. las
3. el
4. el
5. el
6. la
7. la
8. el
9. el
10. el
11. el
12. la
13. la
14. la
15. el

B. **Palabras nuevas**

1. bebidas
2. carnes y comida de mar
3. frutas
4. verduras y legumbres
5. bebidas
6. carnes y comida de mar
7. frutas
8. verduras y legumbres
9. verduras y legumbres
10. bebidas

C. 1. desayuno
2. cena/almuerzo
3. almuerzo
4. cena
5. desayuno

D. 1. desayunar
2. almorzar
3. cenar
4. hervir
5. servir
6. hornear
7. preparar
8. comer
9. saber a
10. sazonar
11. asar
12. calentar
13. cocinar
14. fritar/freír
15. adobar

E. 1. hierve
2. prepara
3. bebe
4. almuerza
5. cenamos
6. hornea
7. desayuna
8. como
9. asan
10. calientas

## Práctica

A. 1. pollo
2. verduras
3. menú
4. pastel
5. hornear
6. ensalada
7. ajos
8. aceite de oliva
9. vino
10. contenta

B. 1. las bebidas energizantes
2. de almendras
3. vino
4. las papas fritas
5. té
6. maíz
7. piñas
8. pavo
9. arroz
10. pescado

C. 1. G: cerveza
2. E: lechuga
3. C: naranja
4. B: zanahoria
5. J: pescado
6. D: pavo
7. I: pimienta
8. F: maíz
9. H: aceite
10. A: leche

## Practique los pronombres de objeto directo

1. a Amelia/a
2. no/a/alguien
3. stress/verb
4. lo/la/los/las
5. lo veo/los
6. precede/follow
7. infinitive/indicative
8. both are correct
9. a/camareras

## Práctica

A. 1. las
2. la
3. lo
4. las
5. las
6. lo
7. lo
8. la
9. lo
10. los

B. 1. al
2. a
3. –
4. a
5. al

C. 1. sí lo tomo/no lo tomo
2. sí los como/no los como
3. sí lo caliento/no lo caliento
4. sí lo preparo/no lo preparo
5. sí la bebo/no la bebo
6. me
7. lo/le (Spain)
8. me
9. los/les (Spain)
10. te

## Practique el pretérito

1. meaning/com-/v-
2. nosotros/tú/yo
3. hablé/habló
4. viví/vivió
5. present/preterite
6. apagué/gu
7. past/I paid
8. creyó/y
9. toqué/qu
10. comencé/c
11. leyeron
12. one/acento

## Práctica

A. 1. prepararon
2. salió
3. habló
4. bebieron
5. horneó
6. adobé
7. compraron
8. pagué
9. limpiamos
10. comí

B. Una invitación especial

1. decidió
2. acompañé
3. volvimos
4. ayudé
5. preparó
6. horneamos
7. llegaron
8. compraron
9. bebieron
10. tomaron

C. 1. Sí ya la cociné.
   2. Lola se lo bebió.
   3. No, no los invité.
   4. Sí lo cociné.
   5. Roberto las lavó.

## Practique el acento

1. one/nueve
2. the last/vowel
3. last/n and s
4. last/vowel/n or s
5. consonant
6. two/last
7. diphthong/a, o
8. he/the
9. you/your
10. yes/if
11. more/but
12. veintidós

## Práctica

1. agua
2. café
3. azúcar
4. comer
5. difícil
6. pastel
7. adobar
8. maíz
9. tú
10. pan
11. horneo/horneó
12. mi
13. están
14. feliz
15. mineral
16. tomates
17. menú
18. él
19. atún
20. cena
21. éxito
22. preparo/preparó
23. día
24. novio
25. plátano
26. **practique/**practiqué
27. desayuno/desayunó
28. simpático
29. comida
30. el
31. sé

# Lesson 8

## Practique las palabras nuevas

A. 1. la
   2. el
   3. el
   4. la
   5. la
   6. el
   7. la
   8. la
   9. el
   10. el
   11. la
   12. el
   13. la
   14. la
   15. la

B. Fiestas y celebraciones.

   1. El Año Nuevo
   2. El Día de La Madre
   3. El Día de Los Muertos
   4. El Día de Acción de Gracias
   5. La Navidad
   6. La Nochebuena
   7. La Pascua
   8. El Día de Las Brujas
   9. El Día de La Independencia
   10. El Día de Los Enamorados

C. 1. entretenido/a
   2. triste
   3. vacío/a
   4. ateo/a
   5. borracho/a

D. 1. se disfrazó
   2. brindaron
   3. toqué
   4. jugaste
   5. lo pasamos bien
   6. celebró
   7. comimos
   8. tomaste
   9. bailaron
   10. disfrutamos

## Práctica

A. 1. los días festivos
   2. Isabel
   3. Ana
   4. Diego
   5. El Día de La Independencia
   6. El Día de Acción de Gracias
   7. Argentina
   8. Chile
   9. religiosas
   10. El Viernes Santo
   11. batallas
   12. Batalla de Ayacucho
   13. El Día de Las Glorias Navales
   14. El Día de Acción de Gracias
   15. La Navidad

B. 1. El Día de Las Glorias Navales
   2. El Día de Acción de Gracias
   3. La Batalla de Ayacucho
   4. El Día de Las Brujas
   5. El Día de Los Muertos

## Practique el pretérito

1. dorm-/durm-/u
2. ped-/pid-/i/pidió
3. dormir/murió/murieron
4. ie/siento/i/sintió
5. third/preterite
6. vuelvo/vuelve/volvió
7. ue/duerme/u/durmió/durmieron

## Práctica

A. 1. sintió/sentí
   2. murió
   3. sirvió
   4. pidió/pedimos
   5. durmió
   6. vistió/vestí
   7. murieron
   8. prefirió/preferiste
   9. repitió/repetí
   10. divirtieron

B. 1. practiqué
   2. disfrazó
   3. salió
   4. pusiste
   5. visitaron
   6. compraron
   7. despertó
   8. divertimos/divirtió
   9. pedí
   10. volvió

## Practique el pretérito

1. present/I say
2. supe
3. hic-/hiz-
4. i/-eron
5. j/condujeron

6. puso
7. trajeron
8. from the context
9. anduve

10. tener/detuvo
11. I was/I went/ir
12. -ar/dieron
13. acento/dio/fue

## Práctica

A. 1. fue
2. trajimos
3. vinieron
4. quisieron/pudieron

5. tuviste
6. hubo
7. supo

8. estuvo
9. hizo
10. dijo

B. 1. anduvo
2. condujo
3. estuvo
4. tuvo

5. llegó
6. dejó
7. se puso

8. hicieron
9. trajeron
10. dijo

## Practique los pronombres de objeto

1. indirect object
2. le/les/reflexive
3. follow/indicative

4. indicative/infinitive
5. se/se lo regalo
6. la

## Práctica

A. 1. le
2. me
3. les

4. nos
5. le
6. me

7. le
8. os
9. te/le

B. 1. Yo le compré un regalo a mi padre.
2. Mi madre me envió un libro.
3. Tu mejor amigo/a te dijo la verdad.
4. Samuel te dio su número de teléfono.
5. Daniel le dio un ramo de flores a su novia.
6. Los estudiantes le enviaron un correo electrónico al profesor Ramos.
7. Camila me dio una idea.

8. El profesor les leyó un libro a los estudiantes ayer.

9. El profesor Soto me hizo una pregunta en clase ayer.

10. Ellos nos prestaron $200.

C. 1. Yo se lo envié ayer.

   2. Olivia se la preparó.

   3. La profesora se la explicó.

   4. Mis padres me lo regalaron.

   5. Mi hermano se las trajo.

# 9 La rutina diaria de la familia Mendoza

## (*The Daily Routine of the Mendoza Family*)

## PALABRAS NUEVAS

| | | | |
|---|---|---|---|
| **Algunas partes del cuerpo** | some parts of the body | **el baño** | bathroom |
| | | **el cepillo de dientes** | toothbrush |
| **la boca** | mouth | **el cepillo para el pelo** | hairbrush |
| **la cabeza** | head | | |
| **la cara/el rostro** | face | **el champú** | shampoo |
| **el cuerpo** | body | **el closet** | closet |
| **los dientes** | teeth | | |
| **las manos** | hands | **la crema de afeitar** | shaving cream |
| **los ojos** | eyes | | |
| **el pelo** | hair | **el despertador** | alarm clock |
| **los pies** | feet | **la ducha** | shower |
| **las uñas** | nails | **el espejo** | mirror |
| | | **el inodoro** | toilet |
| **La casa y los elementos de arreglo personal** | house and personal grooming items | **el jabón** | soap |
| | | **el lavamanos/ lavabo** | sink |

| | | | |
|---|---|---|---|
| el maquillaje | makeup | ponerse feliz | to become happy |
| la máquina de afeitar | shaver | preocuparse por | to worry (about) |
| | | probarse | to try on |
| la pasta dental/ la crema dental | toothpaste | quedar (se) | to be left behind/to stay |
| la peinilla/el peine | comb | quitarse | to take off |
| el perfume | perfume | romper (se) | to break |
| | | secarse | to dry oneself |
| | | sentarse | to sit down |
| el secador de pelo | hair dryer | sentirse | to feel |
| | | vestirse | to get dressed |

| | | | |
|---|---|---|---|
| **Verbos** | *Verbs* | | |
| acabar (se) | To run out of | *Adjetivos* | *Adjectives* |
| acordarse (de) | to remember | atrasado(a) | late |
| acostarse | to go to bed | claro(a) | clear |
| afeitarse | to shave | elegante | elegant |
| alistarse/arreglarse | to get ready | limpio(a) | clean |
| bañarse | to take a bath | feliz | happy |
| caer (se) | to fall | gracioso(a) | funny |
| cepillarse el pelo | to brush one's hair | moderno(a) | modern |
| cepillarse los dientes | to brush one's teeth | oscuro(a) | dark |
| | | próximo(a) | next, coming |
| dañar (se) | to damage/break | puntual | punctual |
| despertarse | to wake up | simpático(a) | nice, pleasant |
| dormirse | to go to sleep/to fall sleep | típico(a) | typical |
| | | varios(as) | several, various |
| ducharse | to take a shower | | |
| | | *Expresiones* | *Expressions* |
| enojarse (con) | To get angry (with) | **así que** | so |
| irse | to go away/to leave | **a veces** | sometimes |
| | | casi | almost |
| lavarse la cara | to wash one's face | **con mucho gusto** | it's a pleasure |
| lavarse las manos | to wash one's hands | | |
| levantarse | to get up | **junto a** | close to, near |
| llamarse | to be called/to be named | **por casualidad** | by chance |
| | | temprano | early |
| maquillarse | to put on makeup | **más temprano** | earlier |
| olvidar (se) | to forget | tarde | late |
| peinarse | to comb one's hair | **más tarde** | later |
| perder (se) | to lose | | |
| pintarse las uñas | to paint one's nails | | |
| ponerse | to put on | | |

# PRACTIQUE LAS PALABRAS NUEVAS

**ANSWERS**
**p. 219**

A. Write *el/los* or *la/las* before each noun.

1. _____ jabón
2. _____ ducha
3. _____ lavamanos
4. _____ uñas
5. _____ espejo

6. _____ champú
7. _____ maquillaje
8. _____ dientes
9. _____ peinilla
10. _____ cara

**ANSWERS**
**p. 219**

B. Complete with the right part of the body associated with the sentence.

1. Nos cepillamos _____ todas las mañanas con la crema dental.
2. Nos miramos _____ en el espejo para maquillarnos.
3. Usamos el champú para lavarnos _____.
4. Nos pintamos _____ de las manos de color rojo (*red*).
5. Nos bañamos _____ con jabón.

**ANSWERS**
**p. 219**

C. Translate the reflexive verb into English.

1. secarse _____
2. vestirse _____
3. cepillarse el pelo _____
4. lavarse las manos _____
5. maquillarse _____

6. peinarse _____
7. probarse _____
8. ducharse _____
9. afeitarse _____
10. arreglarse _____

# DIÁLOGO   Una rutina diaria típica en casa de los Mendoza

*La familia Mendoza es chilena con días muy ocupados. Hoy no es una excepción.*
*Leonardo y Teresa son los padres de Martín y Ximena, dos chicos muy activos.*
*Leonardo y Teresa conversan sobre su rutina para el día*

LEONARDO:   ¡Buenos días, amor! ¿Dormiste bien?

TERESA:   ¡Buenos días! Sí dormí muy bien gracias. Recuerda que hoy tenemos otro día súper atareado.

LEONARDO:   Yo necesito levantarme ya porque hoy debo llegar a la oficina antes de las 8:00 A.M. para una reunión con los empleados. Así que me ducho, me visto, tomo un café y salgo para el trabajo.

TERESA:   Sí amor, yo también voy a levantarme pronto porque Ximena necesita ir al colegio hoy un poco más temprano para su entrenamiento con el equipo de voleibol. Ella necesita despertarse antes de las 5:30 A.M. para tener tiempo para ducharse, maquillarse y cepillarse el pelo.

LEONARDO: ¿A qué hora Ximena tiene su entrenamiento hoy? ¿Sabes si se acostó muy tarde ayer? Sé que hoy tiene un examen muy difícil en su clase de biología.

TERESA: Creo que el entrenamiento empieza a las 6:45 A.M. Ayer Ximena se acostó como a las 11:30 P.M. Yo la escuché por la noche cuando entró al baño para cepillarse los dientes. También tengo que despertar a Martín porque necesita ducharse, vestirse y cepillarse los dientes muy bien porque hoy tiene cita con el odontólogo por la mañana. Y después de su cita necesito llevarlo al colegio.

LEONARDO: Amor, tu día parece más ocupado que el mío. Si quieres, antes de irme para el trabajo, yo te ayudo a preparar el desayuno para los chicos.

TERESA: Sí mi amor, muchas gracias por tu ayuda. Mientras tanto yo voy a ducharme muy rápido, luego voy a despertar a Ximena, y también a Martín. Así ellos también se duchan, se alistan y se desayunan muy bien antes de salir para sus actividades del día.

LEONARDO: Y después de llevar a Martín al colegio, ¿Vas a tener tiempo para ti?

TERESA: Espero que sí. Creo que voy a cepillarme el pelo, maquillarme y pintarme las uñas. Hoy tengo una reunión en el colegio de Ximena y quiero ir muy bien presentada.

# DIALOGUE  *A Typical Daily Routine at the Mendozas' House*

*The Mendoza family is Chilean with very busy days. Today is no exception. Leonardo and Teresa are the parents of Martín and Ximena, two very active children. Leonardo and Teresa talk about their routine for the day*

LEONARDO: *Good morning, darling! Did you sleep well?*

TERESA: *Good morning! Yes, I slept very well, thank you. Remember that today we have another super busy day.*

LEONARDO: *I need to get up now because today I have to get to the office before 8:00 A.M. for a meeting with the employees. So, I need to shower, get dressed, have a coffee and leave for work.*

TERESA: *Yes sweetie, I also need to get up early because Ximena has to go to school a little earlier today for her training with the volleyball team. She needs to wake up before 5:30 A.M. to have time to shower, put on makeup, and brush her hair.*

LEONARDO: *What time does Ximena have her training today? Do you know if she went to bed very late yesterday? I know she has a very difficult test in her biology class today.*

| | |
|---|---|
| TERESA: | *I think her training starts at 6:45 A.M. Yesterday Ximena went to bed around 11:30 A.M. I heard her at night when she went into the bathroom to brush her teeth. I also have to wake up Martín because he needs to shower, get dressed and brush his teeth very well because he has a dentist's appointment in the morning today. And after his appointment I need to take him to school.* |
| LEONARDO: | *Sweetie, your day seems busier than mine. If you want, before I leave for work, I'll help you prepare breakfast for the kids.* |
| TERESA: | *Yes, my darling, thank you very much for your help. Meanwhile, I'm going to shower very quickly, then I'm going to wake up Ximena, and also Martín. This way they also shower, get ready and have a very good breakfast before leaving for their day's activities.* |
| LEONARDO: | *And after taking Martín to school, are you going to have time for yourself?* |
| TERESA: | *I hope so. I think I'm going to brush my hair, put on makeup, and paint my nails. Today I have a meeting at Ximena's school, and I want to be very well presented.* |

# PRÁCTICA

**A.** *Una rutina típica en casa de los Mendoza.* **Complete the story using the information from the dialogue. For this section use the verbs in the present tense form.**

Teresa y Leonardo es una pareja de padres chilenos con unos días muy ocupados. Leonardo _____ (1) pronto porque debe llegar a la oficina antes de las 8:00 A.M. Antes de salir para su trabajo, Leonardo _____ (2), _____ (3) y toma un café. Ximena _____ (4) antes de las 5:30 A.M. porque tiene entrenamiento de voleibol en su colegio. Ella se ducha, _____ (5) y _____ (6) el pelo. Teresa también despierta a Martín temprano. Él se ducha, _____ (7) y _____ (8) los dientes muy bien porque tiene cita en el odontólogo. Después de llevar a Martín al colegio, Teresa se cepilla el pelo, _____ (9) y _____ (10) las uñas porque tiene una reunión en el colegio.

**B.** Circle the answer that best completes the sentence.

**1.** Para cepillarse los dientes se necesita *(el champú, el jabón, la pasta dental, la peinilla).*

**2.** Para peinarse se usa *(la peinilla, el inodoro, el cepillo de dientes, la máquina de afeitar).*

3. Para lavarse el pelo se usa *(el jabón, la crema dental, el champú, la crema de afeitar)*.

4. Para lavarse las manos se necesita *(el jabón, el champú, la peinilla, el cepillo)*.

5. Las personas se duchan en *(el baño, la ducha, el inodoro, el lavamanos)*.

# GRAMMAR I Los pronombres y formas reflexivas (*Reflexive Constructions and Reflexive Pronouns*)

A. Certain verbs in both Spanish and English are reflexive. The object of a reflexive verb is the same person or thing as the subject. The reflexive verbs indicate what people do to or for themselves.

EXS: NONREFLEXIVE: **Teresa despierta a Martín.** (*Teresa wakes up Martín.*) Two different subjects: Teresa and Martín.
REFLEXIVE: **Martín *se despierta.*** (*Martín wakes up.*) Only one subject: Martín

B. Memorize the reflexive construction in the chart.

| Lavarse *(to wash oneself)* | | | |
|---|---|---|---|
| **Subject Pronoun** | **Reflexive Pronoun** | **Verb** | **(English)** |
| yo | me | lavo | I wash myself |
| tú | te | lavas | you wash yourself |
| él | se | lava | he washes himself, it washes itself |
| ella | se | lava | she washes herself, it washes itself |
| Ud. | se | lava | you wash yourself |
| Nosotros/as | nos | lavamos | we wash ourselves |
| vosotros/as | os | laváis | you (all) wash yourselves (Spain) |
| ellos/ellas | se | lavan | they wash themselves |
| Uds. | se | lavan | you (all) wash yourselves (Latin America) |

Note that:

1. Reflexive pronouns precede the conjugated verb but follow the infinitive, just like the direct object pronouns. When the reflexive verb follows the infinitive, it is attached to it.

EXS: **Yo *me* lavo.** (*I wash myself.*)

**Yo *me* voy a lavar.**
**Yo voy a lavar*me.*** }  (*I'm going to wash myself.*)

2. *Se* is the reflexive pronoun for all third-person subjects, singular and plural: él/ellos, ella/ellas, Ud./Uds. The third-person reflexive pronoun *se* can mean *himself, herself, itself, oneself, yourself,* **yourselves,** and *themselves.*

    EXS: **Ximena *se* despierta.** (*Ximena wakes up herself.*)
    **Ximena y Martín *se* despiertan.** (*They wake up themselves.*)

3. In English the reflexive pronoun always follows the verb. It is formed with *-self* and *-selves.*

4. In negative constructions, place reflexive pronoun after the word **no.**

    EXS: Leonardo **no** *se levanta* temprano.
    Teresa **no** *se maquilla* hoy.

5. The pronoun **se** when is attached to the end of an infinitive indicates the verb is *reflexive.* EX: lavar*se*

C. **Emphatic reflexive.** Reflexive pronouns are used with intransitive verbs such as **ir, salir, llegar,** and so on, to show that the action has been planned to be completed.

    EXS: *Me* **voy a casa a las tres.** (*I'm going home at three.*)
    **Voy a casa a las tres.** (*I'm going home at three.*)

This is also done with some transitive verbs to show the same kind of emphasis on completion of action.

    EXS: **Ximena *se* desayuna muy bien.** (*Ximena has a very good breakfast.*)
    **Ximena desayuna muy bien.** (*Ximena has a very good breakfast.*)

D. Not all verbs that are reflexive in Spanish are reflexive in the corresponding English. In English, a reflexive pronoun is often used only for emphasis. For example, you could say *Did you wash?* or *Did you wash yourself?* in English, but in Spanish the corresponding verb *lavarse* is always reflexive: **¿Te lavaste?**

E. Some verbs change meaning in the reflexive and non-reflexive forms: **acostar (a alguien)** *(to put someone else to be or to sleep)* **acostarse** *(to go to bed oneself).*

| | |
|---|---|
| **dormir** (to sleep) | **dormirse** (to fall asleep) |
| **despertar** (to wake someone else up) | **despertarse** (to wake u) |
| **levantar** (to raise/to lift) | **levantarse** (to get up) |
| **llamar** (to call) | **llamarse** (to be called/named) |
| **poner** (to put) | **ponerse** (to put on one's clothes, to dress) |
| **quitar** (to take away) | **quitarse** (to take off) |

F. Here is a list of some common reflexive verbs.

abrocharse (to fasten)
acostarse (ue) (to go to bed)
afeitarse (to shave oneself)
bañarse (to take a bath)
cepillarse (to brush one's hair)
despertarse (ie) (to wake up)
divertirse (ie) (to have fun, amuse oneself)
Dormirse (to fall sleep)
ducharse (to take a shower)
enojarse (to get angry [with])
lavarse (to wash oneself)

levantarse (to get up)
llamarse (to be named, called)
peinarse (to comb one's hair)
ponerse (to put on one's clothes)
preocuparse (por) (to worry [about])
quedarse (to stay)
quitarse (to take off one's clothes, to undress)
secarse (to dry oneself)
sentarse (ie) (to sit down)
sentirse (ie) (to feel)
vestirse (i) (to get dressed)

# PRACTIQUE LOS REFLEXIVOS

**ANSWERS
p. 220**

A. **Complete with the right answer.**

1. A reflexive pronoun repeats the _____ of the sentence. The reflexive pronoun for *yo* is _____, and for *tú* is _____.

2. There is only one reflexive pronoun for all third-person subjects: _____. This is the same pronoun used to translate *one* in impersonal sentences such as *One speaks Spanish:* _____.

3. Which action is more emphatic, **Ya vas a casa** or **Ya te vas a casa?** _____.

4. *Se* is obligatory when the subject of the sentence is an inanimate noun, such as *mano* in **las manos** _____ **lavan con agua y jabón.**

5. Such personal actions as **bañarse, lavarse, sentarse,** require the _____ pronoun when the action is performed on oneself.

6. Notice the difference between *sentarse* and *sentirse*; the first one is an -**ar** verb and the second, -**ir.** How would you say *she is sitting?* **Ella** _____, and *She is feeling. . .?* **Ella** _____

**ANSWERS
p. 220**

B. **Fill in the blank with the present indicative of the reflexive verbs in parentheses.**

1. Leonardo _____ todas las mañanas con su máquina de afeitar (*to shave*).

2. Yo _____ temprano todos los días. (*to go to bed*)

3. ¿A qué hora _____ usted normalmente? (*to wake up*)

4. Mi amiga Lola siempre _____ mucho para ir a las fiestas. (*to put on makeup*)

5. Vosotros _____ tarde todos los viernes. (*to go to bed*)

6. Después de bañarse, Teresa _____. (*to brush her hair*)

7. Ellas _____ un suéter (*sweater*) porque hace fresco. (*to put on*)

8. Mi hermana y yo siempre _____ muy elegantes. (*to get dressed*)

9. Antes de acostarte, siempre _____ la ropa (*clothes*) para ponerte la pijama. (*to take off*)

10. Mi papá y mi tío _____ antes de salir para la reunión. (*to get ready*)

**ANSWERS**
**p. 220**

C. **La rutina de mi familia. Fill in the blank with the right reflexive pronoun.**

En mi casa somos cinco miembros: mi papá, mi hermano Eduardo; mis hermanas Viviana, Elsa y yo. Nuestra mamá murió (*passed away*) hace dos años. La rutina de nosotros es muy diferente. Mi papá _____ (1) levanta muy temprano todos los días. Él _____ (2) despierta a las 5:00am. Viviana y Eduardo también _____ (3) levantan temprano porque necesitan ir a trabajar. Elsa va a la universidad así que _____ (4) despierta como a las 6:30 A.M. A mí me gusta correr, así que yo _____ (5) despierto a las 6:00 A.M. todos los días. Yo _____ (6) baño después de correr y luego _____ (7) visto con ropa informal para ir a mis clases. Mi hermano _____ (8) viste muy elegante porque trabaja en una compañía muy importante. El _____ (9) afeita antes de duchar _____ (10). Después de vestir _____ (11), se desayuna y sale para el trabajo. A Viviana le gusta maquillarse _____ (12). Yo no _____ (13) maquillo porque no tengo mucho tiempo. Nosotros _____ (14) lavamos las manos siempre antes de comer. ¿A qué hora tú _____ (15) despiertas? ¿Te gusta maquillar _____ (16) todos los días? ¿_____ (17) bañas por la mañana o por la tarde? ¿_____ (18) vistes muy elegante para ir a trabajar?

**ANSWERS**
**p. 220**

D. **Reflexive or non-reflexive. Write reflexive (R) or non-reflexive (NR) in the blank.**

1. La mamá despierta a los niños a las 7:00 A.M. todos los días. _____

2. Teresa se mira en el espejo para peinarse. _____

3. Ximena llama a su novio por teléfono todos los días. _____

4. Tú te quitas el maquillaje todas las noches antes de acostarte. _____

5. La abuelita le quita el gorro (*hat*) a su nieto. _____

6. Sofía se viste muy elegante para ir al trabajo. _____

7. La niñera (*babysitter*) duerme a los niños a las 8:30 P.M. _____

8. Usted pone la chaqueta en el closet. _____

9. Tú te secas después de bañarte. _____

10. Nosotros nos dormimos temprano. _____

---

# GRAMMAR II   El SE de situaciones accidentales (*Accidental SE for Unplanned Occurrences*)

A. **Unplanned or accidental occurrences.** When we talk about an action that is or was not planned, especially something unwanted or unpleasant, we use ***the accidental se*.** The SE, in this case, indicates that an action happens by accident. It also implies that the accident or unplanned event is not the direct responsibility of the person. We don't plan actions like forgetting, falling, dropping, or breaking. These actions seem to "just happen."

B. In this type of construction, the direct object of the sentence becomes the subject, and it agrees with the verb, not with the indirect object pronoun. To use the accidental reflexive, we have the following order in the sentence:

*SE + (indirect pronoun) + conjugated verb + noun*

EX: *Se me cayó* el jabón. (I <u>dropped</u> the soap.)

In this example *jabón* is the subject of *cayó,* and *me* is the indirect object. The literal translation is *The soap dropped itself on me.* If we change *soap* to the plural **jabones,** *cayó* has to change to ***cayeron.*** The full sentence is **Se me cayeron los jabones.** More examples:

¿Se *te olvidó* el libro? (*Did you forget the book?*)
¿Se *te olvidaron* los libros? (*Did you forget the books?*)
A Teresa *se le rompió* el cepillo. (*Teresa's brush broke.*)

C. Some examples of verbs that use the accidental SE for unplanned occurrences are: **acabar** (*to run out*), **caer** (*to fall*), **dañar** (*to damage/break*), **olvidar** (*to forget*), **perder** (*to lose*), **quedar** (*to be left behind*), **romper** (*to break something*)

D. **Accidental SE + indirect pronouns.** If a sentence has a personal name or a personal pronoun, it is necessary to use the preposition **A** + name or personal pronoun at the beginning of the sentence before the accidental SE.

EX: **A Paula** *se le* perdió la llave del carro. (*Paula lost her car key.*)
   **A nosotras** *se nos* acabó el champú. (*We ran out of shampoo.*)
   (**A mí**) se me quedó la llave en casa. (*I left the key at home.*)
   (**A ti**) se te quedaron las llaves en casa. (*You left the keys at home.*)
   (**A Teresa**) se le perdieron los aretes. (*Teresa lost her earrings.*)

(**A nosotros/as**) **se nos** olvidó la cita con el odontólogo. (*We forgot the appointment with the dentist.*)

(**A vosotros/as**) **se os** dañó el inodoro. (*Your toilet was damaged.*)

(**A ellos/as**) **se les** acabó el champú. (*They ran out of shampoo.*)

**Practique el *se* accidental. Complete the sentence by using the SE of accidental occurrences and the correct indirect pronoun (me/te/le/les/nos/os).**

1. A nosotros _____ _____ acabó el jabón de manos.

2. A ti _____ _____ rompió la botella del champú.

3. A vosotros _____ _____ olvidaron las llaves en la casa.

4. A mí _____ _____ perdió el anillo *(ring)* de oro.

5. A Emilia _____ _____ quedaron las toallas en la playa.

6. A David y a José _____ _____ dañó la ducha.

7. A mis padres _____ _____ acabó la paciencia.

8. A ti y a mí _____ _____ olvidaron las gafas de sol.

9. A vosotras _____ _____ quedó el cepillo en el hotel.

10. A Pedro _____ _____ dañó la tableta.

# GRAMMAR III     El pretérito de los verbos reflexivos (*The Preterite of Reflexive Verbs*)

**A.** Memorize the preterite of the reflexive verbs in the chart.

| Lavarse *(to wash oneself)* | | | |
|---|---|---|---|
| **Subject Pronoun** | **Reflexive Pronoun** | **Verb** | **(English)** |
| yo | me | lavé | I washed myself |
| tú | te | lavaste | you washed yourself |
| él | se | lavó | he washed himself, it washed itself |
| ella | se | lavó | she washed herself, it washed itself |
| Ud. | se | lavó | you washed yourself |
| nosotros/as | nos | lavamos | we washed ourselves |
| vosotros/as | os | lavasteis | you (all) washed yourselves *(Spain)* |
| ellos/ellas | se | lavaron | they washed themselves |
| Uds. | se | lavaron | you (all) washed yourselves *(Latin America)* |

# Practique los reflexivos en pretérito

ANSWERS
p. 220

Fill in the blank with the preterite of the verb in parentheses.

1. Mi mamá _____ (to wake up) muy temprano hoy.

2. Yo _____ (to get up) un poco más tarde (later).

3. Mi hermano y yo _____ (to take a shower) muy rápido para salir a tiempo para nuestras clases.

4. Tú _____ (to get dressed) con una sudadera porque quieres hacer deporte.

5. Mi hermana _____ muy bonita para ir a su trabajo. (to put on makeup)

6. Eduardo y Jorge _____ (to put on) la ropa de trabajo porque ellos trabajan en un taller de mecánica (garaje) para carros.

7. Tú y yo _____ (to sit) en el sillón de la sala para descansar.

8. Vosotros _____ (to get mad) con Eduardo y Valentina porque ellos no hicieron sus camas ayer.

9. Yo _____ (to go to bed) tarde anoché.

10. Mi amigo Pedro _____ (to fall sleep) viendo televisión.

# PRÁCTICA

ANSWERS
p. 220

A. Unplanned or accidental occurrences of *se*. Write in Spanish the following sentences. Pay attention to the order of the sentence and make the verbs preterite.

Modelo: Eduardo forgot his smart watch at home. *(olvidar)*

*A Eduardo se le olvidó su reloj inteligente en casa.*

1. I dropped the soap. _____ *(caer)*

2. Teresa broke the comb. _____ *(romper)*

3. Martín forgot his glasses. *(gafas)* at home _____ *(olvidar)*

4. Ximena lost her earrings. *(aretes/pendientes)* _____ *(perder)*

5. Leonardo broke the sink. _____ *(romper)*

6. Ana left the book at home. _____ *(quedar)*

7. Martín and Ximena lost their keys *(llaves)*. _____ *(perder)*

8. Teresa ran out of shampoo. _____. *(acabar)*

9. We forgot our appointment *(cita)*. _____ *(olvidar)*

10. Leonardo left the computer at home. _____ *(quedar)*

**ANSWERS**
**p. 221**

**B.** Fill in the blanks with the correct form of the verb in the preterite. If the verb is reflexive, don't forget to write the respective reflexive pronoun: *me/te/se/nos/os.*

1. Esta mañana (yo) no _____ porque no tuve tiempo. (*bañarse*)
2. ¿A qué hora _____ (tú) ayer? (*acostarse*)
3. Ellas _____ tarde el domingo pasado. (*levantarse*)
4. Vosotros _____ cereal esta mañana. (*desayunar*)
5. Juan _____ en su clase de filosofía. (*dormirse*)
6. Anoche nosotros solamente _____ seis horas. (*dormir*)
7. Diana y Gabriela _____ su vestido elegante para el concierto. (*ponerse*)
8. Mi papá _____ la chaqueta cuando _____ a la casa. (*quitarse/entrar*)
9. Martín _____ todos los chocolates. (*comerse*)
10. Leonardo y yo _____ para la oficina a las siete de la mañana. (*salir*)

**ANSWERS**
**p. 221**

**C.** Change the present to the preterite in the following story.

Esta mañana (1) *me despierto* a las siete y cuarto de la mañana, (2) *me levanto* de la cama, y (3) *me baño* con agua bien caliente. Después (4) *me seco* con la toalla, y (5) *me visto* rápidamente. (6) *Me desayuno* con café con pan, y (7) *salgo* de la casa para la universidad. (8) *Llego* a la clase a las ocho menos cinco, y (9) *oigo* las explicaciones del profesor. . . A las doce (10) *almuerzo* una ensalada en la cafetería, y por la tarde (11) *vuelvo* a clase con mis amigos. Mi clase de la tarde (12) *comienza* a la dos en punto. El profesor (13) *explica* por qué el Imperio Romano (14) *se cae* desastrosamente y (15) *se destruye* en poco tiempo.

| 1. _____ | 6. _____ | 11. _____ |
| 2. _____ | 7. _____ | 12. _____ |
| 3. _____ | 8. _____ | 13. _____ |
| 4. _____ | 9. _____ | 14. _____ |
| 5. _____ | 10. _____ | 15. _____ |

**ANSWERS**
**p. 221**

**D.** Complete the following chart with the indirect pronoun and the verb in the preterite. (Remember if the object is in plural, the verb should be in the plural too.)

| A + noun/pronoun | SE | Indirect Object Pronoun | Verb | Subject |
|---|---|---|---|---|
| *A mí* | *se* | *me* | (*forgot*) = olvidaron | *las llaves.* |
| 1. A Martín | se | | (*left*) = | el libro. |
| 2. A Teresa y a Leonardo | se | | (*ran out of*) = | el jabón. |
| 3. A Ximena | se | | (*lost*) = | los aretes. |
| 4. A nosotros | se | | (*broke*) = | el vidrio. (*glass*) |

# 10 Las finanzas y el presupuesto
## (*Finances and Budgeting*)

## PALABRAS NUEVAS

| | | | |
|---|---|---|---|
| el acceso en línea | online access | el cheque[1] | check |
| las acciones | stocks | la chequera/el talonario | checkbook |
| los ahorros | savings | | |
| las alertas | alerts | la contraseña | password |
| la aplicación | app | el crédito | credit |
| los aranceles | tariffs | el crédito bancario | bank credit |
| la autorización | authorization | la cuenta | account |
| el balance/el saldo | balance | cuenta corriente | checking account |
| la banca en línea | online banking | cuenta de ahorros | savings account |
| el banco | bank | el cupo | limit |
| la billetera | wallet | el depósito | deposit |
| la billetera digital | digital wallet | la deuda | debt |
| el billete | bill, ticket | el dinero | money |
| la bolsa de valores | stock market | la divisa | foreign money |
| el/la cajero(a) | cashier | el documento | document |
| el cajero automático | the ATM | el extracto bancario | bank statement |
| la cartera | wallet, purse | la factura[2] | bill, invoice |
| el CDT (Certificado de Depósito a Término) | CD | las finanzas | finances |
| | | las ganancias | earnings/profits |
| | | la ganga | bargain |
| | | el gasto | expense |
| el centavo | cent | | |
| el certificado bancario | bank certificate | | |

| | | | |
|---|---|---|---|
| el giro (postal) | money order | aumentar | to increase |
| giro internacional | international money order | cargar | to load, charge |
| la hipoteca | mortgage | cerrar sesión | to log out |
| la huella digital | fingerprint | cobrar | to charge |
| el impuesto | tax | convenir (ie) | to suit |
| el interés | interest | deber dinero | to owe money |
| los métodos de pago | payment methods | depositar | to deposit |
| | | descubrir | to discover |
| la moneda | currency, coins, cash | descargar | to download |
| | | digitar | to enter |
| el número de la clave | pin number | disfrutar de | to enjoy |
| los pagos | payments | encantar | to like, please |
| las pérdidas | losses | encontrar (ue) | to find |
| el préstamo | loan | faltar | to miss |
| el presupuesto | budget | ganar | to win, earn |
| el reconocimiento facial | face recognition | gastar | to spend |
| | | gustar | to like |
| el reconocimiento de voz | voice recognition | hacer fila | to stand in line |
| | | importar[5] | to matter |
| el retiro | withdrawal | ingresar | to enter |
| el salario[3]/el sueldo | salary | iniciar sesión | to login |
| la sede principal | headquarters | interesar | to interest |
| el servicio al cliente | costumer service | invertir | to invest |
| la solicitud | request | manejar el presupuesto | to manage the budget |
| la sucursal | branch | | |
| la sucursal bancaria | bank branch | mejorar | to improve |
| la sucursal virtual del banco | virtual bank branch | meter | to put into |
| | | ofrecer | to offer |
| la tarjeta de crédito | credit card | pagar | to pay |
| la tarjeta débito | debit card | parecer[6] | to seem |
| el teléfono inteligente | smartphone | perder | to lose |
| los trámites | procedures | prestar | to lend |
| los trámites digitales | digital procedures | quejarse | to complain |
| | | reducir | to reduce |
| la transacción | transaction | retirar | to withdraw |
| la transferencia de dinero | money transfer | revisar | to review |
| | | sacar | to take out |
| el valor[4] | value, stock | sobrar | to be left (over) |
| las ventajas | advantages | solicitar | to request |
| | | tener control | to have control |
| *Verbos* | *Verbs* | valer | to be worth |
| agradar | to please | valer la pena | to be worthwhile |
| ahorrar | to save | valorizarse | to value |

| *Adjetivos* | *Adjectives* | al mes | per month |
|---|---|---|---|
| actual[7] | present/current | a tiempo | on time |
| adinerado(a) | wealthy | a plazos | in installments |
| arancelario | to do with tariffs | a propósito | by the way |
| bancario | banking | al contado | pay cash |
| barato(a) | cheap | cuota de manejo | handling fee |
| costoso(a)/caro(a) | expensive | deudor(a) moroso(a) | slow payer |
| crédito hipotecario | mortgage credit | estar al día | to be up to date |
| deudor(a) | debtor | pagar con tarjeta | pay with credit |
| disponible | available | de crédito | card |
| efectivo | in cash (with cash) | pagar con tarjeta | pay with debit |
| gratis | free | débito | card |
| monetario(a) | monetary | pagar en efectivo | pay in cash |
| necesario(a) | necessary | pagar poco a poco | pay little by little |
| pobre | poor | usar el teléfono para | tap your phone to |
| serio(a) | serious | pagar | pay |
| valioso(a) | valuable | sinfín | endless/wide range |
| | | sobre todo[8] | above all |
| *Expresiones* | *Expressions* | | |
| a fines de/ al final de | at the end of | | |
| al año | per year | | |

## NOTAS

1. *Cheque* is the word used in Latin America for *check*, *talón* is the word used in Spain. *Checkbook* is *talonario* in Spain, and *chequera* in Latin America. Cheques are not as widely used today as they were in previous years, especially among younger generations, who prefer digital transactions. They will likely go out of use in the near future.

2. *Factura* is the commercial word for *bill*, just like *invoice*. We use *cuenta* when the bill is small, such as those you get in a restaurant, drugstore. Do not confuse it with *billete*, which is used for currency bills as well as for travel tickets.

3. *Salario* was used originally for *low wages*, while *sueldo* was used for *high wages*. Nowadays the two words are interchangeable for *salary*.

4. *Valor* means *value* in general as well as *stock* in the stock market. *La bolsa de valores* translates *the stock market*.

5. *Importar* can be two different things: *to import* (from another country), and *to matter*. With the first meaning, we use *importar* like *hablar*, with different subjects: **yo, tú**, and so on. With the second meaning *to matter*, it is used in the third person, like *gustar*, which is explained in the Grammar II section of this lesson.

6. *Parecer* means *to seem, to look like*; the reflexive *parecerse a* means *to take after, resemble*.

   EXS: *¿Te parece* bien el precio? (*Does the price look okay to you?*)
   Yo *me parezco* a mi padre. (*I take after my father.*)

7. *Actual* means *present, now (current)*, whereas English *actual* means **real, verdadero**. The same principle applies to **actualmente**, meaning *presently, now*, whereas *actually* is **verdaderamente**.

8. *Sobretodo* is an adverb meaning *above all*.

# PRACTIQUE LAS PALABRAS NUEVAS

**ANSWERS
p. 221**

**A.** Write *el, la, los,* or *las* before each noun.

1. ____ aplicación
2. ____ aranceles
3. ____ transacción
4. ____ deuda
5. ____ hipoteca
6. ____ sucursal
7. ____ impuestos
8. ____ trámites
9. ____ ahorro
10. ____ divisas
11. ____ cajero
12. ____ finanzas

**ANSWERS
p. 221**

**B.** *Word families.* Write the verb in infinitive related to each of the following nouns.

1. ahorros _____
2. ganancias _____
3. pérdidas _____
4. deuda _____
5. pagos _____
6. gastos _____
7. préstamo _____
8. depósito _____
9. retiro _____
10. solicitud _____

**ANSWERS
p. 221**

**C.** Fill in the blanks with one of the following words or expressions.

| | | | | |
|---|---|---|---|---|
| ahorrar | sueldo | contraseña | moneda | préstamo |
| a plazos | sucursal | transferencia | en efectivo | aplicación |
| cajero automático | pérdidas | crédito hipotecario | chequera | tarjeta de crédito |

1. Necesito pedir un _____ del banco para comprar un carro nuevo.

2. Muchos jóvenes necesitan _____ mucho dinero para poder pagar sus estudios en la universidad.

3. En Latinoamérica las personas compran muchas cosas _____. Así tienen más flexibilidad para pagar poco a poco con intereses.

4. La _____ de México es el peso, y la de España es el euro.

5. En la actualidad es muy normal pagar con _____ todas las compras. Mucha gente no paga con efectivo.

6. La mayoría de las personas en la actualidad prefieren usar la _____ virtual del banco que ir en persona a una de sus oficinas.

7. Para sacar dinero de su cuenta muchas personas prefieren usar el _____ porque es rápido y a veces no se necesita salir del carro.

8. Mis tíos necesitan solicitar un _____ del banco para comprar una nueva casa.

9. Tengo que descargar la nueva _____ de mi banco para hacer las transacciones bancarias usando mi teléfono.

10. La bolsa de valores tuvo muchas _____ esta semana. Algunas acciones perdieron mucho dinero.

11. Claudia necesita hacer una _____ de dinero al banco de su hermana en México para ayudarla.

12. Me gusta pagar la cuenta de un restaurante _____ y no con tarjeta de crédito.

13. Ya casi nadie usa una _____. La mayoría de las personas prefieren pagar usando su teléfono o con sus tarjetas de créditos. No hay muchas personas que usen cheques ahora.

14. El _____ de una persona en Latinoamérica es muy bajo comparado con Estados Unidos o Europa. Muchos empleados ganan el equivalente a menos de $600 dólares al mes.

15. Para usar la sucursal virtual del banco es necesario ingresar o digitar una _____ primero.

**ANSWERS p. 221**

D. Complete each sentence with one of the verbs below. Use the preterite tense.

| ahorrar | digitar | invertir | prestar | gastar |
|---------|---------|----------|---------|--------|
| depositar | solicitar | pagar | reducir | cerrar |

1. Francisco _____ un préstamo al banco para poder comprar un apartamento en Costa Rica.

2. Ayer _____ mi clave cuando usé el cajero automático para retirar dinero.

3. Tú _____ tu tarjeta de crédito a tiempo para que no te cobren intereses.

4. Vosotros _____ los gastos de este mes. Eso está muy bien para mejorar el presupuesto.

5. Nosotros _____ en acciones de oro (*gold*) porque se valorizan bien.

6. Elizabeth le _____ 500 dólares a su hermano para su viaje.

7. Yo _____ la sesión de mi sucursal virtual del banco después de hacer la transacción.

8. Alfredo _____ mil dólares en su cuenta de ahorros.

9. Julián no ahorró nada; al contrario, lo _____ todo.

10. Mis padres _____ mucho dinero para poder viajar a Europa.

**ANSWERS**
**p. 221**

E. Write *true* or *false* (T/F).

1. _____ Abrimos una cuenta de ahorros en un supermercado.
2. _____ Una cuenta corriente ofrece más interés que una cuenta de ahorros.
3. _____ Lo contrario de ahorrar es gastar.
4. _____ Para usar la sucursal virtual del banco hay que ir en persona.
5. _____ Retirar dinero y sacar dinero son sinónimos.
6. _____ La moneda de México es el euro.
7. _____ En la actualidad muchas personas usan los cheques para pagar todo.
8. _____ Si Ud. compra a plazos, tiene que pagar facturas todos los meses.
9. _____ En algunos estados de los Estados Unidos no se pagan impuestos federales.
10. _____ Una hipoteca es un préstamo grande que hace un banco para pagar una casa.

# DIÁLOGO   Hablando de bancos y de finanzas

*César y José son dos jóvenes ecuatorianos que conversan en un café de Quito sobre sus bancos y finanzas.*

CÉSAR:  José, te conté que cambié de banco.

JOSÉ:  ¿Por qué cambiaste de banco? ¿Alguna razón en particular?

CÉSAR:  Mi antiguo banco no está al día con la tecnología y tú sabes que a mí me gusta hacer todo en línea. A mí me parece muy importante poder hacer todas mis transacciones y transferencias bancarias usando mi teléfono o mi computador portátil.

JOSÉ:  Sí lo entiendo. También soy así. Prefiero la comodidad de no tener que ir en persona a un banco. Soy muy práctico también. ¿Y qué banco escogiste?

CÉSAR:  Escogí un banco que se llama Nuevo Banco. Es un banco digital que me conviene porque tiene un sinfín de ofertas financieras para jóvenes como nosotros. Creo que la sede principal de este banco está en Brasil.

JOSÉ:  ¿Cuáles ventajas tiene este banco digital?

CÉSAR:  Primero, me encanta que puedes manejar y tener control de tu dinero y de tus finanzas. Además, es muy fácil abrir una cuenta de ahorros. El banco te permite ajustar el límite o cupo de tu tarjeta de acuerdo con tus finanzas y el dinero que tengas.

JOSÉ:  Me parece muy conveniente. ¿Cobran mucho por hacer transferencias?

CÉSAR:  No cobran nada por hacer transferencias. Además, no tienen cuota de manejo. Con este sistema bancario puedes aprender mucho a manejar tus finanzas y tu presupuesto muy bien.

JOSÉ: Creo que otra gran ventaja es que no tienes que hacer filas largas en un banco que son tan comunes aquí en Quito. A mí me molesta esperar mucho tiempo en una fila.

CÉSAR: Eso es verdad. En este banco digital todo el manejo lo haces en línea y el banco está a tu servicio las 24 horas. Además, el banco tiene controles de seguridad muy buenos.

JOSÉ: Creo que yo también voy a mirar las opciones que ofrece tu banco porque me parecen muy positivas.

CÉSAR: Sí tienes alguna pregunta me dices. Yo acabo de abrir otra cuenta de ahorros y fue muy fácil. El banco digital me ayuda a tener un mejor control y manejo de mi dinero.

# DIALOGUE  *Talking about Banks and Finance*

*César and José are two young Ecuadoreans who talk in a cafe in Quito about their banks and finances.*

CÉSAR: *José, did I tell you that I changed my bank?*

JOSÉ: *Why did you change your bank? Any reason?*

CÉSAR: *My old bank is not up to date with technology, and you know that I like to do everything online. I find it very important to be able to do all my transactions and bank transfers using my phone or my laptop.*

JOSÉ: *Yes, I understand. I like that too. I prefer the convenience of not having to go to a bank in person. I am very practical too. And which bank did you choose?*

CÉSAR: *I chose a bank called Nuevo Banco. It is a digital bank that suits me because it has a wide range of financial offers for young people like us. I believe that the main headquarters of this bank is in Brazil.*

JOSÉ: *What advantages does this digital bank have?*

CÉSAR: *First, I like being able to manage and have control of my money and finances. Plus, it's very easy to open a savings account. The bank allows you to adjust the limit or quota of your credit card according to your finances and the money you have.*

JOSÉ: *It seems very convenient to me. Do they charge a lot for making transfers?*

CÉSAR: *They don't charge anything for making transfers. Additionally, they have no handling fee. With this banking system you can learn a lot about managing your finances and budget very well.*

JOSÉ: *I think another great advantage is that you don't have to wait in long lines at a bank that are so common here in Quito. It annoys me waiting a long time in a line.*

CÉSAR: *That's true. You do all the handling online and the bank is at your service 24 hours a day. Additionally, the bank has very good security controls.*

JOSÉ: *I think I'm also going to look at the options your bank offers because they seem very positive to me.*

CÉSAR: *If you have any questions, tell me. I just opened another savings account, and it was very easy. The digital bank helps me have better control and management of my money.*

# PRÁCTICA

**A.** Complete the story with the information from the dialogue.

José cambió su _____ (1) porque no está al día con la tecnología. A José le gusta hacer todas las _____ (2) bancarias en su teléfono o en su portátil y por eso necesita un banco más eficiente y más moderno. César escogió el banco que se llama _____ (3). Es un banco digital con un sinfín de ofertas _____ (4). La _____ (5) principal del banco está en Brasil. A César le gusta este banco porque puede tener _____ (6) de su dinero y de sus finanzas. Además, el banco le permite ajustar el tope o límite de su _____ (7). Otra de las grandes ventajas del banco es que no cobra por _____ (8) y las transferencias son _____ (9). Otro beneficio para César es que no tiene que ir a un banco en persona y hacer largas _____ (10), lo cual es muy conveniente.

**B.** Complete each sentence with an appropriate word from the chapter word list.

1. Para comprar una casa necesitamos solicitar un _____ del banco, a menos que paguemos por la casa al contado.

2. Visa, MasterCard y American Express son tres _____ muy populares.

3. Para pagar con cheques necesito que el banco me envíe una _____.

4. El _____ mínimo de los trabajadores en Ecuador al mes es de 470.00 dólares.

5. Lo contrario de *ahorrar* es _____.

6. Muchos bancos de Estados Unidos pagan un pequeño _____ por el dinero que se deposita en la cuenta de ahorros.

7. En muchos países del mundo muchos estudiantes solicitan un _____ para poder pagar sus estudios en una universidad.

8. ¿Qué prefiere usted cuando va a una tienda, pagar en efectivo o pagar con _____?

9. Muchas personas tienen su dinero invertido en la _____ porque así obtienen ganancias graduales.

10. El _____ es una forma práctica y conveniente para retirar dinero del banco y muchas veces se puede usar sin tener que salir del carro.

C. Circle the word that best completes the sentence.

1. Pagué la factura con (una moneda, una cuenta, un cheque, una contraseña).

2. Para pagar en efectivo por una compra se necesita tener (tarjeta de crédito, dinero, valores, intereses).

3. Una cuenta de ahorros nos ayuda a (ahorrar, gastar, invertir, perder) dinero.

4. Si quieres invertir tu dinero para obtener ganancias graduales, debes ponerlo en (una cuenta de ahorros, un cajero automático, una cuenta corriente, la bolsa de valores).

5. Para tener más seguridad al ingresar a la sucursal virtual del banco e iniciar una sesión es necesario tener una (cuenta, contraseña, factura, tableta)

---

# GRAMMAR I   El objeto indirecto con verbos como gustar
## (*The Indirect Object with Verbs like gustar*)

A. **Gustar** is used in Spanish to express likes and dislikes. Unlike regular verbs ending in AR, the verb *gustar* follows a different form of conjugation and requires indirect object pronouns. It is not used the same way as the English verb *to like*.

The sentence *Ese banco me gusta* translates literally as *That bank is pleasing to me* in everyday English, *I like that bank*. **Bank** is the subject and must always have a definite article, a short form of the possessive, or a demonstrative. In other words, the subject of *gustar* is the person or thing that is liked.

If we change *banco* to *bancos,* we have to change the verb to the plural: **Esos bancos me gustan.**

*Me* is an indirect object in *Ese banco me gusta.* The indirect object is obligatory with *gustar* and verbs like it.

To talk about what you like or you don't like *to do* use **gustar + verb in infinitive.**

EX: (**A mí**) *no me gusta gastar* dinero or **A Pablo** *le gusta estudiar* finanzas.

It is important to note that **gustar** is used in singular form when it is followed by a verb in the infinitive form.

When it is followed by a noun, it is necessary to agree with the plural or singular form.

EX: ¿Te *gusta* tu *banco*? Sí pero también me *gustan* otros bancos.

| (A mí) | me | | | | *I like the card(s).* |
|--------|-----|---|---|---|---|
| (A ti) | te | | | | *You like the card(s).* |
| (A ella/él) | le | | gusta(n) la(s) carta(s). | | *She/he likes the card(s)* |
| A nosotros/as | nos | | | | *We like the card(s)* |
| A vosotros/as | os | | | | *You (all) like the card(s)* |
| A ellos/as | les | | | | *They like the card(s)* |

B. There are many verbs in Spanish with a construction like that of *gustar.* Here are some of them.

**aburrir** *to bore*  
**apetecer** *to like (food, drink)*  
**convenir (ie)** *to be suitable, be convenient*  
**doler (ue)** *to hurt, ache*  
**encantar** *to like very much*  
**faltar** *to miss, lack*  
**fascinar** *to like a lot/to love*  
**importar** *to matter, be important*  

**interesar** *to interest*  
**molestar** *to bother, annoy*  
**parecer** *to seem, look like*  
**preocupar** *to be concerned (about)*  
**quedar** *to fit/to have something left*  
**sobrar** *to be left*  

C. *Amar, querer,* and *gustar* to express affection and love towards another person. When using these verbs, it is important to note the difference in the conjugations and the use of the object pronouns.

**Amar** expresses a deep, strong love towards a significant other person in your life:

EX: **Yo amo a mi familia.** (*I love my family.*)

If you are expressing your feelings addressing your significant other it is necessary to use the direct object pronoun before the verb.

EX: **Yo *te* amo.** (*I love you.*)  
**¿Tú *me* amas?** (*Do you love me?*)  
**Emilia ama *a Jorge*. Emilia *lo* ama mucho.** (*Emilia loves Jorge.*)  
(*She loves him very much.*)

**Important to note:**

When you want to express in Spanish *to love to do things* or *to love things* you **DO NOT** use the verb *amar* instead you can use the verbs *fascinar* or *encantar.*

EX: *Me encantan* las papas fritas. (*I love French fries.*)  
**A Santiago *le fascina*** hacer ejercicio en el gimnasio. (*Santiago loves to exercise in the gym.*)

*Querer* is a more general verb to express affection.

**Yo *te* quiero mucho.** (*I love you very much.* [*referring to a friend*])

*Gustar* can be used to express if you like or do not like someone. In the following examples the verb needs to be conjugated following the rules of the regular verbs ending in AR.

EX: **Me *gustas* mucho.** (*I like you a lot.*) The literal translation of the sentence would be: *you are pleasing to me.* That is the reason why the verb is conjugated in the second-person singular.
¿**Te *gusto*?** (*Do you like me?*)

D. *Convenir* means both *to agree* and *to be suitable, convenient.* When it means *to agree,* it is conjugated with a regular subject pronoun, like **yo, tú,** and so on. When it means *to be suitable* or *convenient,* it follows the same construction as that of *gustar;* and it is conjugated only in the third person singular and plural.

EXS: **Ella y yo *convinimos* en eso.** (*She and I <u>agreed</u> on that.*)
**Ese banco *te conviene* más.** (*That bank <u>is</u> more <u>convenient to you</u>.*)

E. **Expresión con el verbo *pasar:***
¿**Qué *te pasa*? No me pasa nada. Estoy bien.**
(*What is the matter with you? What is wrong with you?*
*Nothing is wrong with me. I'm fine.*)
¿**Qué le pasa a Mónica? A Mónica no le pasa nada.**
(*What is wrong with Mónica? Mónica is fine.*)
¿**Qué nos pasa a nosotros? A nosotros no nos pasa nada.**
(*What is wrong with us? We are fine.*)

# PRÁCTICA

A. Complete the idea with the right answer.

1. In a sentence like **Me gusta el banco,** the subject is _____, and the indirect object is _____. If we change *banco* to *bancos,* we say _____ los bancos.

2. *Usted* and *Ustedes* are second person in meaning (you), but _____ person grammatically. This is why their indirect objects are the pronouns _____.

3. Which is more emphatic, (a) **Me gusta eso** or (b) **A mí me gusta eso?** _____. Any repetition of information seems to be emphatic.

4. If *Me duele la mano* means *My hand hurts*, it seems obvious that the indirect object *me* has been rendered in English by the word _____.

5. *Parecer (to seem)* needs an indirect object like *gustar*. How would you translate *That idea seems good to me?* Esa idea _____.

**ANSWERS p. 222**

B. Complete the sentences with the verbs suggested. Use the present tense. Don't forget the indirect object pronouns.

1. A mis padres _____ buenos los intereses que da ese banco. (*to seem*)

2. ¿Qué _____a ti? —Pues a mí no _____ nada. (*What is wrong with you?*)

3. A mí _____ usar la sucursal virtual de mi banco. (*to like very much*)

4. A César no _____ invertir dinero en la bolsa de valores en este momento. (*to be suitable/convenient*)

5. A ustedes _____ viajar a Arizona en el invierno. (*to love*)

6. ¿A vosotros no _____ ahorrar dinero para el futuro? (*to matter*)

7. Después de depositar 500 dólares en el banco, a ti no _____ nada en efectivo. (*to be left over*)

8. ¿Te preocupas por mantener un buen presupuesto para el mes? —Claro que sí _____ mucho. (*to be concerned about*)

9. A mi amigo José _____ mucho hacer filas largas en el banco. (*to bother, annoy*)

10. A mi esposa y a mí _____ ahorrar dinero para viajar. (*to like very much/to love*)

**ANSWERS p. 222**

C. Form sentences using the words in the order given. Add any necessary words to complete the sentence correctly. Use the present indicative. Do not forget to include the personal *a*.

Modelo:
*mí/fascinar/inversiones: **A mí me fascinan las inversiones**.*

1. Carlos/interesar/deportes.

   _____

2. Maritza y Guillermo/importar mucho/política/.

   _____

3. vosotras/molestar mucho/ruido *(noise)*/.

   _____

4. ti/quedar/doscientos/dólar/en/billetera/.

   _____

5. nosotros/faltar/un año/para/graduarnos/.

   _____

ANSWERS
p. 222

**D.** Translate the following sentences.

1. I love you.

   _____

2. My friends like to listen to podcasts.

   _____

3. Susana loves to exercise in the gym.

   _____

4. We love our friends.

   _____

5. What's wrong with you today?

   _____

6. You love chocolates.

   _____

7. Juan loves to invest money.

   _____

8. Your problems interest me.

   _____

9. Do you like me?

   _____

10. We have $1,000.00 left in the bank.

    _____

# GRAMMAR II   El imperfecto del indicativo (*The Imperfect Indicative*)

**A.** Unlike the preterite which is used to describe actions that have been completed in the past, the imperfect is used to describe actions that seem to be continuing or incomplete in the past. The imperfect describes what was happening in the past or how things used to be.

**B.** In general, the imperfect is used:

1. **To express habitual or repeated actions** (continuing actions and not a specific time).

   EX: Nosotros **jugábamos** en el parque *todos los fines de semana.*

2. **To express ongoing actions or events that were in progress in the past.**

   EX: Tú **hablabas** por teléfono *mientras (while)* yo **depositaba** el dinero en el banco.

3. **To describe characteristics and conditions in the past.**

   EX: En el pasado **no había** ni cajeros automáticos ni sucursales virtuales.

   EX: Mi abuelita **era** una mujer muy inteligente y bonita.

4. To tell the time *(la hora)* in the past when something happened.

   EX: **Eran** las 9:00 A.M. cuando (yo) llegué al banco.

5. To express a person's age in the past.

   Mi mamá **tenía** 72 años cuando murió.

C. Memorize the imperfect indicative of the verbs in the chart. The only three irregular verbs in imperfect are: **ir** *(to go)*, **ser** *(to be)*, **ver** *(to see)*.

| Subject | *Habl ar* | *Com er* | *Viv ir* | *Ir* | *S er* | *V er* |
|---------|-----------|----------|----------|------|--------|--------|
| yo | habl aba | com ía | viv ía | iba | era | ve ía |
| tú | habl abas | com ías | viv ías | ibas | eras | ve ías |
| él/ella/Ud. | habl aba | com ía | viv ía | iba | era | ve ía |
| Nosotros/as | habl ábamos | com íamos | viv íamos | íbamos | éramos | ve íamos |
| vosotros/as | habl abais | com íais | viv íais | ibais | erais | veíais |
| ellos/ellas/Uds. | habl aban | com ían | viv ían | iban | eran | ve ían |

Note that:

1. The stem of *hablar, comer, vivir,* are the same as for the present: **habl-, com-, viv-**. The endings are **-aba** for the **-ar** verbs, and **-ía** for the **-er** and **-ir** verbs. Notice that *-abas/ías* is the ending for *tú, -aba/ía* for *él/ella/usted, -ábamos/íamos* for **nosotros/as**, abais/íais for **vosotros/as** and *-aban/ían* for *ellos, ellas, Uds.*

2. All verbs are regular in the imperfect indicative except *ir, ser,* and *ver.* As you can see from the chart, the imperfect, of *ir* is *iba* and of *ser* is *era,* which reminds you of the present **tú eres.** *Ver* adds an *e* to the stem **v-** to make **ve,** so the imperfect is *veía* instead of *via.*

3. Notice the accent on the ending *-ia* in all the persons to break up the diphthong, and also the accent in the first-person plural: **hablábamos, éramos, íbamos, veíamos.**

4. Stem-changing verbs do not change the stem in the imperfect. For example, **volver → vuelvo** BUT **volvía; pensar → pienso** BUT **pensaba; pedir → pido** BUT **pedía.**

D. Expressions of time and frequency that often are used with the imperfect:

1. a menudo          *often*
2. antes             *before*
3. a veces           *sometimes/at times*
4. frecuentemente    *often/frequently*
5. generalmente      *generally*
6. mientras          *while*
7. siempre           *always*

EXS: Mis padres y yo *siempre* íbamos a la playa *todos los veranos. (My parents and I used to go to the beach every summer.)*
Mis abuelos **nos** visitaban *a menudo. (My grandparents visited us often.)*

E. **Summary of the use of the imperfect.** The imperfect is a past tense like the preterite, but it is used in a different way. The preterite indicates an entire action completed in the past, whereas the imperfect shows an action going on in the past, with no reference to a beginning or an end. For this reason, the imperfect is usually translated by *was* + (-*ing* form of the verb) in English; in other words, it's an action in progress. Since a habit is an action that repeats itself, the imperfect is used to show a habit.

EXS: Mi madre **hablaba** por teléfono cuando llegué. (*My mother was talking on the phone when I arrived.*)
Los aztecas **comían** mucho maíz. (*The Aztecs used to eat a lot of corn.*)

# PRACTIQUE EL IMPERFECTO

ANSWERS
p. 222

1. Verbs ending in **-ar** take the ending _____ in the imperfect tense. For example, from *gustar* we can say Me _____ ese banco.

2. Verbs ending in **-er** and **-ir** have the same ending for the imperfect: _____. For example, from *beber* we have él _____, and from *salir,* ella _____.

3. The shortest verb in Spanish is **ir** (*to go*), and it is also the most irregular verb. It is **yo fui** (*I went*) in the preterite, and now the imperfect is **yo** _____. How do you say *we were going?* _____.

4. *Ser* (*to be*) is also irregular. Remember **tú eres** in the present. The imperfect shows the same stem: **Yo** _____.

5. *Ver* (*to see, watch*) is also irregular in the imperfect. We say **yo** _____ in imperfect.

6. All persons with the ending **-ía** need an accent to break up the diphthong, like *día.* Verbs ending in **-ar** only carry the accent in the first-person plural. For example, *hablar* has **nosotros** _____; **ir** has _____.

7. We have two tenses to refer to past time: the preterite and the _____. The preterite suggests that the action is completed, finished, whereas the imperfect suggests that the action is _____ in the past.

8. Remember that *hay* (*there is/there are*) is the present of *haber.* How would you say in the imperfect *there was/there were?* _____.

9. If we repeat an action many times, it becomes a habit, as if it were going on forever. For this reason, the _____ is used to show a habit in the past. The adverbs to suggest this repetition are **siempre, muchas veces, a menudo,** and so on.

# PRÁCTICA

**ANSWERS**
**p. 222**

A. Fill in each blank with the correct imperfect tense form of the verb given.

1. Mis abuelos siempre _____ mucho dinero. (*ahorrar*)

2. Cuando _____ *(tener)* ocho años, yo _____ *(ver)* todas las películas de Disney con mi familia.

3. _____ *(ser)* las 10:00 A.M. cuando empezó la reunión virtual con los clientes.

4. ¿Dónde _____ (tú) cuando te llamé anoche? (*estar*)

5. Nosotros antes _____ (*pagar*) todas las compras con cheques ahora sólo pagamos con tarjeta de crédito.

6. Ahora los niños juegan muchos videojuegos antes los niños _____ (*salir*) al parque para jugar.

7. Vosotros ahora usáis el cajero automático para retirar dinero antes sus padres _____ *(retirar)* el dinero en la sucursal del banco.

8. La moneda oficial del Ecuador en la actualidad es el dólar, pero antes los ecuatorianos _____ *(tener)* el sucre como moneda oficial.

9. A mí _____ *(gustar)* montar bicicleta cuando _____ (*ser*) niña.

10. ¿Cuántos invitados _____ en la fiesta de cumpleaños? (*haber*)

**ANSWERS**
**p. 223**

B. Change the verbs from the present to the imperfect. Remember that irregular verbs in the present are not necessarily irregular in the imperfect. (Write the verbs only.)

1. A ti **te conviene** ese préstamo.

   _____

2. César **paga** todo con la tarjeta de crédito.

   _____

3. Ese banco **cobra** muchos intereses por el manejo de la tarjeta de crédito.

   _____

4. ¿Cuánto dinero **te falta** para pagar la cuenta?

   _____

5. Después de pagar la cuenta **me sobran** cinco dólares.

   _____

6. ¿Dónde **inviertes** tu dinero, en el banco o en la bolsa de valores?

   _____

7. José siempre **hace** fila en el banco.

   _____

8. Camila y yo **ahorramos** nuestro dinero en una cuenta de ahorros conjunta.

9. Mi hermano **gasta** mucho dinero en viajes.

   _____

10. El cambio del dólar al peso mexicano **es** muy bueno.

    _____

11. ¿Qué **piensas** hacer con la chequera?

    _____

12. Tú siempre **pagas** al contado todo.

    _____

13. Vosotros **tenéis** muchas acciones en la bolsa de valores.

    _____

14. Ella siempre **sale** a tiempo para el trabajo.

    _____

15. Yo no **conozco** ese banco digital.

    _____

---

## GRAMMAR III — Los verbos hacer y llevar con expresiones de tiempo • Los números ordinales • hacer + (*time expressions*) + **que** + (*present tense*) • **llevar** + (*time expressions*) + (**de**) • (*Ordinal Numbers*)

A.

EXS: 1. **Hace tres años** que vivo aquí.
2. Vivo aquí **hace tres años**.
3. Vivo aquí *desde hace tres años*.

*(I have been living here <u>for three years</u>.)*

We use *hace* + (a time expression) + *que* + (the present tense) (see example 1) to express an action that began in the past and is still going on in the present. We omit *que* when the main verb precedes *hace* (see example 2). This construction can also be used with the preposition *desde* in front of *hace* (see example 3).

EXS: 1. **Hace un mes** que fui a Ecuador.
2. Fui a Ecuador **hace un mes**.

*(I went to Ecuator <u>a month ago</u>.)*

B. We use *hace* + (a time expression) + *que* + (the preterite tense) to express the time that elapsed between an action carried out in the past and the present time (see example 1). We omit *que* when *hace* + (the expression of time) follows the main verb (see example 2).

EXS: Hacía *una hora* que llovía.
Llovía **hacía** *una hora*.
Llovía desde **hacía** *una hora*.

*(It had been raining <u>for one hour</u>.)*

C. The construction *hacía* + (a time expression) + *que* + (the imperfect tense) is used to describe an action that began in the past and continued in the past (see example 1). We omit *que* when *hacía* + (the time expression) follows the main verb (see example 2). This construction can also be used with the preposition *desde* in front of *hacía* (see example 3).

D. *Hace* to express **ago** in Spanish. In order to express the idea of **ago** in Spanish you have two options:

Verb + hace + time  or
Hace + time + que + verb

EXS:

- Paola estudió en la biblioteca hace *media hora*.
- Hace *media hora* que Paola estudió en la biblioteca.
  *(Paola studied in the library half an hour ago.)*

- Ernesto terminó su maestría hace *5 años*.
- Hace *5 años* que Ernesto terminó su maestría.
  *(Ernesto finished his master's five years ago.)*

E. To find out how long an action has been taking place, use:

*Cuánto tiempo + hace + que + present tense of the verb*

EXS: *¿Cuánto tiempo hace que Manuel trabaja en el Banco Interamericano?*
*(How long has Manuel been working at the Interamericano Bank?)*
Hace *tres años* que Manuel trabaja en el Banco Interamericano.
*(Manuel has been working at the Interamericano Bank for three years.)*

To find out how long since an action took place:
¿Cuánto tiempo hace que usted terminó su maestría en negocios?
*(How long has it been since you finished your master's degree in business?)*
Hace *cinco años* que terminé mi maestría en negocios.
*(I finished my master's degree in business five years ago.)*

F. EXS: Ellos *llevan treinta años de* casados. = Hace *treinta años* que ellos se casaron.
*Llevo una hora en la oficina. = Hace una hora que estoy en la oficina.*

*Llevar* + *(a time expression)* is used without any other verb to indicate how long a person or a thing has been in a place. The preposition *de* is added if a job or a condition is added, like **de secretaria, de casado,** and so on.

# PRACTIQUE LAS EXPRESIONES CON HACER PARA EXPRESAR TIEMPO

**ANSWERS**
p. 223

1. *Hace* + (time expression) can be placed before or after the main verb. For example, another way to say *Hace un mes que empecé a trabajar en la compañía* is _____.

2. How do you express in Spanish: *I talked to my mother 20 minutes ago?*

   _____

3. In the sentence *No te veo desde hace un año,* the word _____ can be omitted without changing the meaning.

4. *Hace una hora se fue Juan* is incorrect; the linking conjunction _____ is needed before the main verb, *se fue.*

5. How do you ask this question in Spanish: *How long have you been studying at this university?*

   _____

6. The construction *hacía* + (time expression) requires the main verb to be in the _____ tense.

   EX: Hacía cinco años que José no _____. (*viajar*)

7. *Hacía dos días no trabajaba* is incorrect; the linking conjunction _____ is missing before the main verb *no trabajaba.*

8. How do you translate in English the following sentence: *Tú terminaste el proyecto hace tres horas?*

   _____

9. Another way to say *No trabajaba hacía dos meses* is _____.

10. *Llevar* + (time expression) is another way to convey the idea of being in a place. Another way to say *Hace diez minutos que estoy aquí* with *llevar* is _____.

# PRÁCTICA

**ANSWERS**
p. 223

The following questions are directed to you. Answer them using the cues given.

1. ¿Cuánto tiempo hace que Ud. vive aquí? (*cinco años*)

   _____

2. ¿Cuánto tiempo hace que Ud. viajó a Cuenca, Ecuador? (*ocho años*)

   _____

3. ¿Cuánto tiempo hace que Ud. trabaja en el banco? (*seis meses*)

   _____

4. ¿Cuántos tiempo hace que Ud. salió de su oficina? (*veinticinco minutos*)

   _____

5. ¿Cuántos días hace que Ud. no revisa su cuenta de ahorros? (*dos semanas*)

_____

6. ¿Cuánto tiempo hacía que no invertía dinero? (*un año*)

_____

7. ¿Cuánto tiempo hacía que Ud. no iba a la sucursal del banco? (*siete meses*)

_____

8. ¿Cuánto tiempo hacía que Ud. no retiraba dinero del cajero automático?
(*dos días*)

_____

# NÚMEROS ORDINALES

**A.** These are the ten ordinal numbers in Spanish. They are in numerical order: *first, second,* and so on. They agree in gender and number with the noun. After ten we use ordinary, or cardinal, numbers: **once, doce, trece.**

| | | | | |
|---|---|---|---|---|
| primero(a) | tercero(a) | quinto(a) | séptimo(a) | noveno(a) |
| segundo(a) | cuarto(a) | sexto(a) | octavo(a) | décimo(a) |

**1.** *Primero* and *tercero* drop the *o* when they precede a masculine noun.

EX: **Estamos en el *primer piso*,** no en el tercero.

**2.** The ordinal numbers can precede or follow the noun without change of meaning.

EX: **Leímos *el tercer capítulo*. = Leímos *el capítulo tercero*.** (*We read the third chapter.*)

**3.** To show the order of kings, queens, popes, we use ordinal numbers after the noun in speech, omitting the definite article. In writing we use Roman numerals for regnal and pontifical numbers. Regnal and pontifical numbers are never spelled out in writing.

EXS: **la reina Isabel II** (*segunda*)
      **el rey Carlos III** (*tercero*)

**B.** When giving the date, we use cardinal numbers for days of the month. They are preceded by the article **el,** and the noun **día** is usually omitted. Notice that in English the ordinals are used instead with days of the month.

EX: **Hoy es el (día) *5 (cinco) de marzo*.** (*Today is March [the] fifth.*)

**C.** The only ordinal number ever used for days of the month is **primero;** and even in this case, **uno** in some countries like Spain can be used instead of **primero.**

EX: **Hoy es el *primero* de enero. =** Hoy es el *uno* de enero.

# PRACTIQUE LOS NÚMEROS ORDINALES

**ANSWERS**
**p. 223**

1. The ordinal numbers are adjectives with four endings; they change in gender and _____ according to the noun.

   EX: **libro primero, fila** _____

2. The two numerals that drop the ending **o** are **primero** and _____.
   When is the ending dropped, before or after the masculine noun?
   _____.

3. The ordinal numbers can be placed before or _____ the noun they modify.

   EX: **El primer día** is the same as _____.

4. *Carlos I* is correct for *Charles the First* because Pontifical numbers are _____ in Spanish.

5. There are two ways to say the first of the month: _____.

# 11 Los problemas de salud
## (*Some Health Problems*)

---

## PALABRAS NUEVAS

| *Las partes del cuerpo* | *Parts of the Body* |
|---|---|
| la barbilla/el mentón | chin |
| la boca | mouth |
| el brazo | arm |
| el cabello | hair |
| la cabeza | head |
| la cadera | hip |
| la cara | face |
| las cejas | eyebrows |
| el cerebro | brain |
| la cintura | waist |
| el codo | elbow |
| el corazón | heart |
| el cuello | neck |
| el dedo | finger, toe |
| el diente | tooth |
| la espalda | back (person) |
| el estómago | stomach |
| la frente | forehead |
| la garganta | throat |
| el hombro | shoulder |
| el hueso | bone |
| el labio | lip |
| la mejilla | cheek |

| | |
|---|---|
| la muñeca | wrist; doll |
| el muslo | thigh |
| el músculo | muscle |
| la nariz | nose |
| los nervios | nerves |
| el ojo | eye |
| la oreja | (outer) ear |
| el párpado | eyelid |
| la patilla | sideburn |
| el pecho | breast |
| el pelo | hair |
| las pestañas | eyelashes |
| el pie | foot |
| la pierna | leg |
| la prueba | test/exam |
| los pulmones | lungs |
| la rodilla | knee |
| la sangre | blood |
| el tobillo | ankle |
| la úlcera | ulcer |

| *Los cinco sentidos* | *The Five Senses* |
|---|---|
| el gusto | taste |
| el oído | hearing |
| el olfato | smell |

| | | | |
|---|---|---|---|
| el tacto | touch | el remedio | remedy |
| la visión | sight | el resfriado/ catarro[6] | common cold, catarrh |
| *Otras palabras* | *Other Words* | la salud | health |
| la alergías | allergies | el seguro médico | health insurance |
| el antibiótico | antibiotic | los signos vitales | vital signs |
| el asma | asthma | el síntoma | symptom |
| el centro de salud | clinic | el sistema inmunológico | immune system |
| el/la cirujano(a) | surgeon | | |
| la clínica | clinic | la tarjeta | card |
| la consulta | doctor's consultation | la temperatura | temperature |
| el consultorio | doctor's office | la tensión arterial | blood pressure |
| la cura[1] | cure | el termómetro | thermometer |
| el/la dentista | dentist | la tos | cough |
| la dirección/el domicilio | address; home address | la vacuna | vaccine |
| | | la venda/el vendaje/ la curita/el esparadrapo | bandage, sticking plaster |
| el dolor | pain | | |
| la enfermedad | sickness/illness | la vitamina | vitamin |
| el/la enfermero(a) | nurse | | |
| ela enfermo(a) | ill/sick person | **Verbos** | *Verbs* |
| los escalofríos | chills, shivering | adelgazar(se) | to lose weight |
| el estrés[2] | mental stress | alegrarse | to be glad about |
| el examen médico | physical exam | aliviar | to relieve |
| la farmacia | pharmacy | arreglar | to arrange |
| la fatiga | fatigue | caerse | to fall |
| la fecha de nacimiento | birthdate | calmar[7] | to calm |
| | | calmarse | to calm down |
| la fiebre | fever | cubrir | to cover |
| la gripa/gripe[3] | flu | cuidarse | to take care of |
| el hospital | hospital | curar | to cure, heal |
| la indigestión | indigestion | descansar | to rest |
| la inyección | shot/injection | desmayarse | to faint |
| el jarabe | syrup | doler | to hurt/ache |
| el mareo[4] | dizziness, nausea | enfermarse | to get sick |
| el medicamento | medication | engordar(se) | to gain weight |
| la medicina | medicine | enyesar | to put in plaster |
| la náusea | nausea | estornudar | to sneeze |
| el/la optómetra | optometrist | estresarse | to stress |
| el/la paciente | patient | examinar | to examine/to test |
| la pastilla | tablet/pill | fortalecer | to strengthen |
| el/la pediatra | pediatrician | fracturarse | to fracture/to break |
| el peligro | danger | fumar | to smoke |
| la píldora | pill | inhalar | to inhale |
| la póliza | policy | marearse | to get dizzy |
| la presión arterial | blood pressure | molestar[8] | to bother, annoy |
| la radiografía | X-ray | | |
| la fórmula/receta[5] | Prescription; recipe | | |

| quitar[9] | to remove | obeso(a) | obese |
| quitarse | to take off/to move away, stay away | pálido(a) | pale |
| | | pulmonar | related to lungs |
| recetar/formular | to prescribe | saludable/sano(a) | healthy |
| respirar | to breath | sintomático(a) | symptomatic |
| salir negativo(a) | to come out negative | | |
| salir positivo(a) | to come out positive | *Expresiones* | *Expressions* |
| sufrir | to suffer | a lo mejor | perhaps |
| tomarse | to take | estar asegurado(a) | be insured |
| torcerse | to twist | estar embarazada | to be pregnant |
| toser | to cough | estar enfermo(a) | to be sick |
| | | estar estresado(a) | to be stressed |
| *Adjetivos* | *Adjectives* | guardar cama | to stay in bed |
| alérgico(a) | allergic | hacer inhalaciones | to inhale |
| calmado(a) | calm | llenar una receta | to write out a prescription |
| congestionado(a) | congested | | |
| delgado(a) | thin/slim | menos mal | thank goodness |
| débil | weak | no tener remedio | to have no solution |
| embarazada | pregnant | sentirse mejor/peor | to feel better/worse |
| enfermo(a) | sick, ill | ser alérgico(a) | to be allergic (to) |
| estomacal | related to the stomach | tener dolor (de) | to have pain/ache |
| | | tener fiebre | to have a fever |
| estresado(a) | stressed | tener mareos | to be dizzy |
| estresante | stressful | tener tos | to have a cough |
| fracturado(a) | broken | tomar asiento | to take a seat |
| grave | serious/grave | tomar la temperatura | to take the temperature |
| médico(a) | medical | | |

## NOTAS

1. *Cura* means *cure* as a feminine noun: **la cura.** However, *el cura* means *the priest,* as the person who "cures souls." Una *curita* o una *venda curita* is a sticking plaster.

2. *Estrés* was approved by the Real Academia for their dictionary in 1984 as the equivalent of *mental stress.* Hispanics have added the verb *estresar* and the adjective *estresante* and *estresado/a.*

3. *Gripe* is feminine in all forms of Spanish, but in some countries, they use **la gripa.** The official word for this illness is *influenza,* an Italian term.

4. *Mareo* is *dizziness.* It comes from *mar* (*sea*), but it applies to any kind of dizziness. The plural *mareos* is more common than the singular. The verb for *to get dizzy* is *marearse* as well as the expressions *tener mareos* and *dar mareos.*

5. *Receta* is not only *medical prescription,* but also (*cooking*) *recipe.* In other countries *medical prescription* is translated as a *fórmula médica.*

6. *Resfriado* is one of the many words for the common cold. Other words used in different countries are *resfrío, catarro, constipado.* Pay attention that in English

the word *constipated* refers to a digestive (bowel) problem. In Spanish *constipation* is *estreñimiento*.

7. *Calmar* means *to calm*, and the reflexive *calmarse* is *to calm down*. *Calma* is *calm* as well as *slowness*. *Tener calma* is *to be slow* as well as *to quieten down*.

8. *Molestar* is not *to molest* as the spelling suggests, but *to bother, annoy*. *To molest* is rendered as *abusar sexualmente*.

9. *Quitar* is not *to quit* as the spelling suggests; it means *to take away, remove, steal*. The reflexive *quitarse* is *to take off, to move away, stay away, disappear*. Notice that *quitarse, molestar, aliviar, calmar,* are conjugated like *gustar*, with an indirect object.

EX: **A mí se me quitó la tos con el jarabe.** (*My cough disappeared with the syrup.*)

# PRACTIQUE LAS PALABRAS NUEVAS

**ANSWERS p. 224**

A. Write *el, la, los,* or *las* before each noun.

| | | |
|---|---|---|
| 1. _____ cerebro | 6. _____ corazón | 11. _____ sangre |
| 2. _____ síntoma | 7. _____ alergias | 12. _____ nervios |
| 3. _____ salud | 8. _____ tos | 13. _____ pulmones |
| 4. _____ presión | 9. _____ garganta | 14. _____ náuseas |
| 5. _____ fiebre | 10. _____ inyección | 15. _____ enfermedad |

**ANSWERS p. 224**

B. Complete each sentence with one of the idioms below. Make the necessary adjustments.

| | | |
|---|---|---|
| *está enfermo/a* | *está estresado/a* | *tener calma* |
| *tenía mucha fiebre* | *tiene dolor de* | *sentirse mejor* |
| *guardar cama* | *está embarazada* | *tienen tos* |
| *es alérgico/a* | | |

1. El médico me dijo que debo _____ para descansar y sentirme mejor pronto.

2. Santiago no fue al colegio hoy porque _____. Su temperatura era de 104°F.

3. Mireya _____ cabeza hoy por eso necesita tomarse una pastilla para aliviarse.

4. La situación económica en el país no está bien y nosotros debemos _____ para no enfermarnos.

5. Marcelita está muy feliz porque _____. Ella siempre soñó con tener un bebé.

6. Pedro está en el consultorio del médico porque _____. Se siente cansado, está congestionado y parece que está un poco débil.

7. La doctora Ramírez _____ porque tiene muchos pacientes hoy y no tiene tiempo para descansar.

8. Uno de los síntomas de la gripa es que las personas _____.

9. Natalia _____ a los productos lácteos por eso no puede tomar leche y prefiere tomar leche de almendras.

10. Para _____, César hace ejercicios tres veces por semana.

**ANSWERS p. 224**

C. Complete each sentence with one of the words below. Make the necessary adjustments.

| jarabe | fatiga | pulmones | receta | presión | vacunas |
| farmacia | póliza | radiografía | | | vitamina |

1. Es necesario hacerte una _____ para ver si el hueso está roto o fracturado.

2. Las _____ son muy importantes para proteger la vida de los niños.

3. Las naranjas y limones tienen mucha _____ C, la cual ayuda a fortalecer el sistema inmunológico.

4. En Estados Unidos es muy importante tener una _____ de seguros para cubrir todos los gastos médicos.

5. Vamos a la _____ a comprar las medicinas.

6. Respiramos el aire por la boca y la nariz, pero los órganos encargados de procesar ese aire son los _____.

7. Mi tía sufre de _____ arterial muy alta por eso ella necesita tomar medicamentos.

8. Si sientes mucha _____, debes descansar unos minutos.

9. Danilo toma _____ cada vez que tiene tos.

10. El médico me escribió una _____ para llevarla a la farmacia.

**ANSWERS p. 224**

D. Write a synonym for each word or expression.

1. resfriado/a _____ 4. contento/a _____
2. gripe _____ 5. cansado/a _____
3. pastilla _____

**ANSWERS p. 224**

E. Write the noun that corresponds to each adjective.

1. alérgico/a _____ 6. pulmonar _____
2. estresado/a _____ 7. saludable _____
3. estomacal _____ 8. calmado/a _____
4. enfermo/a _____ 9. asegurado/a _____
5. fracturado/a _____ 10. sintomático/a _____

# DIÁLOGO   En el consultorio médico

*La señora Elsa Murcia no se siente bien y va al consultorio de su doctora.*

SEÑORA MURCIA:    Buenos días. Tengo cita con la doctora Vargas.

RECEPCIONISTA:    ¿Me da su nombre, por favor?

SEÑORA MURCIA:    Elsa Murcia.

RECEPCIONISTA:    ¿Fecha de nacimiento?

SEÑORA MURCIA:    16 de junio de 1965.

RECEPCIONISTA:    ¿Tiene usted seguro médico?

SEÑORA MURCIA:    Sí, aquí tiene mi tarjeta con la póliza del seguro.

RECEPCIONISTA:    Gracias. Espere por favor. Ya la llaman.

■ ■ ■

ENFERMERA:    Buenos días, señora Murcia.

SEÑORA MURCIA:    Buenos días, señorita.

ENFERMERA:    Le voy a tomar primero la temperatura y luego la tensión arterial.

SEÑORA MURCIA:    Yo sufro de hipertensión, siempre tengo la tensión alta.

ENFERMERA:    Su temperatura es de 104, quiere decir que tiene mucha fiebre. Y la tensión la tiene alta también 140/90. Lo normal es 120/80.

SEÑORA MURCIA:    Sí, no me siento muy bien hoy.

ENFERMERA:    Espero que se sienta mejor pronto. La doctora la verá en unos minutos.

■ ■ ■

DOCTORA:    Buenos días, señora Murcia. ¿Cómo está usted?

SEÑORA MURCIA:    Buenos días, Doctora Vargas. Le cuento que no me siento muy bien. Tengo dolor de garganta, congestión nasal, escalofríos, dolor de cuerpo, y tos. Además, tengo náuseas.

DOCTORA:    Sí veo que tiene bastante fiebre y tiene la presión alta.

SEÑORA MURCIA:    ¿Cree usted que tengo gripe?

DOCTORA:    Voy a tomarle una prueba para la gripe o influenza.*(unos minutos más tarde)*

SEÑORA MURCIA:    ¿Cómo salió la prueba?

DOCTORA:    Salió positiva. Sí tiene gripe. Necesita tomarse estos medicamentos que le voy a formular. También necesita mucho descanso y tomar muchos líquidos.

SEÑORA MURCIA:    ¿Necesito antibióticos?

DOCTORA:    Sí, por cinco días. Me parece que tiene una gripe fuerte. Con estos medicamentos usted va a sentirse mejor dentro de poco.

SEÑORA MURCIA:    Se lo agradezco mucho, doctora.

DOCTORA:    Bueno, a la cama y a descansar. Y siga las instrucciones para tomarse los medicamentos. Recuerde comunicarse con nosotros si no se siente mejor.

# DIALOGUE   *At the Doctor's Office*

*Elsa Murcia isn't feeling well and goes to her doctor's office.*

| | |
|---|---|
| MRS. MURCIA: | Good morning. I have an appointment with Dr. Vargas. |
| RECEPTIONIST: | May I have your name, please? |
| MRS. MURCIA: | Elsa Murcia. |
| RECEPTIONIST: | Date of birth? |
| MRS. MURCIA: | June 16, 1965. |
| RECEPTIONIST: | Do you have health insurance? |
| MRS. MURCIA: | Yes; here's the card with the policy number. |
| RECEPTIONIST: | Thank you. Please wait. They will call you in a moment. |

■ ■ ■

| | |
|---|---|
| NURSE: | Good morning, Mrs. Murcia. |
| MRS. MURCIA: | Good morning, Miss. |
| NURSE: | I'm going to take your temperature first and then your blood pressure. |
| MRS. MURCIA: | I suffer from hypertension; my blood pressure is always high. |
| NURSE: | Your temperature is 104, which means you have a high fever. And your blood pressure is also high, 140/90. Normal is 120/80. |
| MRS. MURCIA: | Yes; I'm not feeling very well today. |
| NURSE: | I hope you feel better soon. The doctor will see you in a few minutes. |

■ ■ ■

| | |
|---|---|
| DOCTOR: | Good morning, Mrs. Murcia. How are you? |
| MRS. MURCIA: | Good morning, Dr. Vargas. I'm not feeling very well. I have a sore throat, nasal congestion, chills, body aches, and a cough. I'm also nauseous. |
| DOCTOR: | Yes, I see you have a high fever and high blood pressure. |
| MRS. MURCIA: | Do you think I have the flu? |
| DOCTOR: | I'm going to test you for the flu. (a few minutes later) |
| MRS. MURCIA: | How did the test come out? |
| DOCTOR: | It came out positive. Yes, you have the flu. You need to take these medications I'm going to prescribe you. You also need plenty of rest and plenty of fluids. |
| MRS. MURCIA: | Do I need antibiotics? |
| DOCTOR: | Yes, for five days. I think you have a bad flu. With these medications, you'll feel better soon. |
| MRS. MURCIA: | Thank you very much, doctor. |
| DOCTOR: | Well, go to bed and rest. And please follow the instructions for taking your medications. Remember to contact us if you don't feel better. |

# PRÁCTICA

ANSWERS
p. 224

A. **La señora Murcia en el consultorio de la Doctora Vargas. Complete the story using the information from the dialogue.**

La señora Murcia va al consultorio de la Doctora (1) _____ porque no se siente bien hoy. Cuando llega al consultorio la recepcionista le pregunta el nombre y la (2) _____. Después la recepcionista le pregunta si ella tiene (3) _____ médico. La recepcionista le pide que espere un momento. Después la señora Murcia ve a la (4) _____. Ella le toma la (5) _____ y la (6) _____. La enfermera le dice a la señora Murcia que ella tiene una (7) _____ muy alta: de 104. Cuando la señora Murcia habla con la doctora Vargas le dice que algunos de sus (8) _____ son congestión nasal, dolor de cuerpo, dolor de (9) _____ y (10) _____. La doctora le hace una (11) _____ para saber si la señora Murcia tiene la (12) _____. El resultado de la prueba sale (13) _____. La doctora cree que se trata de un caso de gripe serio. Por eso le dice que debe descansar, tomar muchos líquidos y le receta (14) _____ por cinco días. La doctora le dice que con los (15) _____ pronto va a sentirse mejor.

ANSWERS
p. 224

B. **Answer** *true* **or** *false* **(T/F).**

1. _____ La enfermera necesita saber la fecha de nacimiento de la señora Murcia.

2. _____ La señora Murcia va al consultorio de la doctora Sánchez.

3. _____ La fecha de nacimiento de la señora Murcia es el 16 de junio de 1965.

4. _____ La enfermera le toma la temperatura y la presión arterial a la señora Murcia.

5. _____ La señora Murcia no tiene fiebre.

6. _____ La Doctora Vargas le hace una prueba para el embarazo.

7. _____ Algunos de los síntomas que tiene la señora Murcia son tos, congestión nasal, escalofríos y dolor de cuerpo.

8. _____ La prueba de la gripe salió positiva.

9. _____ La doctora piensa que la señora Murcia tiene una fractura.

10. _____ La doctora le receta unos antibióticos y le manda guardar cama por unos días.

ANSWERS
p. 224

C. **Complete each sentence with an appropriate word.**

1. Lo contrario de *salud* es _____.

2. Lo contrario de *(paciente) enfermo* es _____.

3. Con una _____ se pueden ver los huesos de una persona.

4. La enfermera toma la _____ para ver si uno tiene fiebre.

5. Lo contrario de *curarse* es _____ .

**ANSWERS**
**p. 224**
D. Write sentences using the following words in the order given. Make the necessary changes and add articles, prepositions, and so on. Use the present tense of the indicative.

1. síntoma/la señora Murcia /ser/tos/congestión nasal/y/dolor de garganta.

   _____

2. Carmencita/estar/pálido/porque/tener/gripe /.

   _____

3. Tú/tener/dolor/estómago /.

   _____

4. a Ud/doler/todo/cuerpo/porque/estar/enfermo /.

   _____

5. Nosotros/tomar/jarabe/para/tos/.

   _____

# GRAMMAR I   Contraste entre el pretérito y el imperfecto (*The Preterite and Imperfect in Contrast*)

A. Use of the preterite

There are two tenses in the indicative to refer to an action in the past: the preterite and the imperfect. In order to understand the difference, we must think of an action as having three stages: beginning, middle, and end. We use the preterite to mark the beginning or end of an action, or to show the whole action as a completed event.

EXS: **Ayer** la señora Murcia *fue* al consultorio de la Doctora Vargas a las 9:00 A.M. (*Yesterday Mrs. Murcia <u>went</u> to Dr. Vargas' office at 9:00 A.M.*) (Emphasis on the *beginning*: She went at nine, and we don't know how long the appointment took.)
La señora Murcia **llegó** a las 8:30 A.M. *(Mrs. Murcia <u>arrived</u> at 8:30 A.M.)* (Emphasis on the *end*: There is no action after 8:30 A.M.)
Camilo *vivió* en Costa Rica. *(Camilo <u>lived</u> in Costa Rica.)* (The whole action is completed.)

B. Uses of the imperfect

1. *Basic idea.* The imperfect shows the action in the middle or in progress, without any reference to the beginning or end. The English progressive form *was* + (-*ing* form of the verb) translates the imperfect best. Consider this tense as showing an action in its middle stage.

EXS: **Cuando ella llegó,** la doctora *no estaba* allí. (*When she arrived, the doctor <u>wasn't</u> there.*) (Her arrival occurred *in the midst* of the doctor not being there.)
Ella *trabajaba* en el hospital **en ese tiempo.** (*She <u>was working</u> at the hospital at that time.*) (She was *in the midst of working* there at some time in the past.)

2. *Habit.* We use the imperfect to indicate a habit in the past, since a habit is an action that occurs repeatedly as if it had no beginning or end. Its English equivalent is *used to* (+ verb).

EX: Mi tío Joaquín *fumaba* mucho. (*My uncle Joaquín <u>used to smoke</u> a lot.*)

3. *Description.* To describe people, things, or places in the past, we use the imperfect, even when the situation no longer exists.

EXS: La clínica *estaba* cerca de la estación del tren. (*The clinic <u>was</u> near the train station.*)
*Llovía* cuando **llegó** al consultorio de la doctora. (*<u>It was raining</u> when she arrived to the doctor's office.*)

4. *Time and age.* To tell time and age with *ser* and *tener,* respectively, the imperfect must be used. The preterite cannot be used in these instances, perhaps because "time" is always in the middle of its course and cannot be stopped.

EXS: Cuando llegó *eran* **las ocho y media de la mañana.** (*It <u>was</u> 8:30 A.M. when she arrived.*)
Cuando murió mi mamá *tenía* **setenta y dos años.** (*My mother <u>was</u> seventy-two when she died.*)

C. Combination of imperfect and preterite
It is very common to use the imperfect to indicate the background for the preterite, that is, to show an ongoing action in the background (imperfect) when something else happened in the foreground (preterite). Once again, the imperfect is better translated by the progressive form in English, and the preterite by the *-ed* past tense form.

EX: Cuando la enfermera *me examinaba,* la doctora **la llamó.** (*The doctor <u>called</u> the nurse when she <u>was examining</u> me.*)

# PRACTIQUE EL IMPERFECTO Y EL PRETÉRITO

**ANSWERS**
**p. 225**

1. An action or event has three stages: beginning, _____, and
   _____.

2. The word *imperfect* suggests that something was going on, but is still incomplete or unfinished. Actually, the imperfect tense shows the _____
   of an action, without reference to its beginning or _____.

3. The preterite shows the action as a whole upon completion, but this tense
   often points out either the _____ or the _____ of
   the action.

4. To describe places, people, and things in the past, we use the _____,
   because a description doesn't seem to have limits.
   EX: Roma _____ (*was*) una ciudad grande y _____ (*had*)
       monumentos muy bellos.

5. A habit is something unfinished and suggests repetition, as if it were in a
   middle stage. For this reason, we use the _____ for a habit
   in the past.
   EX: Mi abuelo _____ mucho café cuando _____ joven.
       (*beber/ser*)

6. Sometimes we picture a habit as a unit, a sum of many single actions. In
   this case we use the preterite. For example, Mi tía Inés _____ en
   muchas competencias de atletismo por muchos años. (*participar*)

7. To tell time in the past, do we use the imperfect or the preterite?
   _____. This is perhaps because time has no limits, it cannot
   be stopped.
   EX: Cuando llegué a la cita médica, ya _____ las diez de la mañana.

8. To tell someone's age with *tener*, do we use the imperfect or the preterite?
   _____.
   EX: Mi abuelita _____ dieciocho años cuando se casó.

9. The progressive form, as in *I was working*, shows the ongoing nature of the
   action. Is it best translated by the imperfect or the preterite? _____.

10. The ending *-ed*, as in *I walked two miles*, usually suggests the completion
    of an action. Is it best translated by the imperfect or the preterite?
    _____.

11. Very often the imperfect indicates the background for the preterite—that is, it
    shows an action that continued in the background (imperfect) when
    something else happened in the foreground (preterite).
    EX: Carlota _____ por la calle cuando _____ el accidente.
        (*ir/tener*)

# PRÁCTICA

ANSWERS
p. 225

**A.** Answer the questions in the preterite and in the imperfect, using the cues in parentheses.

1. ¿Dónde vivía su familia cuando usted nació? (*San José*)

   _____

2. ¿Cuántos años tenía su abuelo cuando murió? (*ochenta años*)

   _____

3. ¿Qué hora era cuando llegaste a tu cita médica? (*10:00 A.M.*)

   _____

4. ¿Quién llamó cuando yo estaba en el hospital? (*Estela*)

   _____

5. ¿Quién te tomó la presión arterial y la temperatura? (*la enfermera*)

   _____

6. ¿Con quién habló usted primero cuando llegó al consultorio? (*la recepcionista*)

   _____

ANSWERS
p. 225

**B.** Complete each sentence, using the imperfect or the preterite of the verbs in parentheses. (Remember that the imperfect is like the background of a picture and the preterite, the foreground.)

**En el siguiente párrafo se habla de la vida de la Doctora Vargas.**

La Doctora Sofía Vargas _____ (1 nacer) en San José, Costa Rica en 1972. Su abuela materna _____ (2 ser) inglesa y con ella _____ (3 aprender) el inglés al mismo tiempo que el español. Desde muy niña le _____ (4 gustar) jugar a ser una doctora y siempre _____ (5 entretenerse) curando a sus muñecas *(dolls)*. Cuando _____ (6 tener) quince años ella _____ (7 decidir) que quería estudiar medicina. La doctora Vargas _____ (8 comenzar) sus estudios de Medicina en San José y los _____ (9 continuar) en los Estados Unidos. Después de que _____ (10 terminar) sus estudios graduados, _____ (11 ir) a Londres y a España. Entre los años 2010 y 2020 la Doctora Vargas _____ (12 servir) en la organización Doctores sin Fronteras. Finalmente, ella _____ (13 hacer) su internado en un hospital de la ciudad de Heredia. Allí ella _____ (14 poder) hacer rotaciones en las áreas de pediatría y cirugía. Su experiencia _____ (15 ser) excelente.

**C.** *Dos estudiantes americanas en Costa Rica.* Complete the story with the preterite or imperfect of the verbs given. Read the entire paragraph first to get an understanding of the story; this will help you determine the correct tense.

Cuando Emily y yo _____ (1 *llegar*) ayer al hotel, ya _____ (2 ser) las once y media de la noche. Nosotras _____ (3 estar) muy cansadas del viaje, _____ (4 ducharse) y _____ (5 acostarse) en seguida. Esta mañana _____ (6 despertarse) temprano, y _____ (7 desayunar) muy bien. El día _____ (8 estar) nublado *(cloudy)*, pero _____ (9 hacer) mucho calor. Nosotras _____ (10 tomar) un taxi para ir a la Universidad Nacional. Después de varias horas de recorrer el campus de la universidad, _____ (11 estar) muy cansadas y _____ (12 tener) mucha hambre. _____ (13 ser) las 12:30 P.M. cuando _____ (14 ir) a almorzar al restaurante de la universidad. Mientras *(while)* _____ (15 almorzar) en el restaurante, _____ (16 comenzar) a llover y _____ (17 tener) que volver al hotel en autobús porque no conseguimos taxi. El autobús nos _____ (18 llevar) por muchas calles donde _____ (19 hacer) muchas paradas. Después de llegar al hotel, _____ (20 quedarse) dormidas hasta el otro día.

# GRAMMAR II El futuro del indicativo de los verbos regulares (*Future Indicative of Regular Verbs*)

**A.** The future tense is used to express a future action, event, or state. Unlike English that uses the auxiliary verb *will* or *shall*, in Spanish the simple future tense consists of one conjugated verb.

**B.** Memorize the future indicative forms of the verbs in the chart.

| Subject | *Hablar* | *Comer* | *Vivir* | *Ser* | *Estar* |
|---|---|---|---|---|---|
| yo | hablar é | comer é | vivir é | ser é | estar é |
| tú | hablar ás | comer ás | vivir ás | ser ás | estar ás |
| él/ella/Ud. | hablar á | comer á | vivir á | ser á | estar á |
| nosotros/as | hablar emos | comer emos | vivir emos | ser emos | estar emos |
| vosotros/as | hablar éis | comer éis | vivir éis | ser éis | estar éis |
| ellos/ellas/Uds. | hablar án | comer án | vivir án | ser án | estar án |

Note that:

1. The *infinitive* is the *future stem* for each verb: **hablar, comer, vivir, ser, estar.**

2. The endings are the same for all five verbs: **é, ás, á, emos, éis, án.**

3. Except for **-emos,** all the endings have an accent: **comeré** BUT **comeremos.**

4. The future endings are the same for regular and irregular verbs. Pay attention to the following verbs with an irregular stem in the future tense. It is important to memorize them.

   **decir = dir**

   **haber = habr**

   **hacer = har**

   **poder = podr**

   **poner = pondr**

   **querer = querr**

   **saber = sabr**

   **salir = saldr**

   **tener = tendr**

   **venir = vendr**

   EXS:  La doctora Vargas *vendrá* en unos minutos.
   (Dr Vargas *will come* in a few minutes.)
   Las enfermeras nos *pondrán* una vacuna contra la gripa.
   (The nurses *will give* us a flu shot.)
   Tú *saldrás* del hospital en una semana.
   (You *will be leaving* the hospital in a week.)

C. **Use of the future indicative and other ways of expressing future time**

   1. We use the future indicative to indicate an action that is supposed to occur at some time after the present moment.

      EX: La doctora *llegará* más tarde. (*The doctor will arrive later.*)

   2. A future action may also be expressed by the use of the present indicative.

      EX: La doctora *llega* más tarde. (*The doctor will arrive later.*)

   3. Frequency of usage of the three different ways of expressing future time varies from country to country. For example, the future indicative is used much more in Spain than in Latin America, where use of *ir a* plus the main verb prevails.

**D. Near future:** The construction *ir + a + infinitive* is used to express actions that are going to happen in the future. It is equivalent to English to be going + infinitive.

*Its use is widespread in many countries within everyday speech.*

EX: Yo *voy a ir* a la cita médica *mañana*. (I' *m going to go* to my doctor's appointment tomorrow.)

**E. Future of probability**

The future indicative is also used to indicate amazement or probability at the present time. Its English equivalent often has expressions like *I wonder, probably, can, must be.*

EXS: Sonia no vino a clase hoy. *Estará* enferma. (*Sonia didn't come to class today. Probably she is sick.*)
¿Qué hora *será*? (*I wonder what time it is [what time it can be].*)
No tengo reloj. *Serán* las tres de la tarde. (*I don't have a watch. It must be three o'clock in the afternoon.*)

**F. Some expressions of time with future tense.**

1. **A partir de la próxima semana/a partir del lunes/a partir del próximo año/a partir del primero de abril.** *(Starting next week/starting Monday/starting next year/from April 1st.)*

2. **Dentro de un tiempo.** *(in a while).*

3. **El lunes (martes, miércoles, etc.) que viene.** *(next Tuesday, Wednesday, etc.)*

4. **El próximo año, mes, etc.** *(Next year, month, etc.)*

5. **El próximo lunes, martes, etc.** *(next Monday, Tuesday, etc.)*

6. **En dos días, semanas, meses, etc.** *(in two days, weeks, months, etc.)*

7. **Esta noche** *(tonight)*

8. **Este fin de semana.** *(this weekend)*

9. **Hoy por la tarde.** *(this afternoon)*

10. **La próxima semana** *(next week)*

11. **Mañana** *(tomorrow).*

    EX: Te llamo **mañana** *(I will call you tomorrow.)*
    Pay attention that **mañana** also means morning: *por la mañana (in the morning)*

12. **Mañana por la mañana.** *(tomorrow morning)*

13. **Mañana por la noche.** *(tomorrow night)*

14. **Pasado mañana** *(the day after tomorrow)*

15. **Más tarde.** *(later)*

# PRACTIQUE EL FUTURO

**ANSWERS p. 225**

1. The stem of the future is the whole _____. For example, the stem of *tomarán* is _____; the stem of *seremos* is _____.

2. The endings are the same for all the verbs, but each person has a different ending. For example, *-é* means _____, *-ás* means _____, *-eis* means _____.

3. All the endings have an accent mark except the ending _____.

4. English usually needs the auxiliary *will* or the contracted *'ll* to form the future tense. How do you say *we'll visit* in Spanish? _____.

5. The word *future* is interpreted as an action that will take place after the _____ moment.

6. The future tense is not the only way to express a future action. In Spanish we can use the _____ tense as well as the future tense forms. For example, *Ella llegará mañana* is the same as *Ella _____ mañana.*

7. Another way to indicate a future action is using the present of the auxiliary _____ followed by *a* and by the infinitive of the main verb. For example, *Ella nos va a hablar mañana* carries the same idea as *Ella nos _____ mañana.*

8. To indicate that an action is probable at the present time, we could use one of the several adverbs such as *posible, probable, tal vez* (*maybe*), *quizás* (*perhaps*). However, in Spanish we can use the future tense to indicate the same idea of probability. For example, *Tal vez Mario está enfermo* could be rendered as <u>*Mario _____ enfermo.*</u>

# PRÁCTICA

**ANSWERS p. 225**

A. Write the following expressions in Spanish.

1. Tomorrow morning: _____
2. This weekend: _____
3. The day after tomorrow: _____
4. Starting next week: _____
5. Tonight: _____
6. Later: _____
7. In a while: _____
8. This afternoon: _____
9. Next Tuesday: _____
10. In five months: _____

**ANSWERS p. 225**

B. Complete each sentence with the correct future tense form.

1. La enfermera le _____ (tomar) la temperatura al paciente.
2. ¿Dónde _____ (trabajar-tú) el próximo año?

3. ¿Cuándo _____ (venir) Pablo y Martín?

4. _____ (salir-yo) pronto para ir a mi cita con el dentista.

5. Con este sol y este clima vosotras _____ (calentarse) muy rápido.

6. ¿Cuántos pacientes _____ (haber) en este hospital?

7. La doctora _____ (hacer) lo posible para ayudar a las personas enfermas.

8. Ustedes _____ (poder) venir también a la reunión sobre los nuevos tratamientos para la tensión.

9. La señora Murcia _____ (ver) a la doctora hoy por la tarde.

10. El próximo verano (nosotros) _____ a Costa Rica para estudiar medicina en la universidad. (viajar)

11. Después de la clase Esteban _____ con su novia. (encontrarse)

12. Lucía _____ con muletas por dos semanas. (caminar)

13. Los médicos te _____ el tobillo. (enyesar)

14. Los antibióticos te _____ a sentirte mejor pronto. (ayudar)

15. La doctora le _____ (dar) una receta médica al paciente.

**ANSWERS p. 226**

C. Let's practice *near future*: IR + A + Verb infinitive form. ¿Qué van a hacer estas personas?

**Modelo:** Alberto/correr 3 millas/por la tarde:

*Alberto **va a correr** tres millas por la tarde. (Alberto is going to run 3 miles this afternoon.)*

1. La señora Murcia/hablar con la doctora/más tarde

   _____

2. Julio/salir con sus amigos/el sábado por la noche.

   _____

3. Ximena y Andrea/asistir a una reunión/hoy por la tarde.

   _____

4. Nosotros/caminar por la playa/este fin de semana

   _____

5. Vosotras/trabajar en el consultorio/hasta tarde.

   _____

6. Tú/leer una novela interesante/el domingo por la tarde.

   _____

7. Yo/caminar con mi perro/esta tarde.

   _____

8. David/tomarse los antibióticos/durante los próximos cinco días.

   _____

9. La doctora Vargas/trabajar en el hospital/el fin de semana.

   _____

10. Ustedes/ir a la farmacia/por los medicamentos.

   _____

# GRAMMAR III   Las comparaciones de desigualdad (*Comparisons of Inequality*)

**A.** Comparisons with nouns, adjectives, and adverbs

| Spanish Structure | | | English Equivalent | | |
|---|---|---|---|---|---|
| más menos  +  { | (noun)<br>(adjective)<br>(adverb) | + **que** | more<br>less, fewer | + { | (noun)<br>(adjective)  +  **than**<br>(verb) |

EXS:

- Comparison with nouns:
  más/menos + noun + que
  Ella tiene *más <u>problemas</u> que* yo. (*She has more <u>problems</u> than I do.*)
- Comparison with adjectives:
  más/menos + adjective + que
  José es *más <u>alto</u> que* yo. (*José is <u>taller</u> than me.*)
- Comparison with adverbs:
  más/menos + que + adverb
  Caminas *menos <u>rápido</u> que* yo. (*You walk less <u>quickly</u> than I do.*)

Note that in English short adjectives and adverbs take the comparative ending -*er* rather than the adverb *more: happier, faster, funnier.*

**B.** Comparisons with numbers and amounts

| Spanish Structure | English Equivalent |
|---|---|
| **más menos  +  de  +** (number, amount) | more      +     than  +  (number, amount)<br>less, fewer |

EXS:  Adelgacé *más de* veinte libras. (*I lost <u>more than</u> twenty pounds.*)
Comí *más de* lo que quería. (*I ate <u>more than</u> I wanted.*)

**C.** Emphatic way to indicate an exact amount
no + (verb) + **más que** + (amount) → only + (verb) + (amount)
EXS:  1. No tengo *más que* cinco pesos. (*I have <u>only</u> five pesos.*)
2. Tengo *exactamente* cinco pesos. (*I have <u>exactly</u> five pesos.*)
Example 1 is more emphatic and more idiomatic than example 2.

**D.** Comparisons with verbs

| Spanish Structure | | | English Equivalent | | | |
|---|---|---|---|---|---|---|
| (subject)  +  (verb)  +  **más**<br>**que**<br>**menos**<br>**que** |  | + (Subject) | (subject)  +  (verb)  +  more  +  (Subject)<br>than<br>less<br>than |  |  |  |

EXS:  Ella **trabaja** *más que* yo. (*She works <u>more than</u> I do.*)
Ella **pagó** *menos que* yo. (*She paid <u>less than</u> I did.*)

# PRACTIQUE LOS COMPARATIVOS

p. 226

1. The expressions *más que* and *menos que* are used to compare nouns, verbs, adjectives, and _____.
   EX: Ellos corrieron _____ yo. (*more than*)

2. To compare numbers and general amounts, the expression _____ is used instead of *más que*, and _____ is used instead of *menos que.*

3. How do you complete the sentence *¿Bebió usted* _____ *cuatro vasos de agua ayer?* (*more than*)

4. How do you complete the sentence *En mi familia tenemos* _____ *20 parientes?* (*more than*)

5. Sometimes it's necessary to compare a general amount rather than an exact number. For example, the idea of *more than you think* is translated into Spanish as _____ lo que Ud. piensa.

6. The English ending -*er* added to an adjective or adverb is translated into Spanish by the full word _____. For example, *She is taller than I am* becomes in Spanish **Ella** es _____ **yo.**

7. In Spanish *un, una,* are indefinite articles as well as numbers for *one.* Therefore, it's a mistake to say *Tienes más que un computador.* It should be *Tienes* _____ *un computador.*

8. If I say *No tengo más que dos pesos,* how many pesos do I have exactly? _____

9. If I say *No tengo más de dos pesos,* I probably have fewer than _____, somewhere between one and two.

10. *Compraron exactamente tres termómetros is equivalent but less emphatic than No compraron* _____ *tres termómetros.*

# PRÁCTICA

**ANSWERS**
p. 226

A. Complete the sentences with the comparative forms.

1. La recepcionista se fue a casa _____ temprano _____ la enfermera. (*earlier than*)

2. ¿Tiene Ud. _____ veinte dólares en la billetera para pagar la consulta? (*more than*)

3. No puedo comprar los medicamentos hoy porque tengo _____ diez dólares. (*less than*)

4. Tú examinas a _____ pacientes _____ yo. (*more than*)

5. Nosotros trabajamos _____ horas _____ ustedes. (*less than*)

6. Mi esposa es _____ alta _____ yo. (*taller*)

7. La doctora Vargas trabaja _____ lo que Ud. se imagina. (*more than*)

8. Uds. compraron _____ medicamentos _____ la señora Murcia. (*less than*)

9. En realidad siempre comemos _____ lo que necesitamos.
   (*more than*)

10. Vosotros camináis _____ rápido _____ nosotros.
    (*faster than*)

**ANSWERS p. 226**

B. **Combine the sentences according to the example. Use the word in parenthesis to express the comparison.**

   EX: Ana compró tres medicamentos. Yo compré dos medicamentos.
   (*medicamentos*)
   *Ana compró **más medicamentos que** yo.*

   1. Pablo se rompió dos huesos en el accidente. María se rompió un hueso.
      (*huesos*) (*more than*)

      _____

   2. Mario estuvo enfermo y tuvo 102°F de temperatura. Sonia también estuvo enferma y tuvo 104°F de temperatura. (*fiebre*) (*less than*)

      _____

   3. Marcos tiene seis pies de alto. Laura tiene cinco pies y medio. (*Use the Spanish equivalent of "taller."*)

      _____

   4. Sara estudia mucho, pero su hermana Nora estudia poco. (*estudiar*)
      (*less than*)

      _____

   5. Tú trabajas cinco horas en el hospital todos los días. Yo trabajo 10 horas todos los días. (*horas*)(*more than*)

      _____

**ANSWERS p. 226**

C. **¿Qué piensas? (*What do you think?*) Write sentences with comparisons according to your own opinion. Use the word in parenthesis.**

   1. las mujeres/los hombres (*estar ocupados*)

      _____

   2. los carros 4×4/los carros híbridos (*ser mejores*)

      _____

   3. jugar voleibol/jugar tenis (*ser más fácil*)

      _____

   4. las futbolistas (*soccer players*)/las jugadoras de voleibol (*fracturarse*)

      _____

   5. los perros/los gatos (*amistosos = friendly*)

      _____

   6. En el consultorio de la doctora hay _____ _____ siete pacientes. (*more than*)

   7. Costa Rica tiene _____ _____ 6 millones de personas.
      (*less than*)

# 12 Los buenos hábitos y el deporte
## (*Good Habits and Sport*)

## PALABRAS NUEVAS

| | | | |
|---|---|---|---|
| la alimentación | diet | la carrera | race |
| la autoestima | self-esteem | . . .de carros | car race |
| el balón | ball | la cesta | basket |
| . . . de baloncesto | basketball ball | la cirugía | surgery |
| . . . de fútbol | soccer ball | la competencia | competition |
| . . . de voleibol | volleyball ball | el deporte | sport |
| el bate | bat | el/la deportista | athlete |
| la bicicleta | bicycle | la depresión | depression |
| el bienestar | well-being | la disciplina | discipline |
| el boliche | bowling | el/la entrenador(a) | coach/trainer |
| el calambre | cramp | el entrenamiento | training |
| el calmante | sedative/painkiller | el equipo | team |
| el campeonato | championship | el estadio | stadium |
| el campo | field | el estado de ánimo | mood |
| . . .de fútbol | soccer field | el/la finalista | finalist |
| . . .de golf | golf course | el gimnasio | gym |
| la cancha | court | el/la gimnasta | gymnast |
| . . . de baloncesto | basketball court | el/la golfista | golf player |
| . . .de béisbol | baseball field | el/la jugador(a) | player |
| . . .de fútbol | soccer field | la maratón | marathon |
| . . .de tenis | tennis court | la media maratón | half marathon |
| . . .de voleibol | volleyball court | el/la maratonista | marathon runner |

| | |
|---|---|
| los palos de golf | golf clubs |
| el partido/juego | game |
| los patines | skates |
| . . . para el hielo | ice skates |
| la pelota | ball |
| . . . de béisbol | baseball ball |
| . . . de golf | golf ball |
| . . . de tenis | tennis ball |
| las pesas | weights |
| la pista de atletismo | track and field track |
| la pista de carreras | race track |
| la pista de patinaje | skating rink |
| los primeros auxilios | first aid |
| la raqueta | racket |
| el/la tenista | tennis player |
| el torneo | tournament |
| el tratamiento | treatment |

| *Algunos deportes* | *Some Sports* |
|---|---|
| el atletismo | track and field |
| el baloncesto | basketball |
| el béisbol | baseball |
| el ciclismo | cycling |
| el correr | jogging/running |
| el esquí | ski |
| el fútbol | soccer/football |
| el fútbol americano | American football |
| la gimnasia | gymnastics |
| el golf | golf |
| el levantamiento de pesas | weightlifting |
| la natación | swimming |
| el parapente | paragliding |
| el patinaje | skating |
| . . .sobre el hielo | ice skating |
| el pickleball | pickleball |
| el senderismo | hiking |
| el tenis | tennis |
| el tenis de mesa | ping pong |

| *Verbos* | *Verbs* |
|---|---|
| anotar/marcar | to score |
| ayudar | to help |
| batear | to bat |
| bucear | to dive/diving |
| caminar | to walk/walking |

| | |
|---|---|
| competir | to compete |
| correr | to run/running |
| dejar de | to stop doing something |
| encestar | to score a basket |
| entrenar | to train/training |
| escalar | to climb/climbing |
| hidratarse | to hydrate |
| lanzar | to throw |
| lastimarse | to get hurt |
| levantar pesas | to lift weights |
| nadar | to swim |
| patear | to kick |
| prepararse | to prepare |
| saltar | to jump |
| vencer | to defeat |

| *Adjetivos* | *Adjectives* |
|---|---|
| activo(a) | active |
| extenuado(a) | exhausted |
| herido(a) | injured |
| sedentario(a) | sedentary |
| victorioso(a) | victorious |

| *Expresiones* | |
|---|---|
| al aire libre | outdoors |
| el tiempo libre | free time |
| empatar un partido | to tie in a game |
| entrenar con juicio | to train wisely/with discipline |
| estar a dieta | to be on a diet |
| estar en buena forma | to be in good shape |
| ganar un partido | to win a game |
| hacer calentamiento | to warm up |
| hacer ejercicios | to workout/to exercise |
| hacer estiramiento(s) | to stretch |
| hacer parapente | paragliding |
| hacer senderismo | hiking |
| lanzar la pelota | to throw the ball |
| mantenerse en forma | to stay in good shape |
| perder un partido | to lose a game |
| ponerse manos a la obra | to get down to business |

**NOTAS**

1. *Balón* is characterized by having a valve to be inflated. It will always be propelled by some part of the body and its size is larger than a *pelota*.

    EX: balón de fútbol (*soccer ball*) vs. pelota de tenis (*tennis ball*).

2. *Campo* refers to the *field* where athletes play some sports, but *campo* also means *countryside*.

3. *Carrera* in sports means *race* but it also means *career* in regard to a profession.

4. *Fútbol*, as a single word, refers to *soccer* (term used mainly in United States and Canada), and *football* (British English). *Fútbol americano* refers to *American football* in English.

5. *Cancha de fútbol* and *campo de fútbol* are both correct. In countries like Spain, *cancha* refers to a closed space and *campo* to an open space, such as an open field.

6. *Deportista, finalista, golfista, maratonista* are some of the few words ending in *ista* in Spanish. These nouns have the same ending for masculine and feminine. The article can be used to clarify if the noun is feminine or masculine. EX: *la* deport*ista*, *el* maraton*ista*.

    For the plural equivalent just add the s. EX: *los* deport*istas* o *las* deport*istas*

# PRACTIQUE LAS PALABRAS NUEVAS

**ANSWERS
p. 226**

**A.** Write *el, la, los,* or *las* before each noun.

| | | |
|---|---|---|
| 1. _____ autoestima | 6. _____ depresión | 11. _____ deportes |
| 2. _____ patinaje | 7. _____ cancha | 12. _____ maratón |
| 3. _____ natación | 8. _____ estadio | 13. _____ tenista |
| 4. _____ gimnasta | 9. _____ palos de golf | 14. _____ bienestar |
| 5. _____ golfistas | 10. _____ deportista | 15. _____ jugadoras |

**ANSWERS
p. 227**

**B.** ¿Cuál deporte es? Complete each sentence with one of the sports below.

| | | |
|---|---|---|
| *béisbol* | *baloncesto* | *tenis* |
| *fútbol* | *patinaje* | *ciclismo* |
| *natación* | *maratón* | *golf* |
| *fútbol americano* | | |

1. En cada equipo hay 5 jugadores que lanzan el balón a una cesta:

    _____

2. En este deporte los jugadores no pueden usar las manos sólo pueden usar los pies para patear el balón. El único que puede usar las manos es el arquero:

    _____

3. Hay nueve jugadores en cada equipo y usan un bate y una pelota:

    _____.

4. Para jugar este deporte se necesita una raqueta y una pelota:

    _____.

5. Para competir en este deporte se necesita una piscina:

_____

6. Los deportistas compiten con patines en este deporte:

_____.

7. Para practicar este deporte se necesita una bicicleta:

_____

8. Para participar en esta competencia de atletismo, los atletas necesitan correr muchas millas para poder terminarla:

_____

9. Tiger Woods es uno de los deportistas más famosos de este deporte:

_____

10. El equipo New England Patriots es muy famoso es este deporte:

_____.

**ANSWERS**
**p. 227**

C. ¿La cancha o el campo?

1. _____ de baloncesto.
2. _____ de béisbol.
3. _____ de voleibol.
4. _____ de fútbol.
5. _____ de golf.

**ANSWERS**
**p. 227**

D. Match the following verbs with the right sport.

1. encestar: _____
2. patear: _____
3. batear: _____
4. patinar: _____
5. correr: _____

# DIÁLOGO  Es bueno que nos pongamos en forma para la maratón

*Catalina, Raquel y Ema están preocupadas porque no están en forma y quieren participar en la maratón de Montevideo, Uruguay. Conversan en el gimnasio sobre sus hábitos y lo que necesitan hacer para prepararse bien para la maratón.*

CATALINA:  Chicas, estoy preocupada. No nos quedan muchos meses para la maratón de Montevideo y yo no me siento muy bien preparada.

RAQUEL:  Yo estoy en las mismas. Sé que necesito correr y entrenar con más disciplina. ¿Por qué no hacemos un calendario de entrenamiento entre las tres?

| | |
|---|---|
| EMA: | Me parece excelente idea. Yo también necesito entrenar con juicio. ¿Qué días de la semana y a qué hora les conviene entrenar? |
| CATALINA: | Es importante que entrenemos más o menos por 15 semanas para que estemos listas para la competencia. |
| RAQUEL: | Son muchas semanas, pero tenemos que hacerlo si queremos terminar la maratón sin problemas mayores. |
| EMA: | A mí me conviene correr los martes, jueves y domingos. Podemos también hacer ejercicios en el gimnasio. |
| CATALINA: | Esos días me parecen bien a mí también. Algo muy importante que tenemos que tener en cuenta es hacer suficiente estiramiento antes de empezar a correr para evitar calambres. |
| RAQUEL: | Estoy de acuerdo con los días también. Es importante que para cada entrenamiento llevemos suficiente agua para hidratarnos. Ustedes saben que el cuerpo pierde mucha agua cuando se corren muchas millas. |
| EMA: | ¿Les parece si levantamos pesas los lunes? Creo que nos ayudaría a fortalecer los músculos. |
| CATALINA: | Levantar pesas ayuda mucho. También es bueno que mantengamos una dieta balanceada de alimentación y durmamos bien. |
| RAQUEL: | Sí es verdad. El entrenamiento es intenso. Para las primeras cuatro semanas debemos correr aproximadamente de 20 a 30 millas y estoy preocupada porque yo no estoy en forma. |
| EMA: | No te preocupes que todas nos vamos a ayudar para prepararnos bien y estar en forma para la maratón. Estoy muy emocionada porque va a ser mi primera maratón. |
| CATALINA: | ¡Genial! Sé que vamos a disfrutar entrenar juntas y vamos a estar muy felices de poder participar en esta maratón tan importante. |
| RAQUEL: | ¡Pues manos a la obra! ¡A entrenar se dijo! |
| EMA: | ¡Listo! Nos vemos mañana para empezar. |

# DIALOGUE   *It is good that we get in shape for the marathon*

*Catalina, Raquel, and Ema are worried about not being in shape and they want to participate in the Montevideo Marathon in Uruguay. They talk at the gym about their habits and what they need to do to prepare well for the marathon.*

| | |
|---|---|
| CATALINA: | *Hey guys, I'm worried. We don't have many months left until the Montevideo Marathon, and I don't feel very well prepared.* |
| RAQUEL: | *I'm in the same boat. I know I need to run and train with more discipline. Why don't the three of us create a training schedule?* |
| EMA: | *I think it's a great idea. I also need to train wisely. What days of the week and at what time are best for you to train?* |
| CATALINA: | *It's important that we train for about 15 weeks so we're ready for the competition.* |

| | |
|---|---|
| RAQUEL: | *That's a long time, but we have to do it if we want to finish the marathon without any major problems.* |
| EMA: | *It's best for me to run on Tuesdays, Thursdays, and Sundays. We can also work out at the gym.* |
| CATALINA: | *Those days are fine for me too. Something very important we have to keep in mind is to stretch enough before starting to run to avoid cramps.* |
| RAQUEL: | *I agree about those days too. It's important that we carry enough water for each workout to hydrate ourselves. You know that the body loses a lot of water when running many miles.* |
| EMA: | *What do you think about lifting weights on Mondays? I think it would help us strengthen our muscles.* |
| CATALINA: | *Lifting weights helps a lot. It's also good to maintain a balanced diet and get enough sleep.* |
| RAQUEL: | *Yes, that's true. The training is intense. For the first four weeks, we have to run approximately 20 to 30 miles, and I'm worried because I'm not in shape.* |
| EMA: | *Don't worry, we'll all help each other prepare well and be in shape for the marathon. I'm very excited because it's going to be my first marathon.* |
| CATALINA: | *Great! I know we're going to enjoy training together and we're going to be very happy to be able to participate in this important marathon.* |
| RAQUEL: | *So, let's get to work! Let's train!* |
| EMA: | *I am ready! See you tomorrow to get started.* |

# PRÁCTICA

A. **Es bueno que nos pongamos en forma para la maratón. Complete the story using the information from the dialogue.**

Catalina, Raquel y Ema van a participar en una (1) _____ en la ciudad de (2) _____ en Uruguay. Las tres están preocupadas porque piensan que no están en (3) _____ y no les quedan muchos meses para (4) _____. Las tres prefieren los martes, jueves y (5) _____ para correr, pero los lunes para _____ (6). Catalina cree que es importante que entrenen aproximadamente por (7) _____ semanas. Raquel considera que es necesario que lleven suficiente (8) _____ para hidratarse durante los entrenamientos. Raquel sugiere correr de (9) _____ las primeras cuatro semanas. Ema está muy emocionada porque va a ser su (10) _____ maratón. Las tres están muy felices de entrenar y participar juntas.

B. **Answer *true* or *false* (T/F).**

1. _____ La maratón de Montevideo va a ser la primera para Ema.

2. _____ Las tres amigas van a participar en la media maratón.

3. _____ Catalina sugiere correr 10 millas las primeras cuatro semanas.

4. _____ Raquel recomienda hidratarse muy bien durante los entrenamientos.

5. _____ Ellas escogen los lunes, miércoles y sábados para correr.

**ANSWERS p. 227**

**C. Write the expression in Spanish.**

1. _to stay in good shape_: _____.
2. _to work out_: _____.
3. _to get down to business_: _____.
4. _to stretch_: _____.
5. _hiking_: _____.
6. _to be on a diet_: _____.
7. _outdoors_: _____.
8. _to warm up_: _____.
9. _paragliding_: _____.
10. _to win a game_: _____.

**ANSWERS p. 227**

**D. Circle the word that completes the idea correctly.**

1. Para hidratarse en una competencia es importante beber:
   a. cerveza.  b. vino  c. agua  d. leche
2. Una maratón tiene un recorrido de:
   a. 13 millas  b. 35.5 millas  c. 20 millas  d. 26.2 millas
3. Para mantener una buena salud y estar en forma, es necesario:
   a. beber mucho café  b. hacer ejercicios  c. Comer papas fritas
   d. ver mucha televisión
4. Tener una dieta balanceada quiere decir:
   a. comer muchos carbohidratos  b. comer mucha grasa
   c. comer frutas, verduras y proteínas con moderación
   d. tomar mucha leche
5. Para fortalecer los músculos, es bueno:
   a. levantar pesas  b. caminar  c. jugar tenis de mesa  d. nadar

# GRAMMAR I  Las comparaciones de igualdad • Los superlativos (_Comparisons of Equality • Superlatives_)

**A.** _Comparisons of equality_ are used to indicate that two people, things, or activities are equal in some way.

**B.** Comparisons with adjectives and adverbs

| Spanish Structure | English Equivalent |
|---|---|
| **tan** + (adjective) (adverb) + **como** | as + (adjective) (adverb) + as |

EXS:

Adjective: María es **tan** <u>alta</u> **como** yo. (_Mary is <u>as</u> tall <u>as</u> I am._)

Adverb: Ella corre **tan** <u>rápido</u> **como** yo. (_She runs <u>as</u> fast <u>as</u> I do._)

C. Comparisons with verbs

(verb) + **tanto** + **como** → (verb) + as much as

EXS:  Mario **no camina** *tanto como* tú. (*Mario doesn't walk <u>as much as</u> you do.*)
Ella **nada** *tanto como* yo. (*She swims <u>as much as</u> I do.*)

D. Comparisons with nouns

| Spanish Structure | English Equivalent |
|---|---|
| **tanto/tanta tantos/tantas** + (noun) + **como** | as much as many + (noun) + as |

Note that *tanto, tanta, tantos,* and *tantas* agree with the noun in gender and number.

EXS:  No tengo *tanto* dinero *como* tú. (*I don't have <u>as much</u> money <u>as</u> you.*)
No corro *tantas* horas *como* tú. (*I don't run <u>as many</u> hours <u>as</u> you.*)

E. Superlatives

Superlatives are used to express the highest or lowest degree of comparison among three or more entities.

Study the following examples carefully.

EXS:  **Juan es** *el más* alto **de** la clase. (*Juan is <u>the</u> tallest <u>in</u> the class.*)
**Valentina es** *la más* alta **de** la clase. (*Valentina is <u>the</u> tallest <u>in</u> the class.*)

Note that the articles (**el, la**) and the adjectives (**alto, alta**) have to agree with the nouns in gender and number. However, the most common mistake is to translate *in* by Spanish **en** instead of **de**.

EX:  **Marcos corre** *lo más* rápido posible. (*Mark runs <u>as fast as</u> possible.*)

In this case, the neuter article *lo* has no translation in English, just as the second *as* of the English equivalent has no translation in Spanish.

F. **Irregular comparatives and superlatives**

1. A few adjectives in Spanish—such as **bueno, malo, grande,** and **pequeño**—have the ending *-or* for the comparative (parallel to English *-er*). They can also form the comparative by using their regular forms in combination with other words: **más** + (adjetivo) + **que.** For example, **mejor que** = **más bueno que.**

These adjectives also have an irregular superlative besides **muy** + (adjective).

| Adjective | Comparative | Superlative | (English) |
|---|---|---|---|
| bueno | mejor | óptimo | good, better, best |
| malo | peor | pésimo | bad, worse, worst |
| grande | mayor | máximo | big, bigger, biggest |
| pequeño | menor | mínimo | small, smaller, |
| joven | menor | | smallest |
| viejo/a | mayor | | |

2. *Mayor* translates *older/oldest* when talking about people, and *menor* translates *younger/youngest*. In some countries *mayor* is used for *very old* (like a very old person), and as a noun *los mayores* means *ancestors*. *Antiguo/a* translates as *ancient* (*very old from a historical point of view*).

EXS: Mi hermana *es menor que* yo. (*My sister is <u>younger than</u> I am.*).

Las ruinas de Tikal en Guatemala son *más antiguas que* las ruinas de Machu Pichu en Perú. *(The ruins of Tikal in Guatemala are older than the ruins of Machu Picchu in Peru.)*

3. *Mejor* vs. *más bueno*: *Mejor* is the correct way to express *better*. It is used to indicate that something or someone is superior in quality or value. In some regions or colloquial contexts, *más bueno* may be used to refer to someone who is very kind or friendly (the character of the person).

EX: La señora María es *más buena* que la señora Alicia. La señora María tiene un buen corazón y ayuda a muchas personas todo el tiempo.

4. *Peor* vs. *más malo*: *Peor* is the correct way to express *worse*. In some regions or colloquial contexts, *más malo* may be used to refer to someone who is very malicious or unkind (the character of the person).

EX: Ese hombre es *más malo* que un criminal. Actúa de manera horrible con todas las personas.

G. *The superlative* expresses the idea of being the best in English. In order to form the absolute superlative, drop the final vowel of the adjective and add **ísimo/ísima/ísimos/ísimas.** Pay attention to gender and number agreement.

Juan está *altísimo*. = Juan está muy alto. *(Juan is very tall.) (adjective)*

EXS:

1. Miguel corre **rápido.** *(adverb)*

   *Rápido > rápid > rapidísimo*

   Miguel corre *rapidísimo*

   The accent changes to the ending ísimo/a/s

2. Esta competencia de atletismo está **difícil.**

   *Difícil > dificilísima*

   Esta competencia está *dificilísima*.

   Remember that if the adjective ends in a consonant, add *ísimo/a/s* directly to the singular form of the adjective.

# PRACTIQUE LA GRAMÁTICA

**ANSWERS**
**p. 227**

1. The comparatives tan, tanto, tanta, tantos, and tantas are completed with the word _____, which translates *as* in English.

   EX: Caminé **tanto** _____ tú.

2. *Tanto, tanta,* show the same gender and _____ the noun they modify.

   EX: *Tenemos _____ balones de fútbol* **como** *ustedes.* (*We have as many soccer balls as you do.*)

3. *Tan* is the short form of **tanto,** and it is used only in front of adjectives and

   _____.

   EX: *Tu equipo es _____ bueno* **como** *el mío.* (*Your team is as good as mine.*)

4. What English word is not translated in the expression *as much as?*

   _____

   EX: *I run as much as you do.* = *Corro _____ tú.*

5. How do you translate *older* if we are talking about people? _____.
   The same word is used for *oldest* with the articles *el, la, los, las.*

   EX: *Mi abuela es _____ de la familia.* (*oldest*)

6. How do you say *younger* in Spanish? _____. This word will
   change to the plural, for example, *Tengo dos hermanas _____ que yo.* (*younger*)

7. We can use the word _____ instead of **más bueno** to express **better,**
   and the word _____ instead of **más malo** to express **worse.**

   EX: *Tu equipo de baloncesto es _____ el mío.* (*better than*)

8. *Another way to say the superlative muy rápido in one word is _____.*

   EX: *Carlos camina _____. (very fast)*

9. How do you complete the sentence **Anita es la atleta más rápida**
   _____ **la competencia**? This means that the English equivalent *in* is
   not **en** in Spanish but _____.

10. The maximum speed on United States highways used to be fifty-five miles per hour.
    It is now seventy-five miles per hour in some states. You would tell a Spanish
    tourist that *La velocidad _____ es setenta y cinco millas por hora.*

# PRÁCTICA

ANSWERS
p. 227

A. Complete the sentence with the correct word.

   1. Sofía es _____ (*tan/tanta*) alta como su hermana, las dos miden
      cinco pies.

   2. El partido de voleibol que vimos ayer fue (*mejor/más bueno*)
      _____ que el partido que vimos la semana pasada. Me gustó
      muchísimo.

   3. El equipo de fútbol de Uruguay tiene _____ (*tantas/tantos*)
      jugadores buenos _____ (*como/que*) el equipo de fútbol de Paraguay.

   4. Alejandro es _____ (*más/mayor*) _____ (*como/que*)
      yo. Yo tengo 17 años y él tiene 25 años.

   5. Mi condición física está (*peor/más mala*) _____ que la tuya. No
      puedo hacer ejercicios todos los días y siempre me canso.

6. Emilio, corres _____ (*tanto/tantos*) _____
   (*que/como*) los otros atletas de tu equipo.

7. El campo de fútbol de mi universidad está en _____ (*peores/más mala*) condiciones _____ (*que/como*) el campo de fútbol de tu universidad.

8. Antonio ganó _____ (*tantos/tantas*) competencias _____ (*que/como*) yo.

9. El campo de golf es _____ (*más/tan*) grande _____ (*que/como*) la cancha de tenis.

10. El equipo de Cross-country practica (*más/tantas*) _____ horas que el equipo de béisbol. El equipo de Cross-country practica cuatro horas por día y el de béisbol tres.

**ANSWERS p. 227**

B. Change the comparisons from *más/menos . . .que* to *tan/tanto(s)/tanta(s). . . como*.

1. Nosotros entrenamos más que ellos.

   _____

2. Tú eres más alto que yo.

   _____

3. Paola nada menos horas en la piscina que Eugenia.

   _____

4. Miguel escala más montañas que Daniel.

   _____

**ANSWERS p. 228**

C. Translate into Spanish.

1. Running is as good as walking.

   _____

2. Exercising is better than doing nothing.

   _____

3. My coach (female) is as tall as me.

   _____

4. Sara trains in the gym as much as you (do).

   _____

5. We drink as much water as they (do).

   _____

6. Eduardo is very tall.

   _____

7. Juliana is very fast.

   _____

8. Mónica and Doris are younger than me.

   _____

9. Ricardo and César are older than you.

_____

10. This competition is very hard.

_____

# GRAMMAR II    Presente del subjuntivo de los verbos regulares y de los verbos que cambian de raíz • Usos del presente del subjuntivo (*Present Subjunctive of Regular and of Stem-Changing Verbs • Uses of the Present Subjunctive*)

I. Present subjunctive of regular and of stem-changing verbs

A. Unlike the indicative mood that is used to state facts and to express actions or states that the speaker considers to be real or definitive; the subjunctive mood is used to state the speaker's attitude toward events, as well as actions that the speaker considers as hypothetical or uncertain.

B. Memorize the present subjunctive of the verbs in the chart.

| Subject | *habl ar* | *com er* | *volv er* | *pens ar* | *ped ir* |
|---|---|---|---|---|---|
| yo | habl e | com a | vuelv a | piens e | pid a |
| tú | hables | com as | vuelv as | piens es | pid as |
| él/ella/Ud. | habl e | com a | vuelv a | piens e | pid a |
| nosotros/as | habl emos | com amos | volv amos | pens emos | pid amos |
| vosotros/as | habl éis | com áis | volv áis | pens éis | pid áis |
| ellos/ellas/Uds. | hablen | com an | vuelv an | piens en | pid an |

Note that:

• To form the present subjunctive, use the *yo form of the present indicative*, drop the final *-o* and add the subjunctive ending.

  EX:  Caminar> (yo) camino> camin > camine, es, e, etc.

• Verbs ending in **-ar** take the endings **-e, -es, -e, -emos, -éis, -en**, in the present subjunctive; whereas verbs ending in **-er, -ir**, take the endings **-a, -as, -a, -amos, -áis, -an**. The formal commands show the same switch of vowels: a → e, e → a.

• Stem-changing verbs show the same changes in the present subjunctive as in the present indicative: o → ue (**volver**)/e → ie (**pensar**).

• Verbs like **pedir, vestir,** and **seguir,** change *e* to *i* in all the persons.

• *Morir* and *dormir* change *o* to *ue* in all the persons except in the first- and second-person plural, where *o* changes to *u*: **duerma, duermas, duerman,** BUT **durmamos, durmáis**.

- Verbs like *sentir, divertir, convertir, preferir, sugerir, mentir,* show a double change: *e* changes to *ie* in all the persons except in the first and second plural, where *e* changes to *i*: **sienta, sientas, sientan,** BUT **sintamos, sintáis.**

C. The spelling rules for verbs in the present subjunctive are the same as those for verbs in the formal command.

1. *z → c* in front of *e*: comenzar → comience
2. *c → z* in front of *a*: convencer → convenza
3. *g → gu* in front of *e*: llegar → llegue
4. *gu → g* in front of *a*: seguir → siga
5. *c → qu* in front of *e*: tocar → toque
6. *g → j* in front of *a*: recoger → recoja (*pick up*)

II. Uses of the present subjunctive

The present subjunctive is generally used to express:

1. Will and influence
   EX: **La doctora Vargas *le recomienda* a la señora Murcia que descanse.**
2. Expectations, desires, and hope
   EX: **Mis padres *quieren* que yo estudie medicina.**
3. Requests and orders
   EX: **El entrenador *les pide* a los deportistas que levanten pesas.**
4. Emotion, opinions and attitudes
   EX: **A nosotros *nos molesta* que las personas fumen.**
5. Doubt, disbelief, denial
   EX: **Carlos *duda* que su hijo gane la carrera.**
6. Nonexistence
   EX: ***No hay deporte* que no sea difícil.**

III. The present subjunctive is used in sentences that have two clauses: the main clause (*with the verb in the present indicative*) and a subordinate clause (*with the verb in the present subjunctive*). The main clause has a verb that requires the use of the subjunctive in the subordinate clause. Both clauses are connected by the conjunction *que*.

   EX: **El entrenador quiere <u>que</u> practiquemos todos los días.** (*The coach wants us to practice every day.*)
   Main clause: *el entrenador quiere*
   Connector: *que*
   Subordinate clause: *practiquemos todos los días*
   Notice in the example that there are two clauses, ***each with a different subject***. In order to use the subjunctive mood, both clauses need to have different subjects.

Subject 1: *el entrenador*

Subject 2: *nosotros*

EX: **Es importante que tú hagas ejercicios tres veces por semana.** *(It is important that you exercise three times a week.)*
Main: *es importante* (subject 1: *impersonal*)
Conjuction: *que*
Subordinate: *tú hagas ejercicios* (subject 2: *tú*)

When there is only one subject, use the verb of the subordinate clause in the infinitive instead of the subjunctive.

EX: **Ustedes quieren** *participar* **en la competencia.** *(You want to participate in the competition.)*

When you are using impersonal expressions such as *es necesario, es importante, es bueno,* and *es mejor,* and you are not addressing or speaking about someone in particular, use the infinitive in the subordinate clause instead of the subjunctive.

EXS: **Es mejor** *comer* frutas. *(It is better to eat fruits.)*
**Es mejor que** *comas* frutas. *(It is better that (for) you to eat fruits.)*

**Los doctores recomiendan** *dormir* 8 horas todos los días. *(Doctors recommend sleeping 8 hours every day.)*
**El doctor le recomienda a Camilo que** *duerma* 8 horas todos los días. *(The doctor recommends that Camilo sleep 8 hours every day./The doctor recommends Camilo to sleep 8 hours every day.)*

# PRACTIQUE EL SUBJUNTIVO

1. Verbs ending in **-ar** change the *a* to _____ in the present subjunctive, and verbs ending in **-er, -ir,** change *e* or *i* to _____.
EX: **hablar** → _____. **Vivir** → _____

2. If the verb in the main clause expresses a wish or a request, the subordinate clause should be in _____.

3. To use the subjunctive, it is necessary to have a _____ subject in each clause of the sentence.

4. *Volver* changes the stem **volv-** to _____ in the present indicative as well as in the present subjunctive: **volver → vuelvo →** _____.
However, there is no change in the first- and second-person plural: **volvamos, volváis.**

5. *Sentarse* changes the stem *e* to *ie* in all the persons of the present subjunctive, except nosotros/as and vosotros/as.

EX: Quiero que *te sientes* aquí./Ellos quieren que nosotros *nos sentemos* aquí.
La doctora quiere que la paciente _____ en la sala de espera.
La doctora quiere que vosotras _____ en la sala de espera.

6. *Pedir* changes the vowel *e* in the stem into _____ in all the persons of the present subjunctive: **tú** _____, **nosotros/as** _____.

7. *Dormir* and *morir* show a double change in the present subjunctive: *o* in the stem changes to *ue* in all the persons except in the first and _____: **yo duerma** → **nosotros/as** _____ and **vosotros/as** _____.

8. *Sentir, divertir,* too, show a double change: *e* changes to *ie* in all the persons except in the first and second-person plural, where *e* becomes *i*: **yo sienta** → **nosotros/as** _____.

9. Many verbs have spelling changes because they follow general rules of spelling in Spanish. These same rules apply to the preterite, where we have the ending -*é*. For example, *z* changes to _____ in front of *e*: **comenzar** → **yo** _____.

10. *Seguir* has a silent *u*. This *u* disappears in front of *o* (**sigo**) and in front of _____ in the present subjunctive: **yo** _____.

11. The last *c* of *practicar* and other verbs ending in -**car** change *c* to *qu* in front of the vowel _____ in the present subjunctive. Usted: _____ (**practicar**).

12. Have you noticed that the only difference between the first person of the preterite and the present subjunctive in -**ar** verbs is a written accent? **hablé** → **hable**. Show this contrast with *llegar*: _____ → _____.

# PRÁCTICA

**ANSWERS p. 228**

A. Conjugate the following verbs in the present subjunctive.

1. sentir: que yo. . . _____
2. poner: que nosotros. . . _____
3. marcar: que el equipo. . . _____
4. caminar: que vosotras. . . _____
5. competir: que Luisa y Mireya. . . _____
6. escalar: que tú. . . _____
7. lastimarse: que David. . . _____
8. nadar: que Emilia. . . _____
9. servir: que las jugadoras. . . _____
10. sentarse: que Ernesto. . . _____
11. jugar: que ustedes. . . _____
12. comenzar: que el partido. . . _____
13. beber: que nosotras . . . _____
14. comer: que yo. . . . _____
15. aliviarse: que vosotros. . . . _____

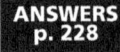

B. You work in your doctor's office. You are repeating what the doctor wants his patients to do and not to do. Use the verbs suggested in the present subjunctive. **El doctor quiere que. . .**

   1. yo _____ una dieta balanceada. *(seguir)*

   2. usted _____ ocho vasos de agua tres al día. *(tomar)*

   3. ella _____ temprano. *(acostarse)*

   4. nosotros _____ mejor de salud. *(sentirse)*

   5. ustedes _____ a verlo en tres días. *(volver)*

   6. tú _____ algunas libras de peso. *(perder)*

   7. mi padre _____ a trabajar menos horas. *(empezar)*

   8. Mi hermano y yo _____ más verduras. *(comer)*

   9. ustedes _____ la cuenta pronto. *(pagar)*

  10. tú no _____ tanto café. *(beber)*

**ANSWERS p. 228**

C. *¿Qué quiere la entrenadora de las jugadoras del equipo de voleibol?* Tell what the coach wants the volleyball players in the team to do or not to do. **La entrenadora quiere que las jugadoras. . .**

   1. no _____ tarde al entrenamiento. *(llegar)*

   2. _____ bien sus ejercicios. *(hacer)*

   3. _____ muchos puntos en el juego. *(marcar)*

 4–5. no _____ ni _____ dulces durante las prácticas. *(dormir/comer)*

   6. _____ con sus compañeras de equipo. *(hablar)*

   7. no _____ chicle durante los partidos. *(chewing gum).* *(masticar* = to chew)

   8. _____ voleibol cuatro días a la semana. *(practicar)*

   9. _____ bien por las noches. *(dormir)*

  10. _____ en los entrenamientos. *(divertirse)*

---

# GRAMMAR III  Los verbos irregulares en el presente del subjuntivo (*Irregular Verbs in the Present Subjunctive*)

A. Memorize the present subjunctive of the verbs in the chart.

| Subject | Sal ir | Conoc er | Ten er | Hu ir |
|---|---|---|---|---|
| yo | salg a | conozc a | teng a | huy a |
| tú | salg as | conozc as | teng as | huy as |
| él/ella/Ud. | salg a | conozc a | teng a | huy a |
| nosotros/as | salg amos | conozc amos | teng amos | huy amos |
| vosotros/as | salg áis | conozc áis | teng áis | huy áis |
| ellos/ellas/Uds. | salg an | conozc an | teng an | huy an |

Note that:

1. *Salir* and *tener* are irregular because they add *g* to the stems, just as they do for the first-person singular of the present indicative.

2. *Conocer* is irregular because it adds *c* to the stem after changing the last letter of the stem from *c* to *z*. Most of the verbs ending in *-cer, -cir*, have this same change: ofrecer, nacer, conducir, seducir, reducir.

3. *Huir* is irregular because it adds *y* to the stem. All the verbs ending in *-uir* have this same change: **construir, destruir, concluir, incluir, excluir.**

B. Memorize this list of the present subjunctive of irregular verbs. The present subjunctive stems stay the same for all the persons, singular and plural.

| caer | **caiga** | hacer | **haga** | saber | **sepa** | valer | **valga** |
|------|-----------|-------|----------|-------|----------|-------|-----------|
| dar | **dé** | huir | **huya** | salir | **salga** | venir | **venga** |
| decir | **diga** | ir | **vaya** | ser | **sea** | ver | **vea** |
| estar | **esté** | oír | **oiga** | traer | **traiga** | haber | **haya** |
| poner | **ponga** | tener | **tenga** | | | | |

1. Notice that **esté, estés, estéis, estén,** need an accent. From *dar* we have *dé* with an accent, which helps to differentiate it from the preposition *de.* The forms **des, de, demos, deis, den,** don't need an accent.

2. The same irregular forms that are used in the present subjunctive are also used in the formal commands: **traer → traiga Ud.** These same forms are used in the negative commands for the familiar *tú:* **traer → no traigas.**

3. Compound verbs show the same irregularities as the simple verbs from which they are derived: **mantener → mantenga/deshacer → deshaga/suponer → suponga.**

# PRACTIQUE EL SUBJUNTIVO

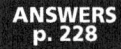
**ANSWERS p. 228**

1. *Preferir* is a stem-changing verb like *sentir.* The present subjunctive of *preferir* is yo _____ and **nosotros/as** _____.

2. *Conocer* and other verbs ending in *-cer, -cir,* are irregular because they add the letter _____ to the stem after changing the last letter of the stem from *c* to _____.

3. *Producir* is like *conocer.* The present subjunctive is **yo** _____; **nosotros/as** _____.

4. *Huir, concluir, destruir,* have the same irregularity: they add _____ to the stem. The subjunctive of *concluir* is **yo** _____.

5. Only two verbs have written accents in the present subjunctive: **estar** and **dar.** From *estar* we have four forms with an accent: _____/_____/_____/_____. And from *dar* we have only one form—that is, **yo, él/ella/Ud.** _____.

6. *Saber* is very irregular because it has **yo sé** in the present indicative, **yo supe** in the preterite, yo _____ in the future, and now yo _____ in the present subjunctive.

7. *Hacer* is another very irregular verb with many stems: **yo hago** in the present indicative, **yo hice** in the preterite, yo _____ in the future, and now yo _____ in the subjunctive.

8. *Decir* is another verb that is irregular in many tenses: **yo digo** in the present indicative, **yo dije** in the preterite, yo _____ in the future, and **yo** _____ in the present subjunctive.

9. From *hacer* we have **yo haga** in the subjunctive. *Satisfacer* is a compound of *hacer* (the old *facer*). The present subjunctive is yo _____.

10. From *tener* we have **tenga** in the subjunctive; from *mantener,* we have _____.

11. From *poner* we have **ponga** in the subjunctive; from *suponer,* we have _____.

# PRÁCTICA

**ANSWERS p. 228**

A. **Imagine that you are a doctor, and you are giving some advice to Mr. Jiménez to improve his health.**

Bueno Señor Jiménez, veo que usted tiene serios problemas de salud. Para mejorar su salud y para sentirse mejor, aquí están mis recomendaciones. (*Use the* **usted** *pronoun for the subjunctive*):

1. Le aconsejo que _____ (dejar) de fumar.
2. Es importante que _____ (beber) mucha agua.
3. Le recomiendo que _____ (caminar) por lo menos veinte minutos todos los días.
4. Le sugiero que _____ (comer) más verduras, vegetales y frutas.
5. Es necesario que no _____ (ver) mucha televisión.
6. Es bueno que _____ (salir) a unas vacaciones con su familia.
7. Quiero que _____ (venir) a visitarme dos veces al mes.
8. Espero que _____ (seguir) mis instrucciones.
9. Quiero que _____ (dormir) por lo menos 8 horas todas las noches.
10. Finalmente, deseo que _____ (sentirse) feliz.

B. You are given infinitives. Fill in the rest of the chart by writing the first person of the present indicative, the third person of the preterite, and the first-person plural of the present subjunctive for each verb. Follow the examples.

| Infinitive | Present Indicative (Yo) | Preterite (Él/ella/usted) | Present Subjunctive (Nosotros/as) |
|---|---|---|---|
| vestirse | me visto | se vistió | nos vistamos |
| sentir | siento | sintió | sintamos |
| 1. dormir | _____ | _____ | _____ |
| 2. servir | _____ | _____ | _____ |
| 3. subir | _____ | _____ | _____ |
| 4. salir | _____ | _____ | _____ |
| 5. nadar | _____ | _____ | _____ |
| 6. conocer | _____ | _____ | _____ |
| 7. seguir | _____ | _____ | _____ |
| 8. tener | _____ | _____ | _____ |
| 9. hacer | _____ | _____ | _____ |
| 10. practicar | _____ | _____ | _____ |
| 11. ir | _____ | _____ | _____ |
| 12. Jugar | _____ | _____ | _____ |
| 13. estar | _____ | _____ | _____ |
| 14. ser | _____ | _____ | _____ |
| 15. acostarse | _____ | _____ | _____ |

# ANSWERS   LESSONS 9–12

## Lesson 9

### Practique las palabras nuevas

A. 1. el   2. la   3. el   4. las   5. el   6. el   7. el   8. los   9. la   10. la

B. 1. los dientes   3. el cabello/el pelo   5. el cuerpo
2. la cara   4. las uñas

C. 1. to dry up   6. to comb one's hair
2. to get dressed   7. to try on
3. to brush one's hair   8. to shower
4. to wash one's hands   9. to shave
5. to put on make up   10. to get ready

## Práctica

## Una rutina típica en la casa de los Mendoza

A. 1. se levanta    3. se viste    5. se maquilla   7. se viste    9. se maquilla

   2. se ducha    4. se despierta   6. se cepilla   8. se cepilla   10. se pinta

B. 1. la pasta dental     3. el champú      5. la ducha

   2. la peinilla       4. el jabón

## Practique los verbos reflexivos

A. 1. subject/me/te      3. ¿ya te vas a casa?     5. reflexive

   2. se/se habla español     4. se            6. se sienta/se siente

B. 1. se afeita          6. se cepilla el pelo

   2. me acuesto      7. se ponen

   3. se despierta     8. nos vestimos

   4. se maquilla      9. te quitas

   5. os acostáis     10. se arreglan

C. 1. se   3. se   5. me   7. me   9. se   11. se   13. me   15. te   17. te

   2. se   4. se   6. me   8. se   10. se   12. se   14. nos   16. te   18. te

D. 1. NR   2. R   3. NR   4. R   5. NR   6. R   7. NR   8. NR   9. R   10. R

## Practique el *se* accidental

   1. se/nos     3. se/os     5. se/le     7. se/les     9. se/os

   2. se/te      4. se/me     6. se/les    8. se/nos   10. se/le

## Practique los reflexivos en pretérito

   1. se despertó     5. se maquilló     9. me acosté

   2. me levanté      6. se pusieron    10. se durmió

   3. nos duchamos    7. nos sentamos

   4. te vestiste      8. os enojasteis

## Práctica

A. 1. (A mí) se me cayó el jabón.

   2. A Teresa se le rompió la peinilla.

   3. A Martín se le olvidaron las gafas en la casa.

   4. A Ximena se le perdieron los aretes (pendientes).

   5. A Leonardo se le rompió el lavamanos.

   6. A Ana se le quedó el libro en casa.

   7. A Martín y a Ximena se les perdieron las llaves.

8. A Teresa se le acabó el champú.
9. (A nosotros) se nos olvidó la cita.
10. A Leonardo se le quedó el computador en casa.

B. 1. me bañé  4. desayunasteis  7. se pusieron  9. se comió
   2. te acostaste  5. se durmió  8. se quitó/entró  10. salimos
   3. se levantaron  6. dormimos

C. 1. me desperté  6. me desayuné  11. volví
   2. me levanté  7. salí  12. comenzó
   3. me bañé  8. llegué  13. explicó
   4. me sequé  9. oí  14. se cayó
   5. me vestí  10. almorcé  15. se destruyó

D. 1. le quedó  2. les acabó  3. le perdieron  4. nos rompió

# Lesson 10

## Practique las palabras nuevas

A. 1. la  4. la  7. los  10. las
   2. los  5. la  8. los  11. el
   3. la  6. la  9. el  12. las

B. 1. ahorrar  3. perder  5. pagar  7. prestar  9. retirar
   2. ganar  4. deber  6. gastar  8. depositar  10. solicitar

C. 1. préstamo  6. sucursal  11. transferencia
   2. ahorrar  7. cajero automático  12. en efectivo
   3. a plazos  8. crédito hipotecario  13. chequera
   4. moneda  9. aplicación  14. sueldo
   5. tarjeta de crédito  10. pérdidas  15. contraseña

D. 1. solicitó  3. pagaste  5. invertimos  7. cerré  9. gastó
   2. digité  4. redujisteis  6. prestó  8. depositó  10. ahorraron

E. 1. F  2. F  3. T  4. F  5. T  6. F  7. F  8. T  9. T  10. T

## Práctica

## Hablando de bancos y de finanzas

A. 1. banco  3. Nuevo Banco  5. sede  7. tarjeta de crédito  9. gratis
   2. transacciones  4. financieras  6. control  8. manejo  10. filas

**B. 1.** crédito hipotecario    **6.** interés
   **2.** tarjetas de crédito    **7.** préstamo
   **3.** chequera    **8.** tarjeta de crédito
   **4.** sueldo/salario    **9.** bolsa de valores
   **5.** gastar    **10.** cajero automático

**C. 1.** un cheque    **4.** la bolsa de valores
   **2.** dinero    **5.** contraseña
   **3.** ahorrar

## Práctica

**A. 1.** banco/me/me gustan    **3.** (b) A mí me gusta eso.    **5.** me parece buena
   **2.** third/le, les    **4.** my

**B. 1.** les parecen    **6.** os importa
   **2.** te pasa/me pasa    **7.** te queda
   **3.** me encanta    **8.** me preocupa
   **4.** le conviene    **9.** le molesta
   **5.** les fascina/les encanta    **10.** nos encanta

**C. 1.** A Carlos le interesan los deportes.
   **2.** A Maritza y a Guillermo les importa mucho la política.
   **3.** A vosotras os molesta mucho el ruido.
   **4.** A ti te quedan doscientos dólares en la billetera.
   **5.** A nosotros nos falta un año para graduarnos.

**D. 1.** Te amo.
   **2.** A mis amigos les gusta escuchar podcasts.
   **3.** A Susana le encanta hacer ejercicios en el gimnasio.
   **4.** Nosotros queremos a nuestros amigos.
   **5.** ¿Qué te pasa a ti hoy?
   **6.** A ti te fascinan (encantan) los chocolates.
   **7.** A Juan le encanta invertir dinero.
   **8.** Me interesan tus problemas.
   **9.** ¿Te gusto?
   **10.** Nos quedan $1000 en el banco.

## Practique el imperfecto

   **1.** -aba/gustaba    **4.** era    **7.** imperfect/going on
   **2.** -ía/bebía/salía    **5.** veía    **8.** había
   **3.** iba/íbamos    **6.** hablábamos/íbamos    **9.** imperfect

## Práctica

**A. 1.** ahorraban    **3.** eran    **5.** pagábamos    **7.** retiraban    **9.** me gustaba/era
   **2.** tenía/veía    **4.** estabas    **6.** salían    **8.** tenían    **10.** había

B. 1. te convenía
   2. pagaba
   3. cobraba
   4. te faltaba
   5. me sobraban

6. invertías
7. hacía
8. ahorrábamos
9. gastaba
10. era

11. pensabas
12. pagabas
13. teníais
14. salía
15. conocía

## Practique las expresiones con hacer para expresar tiempo

1. Empecé a trabajar en la compañía hace un mes.
2. Hace 20 minutos que hablé con mi mamá.
3. desde
4. que
5. ¿Cuánto tiempo hace que estudias en la universidad?
6. imperfect/viajaba
7. que
8. You finished the project three hours ago.
9. Hacía dos meses que no trabajaba.
10. Llevo diez minutos aquí.

## Práctica

1. Hace cinco años que vivo aquí./Vivo aquí desde hace cinco años.
2. Hace ocho años que viajé a Cuenca, Ecuador./Viajé a Cuenca, Ecuador hace ocho años.
3. Hace seis meses que trabajo en el banco./Trabajo en el banco hace seis meses.
4. Hace veinticinco minutos que salí de mi oficina./Salí de mi oficina hace veinticinco minutos.
5. Hace dos semanas que no reviso mi cuenta de ahorros./No reviso mi cuenta de ahorros desde hace dos semanas.
6. Hace un año que no invertía dinero./No invertía dinero desde hace un año.
7. Hacía siete meses que no iba a la sucursal del banco./No iba a la sucursal del banco desde hacía siete meses.
8. Hacía dos días que no retiraba dinero del cajero automático./No retiraba dinero del cajero automático desde hacía dos días.

## Practique los números ordinales

1. number/primera
2. tercero/before
3. after/el día primero
4. Are never spelt out in writing
5. primero/uno

# Lesson 11

## Practique las palabras nuevas

**A.** 1. el     4. la     7. las     10. la     13. los
    2. el     5. la     8. la     11. la     14. las
    3. la     6. el     9. la     12. los     15. la

**B.** 1. guardar cama     4. tener calma     7. está estresada    9. es alérgica
    2. tenía mucha fiebre    5. está embarazada    8. tienen tos     10. sentirse mejor
    3. tiene dolor de     6. está enfermo

**C.** 1. radiografía    3. vitamina    5. farmacia     7. presión     9. jarabe
    2. vacunas     4. póliza     6. pulmones    8. fatiga     10. receta

**D.** 1. catarro        3. tableta        5. agotado/a
    2. gripa         4. feliz

**E.** 1. alergia    3. estómago         5. fractura    7. salud     9. seguro
    2. estrés     4. enfermo (a)/enfermedad    6. pulmón    8. calma    10. síntoma

## Práctica En el consultorio médico

**A.** 1. Vargas           6. tensión (presión) arterial    11. prueba
    2. fecha de nacimiento    7. fiebre                  12. gripe (influenza)
    3. seguro              8. síntomas             13. positivo
    4. enfermera         9. garganta            14. antibióticos
    5. temperatura       10. tos/escalofríos/náuseas    15. medicamentos

**B.** 1. T    2. F    3. T    4. T    5. F    6. F    7. T    8. T    9. F    10. T

**C.** 1. enfermedad         3. radiografía     5. enfermarse
    2. (paciente) saludable    4. temperatura

**D.** 1. Los síntomas de la señora Murcia son tos, congestión nasal y dolor de garganta.
    2. Carmencita está pálida porque tiene gripe.
    3. Tú tienes dolor de estómago.
    4. A usted le duele todo el cuerpo porque está enfermo.
    5. Nosotros tomamos jarabe para la tos.

## Practique el imperfecto y el pretérito

1. middle/end
2. middle/end
3. beginning/end
4. imperfect/era/tenía
5. imperfect/bebía/era
6. participó
7. imperfect/eran
8. imperfect/tenía
9. the imperfect
10. the preterite
11. iba/tuvo

## Práctica

A.
1. Mi familia vivía en San José cuando yo nací.
2. Mi abuelo tenía ochenta años cuando murió.
3. Eran las 10:00 de la mañana cuando llegué a la cita médica.
4. Estela llamó cuando tú estabas en el hospital.
5. La enfermera me tomó la presión arterial y la temperatura.
6. Cuando llegué al consultorio hablé primero con la recepcionista.

B.
1. nació
2. era
3. aprendió
4. gustaba
5. se entretenía
6. tenía
7. decidió
8. comenzó
9. continuó
10. terminó
11. fue
12. sirvió
13. hizo
14. pudo
15. fue

C.
1. llegamos
2. eran
3. estábamos
4. nos duchamos
5. nos acostamos
6. nos despertamos
7. desayunamos
8. estaba
9. hacía
10. tomamos
11. estábamos
12. teníamos
13. eran
14. fuimos
15. almorzábamos
16. comenzó
17. tuvimos
18. llevó
19. hizo
20. nos quedamos

## Practique el futuro

1. infinitive/tomar/ser
2. yo/tú/vosotros/as
3. -emos
4. visitaremos
5. present
6. present/llega
7. ir/hablará (habla)
8. estará

## Práctica

A.
1. mañana por la mañana
2. este fin de semana
3. pasado mañana
4. a partir de la próxima semana
5. esta noche
6. más tarde
7. dentro de un tiempo (momento)
8. esta tarde
9. el próximo martes
10. en cinco meses

B.
1. tomará
2. trabajarás
3. vendrán
4. saldré
5. os calentaréis
6. habrá
7. hará
8. podrán
9. verá
10. viajaremos
11. se encontrará
12. caminará
13. enyesarán
14. ayudarán
15. dará

C. 1. La señora Murcia va a hablar con la doctora más tarde.

2. Julio va a salir con sus amigos el sábado por la noche.

3. Ximena y Andrea van a asistir a una reunión hoy por la tarde.

4. Nosotros vamos a caminar por la playa este fin de semana.

5. Vosotras vais a trabajar en el consultorio hasta tarde.

6. Tú vas a leer una novela interesante el domingo por la tarde.

7. Yo voy a caminar con mi perro esta tarde.

8. David va a tomarse los antibióticos durante los próximos cinco días.

9. La doctora Vargas va a trabajar en el hospital el fin de semana.

10. Ustedes van a ir a la farmacia por los medicamentos.

## Practique los comparativos

1. adverbs/más que    3. más de    5. Más de    7. más de    9. two
2. más de/menos de    4. más de    6. más/más alta que    8. Dos (*Two*)    10. más que

## Práctica

A. 1. más/que    3. menos de    5. menos/que    7. más de    9. más de
2. más de    4. más/que    6. más/que    8. menos/que    10. más/que

B. 1. Pablo se rompió más huesos que María en el accidente.

2. Mario tuvo menos fiebre que Sonia.

3. Marcos es más alto que Laura.

4. Nora estudia menos que Sara.

5. Yo trabajo más horas que tú en el hospital todos los días.

C. 1. Las mujeres están más (menos) ocupadas que los hombres.

2. Los carros híbridos (4 × 4) son mejores que los carros 4 × 4 (híbridos).

3. Jugar voleibol (tenis) es más fácil que jugar tenis (voleibol).

4. Las futbolistas se fracturan más (menos) que las jugadoras de voleibol.

5. Los perros (gatos) son más amistosos que los gatos (perros).

6. más de

7. menos de

# Lesson 12

## Practique las palabras nuevas

A. 1. la            6. la            11. los
2. el            7. la            12. la
3. la            8. el            13. el/la
4. la/el         9. los           14. el
5. los/las      10. el/la         15. las

B. 1. baloncesto 3. béisbol 5. natación 7. ciclismo 9. golf
    2. fútbol 4. tenis 6. patinaje 8. maratón 10. fútbol americano

C. 1. cancha 2. campo 3. cancha 4. campo 5. campo

D. 1. baloncesto 2. fútbol 3. béisbol 4. patinaje 5. atletismo

## Práctica

**Es bueno que nos pongamos en forma para la maratón**

A. 1. maratón 3. forma 5. domingos 7. 15 9. 20 a 30 millas
    2. Montevideo 4. entrenar 6. levantar pesas 8. agua 10. primera

B. 1. T 2. F 3. F 4. T 5. F

C. 1. estar en buena forma 6. estar a dieta
    2. hacer ejercicios 7. al aire libre
    3. ponerse manos a la obra 8. hacer calentamiento
    4. hacer estiramiento(s) 9. hacer parapente
    5. hacer senderismo 10. ganar un partido (juego)

D. 1. (c) agua
    2. (d) 26.2 millas
    3. (b) hacer ejercicios
    4. (c) comer frutas, verduras y proteínas con moderación
    5. (a) levantar pesas

## Practique la gramática

1. como/como 4. the second *as*/ 6. menor/menores 8. rapidísimo/rapidísimo
2. number/tantos    tanto como 7. mejor/peor/ 9. de/de
3. adverbs/tan 5. mayor/la mayor    mejor que 10. máxima

## Práctica

A. 1. tan 3. tantos. . .como 5. peor 7. peores. . . que 9. más. . . que
    2. mejor 4. mayor . . .que 6. tanto . . . como 8. tantas. . .como 10. más. . . que

B. 1. Nosotros entrenamos tanto como ellos.
    2. Tú eres tan alto como yo.
    3. Paola nada tantas horas en la piscina como Eugenia.
    4. Miguel escala tantas montañas como Daniel.

C. 1. Correr es tan bueno como caminar.

2. Hacer ejercicios es mejor que no hacer nada.

3. Mi entrenadora es tan alta como yo.

4. Sara entrena tanto en el gimnasio como tú.

5. Nosotros tomamos tanta agua como ellos.

6. Eduardo es altísimo.

7. Juliana es rapidísima.

8. Mónica y Doris son menores que yo.

9. Ricardo y César son mayores que tú.

10. Esta competencia es (está) dificilísima.

## Practique el subjuntivo

1. e/a/hable/viva
2. subjunctive
3. different
4. vuelv-/vuelva
5. se siente/os sentéis
6. i/pidas/pidamos
7. second-person plural/durmamos/durmáis
8. sintamos
9. c/comience
10. a/siga
11. e/practique
12. llegué/llegue

## Práctica

A. 1. sienta
2. pongamos
3. marque
4. caminéis
5. compitan
6. escales
7. se lastime
8. nade
9. sirvan
10. se siente
11. jueguen
12. comience
13. bebamos
14. coma
15. os aliviéis

B. 1. siga
2. tome
3. se acueste
4. nos sintamos
5. vuelvan
6. pierdas
7. empiece
8. comamos
9. paguen
10. bebas

C. 1. lleguen
2. hagan
3. marquen
4. duerman
5. coman
6. hablen
7. mastiquen
8. practiquen
9. duerman
10. se diviertan

## Practique el subjuntivo

1. prefiera/prefiramos
2. c/z
3. produzca/produzcamos
4. y/concluya
5. esté/estés/estéis/estén/dé
6. sabré/sepa
7. haré/haga
8. diré/diga
9. satisfaga
10. mantenga
11. suponga

## Práctica

A. 1. deje
2. beba
3. camine
4. coma
5. vea
6. salga
7. venga
8. siga
9. duerma
10. se sienta

B. 1. duermo/durmió/durmamos
  2. sirvo/sirvió/sirvamos
  3. subo/subió/subamos
  4. salgo/salió/salgamos
  5. nado/nadó/nademos
  6. conozco/conoció/conozcamos
  7. sigo/siguió/sigamos
  8. tengo/tuvo/tengamos
  9. hago/hizo/hagamos
  10. practico/practicó/practiquemos
  11. voy/fue/vayamos
  12. juego/jugó/juguemos
  13. estoy/estuvo/estemos
  14. soy/fue/seamos
  15. me acuesto/se acostó/nos acostemos

# 13 Una entrevista importante de trabajo

## (*An Important Job Interview*)

---

## PALABRAS NUEVAS

| | | | |
|---|---|---|---|
| la actuación | acting | la criminología | criminology |
| la agricultura | agriculture | el derecho | law |
| la antropología | anthropology | el desempeño | job performance |
| la beca | scholarship | laboral | |
| la bioquímica | biochemistry | el diseño | design |
| el blog | blog | *gráfico* | graphic design |
| el campo de | field of studies | *web y multimedia* | web design and |
| estudios/el área | | | multimedia |
| de estudios | | la educación | education |
| la cardiología | cardiology | *primaria* | elementary education |
| la carrera | career | *secundaria* | secondary education |
| | | los estudios | studies |
| *Las ciencias* | *Sciences* | *globales* | global studies |
| las ciencias de la | health sciences | *internacionales* | international studies |
| salud | | *interdisciplinarios* | interdisciplinary |
| las ciencias | political sciences | | studies |
| políticas | | la empresa | company/business |
| las ciencias | social sciences | la etimología | etymology |
| sociales | | la fábrica | factory |
| la compañía | company | la geología | geology |
| la contaduría | accounting | la hoja de vida/el | resume, curriculum |
| la cosmetología | cosmology | currículo | vitae (CV) |
| el crecimiento | growth | | |

230

| | | | |
|---|---|---|---|
| la ingeniería | engineering | analista | analyst |
| *biomédica* | biomedical engineering | arquitecto(a) | architect |
| *civil* | civil engineering | asesor(a) financiero(a) | financial advisor |
| *eléctrica* | electrical engineering | asistente | assistant |
| *industrial* | industrial engineering | autor(a) | author |
| *del medioambiente* | environmental engineering | bailarín/bailarina | dancer |
| *mecánica* | mechanical engineering | bibliotecario(a) | librarian |
| *química* | chemical engineering | biólogo(a) | biologist |
| *de sistemas y computadores* | computer engineering | bloguero(a) | blogger |
| el incremento | increase, increment | bombero(a) | firefighter |
| la informática | computer science | catedrático(a) | professor |
| la inteligencia artificial | artificial intelligence | campesino(a) | peasant |
| las leyes | laws | candidato(a) | candidate |
| la licenciatura | degree | cantante | singer |
| la lingüística | linguistics | carpintero(a) | carpenter |
| la literatura | literature | científico(a) | scientist |
| las matemáticas | mathematics | cocinero(a) | cook/chef |
| el mercadeo | marketing | conductor(a) | driver/conductor |
| el mercadeo digital | digital marketing | consejero(a) | advisor |
| la meteorología | meteorology | contador(a) | accountant |
| la música | music | cosmetóloga(a) | cosmetologist |
| la pasantía | internship | creador(a) de contenido | content creator |
| el periodismo | journalism | decano(a) | dean |
| el profesorado | faculty | dentista | dentist |
| el puesto (de trabajo) | job position | dermatólogo(a) | dermatologist |
| la química | chemistry | director(a) | director/manager |
| la radiología | radiology | ejecutivo(a) | CEO |
| la sastrería | tailor's shop | diseñador(a) | designer |
| la sociología | sociology | doctor(a) | doctor |
| la teología | theology | empleado(a) | employee |
| la veterinaria | veterinary science | enfermero(a) | nurse |
| | | escritor(a) | writer |
| *Vocabulario de las profesiones y oficios* | *Vocabulary for Professions and Occupations* | estilista | stylist |
| abogado(a) | lawyer | estratega | strategist |
| actor | actor | geólogo(a) | geologist |
| actriz | actress | gerente | manager |
| administrador(a) | manager | *general* | general manager/CEO |
| *...de empresas* | business manager/administrator | *de recursos humanos* | human resources manager |
| agricultor(a) | farmer | influyente | influencer |
| | | ingeniero(a) | engineer |
| | | locutor(a) | announcer |
| | | mecánico(a) | mechanic |
| | | médico(a) | physician/doctor |
| | | meteorólogo(a) | meteorologist |
| | | ministro(a) | minister |

| | | | |
|---|---|---|---|
| músico(a) | musician | despedir | to fire/to dismiss, to say goodbye |
| odontólogo(a) | dentist | dibujar | to draw |
| panadero(a) | baker | dirigir | to lead |
| peluquero(a) | hairdresser | diseñar | to design |
| periodista | journalist | experimentar | to experiment |
| pintor(a) | painter | gestionar | to manage |
| plomero(a) | plumber | hacer experimentos | to experiment |
| policía | police officer | mandar | to command/to order |
| político(a) | politician | manejar | to manage/to administer/to handle/to drive |
| presentador(a) de noticias | presenter news anchor | | |
| presidente | president | otorgar | to grant/to award |
| profesional | professional | participar | to participate |
| profesor(a) | professor/teacher | predecir | to predict |
| psicólogo(a) | psychologist | presidir | to preside |
| publicista | publicist | producir | to produce |
| radiólogo(a) | radiologist | pronosticar | to predict |
| rector(a) | principal/provost, vice-chancellor | solicitar | to apply for/to request |
| responsable de contenidos | content curator | transmitir | to convey/to transmit/ to broadcast |
| sastre | tailor | vigilar | watch over/guard |
| sociólogo(a) | sociologist | | |
| trabajador(a) | worker | | |
| veterinario(a) | veterinarian | *Adjetivos* | *Adjectives* |
| | | administrado(a) | managed/administered |
| | | analizado(a) | analyzed |
| *Verbos* | *Verbs* | apagado(a) | extinct |
| aconsejar | to advise | artístico(a) | artistic |
| actuar | to act | asesorado(a) | advised |
| analizar | to analyze | autoritario | bossy/authoritarian |
| apagar el fuego | to put out the fire | calificado(a) | qualified |
| aplicar el conocimiento | to apply knowledge | creativo(a) | creative |
| | | cuidadoso(a) | careful |
| asesorar | to advise | cultivado(a) | cultivated |
| administrar | to manage | desempleado | unemployed |
| bailar | to dance | detallista | detail-oriented |
| cantar | to sing | dirigido(a) | leaded/guided/ addressed |
| cocinar | to cook | | |
| considerar | to consider | ingenioso(a) | resourceful |
| construir | to build | metódico(a) | methodical |
| contar | to count/to tell | organizado(a) | organized |
| contratar | to hire | otorgado(a) | awarded/granted |
| coser | to sew | paciente | patient |
| crear | to create | producido(a) | produced |
| cultivar | to grow/to cultivate | recursivo(a) | recursive |
| cumplir las leyes | to achieve/to fulfill to comply with the laws | responsable | responsible |
| | | talentoso(a) | talented/gifted |

## NOTAS

1. *Aplicar (to apply)* is a false cognate. When referring *to applying for* a job position or a scholarship, or *to apply for* an institution or university, Spanish uses the verb *solicitar* instead (without translating the preposition *for*). *Aplicar* has a broader meaning in Spanish such as *to include, to put into practice, to administer, to apply something (like a theory, a cream, paint, sanctions, etc.).*

   EXS: Yo **solicité** una beca para estudiar en la universidad. (*I **applied for** a scholarship to study at the university.*)

   La señorita Flores **solicitó** un puesto en la compañía Globatek. *(Miss. Flores **applied for** a position at the Globatek company.)*

   Germán **aplica** todo el conocimiento que tiene en su proyecto. (*German **applies** all the knowledge he has in his project.*)

   La mamá le **aplicó** crema a su hijo para la infección de la piel. (*The mother **applied** cream to her son for the skin infection.*)

2. *Solicitud* is *application* in English.

   EX: Necesito llenar **una solicitud** para entrar a la Universidad Nacional. (*I need to fill out **an application** to enter at La Universidad Nacional.*)

3. *Colegio* means *school* and not *college*. **Colegio** is used in Spanish for an *elementary (primary) or a middle school. A high (secondary) school in Spain is **un instituto**.* For *college* or an institution of higher education, Spanish uses **universidad**. *Escuela* is used in some countries for *elementary or middle school.*

4. *Facultad* means *school* in an institution of higher education, and it doesn't mean *faculty.* EX: The business *school: La **facultad** de Negocios.*

   *Faculty* is **profesorado** in Spanish. EX: *El **profesorado** de la universidad Nacional.*

5. *Hoja de vida* is *resume* in English. Other synonyms are **currículo** or **curriculum vitae** (the Latin expression).

6. *Maestro/a, docente, profesor/a,* and *catedrático/a* are nouns related to education. In Spanish *maestro/a* may be used more when referring to someone that teaches at an elementary school. *Profesor/a* may be used to describe someone that teaches in a high school or a university, and *catedrático/a* is used for someone who teaches mainly in higher education. The word *docente* applies to all who teach. It is a general description related to education.

7. **Rector/a** *(principal)* refers to the person who runs a school.

# PRACTIQUE LAS PALABRAS NUEVAS

**ANSWERS**
**p. 292**

**A.** Write *el, la, los,* or *las* before each noun.

1. _____ diseñadora
2. _____ periodistas
3. _____ campesino
4. _____ influyente

5. _____ políticos
6. _____ dermatóloga
7. _____ policías
8. _____ creadores
de contenido

9. _____ derecho
10. _____ ciencias
11. _____ autor
12. _____ periodista

**ANSWERS**
**p. 292**

**B.** The ending -gy in English is translated in Spanish as *ía*. Write name of the occupation in Spanish.

EX: biology → biología.

1. sociology _____
2. psychology _____
3. anthropology _____
4. cardiology _____
5. dermatology _____
6. etymology _____

7. geology _____
8. theology _____
9. radiology _____
10. neurology _____
11. cosmetology _____
12. criminology _____

**ANSWERS**
**p. 292**

**C.** Complete each sentence with one of the words or expressions below. Make the necessary adjustments.

| | | |
|---|---|---|
| *veterinario/a* | *enfermero/a* | *psicólogo/a* |
| *cirujano/a* | *abogado/a* | *ingeniero/a civil* |
| *administrador/a de empresas* | *escritor/a* | *contador/a* |
| | *meteorólogo/a* | |

1. Este profesional escribe y es muy creativo en el campo literario.

   _____

2. Este profesional observa el comportamiento de las personas y las ayuda con terapias.

   _____

3. Este profesional presenta casos en la corte suprema de justicia.

   _____

4. Este profesional hace operaciones y cirugías en los hospitales.

   _____

5. Este profesional de la salud ayuda a los médicos con los pacientes.

   _____

6. Este profesional puede administrar o dirigir empresas y compañías.

   _____

7. Este profesional diseña y supervisa la construcción de puentes y de vías.

   _____

8. Este profesional analiza la información financiera de una compañía registrando los ingresos y los gastos.

   _____

9. Este profesional estudia el clima y la atmósfera y hace pronósticos sobre los cambios climáticos.

   _____

10. Este profesional ayuda a curar a los animales enfermos.

    _____

**ANSWERS p. 292** D. ¿Cuál es la palabra correcta?

1. _____ de la universidad trabaja en la investigación. (*la facultad/ el profesorado*)
2. _____ de enfermería de la Universidad Nacional es una de las mejores del país. (*la escuela/la facultad*)
3. _____ enseña educación primaria. (*la maestra/la catedrática*)
4. Necesito _____ una beca para estudiar en la Universidad Nacional. (*aplicar/solicitar*)
5. Mis amigos están muy felices estudiando administración de empresas en _____ (*el colegio /la universidad*).

**ANSWERS p. 292** E. ¿Qué trabajo u oficio tiene esta persona?

1. influir a muchas personas con los videos cortos y contenidos que crea para el internet: _____
2. Solucionar un problema con el agua en la casa: _____
3. Cortar y peinar el cabello para ir a una fiesta: _____
4. Cultivar frutas en el campo: _____
5. Manejar un camión para la compañía: _____
6. Apagar un incendio *(fire)*: _____
7. Ayudar y proteger a los ciudadanos *(citizens)* y vigilar que todos cumplan las leyes. _____
8. Hacer y crear vestidos muy elegantes: _____
9. Cocinar en un restaurante: _____
10. Poner maquillaje en la cara: _____
11. Escribir blogs sobre temas de actualidad: _____
12. Presentar la sección de noticias en la televisión: _____
13. Dirigir el funcionamiento de un colegio: _____
14. Enseñar clases en una universidad: _____
15. Cantar en un grupo musical: _____

# DIÁLOGO    Una entrevista importante de trabajo

*Daniela Flores es una ingeniera de sistemas recién graduada de la Universidad Autónoma de México. Hoy tiene una entrevista muy importante de trabajo con el gerente de la compañía Globatek, el señor Antonio Cruz.*

| | |
|---|---|
| SEÑOR CRUZ: | Buenos días, señorita Flores. Me llamo Antonio Cruz y soy el gerente general de la compañía Globatek de México. ¿Cómo está usted? |
| SEÑORITA FLORES: | Muy bien y gracias por invitarme a la entrevista. Es una oportunidad muy importante para mí. |
| SEÑOR CRUZ: | ¿Por qué está interesada en este puesto de trabajo? |
| SEÑORITA FLORES: | Pues cuando estaba buscando trabajo por las páginas del internet encontré que su compañía buscaba un profesional con mis estudios y mi perfil profesional. También me llamó mucho la atención que el trabajo tuviera la opción de trabajar de manera remota. Creo que la flexibilidad laboral es algo que muchos jóvenes de nuestra generación apreciamos mucho. |
| SEÑOR CRUZ: | Muy bien. Señorita Flores, usted menciona en su hoja de vida que tiene experiencia en el campo de la informática y que ha trabajado para su universidad también. ¿Podría explicar cómo fue esa experiencia? |
| SEÑORITA FLORES: | En la universidad tuve la oportunidad de hacer una pasantía con una compañía de sistemas durante tres veranos. Allí tuve la oportunidad de aplicar mis conocimientos en computadores al mismo tiempo que aprendí muchísimo con los ingenieros de planta que trabajaban allí. Creo que, para ser una estudiante, esa fue una gran experiencia para mí. |
| SEÑOR CRUZ: | ¿Señorita Flores, por qué considera que usted es la persona indicada para este puesto? |
| SEÑORITA FLORES: | Como le mencioné anteriormente señor Cruz, y como lo puede ver en mi hoja de vida, soy una persona muy responsable y calificada para este puesto. Mi desempeño académico y profesional han sido excelentes. Tengo excelentes cartas de recomendación. Además, soy una persona a la que le gustan los retos y el crecimiento profesional. |
| SEÑOR CRUZ: | Señorita Flores, ¿me podría decir cuáles son sus expectativas de sueldo con respecto a este trabajo? |
| SEÑORITA FLORES: | Con base en la información que tengo con respecto a los profesionales en mi área, me gustaría empezar ganando unos 18.000 pesos al mes. |
| SEÑOR CRUZ: | Sí, algunos de los ingenieros de nuestra compañía empiezan ganando entre 15 mil y 18 mil pesos al mes. Los incrementos salariales en la compañía se hacen con respecto al desempeño, |

méritos y excelencia del trabajador. ¿Señorita Flores, tiene alguna pregunta para mí?

SEÑORITA FLORES: Sí, gracias, Señor Cruz. Me gustaría saber cuáles son las políticas de la compañía con respecto a las vacaciones y a los beneficios de salud de los nuevos empleados. También quisiera saber si se puede trabajar por fuera del país. Sé que muchos de mis amigos están trabajando remotamente desde diferentes destinos.

SEÑOR CRUZ: La compañía ofrece dos semanas de vacaciones pagadas para los nuevos empleados después de un año completo de trabajo. También todos nuestros empleados están cubiertos con el seguro médico que nuestra compañía ofrece. Con respecto al trabajo remoto desde otro país, necesitaría hablar con la gerente de recursos humanos al respecto en caso de que usted sea contratada para este trabajo.

SEÑORITA FLORES: ¿Para cuándo podría recibir una respuesta sobre este puesto de trabajo?

SEÑOR CRUZ: Tenemos dos candidatos más para entrevista. Así que para la próxima semana ya tendremos la decisión sobre quién será el o la profesional que contrataremos. Muchas gracias, señorita Flores y déjeme decirle que fue un placer conocerla y entrevistarla.

SEÑORITA FLORES: De igual manera señor Cruz. Muchas gracias por la oportunidad para esta entrevista y quedo a la espera de cualquier noticia. Feliz día.

# DIALOGUE   *A Very Important Job Interview*

*Daniela Flores is a recent computer engineering graduate from the Universidad Autónoma de Mexico. Today she has a very important job interview with Mr. Antonio Cruz, the general manager of Globatek.*

MR. CRUZ: *Good morning, Miss Flores. My name is Antonio Cruz, and I am the general manager of Globatek Mexico. How are you?*

MISS FLORES: *Very well and thank you for inviting me to the interview. This is a very important opportunity for me.*

MR. CRUZ: *Tell me Ms. Flores, why are you interested in this position?*

MISS FLORES: *Well, when I was looking for a job online, I found that this company was looking for a professional with my education and professional background. I was also very interested in the fact that the job offered the option of working remotely. I think flexibility regarding the place of work is something that many people of my generation greatly appreciate.*

MR. CRUZ: *Very well. Ms. Flores, you mentioned on your resume that you have experience in the field of computer science and that you have also worked for your university. Could you explain what your experience was like?*

MISS FLORES:    Yes, of course. At university, I had the opportunity to be an intern with a computer company for three summers. There, I had the chance to apply my knowledge of computers while learning a lot from the plant engineers who worked there. I think, as a student, that was a great experience for me.

MR. CRUZ:    Ms. Flores, why do you think you are the right person for this position?

MISS FLORES:    As I mentioned earlier, Mr. Cruz, and as you can see from my resume, I am a very responsible and qualified person for this position. My academic and professional performance has been excellent. I have excellent letters of recommendation. In addition, I am a person who enjoys challenges and professional growth.

MR. CRUZ:    Miss Flores, could you tell me what your salary expectations are for this job?

MISS FLORES:    Based on the information I have regarding professionals in my field, I would like to start earning around 18.000 pesos per month.

MR. CRUZ:    Yes, some of our engineers in this company start earning between 15,000 and 18,000 pesos per month. Salary increases in the company are based on performance, merit, and employee excellence. Miss Flores, do you have any questions for me?

MISS FLORES:    Yes, thank you, Mr. Cruz. I would like to know what the company's policies are regarding vacation and health benefits for new employees. I would also like to know if it is possible to work abroad. I know many of my friends are working remotely from different locations.

MR. CRUZ:    The company offers two weeks of paid vacation for new employees after one full year of work. All our employees are also covered by the health insurance our company offers. Regarding remote work from another country, I would need to speak to the HR manager about this if you are hired for this position.

MISS FLORES:    When can I expect to hear back about this position?

MR. CRUZ:    We still have to interview two candidates. So, we'll make a decision on who we'll hire next week. Thank you very much, Miss Flores, and let me tell you what a pleasure it was to meet and interview you.

MISS FLORES:    Likewise, Mr. Cruz. Thank you very much for the opportunity for this interview, and I look forward to hearing from you. Have a great day.

# PRÁCTICA

**ANSWERS p. 293**

A. **Una entrevista importante de trabajo. Complete the story using the information from the dialogue.**

La señorita Flores es una (1) _____ de sistemas graduada de la universidad (2) _____. Ella tiene una (3) _____ de trabajo importante para la compañía (4) _____ de México. (5) _____

le hace la entrevista y le pregunta la razón por la que ella está interesada en el (6) _____. Ella le dice que buscó el trabajo por el (7) _____. Además, a ella le llama la atención que el trabajo tenga la opción de trabajar de manera (8) _____. En la hoja de vida, la señorita Flores menciona que tiene experiencia en el campo de la (9) _____. También ella puso en su hoja de vida que hizo una (10) _____ con una compañía de (11) _____, durante tres (12) _____. Con respecto al salario, a la señorita Flores le gustaría empezar ganando (13) _____ pesos al mes. El señor Cruz le dice que en la compañía los (14) _____ se hacen con base en el (15) _____, méritos y excelencia del trabajador. La señorita Flores le pregunta al señor Cruz sobre las (16) _____ de la compañía con relación a las (17) _____ y a los (18) _____. El señor Cruz le dice que la compañía ofrece dos (19) _____ de vacaciones a los nuevos empleados y también están cubiertos por el (20) _____.

**ANSWERS p. 293**

B. Circle the best answer.

1. La señorita Flores es una ingeniera (*civil, química, de sistemas, industrial*).

2. La señorita Flores buscó el trabajo en (*el internet, la universidad, el periódico, las redes sociales*).

3. El señor Cruz es (*médico, abogado, gerente general, contador*) de la compañía Globatek.

4. A la señorita Flores le gustaría tener un sueldo de (*18.000, 15.000, 20.000, 10.000*) pesos mexicanos al mes.

5. El señor Cruz dice que su compañía ofrece (*dos, una, tres, cuatro*) semana(s) de vacaciones a los nuevos empleados.

6. La señorita Flores menciona en su hoja de vida que ella hizo (*un trabajo, un estudio, un análisis, una pasantía*) en una compañía durante tres veranos.

7. El señor Cruz dice que tiene (*cinco, tres, uno, dos*) candidato(s) más para entrevistar.

**ANSWERS p. 293**

C. Write the adjectives in Spanish.

1. detail-oriented: _____.

2. recursive: _____.

3. qualified: _____.

4. unemployed: _____.

5. methodical: _____.

6. artistic: _____.

7. authoritarian: _____.

8. resourceful: _____.

9. patient: _____.

10. talented: _____.

# GRAMMAR I   El condicional de los verbos regulares
## (*Conditional Tense of Regular Verbs*)

**A.** The conditional in Spanish is used to express what a person *would do* or what *would happen* in a situation under certain circumstances.

It is used to hypothesize about a situation that is not part of the speaker's present reality. It is a possibility.

**B.** The conditional is similar to the English construction *would + verb*.

**C.** Memorize the conditional forms of the verbs in the chart.

| Subject | *Hablar* | *Comer* | *Vivir* | *Ser* | *Ir* |
|---|---|---|---|---|---|
| yo | hablar ía | comer ía | vivir ía | ser ía | ir ía |
| tú | hablar ías | comer ías | vivir ías | ser ías | ir ías |
| él/ella/Ud. | hablar ía | comer ía | vivir ía | ser ía | ir ía |
| Nosotros/as | hablar íamos | comer íamos | vivir íamos | ser íamos | ir íamos |
| vosotros/as | hablar íais | comer íais | vivir íais | ser íais | ir íais |
| ellos/ellas/Uds. | hablar ían | comer ían | vivir ían | ser ían | ir ían |

Note that:

1. The stem of the conditional, just like the stem of the future tense, is the full infinitive.

   EXS:  hablar → hablaría, comer → comería, vivir → viviría, ser → sería, ir → iría

2. The endings are the same for all the verbs: ía, ías, ía, íamos, íais, ían. Remember that these endings are the same as those of the imperfect tense of -er and -ir verbs. The conditional has one more syllable than the imperfect: comía → comería.

3. Just like the imperfect tense forms (**comía, comías,** and so on), all of the forms of the conditional take an accent mark to break the dipthong: **-ía**.

**D.** Uses of the conditional tense

1. The conditional (*would* + [verb]) is used to indicate an action that is supposed to occur sometime after a moment in the past, just as the future refers to an action that occurs after the time of speaking. The two tenses are parallel.

   EXS:  **Te prometo que *volveré*.** (*I promise you that <u>I will be back</u>.*)
   **Te prometí que *volvería*.** (*I promised you that <u>I would be back</u>.*)

2. We also use the imperfect tense of *ir a* + (verb) to indicate the same idea of the conditional.

   EX:  **Te prometí que *iba a volver*.** = Te prometí que *volvería*.

3. We frequently use the conditional in English to show a habit in the past. This conditional must be translated by the imperfect in Spanish, as we have studied before. The conditional never shows a habit in Spanish.

EX: **Cuando estaba en México, yo siempre *hablaba* español.**
(*When I was in Mexico, I <u>would speak</u> Spanish all the time.*)

E. Conditional of probability
The conditional is also used to indicate an action that was *probable* at a past moment, just as the future tense refers to probability at the present time.

EX: **La señorita Flores no vino a la entrevista. *Se enfermaría*.** (*Miss. Flores did not come to the interview. She <u>probably got sick</u>.*)

# PRACTIQUE EL CONDICIONAL

**ANSWERS**
**p. 293**

1. The stem used in the conditional tense is the full _____. For example, the conditional of the *yo* form of *estar* is _____.

2. The _____ of the conditional are the same for all the verbs: **ía, ías,** and so on.

3. The conditional has the same endings as the _____ tense of verbs ending in -er, -ir. For example, **escribía →** _____.

4. The difference between the imperfect and the conditional forms or -er and -ir verbs is one syllable. The conditional is always longer: **vivía →** _____.

5. We use the conditional to show that an action is supposed to happen after a moment in the _____, just as the future shows an action that takes place after the _____ of speaking.

6. The conditional tense can be replaced by the _____ of *ir a* + (verb). For example, **Me dijo que llegaría tarde. = Me dijo que** _____ **tarde.**

7. The conditional is used in English to show a habit in the past, just like *used to* + (verb). In Spanish the conditional is never used to show a habit. Instead, we use the _____.

8. To indicate probability at the moment of speaking, we use the _____, whereas to show probability in the past, we use the _____.

9. A more idiomatic way of saying *Ella estaba tal vez en la universidad is Ella* _____ *en la universidad*.

# PRÁCTICA

**ANSWERS p. 293**

A. Imagine what these people *would do* if they had their ideal job. Use the conditional form of the verb in parentheses.

Si tuviera (tuvieras, tuviéramos, tuvierais, tuvieran) *(had)* ese trabajo ideal. . .

1. La señorita Flores _____ en diferentes partes del mundo. (*trabajar*)
2. Yo _____ mucho dinero cada mes. (*ganar*)
3. Tú _____ todas tus tarjetas de crédito. (*pagar*)
4. Nosotros _____ un mundo diferente (*construir*)
5. Vosotras _____ más felices. (*ser*)
6. Esteban _____ en Australia. (*vivir*)
7. Marina y Lucrecia _____ de vacaciones todos los veranos. (*salir*)
8. Mis padres _____ a visitarme con más frecuencia. (*venir*)
9. Yo _____ más tarde todos los días. (*levantarse*)
10. Tú y yo _____ lugares exóticos. (*conocer*)
11. Samuel _____ a más personas pobres. (*ayudar*)
12. Ellos _____ mucho sobre inteligencia artificial. (*aprender*)
13. Nuestra situación económica se _____ pronto. (*mejorar*)
14. Ustedes _____ pagar los impuestos sin problema. (*poder*)
15. Vosotros _____ un carro nuevo. (*comprar*)

**ANSWERS p. 293**

B. Change each verb from the present indicative to the conditional. Remember that an irregular verb in the present is not necessarily irregular in the conditional. (You may want to go back to the infinitive.)

1. soy _____
2. otorgo _____
3. estás _____
4. vuelven _____
5. cumplimos _____
6. producís _____
7. conozco _____
8. despedimos _____
9. pago _____
10. aconseja _____
11. escribo _____
12. contratamos _____
13. diriges _____
14. solicitas _____

**ANSWERS p. 294**

C. Now change each verb from the preterite to the conditional. (You may want to go back to the infinitive to get the right stem for the conditional.)

1. entré _____
2. despidió _____
3. fue (*went*) _____
4. fue (*was*) _____
5. pidieron _____
6. solicitó _____
7. aconsejaste _____
8. contrataron _____
9. entrevisté _____
10. hablaron _____
11. estuve _____
12. trabajamos _____

# GRAMMAR II    El futuro y el condicional de los verbos irregulares (*Future and Conditional of Irregular Verbs*)

A. Memorize the future and conditional forms of the irregular verbs in the chart.

| Subject | Saber | | Venir | |
|---|---|---|---|---|
| | **Future** | **Conditional** | **Future** | **Conditional** |
| yo | sabr é | sabr ía | vendr é | vendr ía |
| tú | sabr ás | sabr ías | vendr ás | vendr ías |
| él/ella/Ud. | sabr á | sabr ía | vendr á | vendr ía |
| nosotros/as | sabr emos | sabr íamos | vendr emos | vendr íamos |
| vosotros/as | sabr éis | sabr íais | vendr éis | vendr íais |
| ellos/ellas/Uds. | sabr án | sabr ían | vendr án | vendr ían |

Note that:

1. All the verbs that are irregular in the future show the same irregularities in the conditional, with the same kinds of changes. For example, *sabré* and *sabría* are irregular because they drop the *e*: *saberé → sabré* and *sabería → sabría*.

2. *Vendré* and *vendría* are the irregular forms of *venir*. In this case the *i* is replaced by a *d*: instead of *veniré* the future is *vendré*, and instead of *veniria* the conditional is *vendría*.

B. Memorize the future and conditional forms of the twelve irregular verbs below.

| *Infinitive* | *Future* | *Conditional* | *Infinitive* | *Future* | *Conditional* |
|---|---|---|---|---|---|
| caber | cabré | cabría | querer | querré | querría |
| haber | habré | habría | saber | sabré | sabría |
| hacer | haré | haría | salir | saldré | saldría |
| decir | diré | diría | tener | tendré | tendría |
| poder | podré | podría | valer | valdré | valdría |
| poner | pondré | pondría | venir | vendré | vendría |

C. Compound verbs

The twelve verbs mentioned above have compound forms that show the same irregularities. Here is a partial list that you will encounter at different stages of your learning process. Notice that many of them have cognates in English.

| | | |
|---|---|---|
| **deshacer** to undo melt | **detener** to detain | **componer** to compose, fix |
| **rehacer** to redo, do again | **mantener** to maintain | **exponer** to expose |
| **satisfacer** to satisfy | **obtener** to obtain | **imponer** to impose |
| | **sostener** to sustain | **oponer** to oppose |
| | **convenir** to be convenient | **proponer** to propose |
| **abstener** to abstain | **prevenir** to prevent | |
| **contener** to contain | **provenir** to originate in (provenance) | **suponer** to suppose |

1. The compounds of *decir* are regular in the future and in the conditional.

   bendecir → bendeciré → bendeciría (*I will/would bless*)
   maldecir → maldeciré → maldeciría (*I will/would curse*)

2. *Caber* means to *fit in, to have room for.*

   EX: **En mi carro *caben* cuatro personas**. (*Four people fit in my car.*)

# PRACTIQUE EL FUTURO Y CONDICIONAL

1. The future form of *saber* is not *saberé* but _____. This means that the vowel _____ was dropped.

2. The conditional of *venir* is not *veniria* but _____. This means that the letter *i* was replaced by the letter _____.

3. Every verb that is irregular in the future is also irregular in the _____ For example, from *hacer* we have *haré* and _____.

4. From *querer* we have *quería* in the imperfect. In this case, the conditional is not a syllable longer as in *quererla,* because the vowel *e* is dropped, and the correct form is _____.

5. *Caber* means *to fit in.* How do you say *we won't fit in your car?* **No _____ en tu carro.**

6. *Satisfacer* is a compound of *hacer* (old Spanish *facer*). If the future of *hacer* is *haré,* the future of *satisfacer* is _____.

7. If the future of *tener* is *tendré,* the future of *contener* (*to contain*) is _____, and the conditional _____.

8. If the future of *poner* is *pondré,* the future of *suponer* (*to suppose*) is _____, and the conditional _____.

9. If the conditional of *hacer* is *haría,* the conditional of *rehacer* (*to redo*) is _____, and the future _____.

10. If the conditional of *poner* is *pondría,* the conditional of *oponer* (*to oppose*) is, _____, and the future _____.

# PRÁCTICA

A. Complete each sentence with the correct form of the future.

1. Javier y yo _____ para el aeropuerto a las 5:00 A.M. (*salir*)

2. Pasado mañana _____ una reunión de trabajo en la compañía. (*haber*)

3. El negocio con la compañía alemana _____ muy importante para el futuro de nuestra empresa. (*ser*)

4. El director ejecutivo _____ unas nuevas políticas para la compañía. (*proponer*)

5. Algunos empleados se _____ de participar en la protesta. (*abstener*)

6. La gerente de la compañía _____ a España la próxima semana. (*viajar*)

7. ¿Cuánto _____ los ingenieros de sistemas en México? (*ganar*)

8. Puedes invitar a la gerente de recursos humanos a la reunión; estoy seguro que _____ venir. (*querer*)

9. La señorita Flores solo _____ si van a contratarla hasta la próxima semana. (*saber*)

10. Estamos seguros que el señor Cruz le _____ buenas noticias a la señorita Flores. (*tener*)

**ANSWERS p. 294**

B. *If Señorita Flores got the job, she would do the following. . .* Complete each sentence with the conditional tense of the suggested verb. Use the third-person singular.

1. _____ en un apartamento más grande. (*vivir*)

2. _____ su carro viejo por uno más nuevo. (*cambiar*)

3. _____ con sus amigos con más frecuencia. (*salir*)

4. _____ excelentes resultados para la compañía. (*obtener*)

5. _____ menos estresada. (*estar*)

6. _____ en diferentes lugares del mundo. (*trabajar*)

7. _____ a muchos profesionales importantes en su área de trabajo. (*conocer*)

8. _____ mucho sobre inteligencia artificial. (*aprender*)

9. _____ un buen sueldo. (*recibir*)

10. _____ muchos proyectos interesantes. (*hacer*)

**ANSWERS p. 294**

C. Complete the text with the conditional.

A mi amigo Rafael le fascina la ingeniería civil. Le (1 encantar) _____ poder construir muchos puentes (*bridges*) en la ciudad de México. Dice que los puentes (2 ayudar) _____ a mejorar el tráfico en la ciudad y (3 facilitar) _____ la movilidad de muchas personas que viven en la capital. También, (4 hacer—él) _____ muchas mejoras en la infraestructura vial (*road infrastructure*) de la ciudad. Les (5 explicar—él) a los ciudadanos sobre la importancia de sus proyectos. (6 Unirse—él) _____ con otros ingenieros civiles. Ellos (7 construir) _____ proyectos y (8 mejorar) _____ el sistema vial de la ciudad.

Yo soy ingeniera de sistemas, y (9 tener) _____ interés en aprender más de la informática. (10 preferir) _____ quedarme en una oficina en frente de un computador para desarrollar mis proyectos. Tal vez mis amigos y yo (11 poder) _____ desarrollar más programas de inteligencia artificial.

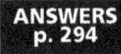

**D.** You have now studied the five tenses of the indicative: present, preterite, imperfect, future, and conditional. This exercise is a summary of these tenses. You have the present and the imperfect. Write the future and the conditional.

| Present | Imperfect | Future | Conditional |
|---------|-----------|--------|-------------|
| 1. vamos | íbamos | _____ | _____ |
| 2. somos | éramos | _____ | _____ |
| 3. estoy | estaba | _____ | _____ |
| 4. dan | daban | _____ | _____ |
| 5. pido | pedía | _____ | _____ |
| 6. veo | veía | _____ | _____ |
| 7. hace | hacía | _____ | _____ |
| 8. digo | decía | _____ | _____ |
| 9. solicito | solicitaba | _____ | _____ |
| 10. venimos | veníamos | _____ | _____ |
| 11. sales | salías | _____ | _____ |
| 12. tenéis | teníais | _____ | _____ |
| 13. vuelves | volvías | _____ | _____ |
| 14. sé | sabía | _____ | _____ |
| 15. ponemos | poníamos | _____ | _____ |
| 16. trabajan | trabajaban | _____ | _____ |
| 17. conoce | conocía | _____ | _____ |
| 18. contrata | contrataba | _____ | _____ |
| 19. puedo | podía | _____ | _____ |
| 20. quiere | quería | _____ | _____ |

# GRAMMAR III    Los mandatos formales. Las conjunciones • La formación y usos de los adverbios terminados en -mente (*Formal Commands. Conjunctions y, e, o, u, sino, pero • Formation and Uses of Adverbs Ending in -mente*)

**A.** Commands are a verbal mode used to tell others to do something. They are used to give orders and commands.

**B.** Commands with regular verbs
To form the commands in Spanish, drop the final -o of the **yo** form of present tense and add -e for *usted* and -en for *ustedes* for -ar verbs. And -a for *usted* and -an for *ustedes* for -er and -ir verbs.

| Habl ar | Com er | Escrib ir | Segu ir |
|---------|--------|-----------|---------|
| habl e Ud. | com a Ud. | escrib a Ud. | sig a Ud. |
| habl en Uds. | com an Uds. | escrib an Uds. | sig an Uds. |

Note that:

1. The pronouns *Ud.* and *Uds.* are not required, but using them is sometimes considered both more polite and more formal.

2. Formal affirmative and negative commands have the same forms.

   EX: hablar → hable Ud. → no hable Ud.

C. Commands with irregular verbs

1. Stem-changing verbs show the same changes in the command forms as in the present indicative.

   EXS: pensar → piense Ud./volver → vuelva Ud./pedir → pida Ud.

2. Verbs with irregularities in the first person singular of the present indicative show the same irregularities in the formal command. Study the following verbs.

   hacer → hago → haga Ud.          decir → digo → diga Ud.
   ofrecer → ofrezco → ofrezca Ud.  huir → huyo → huya Ud.
   poner → pongo → ponga Ud.        oír → oigo → oiga Ud.
   tener → tengo → tenga Ud.        salir → salgo → salga Ud.
                                    venir → vengo → venga Ud.

3. Also study the following verbs.

   ir → voy → vaya Ud./saber → sé → sepa Ud./ser → soy → sea Ud.

D. Spelling changes

1. Verbs with a *z* in the stem change the *z* to *c* before *e*, just as *realizo* changes to *realice*.

   EXS: empezar → empiece Ud/comenzar → comience Ud.

2. Verbs with a *g* at the end of the stem add *u* before *e*.

   EXS: pagar → pague Ud./llegar → llegue Ud.

3. Verbs with the letters *gu* before the -ir infinitive ending drop the *u* before *a*.

   EXS: seguir → siga Ud./conseguir → consiga Ud.

4. Verbs with a *c* before the -ar infinitive ending change the *c* to *qu* before *e*.

   EXS: practicar → practique Ud./sacar → saque Ud.

E. Unstressed object and reflexive pronouns
Unstressed object and reflexive pronouns in commands—such as **me, te, se, lo, la**—follow the affirmative, and precede the negative.

   EXS: decir → dígame → no me diga/lavarse → lávese → no se lave

# PRACTIQUE LOS MANDATOS FORMALES

**ANSWERS p. 294**

Write the following commands. Change the verb in bold to the command form.

1. **Ponerse** ropa apropiada para la entrevista de trabajo.
   *Usted:* _____

2. **Traer** su hoja de vida para la entrevista.
   *Ustedes:* _____

3. **Hacer** una cita con el jefe de la compañía.
   *Ustedes:* _____

4. **Mandar** una carta de agradecimiento.
   *Usted:* _____

5. **Pedir** un incremento de salario.
   *Usted:* _____

**ANSWERS p. 295**

Write the following commands in the negative form.

1. **No salir** tarde de la casa.
   *Usted:* _____

2. **No vestirse** informal para la entrevista.
   *Ustedes:* _____

3. **No hacer** preguntas inapropiadas.
   *Usted:* _____

4. **No usar** el celular durante la entrevista.
   *Ustedes:* _____

5. **No ponerse** nervioso/a.
   *Usted:* _____

# Conjunctions *y, e, o, u, sino, pero* • Formation and Uses of Adverbs Ending in *-mente*

I.  Conjunctions *y, e, o, u, sino, pero*

   A. There are two words in Spanish for the word *and:* y and e. We use *e* when the word that follows begins with the sound [*i*], which corresponds to the letters *i* and *hi.* (Remember that *h* is always silent.)

   EXS: **Daniel *e* Isabel/padre *e* hijo**

   There are a few words that begin with *hie*; in this case *hie* sounds like [*ye*] instead of [*ie*], and the conjunction *y* is used.

   EX: **agua *y* hielo** (*water and ice*)

   B. There are two words in Spanish for the word *or:* o and u. We use *u* when the word that follows begins with the sound [*o*], which corresponds to the letters *o* and *ho.* If the word begins with the diphthong *hue* as in **hueso,** we use *o.*

   EXS: **siete *u* ocho, minutos *u* horas,** BUT **músculos *o* huesos**

C. There are three ways to translate the word *but*: **pero**, **sino**, and **sino que**. In order to use *sino*, two conditions are required:

1. The first part of the sentence must be negative:

   EX: **Ese hombre *no* es ingeniero *sino* contador.** (*That man is <u>not an engineer</u> <u>but</u> an accountant.*)

2. The two parts of the sentence must be parallel—that is, the contrast must be between two nouns, two adjectives, and so on. At the same time those two parts must be on the same level of meaning: two colors, two religions, two affiliations. Otherwise *pero* must be used.

   EXS: **No es cautelosa *sino* metódica.** (*She's not cautious <u>but</u> methodical.*): *cautious* and *methodical* are adjectives.
   *Sino que* is used when each of the two parts of the sentence contains a subject and a verb.

   EXS: **Antonio no trabaja, *sino que* estudia.** (*Antonio doesn't work, <u>but</u> he studies.*)

   BUT **Antonio no quiere estudiar *sino* trabajar.** (*Antonio doesn't want to study <u>but</u> wants to work.*)

II. Formation and uses of adverbs ending in *-mente*

   A. Every descriptive adjective becomes an adverb with the ending **-mente** added to the feminine form of the adjective: **tranquilo → tranquila → tranquilamente/ claro → clara claramente.**

   B. If the adjective has a written accent, this accent is preserved in the adverb. **fácil → fácilmente/rápido → rápida → rápidamente.**

   Actually, these adverbs are the only Spanish compound words with two stresses: one on the adjectival part, the other on the first *e* of *-mente*.

   C. If there are two or more adverbs in a sequence, only the last adverb takes the ending **-mente**, but all of them must be feminine.

   EX: **El señor Cruz habló clara, concisa y amablemente.** (*Mr. Cruz spoke clearly, concisely, and amiably.*)

# PRACTIQUE LA GRAMÁTICA

**ANSWERS p. 295**

1. The usual Spanish translation of *and* is *y*, but if the following word begins with the sound [*i*], we don't use *y* but _____; for example, **padre** _____ **hijo.** There are two possible spellings for the sound [*i*]: _____ and _____.

2. *Hielo* (*ice*) begins with the [*ye*] rather than the [*ie*] sound. Therefore, we say **agua** _____ **hielo.** The same rule applies to *acero* _____ *hierro* (*steel and iron*).

3. We usually translate *or* by *o,* but if the following word begins with the sound [o], we use _____ rather than *o;* for example, **setenta** _____ **ochenta.** The two spellings for the sound [o] are _____ and _____.

4. *Pero* and *sino* mean the same thing: *but.* Most of the time we use *pero.* In order to use *sino,* the first part of the sentence must be _____. If the sentence is affirmative, _____ must be used.

5. Another condition for using *sino* is that the two parts in contrast must be parallel, such as two colors, two nationalities, two professions, and so on.
   EX: **Ella no es contadora** _____ **administradora.**

6. *Sino que* is used when each of the two parts of the sentence contains a _____ and a verb; for example, **Ella no es de México** _____ **es de Chile.**

7. The sentence *María no quiere trabajar* _____ *estudiar* requires *sino* instead of *sino que* because *trabajar* and *estudiar* are two infinitives; they are not full sentences.

8. To form an adverb from an adjective, we add *-mente* to the _____ form of the adjective, the reason being that *la mente* (*mind*) is feminine. If the adjective has only one form for both masculine and feminine, we use that form.
   EX: **triste** → _____

9. If the adjective has a written accent, we _____ that accent.
   EX: **fácil** → _____

10. If we have two or more adverbs in a sequence, only the _____ one takes the ending *-mente,* but all the others must be in the feminine gender.
    EX: **Habla** _____ **y** _____. (*clearly and easily*)

# PRÁCTICA

ANSWERS
p. 295

A. Translate the words in parentheses.

1. Martha _____ Isabel son trabajadoras _____ inteligentes. (*and*)

2. El agua tiene dos elementos: oxígeno _____ hidrógeno. (*and*)

3. ¿Cuántos años tiene tu abuela, setenta _____ ochenta? (*or*)

4. Dos metales importantes son oro _____ hierro. (*and*)

5. Antonio Segovia no era médico _____ odontólogo. (*but*)

6. No me importa si son minutos _____ horas. (*or*)

7. Aquí no está la entrada (*entrance*) de la compañía _____ la salida (*exit*). (*but*)

8. Nosotras no tomamos el autobús _____ tomamos un taxi para llegar más rápido a la universidad. (*but*)

9. Carlos vio el mensaje de texto _____ no lo leyó. (*but*)

10. Irma _____ Nelly son buenas amigas. (*and*)

ANSWERS
p. 295

B. Form adverbs from the following adjectives.

1. rápido _____
2. reciente _____
3. claro _____
4. feliz _____
5. hábil _____
6. suave _____

7. fácil _____
8. difícil _____
9. triste _____
10. común _____
11. actual _____
12. total _____

ANSWERS
p. 295

C. Change adjectives to adverbs ending in *mente*.

EX: **Los trabajadores llegan a trabajar** (*puntual*)
*Los trabajadores llegan a trabajar puntualmente.*

1. Carlos termina su proyecto. . .(*rápido)*.

_____

2. Emilia se graduó de la universidad. . . *(reciente)*.

_____

3. . . .Antonio y David no ganaron la competencia. *(triste)*

_____

4. Vemos . . . cómo ha cambiado la situación política del país. *(claro)*

_____

5. Creo que . . . podremos terminar este examen a tiempo. *(difícil)*

_____

# 14 Necesitamos comprar un nuevo carro

## (*We Need to Buy a New Car*)

## PALABRAS NUEVAS

| | | | |
|---|---|---|---|
| el aceite | oil | el camión | bus (in Mexico) |
| el acelerador | accelerator | el capó | hood |
| el aire acondicionado | air conditioning | el carné[3] | license |
| | | la carretera | road |
| el alquiler de carros | car rental | el carro | car |
| el asistente virtual | virtual assistant | *automático* | automatic car |
| el automóvil[1] | auto | *eléctrico* | electric car |
| la autopista | highway | *híbrido* | hybrid car |
| el autoservicio | self-service | *mecánico* | standard shift |
| la batería | battery | *de trasmisión manual* | manual transmission car |
| el baúl[2] | trunk | | |
| la bocina/el pito | horn | el chofer | driver |
| las bolsas de aire | airbags | el cinturón de seguridad | seat belt |
| el bus | bus | | |
| la calefacción | heating | el concesionario | car dealer, car dealership |
| la calle | street | | |
| la cámara de visión trasera | back-up/rear-view camera | el/la conductor(a) | driver |
| | | el control de crucero | cruise control |
| la cámara | camera | el cruce | intersection |
| *digital* | digital camera | las direccionales | turn signals |
| la camioneta | van/truck | el embotellamiento/ el atasco/ el trancón | traffic jam |
| el camión artículado/ la tractomula | semi-truck | | |

| | | | |
|---|---|---|---|
| la emergencia | emergency | la rueda | wheel |
| los entornos | surroundings | la seguridad | *safety* |
| el espejo retrovisor | rearview mirror | el sensor | sensor |
| la estación de gasolina/la gasolinera/ la bomba de gasolina | gas station | la señal de PARE | stop sign |
| | | las señales de tráfico | traffic signs |
| | | el sistema de seguridad avanzado | advanced security system |
| el estacionamiento | parking | el tablero de mandos | dashboard |
| el faro | headlight | el taller mecánico | mechanic's workshop/ garage |
| el freno | brake | | |
| *de emergencia* | emergency brake | | |
| *de mano* | handbrake | el tanque | tank |
| el galón | gallon | el/la taxista | taxi driver |
| la gasolina | gasoline | el tráfico | traffic |
| la guantera | glove compartment | la transmisión manual, de cambios | standard transmission |
| el kilómetro[4] | kilometer | | |
| la licencia de conducir | driver's license | la velocidad | speed |
| el limpiaparabrisas | windshield wiper | el velocímetro | speedometer |
| la llanta | tire | el vehículo deportivo utilitario | SUV |
| *de repuesto* | spare tire | | |
| la llave del carro | car key | el volante/el timón[6] | steering wheel |
| las luces | lights | los colores | colors |
| *altas* | high lights | amarillo | yellow |
| *delanteras* | headlights | azul | blue |
| el maletero/baúl | trunk (of a car) | *claro* | light blue |
| el mapa | map | *oscuro* | dark blue |
| la marca | car make/brand | *turquesa* | turquoise |
| la matrícula | license plate | blanco(a) | white |
| el/la mecánico(a) | mechanic | gris | gray |
| la milla | mile | marrón/carmelito(a) | brown |
| el modelo | model | morado(a) | purple |
| el motor | engine | naranja/ anaranjado(a) | orange |
| la multa | fine | | |
| el navegador GPS/ Waze | GPS/Waze | negro(a) | black |
| | | plateado(a) | silver |
| el neumático[5] | tire | rojo(a) | red |
| el parabrisas | windshield | rosado(a) | pink |
| el parachoques | bumper | verde | green |
| el parqueadero | parking | | |
| el peaje | toll | *Verbos* | *Verbs* |
| el pedal | pedal | alquilar | to rent |
| la placa | license plate | apagar | to turn off |
| el puente | bridge | aparcar | to park |
| el radio | radio | | |

| | | | |
|---|---|---|---|
| arrancar[7] | to start, root out | *Adjetivos* | *Adjectives* |
| arreglar | to repair/to fix | asegurado(a) | insured |
| bajar la velocidad | to slow down | automático(a) | automatic |
| bajar el volumen | to turn down the volume | cómodo(a) | comfortable |
| | | dañado(a) | broken (not working properly) |
| bajarse de | to get off (the car/ bus, etc.) | descompuesto(a) | |
| chocar | to crash | destruido(a) | destroyed |
| conducir[8] | to drive | eléctrico(a) | electric |
| consumir | to consume | estrellado(a) (carro) | crashed car |
| dar reversa | to reverse | estrellado(a) (cielo) | starry sky |
| dejar de funcionar | to stop working | gastado(a) | worn out |
| descargar/morir | to die (battery of the car) | híbrido | hybrid |
| | | lleno(a) | full |
| desinflar | to deflate | lujoso(a) | luxurious |
| durar | to last | manual[9] | standard shift |
| estacionar(se) | to park | mecánico(a) | mechanical |
| estrellar(se) | to crash | nuevo(a) | new |
| frenar | to brake | roto(a) | broken (in pieces) |
| funcionar | to work | torcido(a) | twisted, bent |
| girar/voltear | to turn | usado(a) | used |
| guiar | to guide | vacío(a) | empty |
| inflar | to inflate | varado(a) | stranded |
| llenar | to fill | | |
|   el tanque | fill the tank | *Expresiones* | *Expressions* |
| manejar | to drive | a. . . millas por hora | at... miles per hour |
| parar/detener(se) | to stop | no alcanzar el presupuesto | does not fit the budget |
| parquear(se) | to park | a todo riesgo | at all risk |
| pincharse | to get a flat tire | de segunda mano | secondhand |
| pitar | to sound the horn | carro de último modelo | brand-new car/ latest model |
| poner las direccionales | to put on the turn signals | la tracción en las cuatro ruedas | four-wheel drive |
| prender el carro | to start the car | | |
| revisar | to check | olerle mal a uno | to smell fishy |
|   el aceite | to check the oil | para colmo de males | to make matters worse |
| subirse a | to get on (the car, bus, etc.) | | |
| | | por ser usted | just for you |
| vararse/quedarse varado(a) | to strand | sacar la mano | to break down |
| | | tocar la bocina/el pito/pitar | to sound the horn |

**NOTAS**

1. *Automóvil* or *auto* is used for *car* in all of the Spanish-speaking world, but different words are preferred in different countries: *carro* is common in Latin America, and *coche* in Spain.

2. *Baúl* is *car trunk* and also *large suitcase.* In Mexico they use *cajuela* for the *car trunk,* and in Spain they use *maletero,* which happens to be the same word for *suitcase carrier* or *porter.*

3. *Carné,* the old *carnet,* is used not only for *driver's license* (*carné de conducir*) but also for any identification document.

4. *Kilómetro* is used in all Hispanic countries. It's 0.62 of a mile; in other words, a mile is 1.6 kilometers.

5. The word *neumático, tire,* reminds us of the times when the tire had an inner tube to inflate. The modern word is *llanta,* which used to be used for the outer part of the tire. In some countries *tires* are called *goma (Puerto Rico),* literally, *rubber.*

6. *Volante* is *steering wheel* of a car, a boat, a tractor, and so on. Lately *timón* is used with the same meaning, although it used to be used only for boats. *Volante* also means *flier,* a "piece of paper that can *fly,*" *volar* in Spanish.

7. *Arrancar* is *to start* (an engine), but the ordinary meaning is *to pull out by the roots* (plants or things).

8. *Conducir* is *to conduct* in all the countries, but in Spain it is used for *to drive vehicles,* which in Latin America is always *manejar. Manejar* also means *to handle.*

9. *Manual* (*un*) as a noun is a *booklet, notebook.* As an adjective it means *by hand,* and it is used for the *standard shift,* along with *mecánico* and *de cambios.*

10. *El bus* or *el autobus* means *bus.* In Mexico, *bus* is *el camión.* In some countries like the Dominican Republic, the Canary Islands, and Puerto Rico, *bus* is called *la guagua. El autocar* is used for long-distance buses in Spain, and *la flota* is used with the same meaning in Colombia.

# PRACTIQUE LAS PALABRAS NUEVAS

**ANSWERS p. 295**

**A.** Write *el, los, la,* or *las* before each noun.

| | | |
|---|---|---|
| 1. ____ direccionales | 6. ____ mapa | 11. ____ taller |
| 2. ____ velocidad | 7. ____ camión | 12. ____ volante |
| 3. ____ parabrisas | 8. ____ peaje | 13. ____ carros |
| 4. ____ navegador | 9. ____ estación | 14. ____ sistemas |
| 5. ____ batería | 10. ____ señales | 15. ____ cinturón |

**ANSWERS p. 295**

**B.** Write a synonym for each of these words.

1. camión (México) _____
2. coche _____
3. estacionar _____
4. licencia _____
5. baúl _____

6. conducir _____
7. matrícula _____
8. neumático _____
9. luces altas _____

**ANSWERS p. 295**

**C.** Complete each sentence with a word or expression from the list of *palabras nuevas*.

1. Para poder manejar un carro necesitas tener este documento siempre:

   _____.

2. Para llenar el tanque del carro con gasolina necesitas ir a este lugar:

   _____.

3. Para parar o detener un carro necesitamos usar:

   _____.

4. Cuando está lloviendo (*raining*) y estamos manejando, se necesita usar:

   _____.

5. Para poder arrancar o prender el coche necesitamos tener:

   _____.

6. Para dar reversa con el automóvil y mirar los entornos es muy conveniente usar:

   _____.

7. Si necesitamos girar o voltear a la izquierda o a la derecha cuando manejamos, es importante poner:

   _____.

8. Para manejar por algunas autopistas importantes los conductores deben pagar un

   _____.

9. Si estamos en invierno es importante usar: _____ para calentar el carro y no sentir frío.

10. Todas las personas que están un coche necesitan ponerse _____ para protegerse en caso de un accidente.

# DIÁLOGO   Necesitamos comprar un nuevo carro

*Lucas y Aurora son una pareja puertorriqueña que necesita comprar un nuevo carro porque el que tienen está muy viejo y se les dañó.*

Lucas:     Aurora, creo que llegó el momento de cambiar de carro. Como sabes, la semana pasada nuestro carro sacó la mano y necesitamos conseguir uno pronto. La trasmisión no funciona, los frenos no están bien y para colmo de males el aire acondicionado dejó de funcionar. Y las llantas están muy gastadas. Además, ese carro ya tenía como cerca de 150 mil millas de recorrido

AURORA: Sí Lucas, entiendo. Nos toca hacer esa inversión y comprar un carro que nos dure. ¿Tienes alguna idea que tipo de carro te gustaría comprar? A mí me parece mejor comprar un carro nuevo y no un carro usado. Además, creo que preferiría una camioneta deportiva 4 × 4.

LUCAS: Recuerda que los carros deportivos están muy costosos y no sé si nos alcanza el presupuesto. Tampoco sabemos cuánto nos pueden ofrecer por el carro viejo. Creo que podríamos comprar un carro usado con pocas millas. A veces esos carros tienen muy buenos precios.

AURORA: Me parece bien mirar las dos opciones y así tomar una decisión sobre cuál carro nos conviene más. ¿Qué características te gustaría que tuviera el carro? Para mí un carro híbrido es muy importante porque el costo de la gasolina está por los cielos.

LUCAS: Yo también preferiría un carro híbrido porque consumen menos gasolina y son muy buenos en general. Algo que me parece que es muy necesario, aunque creo que ahora todos los carros nuevos lo tienen, es el sistema de seguridad avanzado. Es importante que el carro tenga bolsas de aire, cámara digital o de visión trasera, navegador GPS, los sensores laterales para indicar si un carro está cerca. Creo que la nueva tecnología es muy necesaria.

AURORA: Estoy totalmente de acuerdo. ¿Te gustaría algún color en particular? A mí personalmente no me gustan los carros negros ni los carros de color blanco.

LUCAS: Para mí los carros de color azul oscuro me parecen muy elegantes y bonitos. También hay unos carros grises que se ven muy bien. Eso sí no me gustan ni los carros amarillos ni los rosados.

AURORA: Eres muy gracioso. A mí tampoco me gustan esos colores. El azul y el gris me parecen colores muy elegantes. Te parece si empezamos a mirar primero en el internet y el fin de semana podemos visitar varios concesionarios.

LUCAS: Me parece excelente. Creo que así tendremos una primera idea de los precios y los modelos. Y podemos ponernos de acuerdo sobre qué concesionarios visitar primero.

AURORA: Me parece que nos va a ayudar muchísimo cambiar de carro. Voy a traer mi tableta y tú puedes traer tu portátil para empezar a mirar marcas y modelos de carro.

LUCAS: Listo.

# DIALOGUE *We need to buy a new car*

*Lucas and Aurora are a Puerto Rican couple who need to buy a new car because their current one is very old and has broken down.*

LUCAS: Aurora, I think it's time to change our old car. As you know, our car stopped working last week, and we need to get one soon. The transmission isn't working, the brakes aren't working, and to top it all off, the air conditioning stopped working too. And the tires are very worn. Plus, that car already had about 150,000 miles on it.

AURORA: Yes, Lucas, I understand. We have to make that investment and buy a car that will last. Do you have any idea what kind of car you'd like to buy? I think it's better to buy a new car than a used one. Also, I think I'd prefer a 4 × 4 SUV.

LUCAS: Remember, SUVs are very expensive, and I don't know if we can afford it. We also don't know how much they might offer us for the old car. I think we could buy a used car with low mileage. Sometimes those cars are very good value for money.

AURORA: I think it's a good idea to look at both options and then decide which car is best for us. What features would you like the car to have? For me, a hybrid car is very important because the cost of gasoline is sky-high nowadays.

LUCAS: I would also prefer a hybrid car because those cars consume less gas and are very good overall. Something I think is very necessary, although I think all new cars now have them, is an advanced safety system. It's important for the car to have airbags, a digital or rearview camera, a GPS navigator, and side sensors to indicate if a car is nearby. I think new technology is very necessary.

AURORA: I totally agree. Would you like any color in particular? Personally, I don't like black cars or white cars.

LUCAS: I find dark blue in cars very elegant and pretty. There are also some gray cars that look very nice. However, I don't like yellow or pink cars.

AURORA: You're very funny. I don't like those colors either. I think blue and gray are very elegant colors. What do you think if we start looking online first and visit several dealers over the weekend?

LUCAS: I think that's great. I think this way we'll have a good idea of prices and models. And we can agree on which dealers to visit first.

AURORA: I think it'll help us a lot to buy a new car. I'll bring my tablet, and you can bring your laptop so we can start looking at car makers and models.

LUCAS: Done.

## NOTE

*Un carro nuevo* and *un nuevo carro* are expressions with different meanings in Spanish. *Un carro nuevo* means a brand-new car, while *un nuevo carro* could be a used car but a new one for the person who buys it.

# PRÁCTICA

**A. Un nuevo carro para Lucas y Aurora. Complete the story using the information from the dialogue.**

El carro viejo de Lucas y Aurora (1) _____ la semana pasada. El carro ya tenía muchos problemas. (2) _____ no funcionaba, los frenos no estaban bien y (3) _____también dejó de funcionar. Además, el carro ya tenía (4) _____ millas de recorrido. Aurora prefiere comprar una camioneta deportiva (5) _____ y no un carro (6) _____. Lucas considera que los carros deportivos nuevos son muy (7) _____, y no está seguro si tienen el (8) _____ para comprarlo. A Aurora también le parece importante comprar un carro (9) _____ porque consume menos (10) _____. Para Lucas es importante que el carro tenga un (11) _____. Él prefiere un carro con bolsas de aire, (12) _____ de visión trasera, (13) _____ GPS y (14) _____ laterales. A Lucas y a Aurora les gustan los colores (15) _____ y (16) _____ para el carro. A Lucas no le gusta el color (17) _____, ni el rosado. Ellos deciden ver los carros primero por (18) _____ y el fin de semana piensan ir a los (19) _____ para ver los (20) _____ de carros que más les guste.

**B. Answer *true* or *false* (T/F).**

1. _____ Aurora y Lucas tienen un carro último modelo.
2. _____ Aurora prefiere los carros usados y no los nuevos.
3. _____ Lucas considera que los carros deportivos o SUVs son muy baratos.
4. _____ Para Aurora los carros híbridos son mejores porque la gasolina está muy cara.
5. _____ A Lucas le parece importante que el carro tenga un sistema de seguridad avanzado.
6. _____ A Lucas le encanta el color amarillo en los carros.
7. _____ A Aurora le gusta mucho el color rosado.
8. _____ Los dos colores favoritos para carro para los dos son el azul y el gris.
9. _____ Aurora y Lucas van a ver carros primero en el concesionario.
10. _____ Aurora y Lucas van a comprar un carro usado.

C. *Review the subjunctive.* Imagine that you are lending your car to your sixteen-year-old daughter who just got her driver's license. Tell her about the conditions under which she must use it. Use the present subjunctive. Make any necessary changes.

Sarita, puedes usar mi carro por este fin de semana. Pero aquí tienes mis condiciones.

1. Espero que (tú) _____ siempre con mucho cuidado. (*manejar*)
2. Es importante que (tú) _____ bien antes de llegar a una señal de PARE. (*frenar*)
3. Es necesario que (tú) _____ el carro en estacionamientos apropiados. (*estacionar*)
4. Espero que el carro no se _____ en la carretera. (*pinchar*)
5. Ojalá el motor te _____ sin problemas. (*funcionar*)
6. Es bueno que (tú) _____ la bocina sólo cuando sea necesario. (*tocar*)
7. Es importantísimo que siempre (tus amigos y tú) _____ la licencia de manejar. (*llevar*)
8. Espero que el carro te _____ sin dificultad. (*arrancar*)
9. Te recomiendo que nunca _____ a velocidad excesiva. (*conducir*)
10. Te pido que _____ el tanque de gasolina. (*llenar*)

---

## GRAMMAR I  Contraste entre el indicativo y el subjuntivo: información vs. influencia (*Indicative and Subjunctive in Contrast: Information vs. Influence*)

A. In Spanish, a sentence is often composed of two clauses joined by the conjunction *que* (*that*). In this case, the subordinate clause follows *que* and is dependent upon the first clause, which is the main clause.

EX: **Nosotros sabemos** (= *main clause*) **que el carro tiene muchas millas.** (= *subordinate clause*). (*We know that the car has many miles.*)

B. Verbs of information take <u>the indicative</u>.

1. If the main clause contains a verb of information, such as **decir, leer, saber, conocer, informar,** the verb in the subordinate clause must be in the indicative.

EXS: **Ella sabe que Ud. *es mecánico.*** (*She knows [that] you are a mechanic.*)
**Ud. dice que mi carro *necesita* una batería nueva.** (*You say [that] my car needs a new battery.*)

**2.** Here is a partial list of verbs and expressions of information.

| | | |
|---|---|---|
| **conocer** to know | **es cierto que** it's true that | **informar** to inform |
| **contar** to tell | **es claro que** it's clear that | **leer** to read |
| **decir** to say | **escribir** to write | **reconocer** to recognize |
| **declarar** to declare | **es verdad que** it's true that | **saber** to know |

C. Verbs of influence take *the subjunctive*.

**1.** If the main clause contains a verb of influence—that is, a verb that indicates something that is not a fact—the verb in the subordinate clause must be in the subjunctive. By verbs of *influence*, we mean verbs of **advice, command, request, suggestion, preference, desire, hope, permission, prohibition**, and so on.

EX: **Ella quiere que yo *compre* un carro nuevo.** (*She wants me to buy a new car.*)

It is important to note that here the subject of the main clause tries to impose her will on the subject of the subordinate clause. Therefore, they must be different persons. If the subject is the same in both clauses, then we use the infinitive.

EXS: **Ella quiere comprar un carro.** (*She wants to buy a car.*)

*Ella* **quiere que *tú* compres un carro nuevo.** (*She wants you to buy a new car.*)

**2.** Here is a list of some *verbs of influence*.

| | | |
|---|---|---|
| **aconsejar** *to advise* | **impedir** *to prevent* | **preferir** *to prefer* |
| **decir** *to tell* | **insistir** *to insist* | **prohibir** *to forbid* |
| **dejar** *to allow, let* | **mandar** *to order* | **querer** *to want* |
| **desear** *to wish* | **oponerse** *to oppose* | **recomendar** *to recommend* |
| **escribir** *to write* | **ordenar** *to order* | **sugerir** *to suggest* |
| **esperar** *to hope* | **pedir** *to ask for* | **suplicar** *to beg* |
| **gritar** *to scream* | **permitir** *to allow* | |

D. The following verbs take the subjunctive, just like verbs of influence.

**1.** When we say to a person "It's necessary that you do it," we are trying to influence that person; in other words, instead of saying directly "I want you to do it," we are using the impersonal expression to convey the same idea. Therefore, the subjunctive is required in the subordinate clause.

EX: **Es importante que lo hagas.** (*It's important that <u>you do</u> it.*)

2. Here is a partial list of *impersonal expressions of influence*.

| | |
|---|---|
| **es aconsejable** it's advisable | **es malo** it's bad |
| **es bueno** it's good | **es mejor** it's better |
| **es conveniente** it's convenient | **es necesario** it's necessary |
| **es deseable** it's desirable | **es peor** it's worse |
| **es imperativo** it's imperative | **es preciso** it's necessary |
| **es importante** it's important | **está prohibido** it's forbidden |
| **es inútil** it's useless | **es útil** it's useful |

E. Some verbs are both verbs of information and verbs of influence. You may have noticed that a few verbs appear both under letter *B* as verbs of information and under letter *C* as verbs of influence. These verbs are *decir, escribir, insistir, gritar.* Actually, these verbs have a double meaning; for example, *decir* means both to state with words (*information*) and to request something (*influence*). The difference is illustrated by the use of either the indicative or the subjunctive.

EX: INFORMATION: **Papá dice que *eres* bueno.** (*Dad says that you are good.*)
INFLUENCE: **Papá dice que *seas* bueno.** (*Dad requests [asks] that you be good.*)

# PRACTIQUE EL SUBJUNTIVO

ANSWERS
p. 296

1. A clause that depends on another clause is called a _____ clause. The independent clause is called the _____ clause.
2. In English the linking conjunction between the main and the subordinate clauses is *that,* which is omitted very frequently. In Spanish the conjunction is _____ and is never omitted.
3. If the main clause contains a verb of information, the verb in the subordinate clause must be in the _____. For example, Aurora sabe que Lucas _____ comprar un carro. (*querer*)
4. If the main clause contains a verb of influence, the subordinate clause must have its verb in the _____. For example, **Lucas no quiere que Aurora** _____ **un carro costoso.** (*comprar*)
5. By influence we mean verbs that denote imposition of will, from a strong command to a soft suggestion. Usually, these verbs are listed as command, request, desire, wish, prohibition, advice, opposition, and the like.
   EX: **El mecánico sugiere que (nosotros)** _____ **los frenos del carro.** (*cambiar*)
6. If the main clause and the subordinate clause have the same subject, there actually is no subordinate clause. We use the _____ in the second part of the sentence.
   EX: **Mis amigos quieren** _____ **durante el viaje.** (*conducir*)
7. Verbs like *saber, declarar, leer,* denote information. Therefore, the verb in the subordinate clause must be in the _____.

8. If you read a notice at work that says *It is important that all of you...*, you will probably interpret it as an order, even if your name is not mentioned there. Complete this sentence: **Es necesario que ustedes** _____ **el peaje.** (*pagar*)

9. Notice that impersonal expressions like *es bueno* and *es mejor* contain an adjective. If this adjective in the main clause contains a message of information—like *cierto*, *claro*, *verdad*—the subordinate clause must be completed in the _____.

   EX:  **Es cierto que ella** _____ **bien.** (*manejar*)

10. How do you translate **El director dice que Ud. trabaja mucho?** *The director* _____ *a lot.*

11. How do you translate **El director dice que Ud. trabaje mucho?** *The director* _____ *a lot.*

# PRÁCTICA

**ANSWERS p. 296**

A. Complete each sentence with a present indicative or a present subjunctive form of the verb in parentheses.

   1. Lucas quiere que el mecánico _____ el aceite del coche. (*revisar*)
   2. No es necesario que la camioneta _____ de último modelo. (*ser*)
   3. Es verdad que ustedes _____ bien. (*manejar*)
   4. El mecánico espera que el chofer _____ el camión a tiempo para la revisión. (*traer*)
   5. Es cierto que nosotros _____ un carro con muchas millas de recorrido. (*tener*)
   6. El vendedor del concesionario recomienda que Lucas y Aurora _____ un carro híbrido. (*comprar*)
   7. Todos sabemos que los carros eléctricos _____ con electricidad. (*funcionar*)
   8. Lucas espera que el carro _____ un sistema de seguridad avanzado. (*tener*)
   9. Aurora no permite que Lucas _____ un carro amarillo. (*buscar*)
   10. Es mucho mejor que nosotros _____ a un buen concesionario para comprar un carro. (*ir*)
   11. Es importante que el vendedor nos _____ un descuento para la compra de la camioneta. (*hacer*)
   12. Miré en esta página de internet y sé que _____ autos muy baratos en este concesionario. (*haber*)
   13. Prefiero que el carro _____ 4 × 4. (*ser*)
   14. Es cierto que los carros deportivos _____ de moda. (*estar*)
   15. No es bueno mi hija _____ muy tarde del trabajo. (*salir*)

16. El mecánico dice que la batería del bus _____. (*descargarse*)

17. El policía no permite que (nosotros) _____ aquí. (*estacionarse*)

18. ¿Me sugiere Ud. Que (yo) _____ en tren desde Chicago? (*venir*)

19. Mi hijo siempre me pide que le _____ el carro los viernes por la tarde. (*prestar*)

20. Es claro que Aurora _____ bien a Lucas. (*conocer*)

ANSWERS p. 296

B. **What do Aurora and Lucas expect of the new car they want to buy? Complete each sentence using the present subjunctive.**

Queremos que el carro. . .

1. _____ (*ser*) híbrido.
2. _____ (*tener*) bolsas de aire.
3. _____ (*venir*) con sensores.
4. _____ (*estar*) en buenas condiciones.
5. No _____ (*costar*) mucho.
6. _____ (*durar*) muchos años.
7. _____ (*funcionar*) bien.
8. _____ (*ser*) de color azul o gris.
9. No _____ (*consumir*) mucha gasolina.
10. _____ (*ser*) cómodo.
11. _____ (*prender*) de manera remota.
12. _____ (*tener*) calefacción y aire acondicionado.

ANSWERS p. 296

C. **Complete the sentences with one of the ideas given below. Decide to use the indicative or subjunctive according to the rules.**

*necesitar una batería nueva*    *poner el aire*    *conducir*
*comprar un carro nuevo*    *acondicionado*    *llevar el carro al*
   *taller mecánico*

1. A Lucas se le dañó la batería de su carro. Es necesario que él

_____.

2. El mecánico revisó el carro y nos dice que _____.

3. Nuestro carro ya no funciona. Está en muy malas condiciones. Es mejor que nosotros _____.

4. Vamos a ir a Chicago en carro. Vamos a pedirle a Lucas que él

_____.

5. Hace un calor terrible y llevamos dos horas en el carro. Sugiero que (nosotros) _____.

# GRAMMAR II   Los mandatos informales (*Familiar Commands (tú form)*)

A. Regular commands

*Commands* are expressed in the *imperative mood* in Spanish. They are used to give orders, advise, or make requests. You use *familiar commands* (**tú** *form*) when you want to give an order or make request to someone you generally address with the pronoun *tú*. The forms for the *affirmative* familiar commands are different from those for *negative* familiar commands.

1. **Affirmative commands.** The form is identical to the third person singular of the present indicative: **revisar** → **revisa; volver** → **vuelve.**

   EX: *Revisa* el aceite del carro. (*Check the car's oil.*)

2. **Negative commands.** Verbs ending in **-ar** take the ending **-es,** and verbs ending in **-er** and **-ir** take the ending **-as.** A negative is required before the verb.

   EXS: comprar = *No compres* esa camioneta roja. (*Don't buy that red van.*)
   subirse = *No te subas a* ese bus. (*Don't get on that bus.*)

B. Irregular commands

1. All stem-changing verbs have the same changes in the command forms as in their present indicatives.

   EXS: dormir → duerme → no duermas/pedir → pide → no pidas/pensar → piensa → no pienses/volver → vuelve → no vuelvas

2. Most verbs that are irregular in the first person of the present tense show the same irregularity in the negative command.

   EXS: conducir → conduzco → no conduzcas/decir → digo → no digas/ huir → huyo → no huyas/oír → oigo → no oigas/salir → salgo → no salgas/tener → tengo → no tengas

3. Here are ten verbs that are irregular either because they drop the ending **-e** in the affirmative command or because they take unexpected forms.

   | | |
   |---|---|
   | decir → di → no digas | salir → sal → no salgas |
   | hacer → haz → no hagas | ser → sé → no seas |
   | poner → pon → no pongas | tener → ten → no tengas |
   | saber → sabe → no sepas | venir → ven → no vengas |

C. Object pronouns with command forms

Unstressed object pronouns (including reflexive pronouns) follow the affirmative command, and they are attached to it. They precede the verb if the command is negative.

   EXS: **Llámame.** No *me* llames. (*Call me./Don't call me.*)
   **Dímelo.** No *me lo* digas. (*Tell it to me./Don't tell it to me.*)
   **Siéntese.** No *se* siente. (*Sit down./Don't sit down.*)

# PRACTIQUE LOS MANDATOS

**ANSWERS p. 297**

1. We use the command forms (the imperative) to give a direct order. There are two kinds of commands: formal commands, addressed to **Ud.**, and _____ commands, addressed to _____. We already covered the formal commands in the previous unit.

2. The affirmative commands in the *tú* form are the same as the third-person singular forms of the present _____. For example, **estacionar** → _____.

3. For negative commands, verbs ending in **-ar** take the ending _____; verbs ending in **-er** and **-ir** take the ending _____. For example, **revisar** → no _____/**volver** → no _____. A negative sentence always requires a negative word in front of the verb.

4. Stem-changing verbs show the same changes in the command forms as in the present _____. For example, **dormir** → **duermo** → _____.

5. Most verbs that are irregular in the present indicative show the same irregularities in the _____ command forms. Example, **salir** → **salgo** → no _____.

6. A few verbs are irregular in the affirmative command because they show no ending; they drop the *e*. Examples, **venir** → _____; **tener** → _____; **salir** → _____.

7. The word *di* is two different things in Spanish: a) the preterite of *dar,* and it means _____; b) the familiar command form of *decir,* and it means _____. Notice that *di* does not take an accent!

8. *Sé* is also two different things: a) the present of *saber,* and it means _____, b) the familiar command form of *ser,* and it means _____. In both cases it needs an accent.

9. Unstressed pronouns, such as **me, se, lo, la,** follow the _____ commands, but precede the _____ commands.

10. To translate *call me* in Spanish, we follow the same order as in English: _____. However, in *Don't call me* the order is different: **No** _____.

11. Compound verbs follow the same rules as simple verbs. If the familiar command form of *poner* is *pon,* the familiar command form of *suponer* is _____. (It needs an accent because it has two syllables.)

12. If the familiar command form of *tener* is *ten,* the familiar command of *mantener* is _____. If the familiar command form of *venir* is *ven,* the familiar command of *prevenir* is _____.

# PRÁCTICA

ANSWERS
p. 297

**A.** Change the statements to affirmative familiar commands. Write the verb only.

EX: Carlos *me llama* esta noche. = Carlos, llámame. . .

1. Lola *habla* con el vendedor. = Lola, _____
2. Luis *escribe* un mensaje de texto. = Luis, _____
3. José *dice* la verdad. = José, _____
4. Marcos *me hace* un favor. = Marcos, _____
5. Aurora *viene* conmigo al concesionario. = Aurora, _____
6. Esteban *me oye* bien. = Esteban, _____
7. Lucas *sale* temprano hoy. = Lucas, _____
8. Felipe *pone* la gasolina al carro. = Felipe, _____
9. Ramiro *revisa* el aceite del camión. = Ramiro, _____
10. Susana *presenta* la licencia de conducir = Susana, _____

ANSWERS
p. 297

**B.** Now change these statements to negative familiar commands.

1. Luisa no llega tarde. = Luisa, no _____.
2. Guillermo no dice nada. = Guillermo, no _____.
3. Sonia no me llama hoy. = Sonia, no me _____.
4. Anita no me lo compra. = Anita, no me lo _____.
5. Carlos no revisa la trasmisión. = Carlos, no la _____.

ANSWERS
p. 297

**C.** Answer the questions first affirmatively and then negatively. Replace the direct and indirect object nouns with pronouns.

EX: ¿Llevo <u>el carro</u> al mecánico? —Sí, *lléva<u>lo</u>.* —No, *no <u>lo</u> lleves.*
*(Should I take the car to the mechanic? Yes, please take it or do not take it.)*

1. ¿Llamo al concesionario?
   —Sí, _____.          —No, _____.
2. ¿Lleno el tanque de gasolina?
   —Sí, _____.          —No, _____.
3. ¿Reviso los frenos?
   —Sí, _____.          —No, _____.
4. ¿Pongo el aire acondicionado?
   —Sí, _____.          —No, _____.
5. ¿Cambio el aceite?
   —Sí, _____.          —No, _____.

**ANSWERS**
**p. 297**

D. Complete con la forma correcta del mandato informal (I = verbo irregular).

1. _____ (abrir) la puerta, por favor.

2. _____ (revisar) las bolsas de aire.

3. _____ (ir) al concesionario para ver los nuevos modelos. *(I)*

4. No _____ (venir) muy tarde. *(I)*

5. _____ (llegar) temprano al taller.

6. _____ (hacer) los arreglos necesarios. *(I)*

7. _____ (poner) la calefacción porque está haciendo frío. *(I)*

8. No _____ (conducir) muy rápido en la autopista.

9. _____ (llevar) siempre tu licencia de conducir.

10. No _____ (escribir) mensajes de texto cuando manejes.

# GRAMMAR III   Revisión del acento • Los usos de POR y PARA (*A Review of the Written Accent* • *The Uses of POR and PARA*)

A. The written accent (´) is used in Spanish to facilitate reading. It is written on the stressed vowel of a word according to spelling rules that have changed somehow along the years. You should be able to hear the stress in order to apply the rules. Quite a few Hispanics cannot hear it. For example, if you hear the stress on *la* of *lápiz*, you should be able to apply rule number 2 from letter *B* below and write the accent.

B. There are three important rules for the use of the written accent.

1. Words with the stress on the last syllable need an accent mark if the last letter is a vowel or the consonant *n* or *s*. If the word has only one syllable, the rule doesn't apply.

   EXS: **comió, menú, menús, estén, café, dieciséis**
   
     BUT **dio, di, fue, vio, seis, mes**

2. Words with the stress on the next-to-the-last syllable need an accent mark if the last letter is any consonant except *n* or *s*.

   EXS: **árbol, fácil, lápiz, álbum, estándar**

3. Words with the stress two syllables before the last always need an accent. The last letter doesn't matter.

   EXS: **águila, águilas, número, dígame, lávese, área, estéreo, gramática**

C. Following are two special cases for the use of the written accent.

1. Whenever the weak vowel *i* or *u* precedes or follows any of the so-called strong vowels—a, e, or o—the two vowels form one syllable, with the stress on the strong vowel. This combination is called a diphthong. For example, *oi-ga* has two syllables: *oi-ga,* with the stress on the *o*.

When the stress is on the weak vowels, *i* or *u*, the diphthong is broken. This is shown with a written accent: *oído* has three syllables: o-í-do, Ma-rí-a, and so on.

EXS: **oír, día, mío, baúl, dúo, maíz** (BUT **maizal**), **país, países** (BUT **paisano**), **reúnes** (BUT **reunir**), **prohíbo** (BUT **prohibir**), **oí, oíste** (BUT **oigo**)

2. When a word has two or more meanings, one meaning is denoted by the use of an accent mark. Altogether there are ten such words.

| | |
|---|---|
| **aún** (*yet*) vs. **aun** (*even*) | **sé** (*I know, be*) vs. **se** (*himself, herself, etc.*) |
| **dé** (*give*) vs. **de** (*of, 's*) | **sí** (*yes, oneself*) vs. **si** (*if*) |
| **él** (*he*) vs. **el** (*the*) | |
| **más** (*more*) vs. **mas** (*but*) | **té** (*tea*) vs. **te** (*you*) |
| **mí** (*me*) vs. **mi** (*my, mine*) | **tú** (*you*) vs. **tu** (*your*) |

D. Question words take an accent in questions and in exclamatory expressions, such as **¡Qué emoción!** (*How exciting!*) Question words are **cuánto, dónde, cómo, qué, por qué, cuál, quién, para qué**. Question words take an accent even when they are used in indirect questions. A question is indirect because it depends on verbs of asking, knowing, finding out, and the like.

EX: **Quiero saber cómo te llamas.** (*I want to know <u>what</u> your name is.*)

# PRACTIQUE LOS ACENTOS

**ANSWERS p. 297**

1. The accent is written over the _____ vowel of a word.

2. If a word ends in a vowel, we write the accent if the stress is on the _____ syllable, but the word must have _____ or more syllables: **revisaré, oí, champú**.

3. If a word ends in *n, s*, we write the accent if the _____ is on the last syllable. Again, we need at least _____ syllables, because this rule doesn't apply to one-syllable words: **dos → veintidós, mes → entremés, Dios → adiós**.

4. *Fue, dio, vio, vi, di, fui*, used to have an accent. However, in 1959 the Real Academia decided that the accent on a one-syllable word was useless unless the word had two meanings, like *tú* meaning _____ and *tu* meaning _____.

5. *Lápiz* needs an accent because the _____ is on the next-to-the-last syllable, and the last letter is a consonant other than _____, in this case a *z*. The plural **lápices** needs the accent because of a different rule: the stress is on _____ syllables before the last.

6. Foreign words follow the same rules for the accent. For example, *sandwich* gave us *sánduche*, which needs an accent for the same reason that *lápiz, azúcar, Cristóbal, eslálom*, do: the last letter is a consonant, and the stress is on the _____ syllable.

7. Some Spanish speakers say **sánduche**, and this word needs the accent because the stress is _____ syllables before the last, just as in **lápices** and **pirámide**.

8. *Diga* doesn't need the accent, but *dígame* does, because the stress is on *di-*, which is _____ syllables before the last. In a few cases, there are three syllables before the last, and obviously they need the accent: **dígamelo** (*tell it to me*).

9. *Sí* needs an accent when it means: (1) _____, (2)_____. However, *si* does not need an accent (nor stress) when it means _____.

10. *Mi* means _____, whereas *mí* means _____.
    I. EX: A _____ me gusta _____ coche. (*I like my car.*)

11. *Yo sé donde vive usted* is not correct because an accent is missing on _____.

12. We put an accent on a question word that appears in a question or in an exclamatory expression. For example, _____ **carro tan malo!** (*What a terrible car!*)

13. *Día, María, mío, dúo, país, baúl*—they all need an accent for the same reason: the stress is on the weak vowels, *í, ú,* and the _____ is broken.

14. Do you put an accent on *oir*? _____, because the stress is on -ir, as in all the verbs with this same ending. *Oiga* doesn't need the accent because it has two syllables (oi-ga) and the stress is on the vowel _____.

# PRÁCTICA

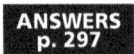
ANSWERS
p. 297

Write the accent when needed.

1. El baul de mi automovil es bastante grande y ayer lo llene de maletas.
2. El mecanico cambio la bateria del camion.
3. Lucas prefirio comprar un coche automatico e hibrido.
4. Tu camion esta en pesimas condiciones.
5. No entiendo por que los carros mecanicos son tan dificiles de manejar.

# USOS DE *POR* Y *PARA*

Spanish has two words that mean *for: por* and *para*. Both prepositions are used under different circumstances. Here are some uses:

A. Uses of *para*

   1. *Purpose, aim, (in order to):*
      EX: Alberto estudió una carrera técnica **PARA** ser mecánico. (*Alberto studied a technical course (in order to) to become a mechanic.*)

2. *Purpose (for, used for):*

   Estas llantas son *PARA* la camioneta blanca. *(These tires are for the white truck.)*

3. *Motion toward a specific destination:*

   EX: Aurora y Lucas salieron *PARA* el concesionario. (*Aurora and Lucas left for the dealer's.*)

4. *For whom or for what something is meant (recipient):*

   EX: Jaime compró un coche *PARA* su hijo. *(Jaime bought a car for his son.)*

5. *Deadlines or definite point in time (by + time):*

   EX: La camioneta estará lista *PARA* el lunes de la próxima semana. (*The truck will be ready by Monday of next week.*)

6. *Compared with, considering (that):*

   EX: *PARA* ser híbrido este carro consume mucha gasolina. (*For a hybrid, this car consumes a lot of gasoline.*)

7. *To give an opinion:*

   EX: *PARA* mí y *PARA* ti los carros automáticos son mejores que los carros de cambios. (*For you and me, automatic cars are better than stick shift cars.*)

8. *To be about, to be on the verge of.*

   EX: Los nuevos modelos de coches están *PARA* llegar. (*The new car models are about to arrive.*)

9. *Estar listo/a para* means *to be ready to:*

   EX: Lucas *ESTÁ LISTO PARA* salir al concesionario. (*Lucas is ready to go to the dealer.*)

B. Uses of *por*

   1. *Motivation, reason (because of, out of, for, on behalf of, on account of).*

      EX: *POR* la lluvia, llegué tarde a la cita. (*I was late for the appointment due (because of) to rain.*)

   2. *Feelings or attitudes of the subject toward a person or thing, also to be for, to be in favor of.*

      EX: *POR* mis padres decidí estudiar ingeniería de sistemas. (*Because of my parents, I decided to study Computer Engineering.*)

   3. The object of an errand, usually with verbs like *ir, venir, mandar, enviar.*

      EX: El taller me envió la cuenta del costo del arreglo del coche *POR* correo. (*The workshop sent me the bill for the cost of the car repair by mail.*)

   4. *Approximate location or time; place of transit (around, in, by, throughout, along).*

      EX: Caminamos *POR* la playa *POR* dos horas. (*We walked along the beach for two hours.*)

   5. *Duration of an action. Por* is frequently omitted in this case.

      EX: Estuve en un embotellamiento de tráfico *(POR)* dos horas. (*I was stuck in a traffic jam for two hours.*)

6. *Substitution, exchange, price.*

EX: Pagamos 35 mil dólares **POR** esa camioneta. (*We paid 35 thousand dollars for that truck.*)

7. *To substitute for es sustituir a.*

EX: Luis trabajó **POR** Miguel porque Miguel estaba enfermo. (*Luis worked for (instead of) Miguel because Miguel was sick.*)

8. *Percentage, rate, multiplication.* Equivalents of *per* and *by.*

EX: Los impuestos de compras en Indiana son del 7 **POR CIENTO** (7%). (*Purchase taxes in Indiana are 7 PERCENT (7%).*)

$5 \times 5 = 25$ (cinco **POR** cinco es igual a veinticinco).

9. *Means, manner, instrument, agent.*

Aurora y Lucas siempre viajan **POR** carro en la autopista. (*Aurora and Lucas always travel by car on the highway*)

C. **Some expressions with** *por*

1. Por adelantado (*in advance*)
2. Por ahora (*for the time being*)
3. Por completo (*completely*)
4. Por consiguiente (*therefore*)
5. Por decirlo así (*so to speak*)
6. Por eso (*for that reason*)
7. Por las nubes (*sky-high price*)
8. Por lo general (*as a general rule*)
9. Por lo menos (*at least*)
10. Por lo tanto (*consequently*)
11. Por lo visto (*apparently*)
12. Por ningún motivo (*under no circumstances*)
13. Por otra parte/por otro lado (*on the other hand*)
14. Por supuesto (*of course*)

# PRACTIQUE LOS USOS DE *POR* Y *PARA*

ANSWERS
p. 297

A. Complete el párrafo con *por* o *para*.

Hoy fui a ver a mi amigo Antonio que trabaja _____ (1) una agencia de viajes. La agencia está _____ (2) la calle Calumet. Fui a la agencia _____ (3) comprar dos pasajes _____ (4) un viaje que vamos a hacer mi hermano y yo a Bolivia. Cuando entré en la agencia tuve que esperar _____ (5) treinta minutos. _____ (6) fin, Antonio llegó y le compré los boletos. El viaje es _____ (7) avión y los pasajes me costaron $950.00 dólares _____

(8) persona. El viaje incluye pasaje de ida y vuelta, hospedaje, comida y excursiones _____ (9) todo el país _____ (10) nueve días. _____ (11) ser un viaje de tantos días, no está caro. El viaje es _____ (12) el próximo sábado y sale de Miami a las 8:30 A.M. Va a ser una experiencia fabulosa _____ (13) nosotros.

**ANSWERS p. 298**

**B.** ¿*Por* o *para*?

1. Mis hijos estudian en la universidad _____ conseguir un buen trabajo.

2. _____ su edad (*age*), se ve muy joven.

3. El agente de seguros me ofreció $500.00 _____ mi póliza de seguros.

4. El accidente ocurrió _____ la cantidad de nieve.

5. Cuando pases _____ mi oficina, sube a visitarme.

6. El mecánico dice que el carro estará listo _____ el próximo martes.

7. _____ mí, los carros eléctricos presentan muchos problemas.

8. Estoy trabajando hoy _____ Luis porque él está enfermo.

9. ¿Este carro es _____ mí? ¡Qué emoción!

10. _____ cierto, ¿Cuánto cuesta la reparación de la camioneta?

11. Mi esposa y yo pagamos mucho dinero _____ ese coche.

12. Tú estuviste en un embotellamiento de tráfico _____ tres horas.

13. Quieres estudiar medicina _____ ganar mucho dinero en el futuro.

14. Mi hermana y yo nos comunicamos _____ WhatsApp.

15. Salimos _____ el aeropuerto a las 5:00 A.M.

# 15 Alojamiento para nómadas digitales

## (*Accommodations for Digital Nomads*)

## PALABRAS NUEVAS

| | | | |
|---|---|---|---|
| las afueras | suburbs, outskirts | el baño | bathroom |
| la alfombra | carpet/rug | el barrio/la colonia | neighborhood |
| el alojamiento | accommodations | la cafetera | coffee maker |
| el alquiler/el arriendo/la renta | rent | la casa | house |
| | | la cocina | kitchen |
| el apartaestudio | studio apartment | la cocina integral | full kitchen |
| el apartamento/ piso | apartment/ condominium | el comedor | dining room |
| | | el congelador | freezer |
| el asador | grill | el conjunto residencial | residential complex |
| el ascensor/elevador | elevator | | |
| la aspiradora | vacuum cleaner | las cortinas | curtains |
| el aviso | notice/ad | los cubiertos | cutlery |
| el aviso de tornado | tornado warning | el dormitorio | bedroom |
| el balcón | balcony | | |

| el edificio de apartamentos | apartment building |
| los electrodomésticos | electrical appliances |
| la entrada | entrance |
| la escalera | ladder |
| las escaleras | stairs |
| la escoba | broom |
| el espacio funcional | functional space |
| el estante | bookshelves/ bookcase |
| el estudio/cuarto de estudio | study/office |
| la estufa | stove |
| el garaje | garage |
| la habitación/la alcoba/la recámara/ el cuarto | room |
| el horno (microondas) | oven (microwave) |
| la inmobiliaria | real estate |
| el inmueble | property |
| el jardín | garden/yard |
| la lámpara/pantalla | lamp |
| la lavadora | washing machine |
| el lavaplatos | dishwasher |
| la luz | light/electricity |
| el mirador | balcony |
| los muebles | furniture |
| el/la nómada | nomad |
| la pared | wall |
| el pasillo/hallway | hallway |
| el patio | patio/yard |
| el piso | floor/storey |
| la planta baja | ground floor |
| los platos | dishes |
| el rascacielos | skyscraper |
| el reciclaje | recycling |
| el refrigerador/la nevera | refrigerator |
| la sala | living room |
| la secadora | dryer |
| el sofá | sofa |
| el sótano | basement |
| la terraza | terrace |
| la ventana | window |
| la vista panorámica | panoramic view |

| la vivienda | housing |
| la zona de trabajo compartido | coworking space/ shared work area |

| *Verbos* | *Verbs* |
| alquilar/arrendar | to rent |
| amoblar | to furnish |
| arreglar | to organize |
| barrer el suelo | to sweep the floor |
| calentar | to warm/to heat |
| cocinar | to cook |
| congelar | to freeze |
| ensuciar | to get (something) dirty |
| hacer desorden/ desordenar | to make mess |
| hacer (tender) la cama | to make the bed |
| hacer quehaceres domésticos | to do household chores |
| hornear | to bake |
| lavar | to wash |
| limpiar | to clean |
| el polvo | to dust |
| pasar la aspiradora/ aspirar el piso | to vacuum |
| poner la mesa | to set the table |
| reciclar | to recycle |
| sacar la basura | to take out the trash |
| secar la ropa | to dry the clothes |

| *Adjetivos* | *Adjectives* |
| amplio(a) | spacious |
| amueblado(a) | furnished |
| desocupado(a) | empty |
| desordenado(a) | messy |
| estrecho(a) | narrow |
| limpio(a) | clean |
| lujoso(a) | luxurious |
| nómada | nomadic |
| ordenado(a)/ organizado(a) | organized/tidy |
| sucio(a) | dirty |
| terminado(a) | finished |

**NOTAS**

1. *Apartamento, piso, departamento* are synonyms that refer to *apartment* or *condominium* or *flat* in English. *Apartamento* and *departamento* are used in Latin America while *piso* is used in Spain. *Casa* is a word that refers to *a house* or *a town home*.

2. *Pisos (floors)* in a building are designated by **ordinal numbers** that are placed before the word *piso*: primer/o (*first*), segundo (*second*), tercer/o (*third*), cuarto (*fourth*), quinto (*fifth*), sexto (*sixth*), séptimo (*seventh*), octavo (*eighth*), novena (*ninth*), décimo (*tenth*).

   EX: Vivo en el *primer piso,* pero mi hermana vive en el *cuarto piso.*

3. After floor #10 in a building, Spanish normally uses cardinal numbers. The numbers are placed after the noun **piso**.

   EX: *piso once, piso doce, piso quince.*

4. In Spain, the first floor of an apartment building, the one at street level, is called *la planta baja* (the ground floor).

# PRACTIQUE LAS PALABRAS NUEVAS

**ANSWERS p. 298**

A. Write *el, los, la,* or *las* before each noun.

| | | |
|---|---|---|
| 1. _____ jardín | 6. _____ lavaplatos | 11. _____ apartamentos |
| 2. _____ sótano | 7. _____ muebles | 12. _____ balcón |
| 3. _____ afueras | 8. _____ escaleras | 13. _____ reciclaje |
| 4. _____ rascacielos | 9. _____ ascensor | 14. _____ nómada |
| 5. _____ secadora | 10. _____ estantes | 15. _____ alojamiento |

**ANSWERS p. 298**

B. Use the following words to complete the idea.

| | | |
|---|---|---|
| la cocina | el comedor | la terraza |
| el baño | la sala | la alcoba |
| el jardín | el garaje | el sótano |

1. La estufa está en _____.
2. La cama está en _____.
3. El carro lo ponemos en _____.
4. El sofá está en _____.
5. La mesa para comer está en _____.
6. Cultivamos flores en _____.
7. Hay una chimenea en _____ en el último piso del edificio.
8. Usamos _____ si hay aviso de tornado.
9. El inodoro está en _____.

C. Write the appliances or devices related to each activity.

1. congelar verduras: _____
2. lavar ropa: _____
3. secar ropa: _____
4. preparar café: _____
5. cocinar: _____
6. calentar comida rápidamente: _____
7. lavar platos: _____
8. hornear: _____

D. Write the word in Spanish.

1. accommodation _____
2. balcony _____
3. housing _____
4. basement _____
5. nomad _____
6. skyscraper _____
7. floor _____
8. wall _____
9. window _____
10. hallway _____

E. *¡Los quehaceres domésticos!* Complete each sentence with the present subjunctive of the verb in parentheses.

Nuestros amigos vienen a visitarnos y es importante que tengamos el apartamento muy limpio.

*Es necesario que nosotros. . .*

1. _____ los platos. (*lavar*)
2. _____ la basura. (*sacar*)
3. _____ la ropa. (*secar*)
4. _____ el polvo. (*limpiar*)
5. _____ el piso de la cocina. (*barrer*)
6. _____ la cena. (*preparar*)
7. _____ el pastel. (*hornear*)
8. _____ la aspiradora por la alfombra. (*pasar*)
9. No _____ desorden. (*hacer*)

# DIÁLOGO   Buscando un apartaestudio en La Paz

*Paula es una chica americana que trabaja para una compañía multinacional de manera remota y tiene la ventaja de trabajar desde cualquier ciudad y país que prefiera con tal de que se ajuste a su horario de trabajo. Ahora Paula quiere trabajar desde La Paz, Bolivia y está buscando un apartaestudio que se acomode a sus necesidades. Ella habla por zoom con la agente de la inmobiliaria, la señorita Laura Méndez.*

PAULA:   Hola Laura. ¡Qué bueno poder conversar contigo por zoom!

LAURA:   Con todo gusto. Dime, ¿estás interesada en trabajar para tu compañía desde La Paz y te gustaría alquilar un apartaestudio?

PAULA: Sí, así es. No conozco La Paz ni ningún lugar en Bolivia y me parece una excelente oportunidad poder trabajar desde allí y al mismo tiempo poder visitar los lugares hermosos que el país ofrece.

LAURA: ¿Por cuánto tiempo piensas trabajar desde La Paz?

PAULA: Creo que me gustaría trabajar por dos meses. Por esa razón necesito un apartaestudio que tenga los requisitos necesarios para mi trabajo y que esté ubicado en un lugar seguro de la ciudad.

LAURA: Sí entiendo. En La Paz se están construyendo edificios de apartamentos muy modernos. Muchos trabajadores nómadas buscan venir y trabajar por un tiempo y así poder conocer el país. En este momento tengo en mi lista un apartaestudio de 45 metros cuadrados en un décimo piso con una vista panorámica de las montañas.

PAULA: ¿Tiene ascensor? Porque sé que La Paz es una de las ciudades más altas del mundo y subir por las escaleras al décimo piso sería terrible para mí.

LAURA: Sí, el edificio tiene tres ascensores. También tiene escaleras de emergencia, por supuesto. El apartamento está amoblado, con terminados muy elegantes y es muy lindo. Tiene refrigerador, lavaplatos, y una torre con secadora y lavadora muy conveniente. Además, en el último piso del edificio hay una terraza con una chimenea y un asador. También el edificio tiene un gimnasio.

PAULA: Estupendo. ¿Y cómo funciona la conexión del internet y el wifi? ¿El edificio tiene una zona de trabajo compartido o coworking?

LAURA: Déjame contarte, la red de internet y el wifi funcionan muy bien. Además, el segundo piso del edificio está diseñado como zona de trabajo en común con computadores, escritorios, sofás y una cocina pequeña con cafetera para prepararse un delicioso café.

PAULA: Me parece excelente. Así puedo conocer a más trabajadores nómadas como yo. ¿Tiene el nombre del conjunto de apartamentos para poder buscarlo por el internet y mirar las fotos?

LAURA: Claro que sí. Yo te mando el enlace del sitio del internet en un correo electrónico.

PAULA: Muchas gracias. ¿Me puedes decir cuánto cuesta el alquiler por mes?

LAURA: Cuesta 9.000 bolivianos al mes. Es decir, el equivalente a 1.300 dólares americanos.

PAULA: Me parece un buen precio. Voy a revisar la información sobre el apartamento y te aviso sobre cualquier decisión que tome al respecto.

LAURA: Está muy bien. Paula, recuerda que Bolivia te espera con los brazos abiertos.

# DIALOGUE  *Looking for a Studio Apartment in La Paz*

*Paula is an American woman who works remotely for a multinational company and has the advantage of working from any city or country she prefers, as long as it fits her work schedule. Now, Paula wants to work from La Paz, Bolivia, and is looking for a studio apartment that suits her needs. She speaks via Zoom with the real estate agent, Miss Laura Méndez.*

PAULA:  *Hi Laura. It's so nice to be able to chat with you via Zoom!*

LAURA:  *Gladly. Tell me, are you interested in working for your company from La Paz and would you like to rent a studio apartment?*

PAULA:  *Yes, that's right. I'm not familiar with La Paz or any other part of Bolivia, and I think it's an excellent opportunity to work from there and at the same time visit the beautiful places the country has to offer.*

LAURA:  *How long do you plan to work from La Paz?*

PAULA:  *I think I'd like to work for two months. For that reason, I need a studio apartment that meets the necessary requirements for my job and is located in a safe part of the city.*

LAURA:  *Yes, I understand. Very modern apartment buildings are being built in La Paz. Many nomadic workers are looking to come and work for a while and get to know the country. Right now, I have a 45-square-meter studio apartment on the tenth floor with a panoramic view of the mountains on my list.*

PAULA:  *Does it have an elevator? Because I know La Paz is one of the highest cities in the world, and climbing the stairs to the tenth floor would be terrifying for me.*

LAURA:  *Yes, the building has three elevators. It also has emergency stairs, of course. The apartment is furnished, with very elegant finishes, and is very nice. It has a refrigerator, dishwasher, and a stacked washer and dryer unit, which is very convenient. Plus, on the top floor of the building, there's a terrace with a fireplace and a grill. The building also has a gym.*

PAULA:  *Great. And how do the internet and Wi-Fi work? Does the building have a shared workspace or coworking space?*

LAURA:  *Let me tell you, the internet and Wi-Fi work very well. Plus, the second floor of the building is designed as a shared work area with computers, desks, sofas, and a small kitchen with a coffee maker to make delicious coffee.*

PAULA:  *I think it's excellent. This way I can meet more nomadic workers like me. Do you have the name of the apartment complex so I can search for it online and look at the photos?*

LAURA:  *Of course. I'll send you the website link in an email.*

PAULA:  *Thank you very much. Can you tell me how much the rent is per month?*

LAURA: *It's 9,000 bolivianos per month. That's the equivalent of 1,300 US dollars.*

PAULA: *I think it's a good price. I'll check the information about the apartment and let you know about any decision I make.*

LAURA: *That's great. Paula, remember that Bolivia awaits you with open arms.*

# PRÁCTICA

**ANSWERS p. 298**

**A.** **Buscando un apartaestudio en La Paz. Complete the story by using the information from the dialogue.**

Paula es una chica (1) _____que trabaja para una compañía multinacional que le permite trabajar desde cualquier ciudad y país que ella prefiera. Paula quiere ahora trabajar desde (2) _____, Bolivia. Por eso habla con (3) _____, una agente inmobiliaria. Laura le pregunta a Paula que por cuánto tiempo ella piensa trabajar en La Paz. Paula le dice que por dos (4) _____. Y por esa razón, Paula necesita un (5) _____ que tenga los requisitos necesarios para trabajar de manera remota. Laura le dice que tiene un apartaestudio de (6) _____ en un (7) _____ piso y que tiene una vista panorámica de las montañas. Paula le pregunta a Laura si el edificio tiene (8) _____ porque ella sabe que La Paz es una de las ciudades (9) _____ altas del mundo. Laura le responde que el edificio tiene (10) _____ ascensores y también cuenta con (11) _____ de emergencia. El apartamento tiene (12) _____, lavaplatos, y una torre con (13) _____ y (14) _____ muy conveniente.

Laura le dice también que la (15) _____ de internet, y el (16) _____ funcionan muy bien. También le cuenta que la (17) _____ de trabajo común está en el (18) _____piso. El precio del alquiler es de 9.000 (19) _____, que es el equivalente a aproximadamente (20) _____dólares americanos.

**ANSWERS p. 299**

**B.** **Answer *true* or *false* (T/F). Think of the correct answer for each false statement.**

1. _____ Paula quiere trabajar de manera remota en Cochabamba, Bolivia.
2. _____ Laura Méndez es la mejor amiga de Paula.
3. _____ Paula es una trabajadora nómada colombiana.
4. _____ El apartamento que Laura tiene en su lista está en el décimo piso.
5. _____ El apartamento está amoblado y tiene 45 metros cuadrados.
6. _____ El edificio solo tiene escaleras y no ascensores.
7. _____ El apartamento tiene un gimnasio y una terraza con asador.
8. _____ La zona de trabajo compartido o coworking está en el cuarto piso.
9. _____ El apartamento tiene una vista panorámica de la playa.
10. _____ El alquiler del apartamento por mes es de 9.000 bolivianos.

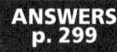

**ANSWERS p. 299**

C. ¿Subjunctive or indicative? Complete with the right form of the verbs in parentheses.

1. Paula quiere alquilar un apartamento que _____ en una zona segura de La Paz. (*estar*)
2. Laura le sugiere a Paula que _____ un apartamento en el décimo piso de un edificio muy moderno. (*mirar*)
3. Para Paula es necesario que el edificio_____ una zona de trabajo común. (*tener*)
4. Para ella también es importante que _____ ascensor en el edificio. (*haber*)
5. Laura le dice a Paula que el internet y el wifi _____ muy bien en el edificio. (*funcionar*)
6. Laura le dice que en el edificio _____ una terraza con asador. (*haber*)
7. Paula sabe que La Paz _____ una de las ciudades más altas del mundo. (*ser*)
8. Para Paula es conveniente que el apartamento _____ lavadora y secadora. (*tener*)
9. Paula espera que el precio del alquiler no _____ muy alto. (*ser*)
10. Laura le dice que el alquiler del apartamento_____ 9.000 bolivianos al mes. (*costar*)

**ANSWERS p. 299**

D. You are going to La Paz for the first time. Listen to your travel agent giving you advice. Complete her statements using the *Ud.* formal command.

1. _____ los boletos a tiempo. (*comprar*)
2. No _____ las cosas para el último momento. (*dejar*)
3. _____ algunos libros sobre el país que va a visitar. (*leer*)
4. _____ los mapas de la región que visita. (*consultar*)
5. No _____ el pasaporte en casa. (*olvidar*)
6. _____ las maletas con anticipación. (*hacer*)
7. No _____ sus documentos ni sus tarjetas de crédito. (*perder*)
8. _____ cuidado con sus maletas. (*tener*)

# GRAMMAR I Contraste entre el indicativo y el subjuntivo: percepción vs. emoción (*Indicative and Subjunctive in Contrast: Perception vs. Emotion*)

A. If the main clause contains a verb or an expression of perception—such as **oír, ver, observar, es obvio**—the verb in the subordinate clause must be in the indicative. There are not many verbs or expressions of perception. They are as follows:

| | |
|---|---|
| **notar** to notice | **es claro** it's clear |
| **observar** to observe | **es evidente** it's evident |
| **oír** to hear | **es obvio** it's obvious |
| **sentir** to feel | **está claro** it's clear |
| **ver** to see | |

EXS: **Tú ves que *el edificio tiene* gimnasio.** (*You see that <u>the building has</u> a gym.*)
**Es obvio que *ella prefiere* trabajar en La Paz.** (*It's obvious that <u>she prefers</u> to work in La Paz.*)

B. If the main clause contains a verb of emotion, the verb in the subordinate clause must be in the subjunctive. Verbs of emotion are those that denote sadness, happiness, like, dislike, surprise, hate, love, fear, pity, anger, gratitude, and so on.

EXS: **Me gusta que *vayas* a Bolivia.** (*I like that you're going to Bolivia.*)
**Es triste que él *esté* enfermo.** (*It's sad that he is sick.*)

If the two clauses have the same subject, the second clause takes the infinitive, although the subjunctive is still possible.

EXS: **Siento mucho no *ir*. . .** (*I'm sorry I am not going. . . .*)
**Siento mucho que no *vaya*. . .** (*I'm sorry I am not going. . . .*)

Here is a partial list of verbs and expressions of emotion:

| | |
|---|---|
| **agradar** to please, like | **es extraño** it's strange |
| **agradecer** to thank | **es maravilloso** it's marvelous |
| **alegrarse** to be glad | **es sorprendente** it's surprising |
| **asustar** to scare | **es triste** it's sad |
| **disgustar** to upset | **es (una) lástima** it's a pity |
| **enojarse** to get angry | **es una pena** it's a pity |
| **gustar** to like | **tener miedo** to be afraid |
| **molestar** to bother | |
| **sentir** to be sorry | |
| **sorprender** to surprise | |
| **temer** to be afraid | |

C. Note that:

1. Sentir means both *to be sorry* and *to feel, to sense*. When it means *to be sorry*, it takes the subjunctive, because being sorry is an emotion. When it means *to feel, to sense*, it takes the indicative, because feeling or sensing is a perception.

EXS: **Siento mucho que *estés* enfermo.** (*I'm sorry that you're are sick.*)
**Siento por el pulso que *estás* enfermo.** (*I feel [sense] by your pulse that you're sick.*)

2. *Ojalá (que)* means *I hope that*, implying an emotion or a wish. It is not a verb; it's an expression originating from Arabic. It always takes the subjunctive, and it may or may not be followed by **que**.

EXS: **Ojalá *llegues* a tiempo.** (*I hope [that] you will be on time.*)

**Ojalá *que tenga* suerte.** (*I hope [that] I will be lucky.*)

# PRACTIQUE LA GRAMÁTICA

**ANSWERS**
**p. 299**

1. If the main clause contains a verb of perception, the subordinate clause must be in the _____.

   EX:  **Es evidente que ella _____ trabajar en Bolivia.** (*querer*)

2. If the main clause contains a verb of emotion, the subordinate clause must be in the _____.

   EX:  **Me alegra que (tú) _____en La Paz.** (*vivir*)

3. In the previous lesson we saw that a verb of information requires the indicative. *Perception* is information through our senses. Also remember that a verb of *influence* requires the _____. Somehow an emotion is an *influence* on somebody, and as such, requires the verb in the _____.

4. Gratitude is an emotion. How would you finish the sentence **Paula te agradece que (tú) _____ un apartamento apropiado.** (*buscar*)

5. *Molestar* is not *to molest* but *to bother*, an emotion of dislike. Complete the sentence **Me molesta que Ud. _____ mucho ruido.** (*hacer*)

6. *Asustar* is an emotion of surprise combined with fear. How do you complete the sentence **Me asusta que ellos _____ a noventa millas por hora?** (*manejar*)

7. *Evidente* is related to *ver* and *video;* it refers to something everybody can see and understand.

   EX:  **Es evidente que él _____ dinero.** (*tener*)

8. *Ojalá* is one of the many words that Spanish inherited from the Arabic language. Originally it meant *may Allah grant that.* However, nowadays it means *I hope that.* Complete the sentence.

   **Ojalá (que) no _____ mañana.** (*llover*)

9. In the expresion *Es una lástima que* (*It's a pity that*), *una* may be omitted. This is an emotion of sadness and compassion, and it requires the verb in _____.

10. *Sentir* means both *to be sorry* and *to feel, sense, hear.* When it means *to be sorry,* it takes the _____; when it means *to feel, sense, hear,* it takes the _____.

# PRÁCTICA

**ANSWERS**
**p. 299**

A. Complete each sentence with a present indicative or a present subjunctive form of the verb in parentheses.

   1. Me sorprende que Paula _____ a La Paz. (*ir*)
   2. Es una lástima que ustedes no _____ ir con ella. (*poder*)
   3. Es obvio que Laura y Paula no _____ en persona. (*conocerse*)
   4. Laura le asegura a Paula que el edificio _____ tres ascensores. (*tener*)

5. Me enoja que los vecinos _____ la música con mucho volumen. (*poner*)

6. ¿Te gusta que yo _____ ese apartamento? (*alquilar*)

7. Todos vemos que Paula _____ lista para trabajar en La Paz. (*estar*)

8–9. Es evidente que Ud. no _____ Bolivia ni _____ mucho de su historia. (*conocer/saber*)

10. Ojalá que el apartamento no _____ muy costoso. (*ser*)

**ANSWERS p. 299**

B. Write sentences with the following words in the order given. Make any necessary adjustments.

1. me sorprende/Paula/querer trabajar/en Bolivia/.

   _____

2. nos alegramos mucho/ustedes/comprar/bueno/apartamento/.

   _____

3. ojalá/nosotros/ganar/mucho/bolivianos/en La Paz/.

   _____

4. es una lástima/tú/no poder/acompañar/a mí/.

   _____

5. nos molesta/vecinos (*neighbors*)/poner/la música/muy alto/.

   _____

# GRAMMAR II Contraste entre el indicativo y el subjuntivo: certeza vs. duda (*Indicative and Subjunctive in Contrast: Certainty vs. Doubt*)

A. Indicative with verbs of certainty

1. If the main clause contains a verb of certainty or belief, the verb in the subordinate clause is in the indicative.

   EXS: **Ud. cree que su amiga** *está* **enferma.** (*You believe your friend is sick.*)
   **Supongo que ella** *está* **enferma.** (*I suppose she is sick.*)

2. Here is a partial list of verbs and expressions of certainty, belief, and sureness.

   | | |
   |---|---|
   | **creer** to believe | **estar convencido** to be convinced |
   | **imaginarse** to imagine | **es verdad** it's true |
   | **parecer** to seem | **no dudar** to not doubt |
   | **pensar** to think | **no hay duda** there is no doubt |
   | **suponer** to suppose | **tener por cierto** to be certain |
   | **es que** the fact is | **tener por seguro** to be sure |

B. Subjunctive with verbs of doubt, disbelief

1. If the main clause contains a verb of doubt, disbelief, denial, the verb in the subordinate clause is in the subjunctive.

EXS:  **Ud. no cree que ella** *esté* **enferma.** (*You don't believe she is sick.*)
   **Es posible que** *llueva* **mañana.** (*It's possible that it will rain tomorrow.*)

2. Here is a partial list of verbs of disbelief, doubt, and denial.

| | |
|---|---|
| **dudar** to doubt | **no es que** it isn't that |
| **es dudoso** it's doubtful | **no estar convencido** to not be convinced |
| **es imposible** it's impossible | **no es verdad** it's not true |
| **es posible** it's possible | **no imaginarse** to not imagine |
| **es probable** it's probable | **no parecer** to not seem |
| **hay duda de** there is doubt | **no pensar** to not think |
| **no creer** to not believe | **no suponer** to not suppose |

3. There is no clear-cut way of being able to tell when the verbs and expressions above express doubt and when they are expressing certainty. Therefore, the rules given do not apply one hundred percent of the time, but lend themselves to interpretation. You may have noticed that many of the verbs and verbal expressions in *B, 2* above are the negative counterpart of the verbs and verbal expressions in *A, 2:* **creer** → **no creer/pensar** → **no pensar/es verdad** → **no es verdad.**

C.  Indicative and subjunctive with adverbs of doubt

The adverbs of doubt are **quizá(s), tal vez, acaso, puede ser,** and they all mean the same: *perhaps, maybe.* They are used with the indicative or subjunctive, depending on the degree of doubt the speaker feels.

EXS:  **Quizás** *llueve* **mañana.** (*Perhaps it will rain tomorrow.*): The speaker is almost sure.
   **Tal vez** *llueva* **mañana.** (*Perhaps it will rain tomorrow.*): The speaker has doubts.

# PRACTIQUE LA GRAMÁTICA

**ANSWERS**
**p. 299**

1. Verbs and expressions of doubt require the verb in the subordinate clause to be in the _____.
   EX:  **Es posible que Laura me** _____. (*visitar*)

2. Verbs of certainty and belief in the main clause require the subordinate clause to be in the _____.
   EX:  **Pienso que (tú)** _____ **razón.** (*tener*)

3. *Suponer* indicates more certainty than doubt. For this reason, it requires the subordinate verb to be in the _____.
   EX:  **Supongo que ella** _____ **bien.** (*estar*)

4. One way to emphasize a statement in English is to add *the fact is that* in front of it. To translate this idea Spanish uses the simple expression _____, which requires the indicative.
   EX:  **Es que Paula** _____ **inglés y español.** (*saber*)

5. To deny a fact with emphasis, in Spanish we use *No es que* + (statement), and the opposite usually follows with *sino que.*

    EX:  **No es que Paula** _____ **colombiana, sino que vivió en Colombia.** (*ser*)

6. Adverbs of doubt such as **quizás, tal vez,** take the _____ if the speaker is almost sure; they take the _____ if he or she is not that sure.

# PRÁCTICA

**ANSWERS**
**p. 299**

A. Complete each sentence with a present indicative or a present subjunctive form of the verb in parentheses.

   1. Pienso que mis padres _____ en casa ahora. (*estar*)

   2. Marta no está convencida de que tú la _____. (*querer*)

   3. Es posible que Paula y Laura _____ a vernos para fin de año. (*venir*)

   4. Me parece muy bien que ustedes _____ trabajando en ese proyecto. (*seguir*)

   5. El agente de la inmobiliaria piensa que el apartamento no _____ grande. (*ser*)

   6. No hay duda de que ellos _____ conocer La Paz. (*desear*)

   7. ¿Por qué dudas de que ella no te _____ el dinero del alquiler? (*dar*)

   8. Suponemos que esta casa _____ en buenas condiciones. (*estar*)

   9–10. No es que yo _____ infalible, pero es que tú siempre _____ tener razón. (*ser/querer*)

**ANSWERS**
**p. 299**

B. Add the expressions in parentheses to form sentences with two clauses.

   EX:  **Paga mucho dinero por arreglar la casa.** (*dudo*)
        **Dudo que pague mucho dinero por arreglar la casa.**

   1. La joven pasa la aspiradora sin problema. (*suponemos*)

   _____

   2. Roberto se ocupa de comprar los electrodomésticos. (*me parece*)

   _____

   3. Los vecinos hacen mucho ruido por la noche. (*es posible*)

   _____

   4. Seguimos derecho hasta la capital. (*es probable*)

   _____

   5. Paula llega a Bolivia en tres días. (*es imposible*)

   _____

**GRAMMAR III** **Contraste entre el subjuntivo y el indicativo: Cláusulas adjetivas y adverbiales** (*Indicative and Subjunctive in Contrast: Adjectival and Adverbial Clauses*)

**A.** Indicative-subjunctive contrast in adjectival clauses: known vs. unknown

   **1.** Compare this pair of sentences:

      **a)** **Tengo una casa que *es* grande.** (*I have a house that is big.*)

      **b)** **Busco una casa que *sea* grande.** (*I'm looking for a house that is big.*)

     In *a)* we have a house that is known, and the verb *es* is in the indicative. In *b)* the house is unknown, and the verb *sea* is in the subjunctive. These clauses are called adjectival because they describe the *house*.

   **2.** Now compare this pair of sentences:

      **a)** **Aquí hay un señor que habla quechua.** (*There is a man here who speaks Quechua.*)

      **b)** **Aquí no hay un señor que hable quechua.** (*There is no man here who speaks Quechua.*)

     In *a)* the speaker states the existence of a man who is known, and therefore the verb has to be in the indicative (**habla**). In *b)* the speaker denies the existence of a man, in other words, the man is unknown. Therefore, the verb has to be in the subjunctive (**hable**).

     More examples follow.

     EXS:  **Quiero un apartamento que tenga balcón.** (unknown)
           **Sé que hay un apartamento que tiene balcón.** (known)
           **¿Hay un apartamento que tenga balcón?** (unknown)

**B.** Indicative-subjunctive contrast in adverbial clauses

   **1. Indicative to show reality.** An adverbial clause explains some circumstances of the main clause: time, location, and so on. If the main clause shows an action that has already occurred, the verb in the subordinate clause is in the indicative because it's a real fact or a definite situation.

     EXS:  **Te vi cuando saliste de la casa.** (*I saw you when you left the house.*)
           **Te saludo cuando llego a casa.** (*I greet you when I arrive home.*)

     Notice that any action in the past is a fact. The present too can be a fact when it's a habit; as such it has happened many times before.

   **2. Subjunctive to show unreality.** A future action is only a possibility; it is not yet a fact. When the main clause is in the future tense, the verb in the subordinate clause has to be in the subjunctive. Remember that the present indicative is often used to show a future action, as you can see in the second example below.

EXS: **Te veré cuando llegues.** (*I'll see you when you arrive.*)
**Te pago cuando me paguen.** (*I'll pay you when they pay me.*)

3. **Adverbial conjunctions.** Here is a list of adverbial conjunctions that may take the indicative or the subjunctive.

| | |
|---|---|
| **aunque** although | **en seguida que** as soon as |
| **como** as | **hasta que** until |
| **cuando** when | **luego que** after |
| **después (de) que** after | **mientras (que)** while |
| **donde** where | **siempre que** whenever |
| **en cuanto** as soon as | **tan pronto como** as soon as |

### NOTES

1. *Mientras* can be used with *que* and without it. The modern tendency is to omit it.

   EX: **Mamá cocina mientras nosotros *vemos* la TV.** (indicative = habit = reality)

2. *Antes que* always takes the subjunctive, even to show reality in the past, or when there is a real habit.

   EX: **Siempre te llamo antes que *salgas*.** (*I always call you before you leave.*)

3. We use *antes que* and *antes de que* with the same meaning. The modern tendency is to omit *de*. Exactly the same happens with *después que* and *después de que*.

C. **Indicative-subjunctive contrast.** Review the uses of the indicative vs. those of the subjunctive.

| Indicative | Subjunctive |
|---|---|
| 1. INFORMATION: | INFLUENCE: |
| Ya sé que *estás* bien. | Espero que *estés* bien. |
| 2. PERCEPTION: | EMOTION: |
| Ya veo que *estás* bien. | Me alegra que *estés* bien. |
| 3. CERTAINTY: | DOUBT: |
| Creo que *estás* bien. | No creo que *estés* bien. |
| 4. KNOWN ELEMENT: | UNKNOWN ELEMENT: |
| Tengo una casa que *tiene* dos pisos. | Busco una casa que *tenga* dos pisos. |
| 5. REAL FACT: | FUTURE FACT: |
| Te invité cuando te *saludé*. | Te veré cuando *llegues*. |

# PRACTIQUE LA GRAMÁTICA

**ANSWERS**
**p. 300**

1. An adjective describes a noun. A subordinate clause that starts with *que* and describes a noun in the main clause is called an _____ clause.

2. The adjectival clause may describe a known noun; in this case the verb is in _____. If the noun described is unknown, the verb in the adjectival clause must be in the _____.

3. To state the existence of a noun presupposes some knowledge of that noun. Complete this sentence: **Aquí hay una pirámide que** _____ **ochocientos años.** (*tener*)

4. A speaker can mention a noun that is hypothetical or nonexistent, and therefore, unknown. Complete this sentence: **No hay un boliviano que no** _____ **español.** (*hablar*)

5. You ask for information about a noun when you don't know about that noun. Complete the sentence: **¿Hay alguna persona que** _____ **quechua?** (*estudiar*)

6. You know about the things you have: your house, your car, and so on. Complete the sentence: **Tenemos un perro que** _____ **mucho.** (*comer*)

7. An adverb gives information about an action; it tells when, where, how. If we use a clause instead of an adverb to describe the verb of the main clause, this will be an _____ clause.

8. If the main clause shows an action that has already occurred, this action is a reality. The verb in the subordinate clause must be in the _____.
   EX:  **Salimos después que la agente inmobiliaria** _____. (*llegar*)

9. A habit is something we repeat many times, and it is therefore a reality. Consequently, the subordinate clause must be in the _____.
   EX:  **Laura siempre toma un café después que** _____. (*almorzar*)

10. A future action is only a possibility; it's not a reality. When the main clause is in the future tense, the subordinate clause must be in _____.
   EX:  **Comeremos después que Laura y Paula** _____. (*llegar*)

11. Complete this sentence: **Vamos a viajar a Bolivia cuando (nosotros)** _____ **dinero.** (*tener*)

12. In the adverb-conjunction *después de que* the preposition _____ is omitted in modern Spanish, and so is the conjunction _____ in *mientras que.*

13. *Antes que* always requires the _____, even in the past when the action has been a reality.

14. Verbs of influence and emotion require the _____, whereas verbs of information and perception require the _____.

# PRÁCTICA

ANSWERS
p. 300

A. Complete each sentence with a present indicative or a present subjunctive form of the verb in parentheses.

1. Conozco un conjunto residencial que _____ muchos árboles. (*tener*)
2. Compré una casa que me _____ mucho. (*gustar*)
3. Necesitamos un/a agente (*team*) que _____ de inmuebles. (*saber*)
4. Teresa tiene una casa que _____ muy linda. (*ser*)
5. Hablé con mi esposa después que _____ el trabajo. (*terminar*)
6. Hablaré con la agente inmobiliaria antes que se _____ a casa. (*ir*)
7. Es cierto que yo sólo _____ inglés y español. (*saber*)
8. No hay muchos bolivianos que _____ quechua. (*hablar*)
9. Paula tiene un amigo que _____ en La Paz. (*vivir*)
10. En Bolivia hay más de 2 millones de personas que _____ quechua. (*saber*)
11. Tengo miedo de que ellos _____ demasiado dinero en el apartaestudio. (*gastar*)
12. Quiero comprar una casa que no _____ muy cara. (*ser*)
13. Haré ese trabajo, aunque no me _____. (*gustar*)
14. Hice el trabajo como usted me _____. (*decir*)
15. Trabajaré toda la tarde hasta que me _____. (*cansar*)

ANSWERS
p. 300

B. Replace the verbs or verbal expressions in the main clause with those in parentheses. Make the necessary changes.

EX: **Tienen una casa grande.** (*buscar*)
**Buscan una casa que sea grande.**

1. Tenemos un jefe que nunca llega tarde. (*querer*)

   _____

2. Hay alguien aquí que estudia quechua en esta ciudad. (*no hay nadie*)

   _____

3. Conocemos a una agente inmobiliaria que vende apartaestudios en La Paz. (*necesitar*)

   _____

4. Hay muchos turistas que viajan a Cochabamba. (*no hay ningún*)

   _____

5. Los trabajadores nómadas viajan por todo el mundo. (*ojalá*)

   _____

ANSWERS
p. 300

C.  Translate the sentences into Spanish.

1.  We don't know anyone who is going.

_____

2.  She needs an apartment that has two bedrooms.

_____

3.  There is no one here who speaks quechua.

_____

4.  Is there anyone here who has a big condominium?

_____

5.  I am looking for a secretary who wants to work.

_____

ANSWERS
p. 300

D.  Use the conjunctions in parentheses to combine the two sentences. Make the necessary changes.

EX:  **Paula se mudará a Bolivia. Ella alquilará un apartamento.** (*después que*)
**Paula se mudará a Bolivia después (de) que alquile un apartamento.**

1.  No te olvides de llamarme. Llegarás a la oficina. (*antes que*)

_____

2.  Laura siempre llama a su jefe. Tiene preguntas. (*cuando*)

_____

3.  Los trabajadores nómadas volverán a la oficina. Visitarán muchos países. (*después que*)

_____

4.  Limpiaré el apartamento. Mis amigos se irán. (*tan pronto como*)

_____

5.  Yo busco la dirección. Ud. revisa la solicitud. (*mientras*)

_____

ANSWERS
p. 300

E.  Complete these sentences with the indicative or subjunctive forms of the verbs in parentheses.

1.  Espero que Ud. _____ el apartaestudio a un buen precio. (*alquilar*)
2.  No entiendo por qué ella _____ a Bolivia mañana. (*irse*)
3.  Puedo hablar con Laura después que (yo) _____ de mi trabajo. (*salir*)
4.  Te contaré muchas cosas cuando (nosotras) _____ a casa. (*llegar*)
5.  No hay nadie aquí que no _____ español. (*hablar*)
6.  Conozco a una muchacha en la oficina que _____ de Cochabamba. (*ser*)
7.  Anita me informa que Ud. _____ a La Paz el verano próximo. (*ir*)
8.  Teresa me sugiere que (nosotros) _____ en la esquina. (*cruzar*)

9. Paula trabajará hasta que se _____. (*cansarse* = get tired)

10. Me sorprende que mis amigos no _____ nada. (*decir*)

11. Es una pena que miles de niños _____ de hambre. (*morir*)

12. Supongo que ustedes _____ responsables en su trabajo. (*ser*)

# ANSWERS   LESSONS 13–15

## Lesson 13

### Practique las palabras nuevas

A. 1. la        4. el/la      7. los/las      10. las
   2. los/las    5. los       8. los          11. el
   3. el         6. la        9. el           12. el/la

B. 1. sociología      4. cardiología     7. geología      10. neurología
   2. psicología      5. dermatología    8. teología      11. cosmetología
   3. antropología    6. etimología      9. radiología    12. criminología

C. 1. escritor/a      4. cirujano/a      6. administrador/a      8. contador/a
   2. psicólogo/a     5. enfermero/a        de empresas          9. meteorólogo/a
   3. abogado/a                          7. ingeniero/a civil    10. veterinario/a

D. 1. el profesorado     3. la maestra        5. la universidad
   2. la facultad        4. solicitar

E. 1. creador/a de contenido/      6. bombero                12. presentador/a
      influyente                   7. (oficial de) policía       de noticias
   2. plomero                      8. sastre                 13. rector/a
   3. estilista/peluquero(a)       9. cocinero(a)/chef       14. catedrático(a)/
   4. agricultor(a)/campesino(a)  10. cosmetóloga/o              profesor(a)
   5. chofer/conductor(a)         11. bloguero/a             15. cantante

## Práctica

## Una entrevista importante de trabajo

A.
1. ingeniera
2. Autónoma de México
3. entrevista
4. Globatek
5. El señor Cruz
6. trabajo
7. internet
8. remota
9. informática
10. pasantía
11. sistemas
12. veranos
13. 18.000 (18 mil)
14. incrementos salariales
15. desempeño
16. políticas
17. vacaciones
18. beneficios de salud
19. semanas
20. seguro médico

B.
1. de sistemas
2. el internet
3. gerente general
4. 18.000
5. dos
6. una pasantía
7. dos

C.
1. detallista
2. recursivo/a
3. calificado/a
4. desempleado/a
5. metódico/a
6. artístico/a
7. autoritario/a
8. ingenioso/a
9. paciente
10. talentoso/a

## Practique el condicional

1. infinitive/estaría
2. endings
3. imperfect/escribiría
4. viviría
5. past/time
6. imperfect/iba a llegar
7. imperfect
8. future/conditional
9. estaría

## Práctica

A.
1. trabajaría
2. ganaría
3. pagarías
4. construiríamos
5. seríais
6. viviría
7. saldrían
8. vendrían
9. me levantaría
10. conoceríamos
11. ayudaría
12. aprenderían
13. mejoraría
14. podrían
15. compraríais

B.
1. ser > sería
2. otorgar > otorgaría
3. estar > estarías
4. volver > volverían
5. cumplir > cumpliríamos
6. producir > produciríais
7. conocer > conocería
8. despedir > despediríamos
9. pagar > pagaría
10. aconsejar > aconsejaría
11. escribir > escribiría
12. contratar > contrataríamos
13. dirigir > dirigirías
14. solicitar > solicitarías

C. 1. entrar > entraría
   2. despedir > despediría
   3. ir > iría
   4. ser > sería
   5. pedir > pedirían
   6. solicitar > solicitaría
   7. aconsejar > aconsejarías
   8. contratar > contratarían
   9. entrevistar > entrevistaría
   10. hablar > hablarían
   11. estar > estaría
   12. trabajar > trabajaríamos

## Practique el futuro y el condicional

1. sabré/e
2. vendría/d
3. conditional/haría
4. querría
5. cabremos
6. satisfaré
7. contendré/contendría
8. supondré/supondría
9. reharía/reharé
10. opondría/opondré

## Práctica

A. 1. saldremos
   2. habrá
   3. será
   4. propondrá
   5. se abstendrán
   6. viajará
   7. ganarán
   8. querrá
   9. sabrá
   10. tendrá

B. 1. viviría
   2. cambiaría
   3. saldría
   4. obtendría
   5. estaría
   6. trabajaría
   7. conocería
   8. aprendería
   9. recibiría
   10. haría

C. 1. encantaría
   2. ayudarían
   3. facilitarían
   4. haría
   5. explicaría
   6. se uniría
   7. construirían
   8. mejorarían
   9. tendría
   10. preferiría
   11. podríamos

D. 1. iremos/iríamos
   2. seremos/seríamos
   3. estaré/estaría
   4. darán/darían
   5. pediré/pediría
   6. veré/vería
   7. hará/haría
   8. diré/diría
   9. solicitaré/solicitaría
   10. vendremos/vendríamos
   11. saldrás/saldrías
   12. tendréis/tendríais
   13. volverás/volverías
   14. sabré/sabría
   15. pondremos/pondríamos
   16. trabajarán/trabajarían
   17. conocerá/conocería
   18. contratará/contrataría
   19. podré/podría
   20. querrá/querría

## Practique los mandatos formales

1. póngase   2. traigan   3. hagan   4. mande   5. pida

## Los mandatos formales en forma negativa

1. no salga     2. no se vistan     3. no haga     4. no usen     5. no se ponga

## Practique la gramática

1. e/e/i/hi
2. y/y
3. u/u/o/ho
4. negative/pero

5. sino
6. subject/sino que
7. sino

8. feminine/tristemente
9. keep/fácilmente
10. last/clara/fácilmente

## Práctica

A. 1. e/e     3. u     5. sino     7. sino     9. pero
   2. e        4. y     6. u       8. sino que  10. y

B. 1. rápidamente       4. felizmente     7. fácilmente     10. comúnmente
   2. recientemente     5. hábilmente     8. difícilmente    11. actualmente
   3. claramente        6. suavemente     9. tristemente     12. totalmente

C. 1. rápidamente       3. tristemente     5. difícilmente
   2. recientemente     4. claramente

# Lesson 14

## Practique las palabras nuevas

A. 1. las     4. el     7. el     10. las     13. los
   2. la      5. la     8. el     11. el      14. los
   3. el      6. el     9. la     12. el      15. el

B. 1. bus/autobus/autocar        4. carné               7. licencia
   2. carro/auto/automóvil       5. maletero/cajuela    8. llanta
   3. parquear                   6. manejar             9. faro

C. 1. licencia (carné) de conducir      6. la cámara digital/la cámara de visión trasera
   2. estación de gasolina/gasolinera   7. las direccionales
   3. los frenos                        8. un peaje
   4. el limpiaparabrisas               9. la calefacción
   5. una llave                         10. el cinturón de seguridad

## Práctica

### Un nuevo carro para Lucas y Aurora

A. 1. sacó la mano
2. La trasmisión
3. el aire acondicionado
4. 150 mil
5. nueva
6. usado
7. costosos
8. presupuesto
9. híbrido
10. gasolina
11. sistema de seguridad avanzado
12. cámara
13. navegador
14. sensores
15. azul
16. gris
17. amarillo
18. internet
19. concesionarios
20. modelos

B. 1. F   2. F   3. F   4. T   5. T   6. F   7. F   8. T   9. F   10. F

C. 1. manejes
2. frenes
3. estaciones
4. pinche
5. funcione
6. toques
7. lleven
8. arranque
9. conduzcas
10. llenes

## Practique el subjuntivo

1. subordinate/main
2. que
3. indicative/quiere
4. subjunctive/compre
5. cambiemos
6. infinitive/conducir
7. indicative
8. paguen
9. indicative/maneja
10. says that you work
11. tells you to work

## Práctica

A. 1. revise
2. sea
3. manejan
4. traiga
5. tenemos
6. compren
7. funcionan
8. tenga
9. busque
10. vayamos
11. haga
12. hay
13. sea
14. están
15. salga
16. se descargó
17. nos estacionemos
18. venga
19. preste
20. conoce

B. 1. sea
2. tenga
3. venga
4. esté
5. cueste
6. dure
7. funcione
8. sea
9. consuma
10. sea
11. prenda
12. tenga

C. 1. lleve el carro al taller mecánico.
2. necesita una batería nueva.
3. compremos un carro nuevo.
4. conduzca.
5. pongamos el aire acondicionado.

## Práctique los mandatos

1. familiar/tú
2. indicative/estaciona
3. -es/-as/revises/vuelvas
4. indicative/duerme
5. negative/salgas
6. ven/ten/sal
7. I gave/tell (say)
8. I know/be
9. affirmative/negative
10. llámame/me llames
11. supón
12. mantén/prevén

## Práctica

A.
1. habla
2. escribe
3. di
4. hazme
5. ven
6. oye
7. sal
8. pon
9. revisa
10. presenta

B.
1. llegues
2. digas
3. llames
4. compres
5. revises

C.
1. llámalo/no lo llames
2. llénalo/no lo llenes
3. revísalos/no los revises
4. pónlo/no lo pongas
5. cámbialo/no lo cambies

D.
1. abre
2. revisa
3. ve
4. vengas
5. llega
6. haz
7. pon
8. conduzcas
9. lleva
10. escribas

## Practique los acentos

1. stressed
2. last/two
3. stress/two
4. you/your
5. stress/n, s/two
6. next-to-the-last
7. two
8. two
9. yes/oneself/if
10. my/me/mí/mi
11. dónde
12. ¡Qué!
13. diphthong
14. yes/o

## Práctica

1. El **baúl** de mi **automóvil** es bastante grande y ayer lo **llené** de maletas.
2. El **mecánico cambió** la **batería** del **camión**.
3. Lucas **prefirió** comprar un coche **automático** e **híbrido**.
4. Tu **camión** está en **pésimas** condiciones.
5. No entiendo por **qué** los carros **mecánicos** son tan **difíciles** de manejar.

## Práctique los usos de *por* y *para*

A.
1. para
2. por
3. para
4. para
5. por
6. por
7. por
8. por
9. por
10. por
11. para
12. para
13. para

**B. 1.** para   **4.** por   **7.** para   **10.** por   **13.** para
**2.** para   **5.** por   **8.** por   **11.** por   **14.** por
**3.** por   **6.** para   **9.** para   **12.** por   **15.** para

# Lesson 15

## Práctique las palabras nuevas

**A. 1.** el   **4.** el/los   **7.** los   **10.** los   **13.** el
**2.** el   **5.** la   **8.** las   **11.** los   **14.** el/la
**3.** las   **6.** el/los   **9.** el   **12.** el   **15.** el

**B. 1.** la cocina   **4.** la sala   **7.** la terraza
**2.** la alcoba   **5.** el comedor   **8.** el sótano
**3.** el garaje   **6.** el jardín   **9.** el baño

**C. 1.** el congelador/el refrigerador   **4.** la cafetera   **7.** el lavaplatos
**2.** la lavadora   **5.** la estufa   **8.** el horno
**3.** la secadora   **6.** el microondas

**D. 1.** el alojamiento   **4.** el sótano   **7.** el piso   **9.** la ventana
**2.** el balcón   **5.** el/la nómada   **8.** la pared   **10.** el pasillo
**3.** la vivienda   **6.** el rascacielos

**E. 1.** lavemos   **4.** limpiemos   **7.** horneemos
**2.** saquemos   **5.** barramos   **8.** pasemos
**3.** sequemos   **6.** preparemos   **9.** hagamos

## Práctica

## Buscando un apartaestudio en La Paz

**A. 1.** americana   **8.** ascensor   **15.** red
**2.** La Paz   **9.** más   **16.** wifi
**3.** Laura Méndez   **10.** tres   **17.** zona
**4.** meses   **11.** escaleras   **18.** segundo
**5.** apartaestudio   **12.** refrigerador   **19.** bolivianos
**6.** 45 metros cuadrados   **13.** secadora   **20.** $1.300
**7.** décimo   **14.** lavadora

B. 1. F    2. F    3. F    4. T    5. T    6. F    7. T    8. F    9. F    10. T

C. 1. esté       3. tenga       5. funcionan       7. es         9. sea
   2. mire       4. haya        6. hay             8. tenga      10. cuesta

D. 1. compre       3. lea          5. olvide       7. pierda
   2. deje         4. consulte     6. haga         8. tenga

## Práctique la gramática

1. indicative/quiere          5. haga            8. llueva
2. subjunctive/vivas          6. manejen         9. subjunctive
3. subjunctive/subjunctive    7. tiene           10. subjunctive/indicative
4. busques

## Práctica

A. 1. vaya       3. se conocen    5. pongan     7. está       9. sabe
   2. puedan     4. tiene         6. alquile    8. conoce     10. sea

B. 1. Me sorprende que Paula quiera trabajar en Bolivia.
   2. Nos alegramos mucho que ustedes compren un buen apartamento.
   3. Ojalá que nosotros ganemos muchos bolivianos en La Paz.
   4. Es una lástima que (tú) no puedas acompañarme (a mí).
   5. Nos molesta que los vecinos pongan la música muy alta.

## Práctique la gramática

1. subjunctive/visite       3. indicative/está      5. sea
2. indicative/tienes        4. es que/sabe          6. indicative/subjunctive

## Práctica

A. 1. están      3. vengan    5. es        7. dé        9. sea
   2. quieras    4. sigan     6. desean    8. está      10. quieres

B. 1. Suponemos que la joven pasa la aspiradora sin problema.
   2. Me parece que Roberto se ocupa de comprar los electrodomésticos.
   3. Es posible que los vecinos hagan mucho ruido por la noche.
   4. Es probable que sigamos derecho hasta la capital.
   5. Es imposible que Paula llegue a Bolivia en tres días.

## Práctique la gramática

| | | |
|---|---|---|
| 1. adjectival | 6. come | 11. tengamos |
| 2. indicative/subjunctive | 7. adverbial | 12. de/que |
| 3. tiene | 8. indicative/llegó | 13. subjunctive |
| 4. hable | 9. indicative/almuerza | 14. subjunctive/indicative |
| 5. estudie | 10. subjunctive/lleguen | |

## Práctica

| A. 1. tiene | 4. es | 7. sé | 10. saben | 13. guste (gusta) |
|---|---|---|---|---|
| 2. gusta (gustó) | 5. terminé | 8. hablen | 11. gasten | 14. dijo |
| 3. sepa | 6. vaya | 9. vive | 12. sea | 15. canse |

B. 1. Queremos un jefe que nunca llegue tarde.
   2. No hay nadie que estudie quechua en esta ciudad.
   3. Necesitamos una agente inmobiliaria que venda apartamentos en La Paz.
   4. No hay ningún turista que viaje a Cochabamba.
   5. Ojalá que los trabajadores nómadas viajen por el mundo.

C. 1. No conocemos a nadie que vaya.
   2. (Ella) necesita un apartamento que tenga dos alcobas (recámaras/dormitorios).
   3. No hay nadie aquí que hable quechua.
   4. ¿Hay alquien aquí que tenga un apartamento grande?
   5. Busco a una secretaria que quiera (desee) trabajar.

D. 1. No te olvides de llamarme antes que llegues a la oficina.
   2. Laura siempre llama a su jefe cuando tiene preguntas.
   3. Los trabajadores nómadas volverán a la oficina después (de) que visiten muchos países.
   4. Limpiaré el apartamento tan pronto como mis amigos se vayan.
   5. (Yo) busco la dirección mientras Ud. revisa la solicitud.

| E. 1. alquile | 4. lleguemos | 7. irá/va | 10. digan |
|---|---|---|---|
| 2. se va | 5. hable | 8. crucemos | 11. mueran |
| 3. salga | 6. es | 9. canse | 12. son |

# Appendixes

## APPENDIX 1 Los modos verbales en español (*Verbal Moods in Spanish*)

El modo verbal (*verbal mood*) is a certain aspect of communication that reflects the speaker's attitude toward what he/she says. In other words, it is the communicative process that the speaker uses to express ideas, emotions, suggestions, orders, etc. In Spanish, there are three verbal moods: **el indicativo** (*the indicative*), **el subjuntivo** (*the subjunctive*), and **el imperativo** (*the imperative*). **El condicional** (*the conditional*) belongs to the indicative mood.

1. **El modo indicativo** is used to express real facts or facts that are considered true, to describe things or phenomena, to express objective ideas, to talk about daily routines or past events, to talk about the future, etc. In Spanish, there are simple verbal tenses: **presente** (*present*), **pretérito** (*preterite/past*), **imperfecto** (*imperfect past*), **futuro** (*simple future*), and **condicional** (*conditional*). There are also some compound verb tenses we did not study in this textbook.

2. **El modo subjuntivo** in Spanish is used to express wishes, opinions, possibilities or hypothetical actions. The most common tenses for the subjunctive are: **presente del subjuntivo** (*present*) and **imperfecto del subjuntivo** (imperfect). In this book we focus on the present subjunctive and not on the imperfect subjunctive.

3. **El modo imperativo** in Spanish is used to give orders, advice, requests, or instructions directly, and is conjugated primarily in the second-person singular (familiar *tú*) and plural (*vosotros*), and in the formal form (*usted*). In this text, we studied the familiar (*tú*) and formal (*usted*) forms of the imperative.

# APPENDIX 2　Regular Verbs

**Infinitive**

habl ar (*to speak*)　　com er (*to eat*)　　viv ir (*to live*)

**Present Participle**

habl ando (*speaking*)　　com iendo (*eating*)　　viv iendo (*living*)

**Past Participle**

habl ado (*spoken*)　　com ido (*eaten*)　　viv ido (*lived*)

## Indicative: Simple Tenses

### PRESENT

| (*I speak, am speaking, do speak*) | (*I eat, am eating, do eat*) | (*I live, am living, do live*) |
|---|---|---|
| habl o | com o | viv o |
| habl as | com es | viv es |
| habl a | com e | viv e |
| habl amos | com emos | viv imos |
| habl áis | com éis | viv ís |
| habl an | com en | viv en |

### IMPERFECT

| (*I was speaking, used to speak, spoke*) | (*I was eating, used to eat, ate*) | (*I was living, used to live, lived*) |
|---|---|---|
| habl aba | com ía | viv ía |
| habl abas | com ías | viv ías |
| habl aba | com ía | viv ía |
| habl ábamos | com íamos | viv íamos |
| habl abais | com íais | viv íais |
| habl aban | com ían | viv ían |

### PRETERITE

| (*I spoke, did speak*) | (*I ate, did eat*) | (*I lived, did live*) |
|---|---|---|
| habl é | com í | viv í |
| habl aste | com iste | viv iste |
| habl ó | com ió | viv ió |
| habl amos | com imos | viv imos |
| habl asteis | com isteis | viv isteis |
| habl aron | com ieron | viv ieron |

### FUTURE

| *(I shall/will speak)* | *(I shall/will eat)* | *(I shall/will live)* |
|---|---|---|
| hablar **é** | comer **é** | vivir **é** |
| hablar **ás** | comer **ás** | vivir **ás** |
| hablar **á** | comer **á** | vivir **á** |
| hablar **emos** | comer **emos** | vivir **emos** |
| hablar **éis** | comer **éis** | vivir **éis** |
| hablar **án** | comer **án** | vivir **án** |

### CONDITIONAL

| *(I would speak)* | *(I would eat)* | *(I would live)* |
|---|---|---|
| hablar **ía** | comer **ía** | vivir **ía** |
| hablar **ías** | comer **ías** | vivir **ías** |
| hablar **ía** | comer **ía** | vivir **ía** |
| hablar **íamos** | comer **íamos** | vivir **íamos** |
| hablar **íais** | comer **íais** | vivir **íais** |
| hablar **ían** | comer **ían** | vivir **ían** |

## Subjunctive: Simple Tenses

### PRESENT

| *(that I [may] speak)* | *(that I [may] eat)* | *(that I [may] live)* |
|---|---|---|
| habl **e** | com **a** | viv **a** |
| habl **es** | com **as** | viv **as** |
| habl **e** | com **a** | viv **a** |
| habl **emos** | com **amos** | viv **amos** |
| habl **éis** | com **áis** | viv **áis** |
| habl **en** | com **an** | viv **an** |

### IMPERFECT

| *(that I [might] speak)* | | *(that I [might] eat)* | | *(that I [might] live)* | |
|---|---|---|---|---|---|
| habl **ara** | habl **ase** | com **iera** | com **iese** | viv **iera** | viv **iese** |
| habl **aras** | habl **ases** | com **ieras** | com **ieses** | viv **ieras** | viv **ieses** |
| habl **ara** | habl **ase** | com **iera** | com **iese** | viv **iera** | viv **iese** |
| habl **áramos** | habl **ásemos** | com **iéramos** | comi**ésemos** | viv **iéramos** | viv **iésemos** |
| hablar **ais** | habl **aseis** | com **ierais** | comi**eseis** | viv **ierais** | viv **ieseis** |
| habl **aran** | habl **asen** | com **ieran** | com **iesen** | viv **ieran** | viv **iesen** |

### COMMANDS

| *(speak)* | *(eat)* | *(live)* |
|---|---|---|
| habl **a** (**tú**) | com **e** (**tú**) | viv **e** (**tú**) |
| habl **e** (**Ud.**) | com **a** (**Ud.**) | viv **a** (**Ud.**) |
| habl **en** (**Uds.**) | com **an** (**Uds.**) | viv **an** (**Uds.**) |
| habl **emos** (**nosotros/as**) | com **amos** (**nosotros/as**) | viv **amos** (**nosotros/as**) |
| habl **ad**/no habl **éis** | com **ed**/no com **áis** | viv **id**/no viv **áis** |
| (**vosotros/as**) | (**vosotros/as**) | (**vosotros/as**) |

## Indicative: Compound Tenses

### PRESENT PERFECT

| *(I have spoken)* | *(I have eaten)* | *(I have lived)* |
|---|---|---|
| h e | h e | h e |
| h as | h as | h as |
| h a  — hablado | h a  — comido | h a  — vivido |
| h emos | h emos | h emos |
| habéis | habéis | habéis |
| h an | h an | h an |

### PAST PERFECT

| *(I had spoken)* | *(I had eaten)* | *(I had lived)* |
|---|---|---|
| hab ía | hab ía | hab ía |
| hab ías | hab ías | hab ías |
| hab ía  — hablado | hab ía  — comido | hab ía  — vivido |
| hab íamos | hab íamos | hab íamos |
| hab íais | hab íais | hab íais |
| hab ían | hab ían | hab ían |

### FUTURE PERFECT

| *(I will have spoken)* | *(I will have eaten)* | *(I will have lived)* |
|---|---|---|
| habr é | habr é | habr é |
| habr ás | habr ás | habr ás |
| habr á  — hablado | habr á  — comido | habr á  — vivido |
| habr emos | habr emos | habr emos |
| habr éis | habr éis | habr éis |
| habr án | habr án | habr án |

### FUTURE PERFECT

| *(I would have spoken)* | *(I would have eaten)* | *(I would have lived)* |
|---|---|---|
| habr ía | habr ía | habr ía |
| habr ías | habr ías | habr ías |
| habr ía  — hablado | habr ía  — comido | habr ía  — vivido |
| habr íamos | habr íamos | habr íamos |
| habr íais | habr íais | habr íais |
| habr ían | habr ían | habr ían |

## Subjunctive: Compound Tenses

### PRESENT PERFECT

| *(that I [may] have spoken)* | *(that I [may] have eaten)* | *(that I [may] have lived)* |
|---|---|---|
| hay a | hay a | hay a |
| hay as | hay as | hay as |
| hay a  — hablado | hay a  — comido | hay a  — vivido |
| hay amos | hay amos | hay amos |
| hay áis | hay áis | hay áis |
| hay an | hay an | hay an |

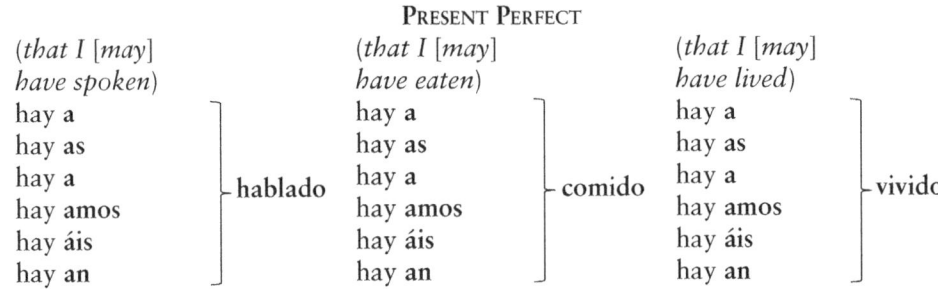

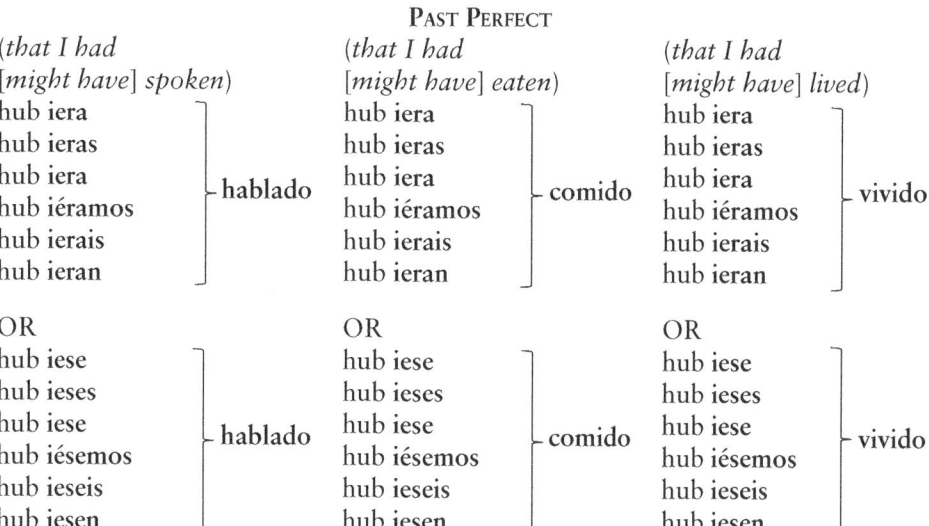

PAST PERFECT

(*that I had
[might have] spoken*)

hub iera
hub ieras
hub iera ⎤
hub iéramos ⎦ hablado
hub ierais
hub ieran

(*that I had
[might have] eaten*)

hub iera
hub ieras
hub iera ⎤
hub iéramos ⎦ comido
hub ierais
hub ieran

(*that I had
[might have] lived*)

hub iera
hub ieras
hub iera ⎤
hub iéramos ⎦ vivido
hub ierais
hub ieran

OR
hub iese
hub ieses
hub iese ⎤
hub iésemos ⎦ hablado
hub ieseis
hub iesen

OR
hub iese
hub ieses
hub iese ⎤
hub iésemos ⎦ comido
hub ieseis
hub iesen

OR
hub iese
hub ieses
hub iese ⎤
hub iésemos ⎦ vivido
hub ieseis
hub iesen

# APPENDIX 3   Irregular Verbs

(Only the tenses in which the verbs are irregular are included here.)

### Andar *to walk, go*
PRETERITE: anduve, anduviste, anduvo, anduvimos, anduvisteis, anduvieron
IMPERFECT SUBJUNCTIVE: anduviera (anduviese), anduvieras, anduviera, anduviéramos, anduvierais, anduvieran

### Caber *to fit*
PRESENT INDICATIVE: quepo, cabes, cabe, cabemos, cabéis, caben
PRETERITE: cupe, cupiste, cupo, cupimos, cupisteis, cupieron
FUTURE: cabré, cabrás, cabrá, cabremos, cabréis, cabrán
CONDITIONAL: cabría, cabrías, cabría, cabríamos, cabríais, cabrían
PRESENT SUBJUNCTIVE: quepa, quepas, quepa, quepamos, quepáis, quepan
IMPERFECT SUBJUNCTIVE: cupiera (cupiese), cupieras, cupiera, cupiéramos, cupierais, cupieran

### Caer *to fall, drop*
PRESENT INDICATIVE: caigo, caes, cae, caemos, caéis, caen
PRESENT SUBJUNCTIVE: caiga, caigas, caiga, caigamos, caigáis, caigan

### Conducir *to drive, conduct*
PRESENT INDICATIVE: conduzco, conduces, conduce, conducimos, conducís, conducen
PRETERITE: conduje, condujiste, condujo, condujimos, condujisteis, condujeron
PRESENT SUBJUNCTIVE: conduzca, conduzcas, conduzca, conduzcamos, conduzcáis, conduzcan
IMPERFECT SUBJUNCTIVE: condujera (condujese), condujeras, condujera, condujéramos, condujerais, condujeran

### Conocer *to know, be acquainted with*
PRESENT INDICATIVE: conozco, conoces, conoce, conocemos, conocéis, conocen
PRESENT SUBJUNCTIVE: conozca, conozcas, conozca, conozcamos, conozcáis, conozcan

### Construir *to build, construct*
PRESENT INDICATIVE: construyo, construyes, construye, construimos, construís, construyen
PRESENT SUBJUNCTIVE: construya, construyas, construya, construyamos, construyáis, construyan

### Dar *to give*
PRESENT INDICATIVE: doy, das, da, damos, dais, dan
PRETERITE: di, diste, dio, dimos, disteis, dieron
IMPERFECT SUBJUNCTIVE: diera (diese), dieras, diera, diéramos, dierais, dieran

### Decir *to say, tell*
PRESENT INDICATIVE: digo, dices, dice, decimos, decís, dicen
PRETERITE: dije, dijiste, dijo, dijimos, dijisteis, dijeron
FUTURE: diré, dirás, dirá, diremos, diréis, dirán
CONDITIONAL: diría, dirías, diría, diríamos, diríais, dirían
PRESENT SUBJUNCTIVE: diga, digas, diga, digamos, digáis, digan
IMPERFECT SUBJUNCTIVE: dijera (dijese), dijeras, dijera, dijéramos, dijerais, dijeran
COMMANDS: di (tú), diga (Ud.), digan (Uds.)
PRESENT PARTICIPLE: diciendo
PAST PARTICIPLE: dicho

### Estar *to be*
PRESENT INDICATIVE: estoy, estás, está, estamos, estáis, están
PRETERITE: estuve, estuviste, estuvo, estuvimos, estuvisteis, estuvieron
PRESENT SUBJUNCTIVE: esté, estés, esté, estemos, estéis, estén
IMPERFECT SUBJUNCTIVE: estuviera (estuviese), estuvieras, estuviera, estuviéramos, estuvierais, estuvieran

### Haber *to have* (*auxiliary*)

PRESENT INDICATIVE: he, has, ha, hemos, habéis, han
PRETERITE: hube, hubiste, hubo, hubimos, hubisteis, hubieron
FUTURE: habré, habrás, habrá, habremos, habréis, habrán
CONDITIONAL: habría, habrías, habría, habríamos, habríais, habrían
PRESENT SUBJUNCTIVE: haya, hayas, haya, hayamos, hayáis, hayan
IMPERFECT SUBJUNCTIVE: hubiera (hubiese), hubieras, hubiera, hubiéramos,
    hubierais, hubieran

### Hacer *to do, make*

PRESENT INDICATIVE: hago, haces, hace, hacemos, hacéis, hacen
PRETERITE: hice, hiciste, hizo, hicimos, hicisteis, hicieron
FUTURE: haré, harás, hará, haremos, haréis, harán
CONDITIONAL: haría, harías, haría, haríamos, haríais, harían
PRESENT SUBJUNCTIVE: haga, hagas, haga, hagamos, hagáis, hagan
IMPERFECT SUBJUNCTIVE: hiciera (hiciese), hicieras, hiciera, hiciéramos,
    hicierais, hicieran
COMMANDS: haz (tú), haga (Ud.), hagan (Uds.)
PAST PARTICIPLE: hecho

### Ir *to go*

PRESENT INDICATIVE: voy, vas, va, vamos, vais, van
IMPERFECT INDICATIVE: iba, ibas, iba, íbamos, ibais, iban
PRETERITE: fui, fuiste, fue, fuimos, fuisteis, fueron
PRESENT SUBJUNCTIVE: vaya, vayas, vaya, vayamos, vayáis, vayan
IMPERFECT SUBJUNCTIVE: fuera (fuese), fueras, fuera, fuéramos, fuerais, fueran
COMMANDS: ve (tú), vaya (Ud.), vayan (Uds.)
PRESENT PARTICIPLE: yendo

### Oír *to hear, listen*

PRESENT INDICATIVE: oigo, oyes, oye, oímos, oís, oyen
PRESENT SUBJUNCTIVE: oiga, oigas, oiga, oigamos, oigáis, oigan

### Poder *to be able to, can*

PRESENT INDICATIVE: puedo, puedes, puede, podemos, podéis, pueden
PRETERITE: pude, pudiste, pudo, pudimos, pudisteis, pudieron
FUTURE: podré, podrás, podrá, podremos, podréis, podrán
CONDITIONAL: podría, podrías, podría, podríamos, podríais, podrían
PRESENT SUBJUNCTIVE: pueda, puedas, pueda, podamos, podáis, puedan
IMPERFECT SUBJUNCTIVE: pudiera (pudiese), pudieras, pudiera, pudiéramos,
    pudierais, pudieran
PRESENT PARTICIPLE: pudiendo

### Poner *to put, place, set*
PRESENT INDICATIVE: pongo, pones, pone, ponemos, ponéis, ponen
PRETERITE: puse, pusiste, puso, pusimos, pusisteis, pusieron
FUTURE: pondré, pondrás, pondrá, pondremos, pondréis, pondrán
CONDITIONAL: pondría, pondrías, pondría, pondríamos, pondríais, pondrían
PRESENT SUBJUNCTIVE: ponga, pongas, ponga, pongamos, pongáis, pongan
IMPERFECT SUBJUNCTIVE: pusiera (pusiese), pusieras, pusiera, pusiéramos,
    pusierais, pusieran
COMMANDS: pon (tú), ponga (Ud.), pongan (Uds.)
PAST PARTICIPLE: puesto

### Querer *to wish, want; love*
PRESENT INDICATIVE: quiero, quieres, quiere, queremos, queréis, quieren
PRETERITE: quise, quisiste, quiso, quisimos, quisisteis, quisieron
FUTURE: querré, querrás, querrá, querremos, querréis, querrán
CONDITIONAL: querría, querrías, querría, querríamos, querríais, querrían
PRESENT SUBJUNCTIVE: quiera, quieras, quiera, queramos, queráis, quieran
IMPERFECT SUBJUNCTIVE: quisiera (quisiese), quisieras, quisiera, quisiéramos,
    quisierais, quisieran

### Saber *to know*
PRESENT INDICATIVE: sé, sabes, sabe, sabemos, sabéis, saben
PRETERITE: supe, supiste, supo, supimos, supisteis, supieron
FUTURE: sabré, sabrás, sabrá, sabremos, sabréis, sabrán
CONDITIONAL: sabría, sabrías, sabría, sabríamos, sabríais, sabrían
PRESENT SUBJUNCTIVE: sepa, sepas, sepa, sepamos, sepáis, sepan
IMPERFECT SUBJUNCTIVE: supiera (supiese), supieras, supiera, supiéramos,
    supierais, supieran

### Salir *to go out, leave*
PRESENT INDICATIVE: salgo, sales, sale, salimos, salís, salen
FUTURE: saldré, saldrás, saldrá, saldremos, saldréis, saldrán
CONDITIONAL: saldría, saldrías, saldría, saldríamos, saldríais, saldrían
PRESENT SUBJUNCTIVE: salga, salgas, salga, salgamos, salgáis, salgan
COMMANDS: sal (tú), salga (Ud.), salgan (Uds.)

### Ser *to be*
PRESENT INDICATIVE: soy, eres, es, somos, sois, son
IMPERFECT INDICATIVE: era, eras, era, éramos, erais, eran
PRETERITE: fui, fuiste, fue, fuimos, fuisteis, fueron
PRESENT SUBJUNCTIVE: sea, seas, sea, seamos, seáis, sean
IMPERFECT SUBJUNCTIVE: fuera (fuese), fueras, fuera, fuéramos, fuerais, fueran

### Tener *to have*

PRESENT INDICATIVE: tengo, tienes, tiene, tenemos, tenéis, tienen
PRETERITE: tuve, tuviste, tuvo, tuvimos, tuvisteis, tuvieron
FUTURE: tendré, tendrás, tendrá, tendremos, tendréis, tendrán
CONDITIONAL: tendría, tendrías, tendría, tendríamos, tendríais, tendrían
PRESENT SUBJUNCTIVE: tenga, tengas, tenga, tengamos, tengáis, tengan
IMPERFECT SUBJUNCTIVE: tuviera (tuviese), tuvieras, tuviera, tuviéramos, tuvierais, tuvieran
COMMANDS: ten (tú), tenga (Ud.), tengan (Uds.)

### Traer *to bring*

PRESENT INDICATIVE: traigo, traes, trae, traemos, traéis, traen
PRETERITE: traje, trajiste, trajo, trajimos, trajisteis, trajeron
PRESENT SUBJUNCTIVE: traiga, traigas, traiga, traigamos, traigáis, traigan
IMPERFECT SUBJUNCTIVE: trajera (trajese), trajeras, trajera, trajéramos, trajerais, trajeran

### Valer *to be worth, cost*

PRESENT INDICATIVE: valgo, vales, vale, valemos, valéis, valen
FUTURE: valdré, valdrás, valdrá, valdremos, valdréis, valdrán
CONDITIONAL: valdría, valdrías, valdría, valdríamos, valdríais, valdrían
PRESENT SUBJUNCTIVE: valga, valgas, valga, valgamos, valgáis, valgan

### Venir *to come, go*

PRESENT INDICATIVE: vengo, vienes, viene, venimos, venís, vienen
PRETERITE: vine, viniste, vino, vinimos, vinisteis, vinieron
FUTURE: vendré, vendrás, vendrá, vendremos, vendréis, vendrán
CONDITIONAL: vendría, vendrías, vendría, vendríamos, vendríais, vendrían
PRESENT SUBJUNCTIVE: venga, vengas, venga, vengamos, vengáis, vengan
IMPERFECT SUBJUNCTIVE: viniera (viniese), vinieras, viniera, viniéramos, vinierais, vinieran
COMMANDS: ven (tú), venga (Ud.), vengan (Uds.)

### Ver *to see, watch*

PRESENT INDICATIVE: veo, ves, ve, vemos, veis, ven
IMPERFECT INDICATIVE: veía, veías, veía, veíamos, veíais, veían
PRESENT SUBJUNCTIVE: vea, veas, vea, veamos, veáis, vean
PAST PARTICIPLE: visto

# APPENDIX 4   Stem-Changing Verbs • Verbs with Spelling Changes

## STEM-CHANGING VERBS

### 1. Single change: e → ie/o → ue

**Pensar** to *think, plan*

PRESENT INDICATIVE: pienso, piensas, piensa, pensamos, penséis, piensan

PRESENT SUBJUNCTIVE: piense, pienses, piense, pensemos, penséis, piensen

**Volver** *to return*

PRESENT INDICATIVE: vuelvo, vuelves, vuelve, volvemos, volvéis, vuelven

PRESENT SUBJUNCTIVE: vuelva, vuelvas, vuelva, volvamos, volváis, vuelvan

Some common verbs of this type are:

| | |
|---|---|
| acordarse (ue) *to remember* | jugar (ue) *to play* |
| acostarse (ue) *to go to bed* | llover (ue) *to rain* |
| cerrar (ie) *to close* | mostrar (ue) *to show* |
| comenzar (ie) *to start, begin* | negar (ie) *to deny* |
| contar (ue) *to count, tell* | nevar (ie) *to snow* |
| costar (ue) *to cost* | perder (ie) *to miss, lose* |
| despertarse (ie) *to wake up* | querer (ie) *to wish, love* |
| doler (ue) *to hurt* | recordar (ue) *to remember, remind* |
| empezar (ie) *to start, begin* | sentarse (ie) *to sit down* |
| encontrar (ue) *to find* | tener (ie) *to have* |
| entender (ie) *to understand* | volar (ue) *to fly* |

### 2. Double change: e → ie, i,/o → ue, u

**Preferir** *to prefer*

PRESENT INDICATIVE: prefiero, prefieres, prefiere, preferimos, preferís, prefieren

PRETERITE: preferí, preferiste, prefirió, preferimos, preferisteis, prefirieron

PRESENT SUBJUNCTIVE: prefiera, prefieras, prefiera, prefiramos, prefiráis, prefieran

IMPERFECT SUBJUNCTIVE: prefiriera (prefiriese), prefirieras, prefiriera, prefiriéramos, prefirierais, prefirieran

PRESENT PARTICIPLE: prefiriendo

**Dormir** *to sleep*

PRESENT INDICATIVE: duermo, duermes, duerme, dormimos, dormís, duermen

PRETERITE: dormí, dormiste, durmió, dormimos, dormisteis, durmieron

PRESENT SUBJUNCTIVE: duerma, duermas, duerma, durmamos, durmáis, duerman

IMPERFECT SUBJUNCTIVE: durmiera (durmiese), durmieras, durmiera, durmiéramos, durmierais, durmieran

PRESENT PARTICIPLE: durmiendo

Other verbs with double changes in the stems are:

**convertir** (ie, i) *to convert*　**morir** (ue, u) *to die*
**divertirse** (ie, i) *to enjoy*　**sentir** (ie, i) *to feel, sense*
*oneself, to have fun*
**mentir** (ie, i) *to lie*

## 3. Change from e → i
**Pedir** *to ask for*

PRESENT INDICATIVE: pido, pides, pide, pedimos, pedís, piden
PRETERITE: pedí, pediste, pidió, pedimos, pedisteis, pidieron
PRESENT SUBJUNCTIVE: pida, pidas, pida, pidamos, pidáis, pidan
IMPERFECT SUBJUNCTIVE: pidiera (pidiese), pidieras, pidiera, pidiéramos, pidierais, pidieran
PRESENT PARTICIPLE: pidiendo

Other verbs with this type of change:

**competir** (i) *to compete*　**seguir** (i) *to follow*
**conseguir** (i) *to obtain*　**servir** (i) *to serve*
**corregir** (i) *to correct*　**vestirse** (i) *to get dressed*
**repetir** (i) *to repeat*

## VERBS WITH SPELLING CHANGES

### 1. Verbs ending in *-zar* change *z* to *c* before *e*.
**Empezar** *to begin*

PRETERITE: empecé, empezaste, empezó, empezamos, empezasteis, empezaron
PRESENT SUBJUNCTIVE: empiece, empieces, empiece, empecemos, empecéis, empiecen

Other verbs with this type of spelling changes are:

**cazar** *to hunt*　**especializarse** *to specialize*
**comenzar** *to start, begin*　**organizar** *to organize*

### 2. Verbs ending in *-cer* change *c* to *z* before *o* and *a*.
**Vencer** *to defeat, conquer*

PRESENT INDICATIVE: venzo, vences, vence, vencemos, vencéis, vencen
PRESENT SUBJUNCTIVE: venza, venzas, venza, venzamos, venzáis, venzan
*Convencer,* to convince, has the same changes as *vencer.*

### 3. Verbs ending in *-car* change *c* to *qu* before *e*.
**Buscar** *to look for*

PRETERITE: busqué, buscaste, buscó, buscamos, buscasteis, buscaron
PRESENT SUBJUNCTIVE: busque, busques, busque, busquemos, busquéis, busquen

Other verbs that end in *-car* and change *c* to *qu* before *e* are:

**explicar** *to explain*   **sacar** *to take out*
**practicar** *to practice*   **tocar** *to touch, play an instrument*

4. **Verbs ending in *-gar* change *g* to *gu* before *e*.**
   **Llegar** *to arrive*
   PRETERITE: llegué, llegaste, llegó, llegamos, llegasteis, llegaron
   PRESENT SUBJUNCTIVE: llegue, llegues, llegue, lleguemos, lleguéis, lleguen

5. **Verbs ending in *-guir* change *gu* to *g* before *o* and *a*.**
   **Seguir** *to follow*
   PRESENT INDICATIVE: sigo, sigues, sigue, seguimos, seguís, siguen
   PRESENT SUBJUNCTIVE: siga, sigas, siga, sigamos, sigáis, sigan
   *Conseguir*, to obtain, and ***distinguir***, to distinguish, follow the same changes.

6. **Verbs ending in *-ger, -gir,* change *g* to *j* before *o* and *a*.**
   **Coger** *to take, grab, seize, catch*
   PRESENT INDICATIVE: cojo, coges, coge, cogemos, cogéis, cogen
   PRESENT SUBJUNCTIVE: coja, cojas, coja, cojamos, cojáis, cojan

   Other verbs ending in *-ger, gir,* with the same changes:

   **corregir** *to correct*   **escoger** *to choose*
   **dirigir** *to direct, go to*   **recoger** *to pick up*
   **elegir** *to elect*

7. **Verbs ending in *-aer, -eer, -uir,* change *i* to *y* when *i* is unstressed and is between two vowels.**
   **Leer** *to read*
   PRETERITE: leí, leíste, leyó, leímos, leísteis, leyeron
   IMPERFECT SUBJUNCTIVE: leyera (leyese), leyeras, leyera, leyéramos, leyerais, leyeran
   PRESENT PARTICIPLE: leyendo

   Other verbs changing *i* to *y:*

   **caer** *to fall*   **excluir** *to exclude*
   **construir** *to build*   **huir** *to flee*
   **creer** *to believe*   **incluir** *to include*
   **destruir** *to destroy*   **traer** *to bring*

# Spanish–English Vocabulary

## A

**abajo** down there

**abogado(a) (el/la)** lawyer

**abordar** to board

**abril** April

**abrir** to open

**abrocharse** to fasten

**abuelo(a) (el/la)** grandfather/ grandmother

**abuelos (los)** grandparents

**aburrido(a)** boring, bored

**acá/aquí** here

**acabar de (+ infinitivo)** to have just . . .

**acabarse** to run out of

**acceso en línea (el)** online access

**acción (la)** action

**acciones (las)** stocks

**aceite (el)** oil

    **aceite de oliva (el)** olive oil

**aceitunas (las)** olives

**acelerador (el)** accelerator

**aceptar** to accept

**acompañar** to accompany

**aconsejar** to advise

**acordarse de** to remember

**acostarse** to go to bed

**acostumbrar(se)** to get used to

**acta (el)** minutes (of a meeting)

**activo(a)** active

**actor (el)** actor

**actriz (la)** actress

**actuación (la)** acting

**actual** present, current

**actuar** to act

**adelgazar(se)** to lose weight

**además** besides, moreover

**adentro** inside

**aderezo (el)** salad dressing, seasoning

**adinerado(a)** wealthy

**adiós** good-bye

**adobar** to marinate

**administración (la)** management

    **administración de negocios (la)** business administration

    **administrador(a) de empresas (el/la)** business manager (administrator)

**administrado(a)** managed/ administered

**administrar** to manage

**aduana (la)** customs

**aerolínea (la)** airline

**aeropuerto (el)** airport

**afeitarse** to shave

**a fines de** by the end of

**afuera** outside

**afueras (las)** suburbs, outskirts

**agencia (la)** agency

**agente (el/la)** agent

**agosto** August

**agradable** pleasant

**agradar** to please

**agradecer** to thank

**agradecido(a)** thankful

**agricultura (la)** agriculture

**agricultor(a)** farmer

**agua (f.) (el)** water

    **agua mineral (el)** mineral water

**aguacate (el), palta (la)** avocado

**ahora** now

**ahorrar** to save

**ahorros (los)** savings

**aire acondicionado (el)** air conditioning

**ajo (el)** garlic

**alberca (la)** pool (*Mexico*), water tank

**alcoba (la)** bedroom

**al contado** cash (*money*)

**alegrarse** to be happy, to be glad

**alegre** happy, glad, cheerful

**alegría** joy, happiness

**alergias (las)** allergies

**alérgico(a)** allergic
   **ser ~** to be allergic
**alerta (la)** alert
**alfombra (la)** carpet, rug
**algo** something
**algunos/as** few, some
**alimentación (la)** diet
**alimentar** to feed
**alimento (el)** food
**alistarse** to get ready
**aliviar** to relieve
**aliviarse** to get relief
**allá/allí/ahí** there, over there
**almorzar** to have (eat) lunch
**almuerzo (el)** lunch
**¡aló!, dígame** hello!
**alojamiento (el)**
   accommodations, lodging
**a lo mejor** perhaps
**alquilar, arrendar** to rent
**alquiler (el), arriendo (el), renta
   (la)** lease, rent
**alquiler de carros (el)** car
   rental
**alrededores (los)** surroundings
**alto(a)** high, tall
**amable** kind, nice
**amarillo(a)** yellow
**amigo(a) (el/la)** friend
**amoblar** to furnish
**amplio(a)** spacious
**amueblado(a)** furnished
**analista (el/la)** analyst
**analizado(a)** analyzed
**analizar** to analyze
**ancho(a)** wide
**andar** to walk
**andén (el)** sidewalk
**anillo (el)** ring
**animado(a)** lively

**animal (el)** animal
**anoche** last night
**anotar** to score
**anteayer** day before yesterday
**antes (de)** beforehand, before
**antibiótico (el)** antibiotic
**anticipación: con ~** ahead
   of time
**antiguo(a)** ancient, former
**antipático(a)** unpleasant
**antropología (la)**
   anthropology
**anual** yearly
**año (el)** year
   **año pasado (el)** last year
**apagar** to turn off
   **apagar el fuego** to put
     out the fire
**apagado(a)** extinct
**aparcar** to park
**aparecer** to appear
**apartaestudio (el)** studio
   apartment
**apartamento (el)/piso (el)**
   apartment, flat, condominium
**aperitivo (el)** aperitif, appetizers
**aplicación (la), aplicativo (el)** app
**aplicar** to put into practice, to
   apply something (theory, cream,
   paint), to administer
**apreciar** to appreciate
**aprender** to learn
**apuntes (los)** notes (take in class or
   in a meeting)
**aquí** here, over here
**aranceles (los)** tariffs
**arancelario(a)** to do with
   tariffs
**árbol (el)** tree
   **árbol de Navidad (el)**
     Christmas tree

**arquitecto(a) (el/la)** architect
**arquitectura (la)**
   architecture (la)
**arrancar** to start, root
**arranque (el)** starter
**arreglar** to arrange, to repair, to
   fix, to straighten up
**arreglarse** to get ready
**arreglo personal (el)** grooming
**arrendar** to rent
**arriba** up there
**arriendo (el), renta (la)** rent
**arroz (el)** rice
**arte (el)** art
**artista (el/la)** artist
**artístico(a)** artistic
**arvejas (las), guisantes (los)**
   green peas
**asado(a)** roasted
**asador (el)** grill
**asar** to barbecue, to roast
**ascensor (el)** elevator
**asegurado(a)** insured
**asesor(a) financiero(a) (el/la)**
   financial advisor
**asesorar** to advise
**asiento (el)** seat
**asignar** to assign
**así que** so
**asistente (el/la)** assistant
   **asistente virtual (el/la)**
     virtual assistant
**asistir** to attend to (a class
   or meeting)
**asma (el)** asthma
**aspiradora (la)** vacuum
   cleaner
**asustar** to scare
**atender (ie)** to attend someone,
   to wait on
**atento(a)** polite, attentive

ateo(a) atheist

aterrizaje (el) landing

aterrizar to land

atletismo (el) athletics

atrasado(a) late, delayed

atún (el) tuna

audio (el) audio

aumentar to increase

aunque although

autoestima (la) self-esteem

autobús (el) bus

automático(a) automatic

automóvil (el) auto

autopista (la) highway

autor(a) (el/la) author

autoritario(a) bossy, authoritarian

autorización (la) authorization

autoservicio (el) self-service

auxiliar de vuelo (el/la)
    flight attendant

ave (cl) bird

a veces sometimes

avería (la) breakdown

averiguación (la) inquiry

avión (el) airplane

avisar to warn, inform

aviso (el) notice, add

aviso de tornado (el) tornado
    warning

ayer yesterday

ayuda (la) help

ayudar to help

azafata (la) stewardess, female
    flight attendant

azúcar (el/la) sugar

azul (el) blue

**B**

bailar to dance

bailarín (el)/bailarina (la)
    dancer

bajar(se) (de) to get off, go down

   bajar de peso to lose
       weight

   bajar la velocidad
       to slow down

   bajar el volumen to turn down
       the volume

bajo(a) low, short

balance (saldo) (el) bank
    balance

balanceado(a) balanced

balancear to balance

balcón (el) balcony

balón (el) ball

baloncesto (el) basketball

banana(o) (la/el), plátano (el)
    banana

banca en línea (la) online
    banking

bancario(a) banking

banco (el) bank

bañarse to bathe, to take a bath

baño (el) bathroom

barato(a) cheap

barbilla (la), mentón (el) chin

barrer to sweep

barrio (el), colonia (la)
    neighborhood

bastante enough

bate (el) bat

batear to bat

batería (la) battery

baúl (el) trunk

beber to drink

bebida (la) drink, beverage

   bebida energizante (la)
       energy drink

bebido(a)/borracho(a)
    drunk

beca (la) scholarship

béisbol (el) baseball

besar to kiss

biblioteca (la) library

bibliotecario(a) (el/la)
    librarian

bicicleta (la) bicycle

bienes raíces (los) real estate

bienestar (el) well-being

bienvenida (la) welcome

billete (el) bill, ticket

billetera (la) wallet
    digital (la) digital wallet

biólogo(a) (el/la) biologist

bisabuelo(a) (el/la) great-
    grandfather/great-grandmother

bisté (el), bistec (el) beef steak

blanco(a) white

blando(a) tender, soft

blog (el) blog

bloguero(a) (el/la) blogger

boca (la) mouth

bocadillo (el) sandwich

bocina (la), pito (el) horn (of a car)

boda (la) wedding

boleto (el) ticket

boliche (el), bolos (los)
    bowling

bolígrafo (el) pen

bolsas de aire (las) airbags

bolsa de valores (la) stock
    market

bolso(a) (el/la) purse

bomba (la) gas pump, bomb

bombero(a) (el/la) firefighter

bonito(a) pretty, beautiful

borracho(a) (el/la) drunk

borrador (el) eraser

borrar to erase

botella (la) bottle

botón (el) button

botones (el) bellboy

brazo (el) arm

breve short, brief

**brillante** bright, brilliant

**brindar** to toast

**brócoli** (el) broccoli

**bronceado(a)** tanned

**broncearse** to get a tan, to tan

**bucear** to dive, diving

**bueno(a)** good, healthy

**bus** (el) bus

**buscar** to look for

## C

**cabello** (el) hair

**cabeza** (la) head

**cabina del avión** (la) airplane cabin

**cadera** (la) hip

**caer(se)** to fall

**café** (el) coffee

**cafetera** (la) coffee maker

**cafetería** (la)/**café** (el) coffee shop (place)

**caja** (la) cash register

**cajero(a)** (el/la) cashier

**cajero automático** (el) the ATM

**cajuela** (la) trunk

**calabacín** (el) zucchini, courgette

**calambre** (el) cramp

**calefacción** (la) heating

**calentar** to heat, to warm

**caliente** hot (temperature)

**calificación** (la) grade

**calificado(a)** qualified

**calle** (la) street

**calma** (la) calm

**calmado(a)** calm

**calmante** (el) painkiller, sedative

**calmar(se)** to calm (down)

**calor** (el) heat

**caloría** (la) calorie

**cama** (la) bed

**doble** (la) double bed, queen size bed

**sencilla** (la) twin, single bed

**cámara** (la) camera

**cámara digital** (la) digital camera

**cámara de visión trasera** (la) back-up, rear-view camera

**camarero(a)** (el/la) waiter, waitress

**camarón** (el) shrimp

**cambiar** to change

**cambio** (el) change

**camino** (el) road, way

**caminar** to walk, walking

**camión** (el) truck, bus (*Mexico*)

**camión articulado** (el)/**tractomula** (la) semi-truck

**camioneta** (la) truck, van

**camisa** (la) shirt

**camiseta** (la) t-shirt

**campeón/campeona** (el/la) champion

**campeonato** (el) championship

**campesino(a)** (el/la) peasant, farmer

**campo** (el) field, countryside

**campo (área) de estudios** (el) field of studies

**cancha** (la) sports court

**canción** (la) song

**candidato(a)** (el/la) candidate

**cantante** (el/la) singer

**cantar** to sing

**capó** (el) hood

**cara** (la), **rostro** (el) face

**característica** (la) characteristic

**cardiología** (la) cardiology

**cardiólogo(a)** (el/la) cardiologist

**cargar** to charge, to load

**carnaval** (el) carnival, Shrove Tuesday

**carne** (la) meat

**carne de res** (la) beef

**carné** (el) license

**caro(a)** expensive

**carpintero(a)** (el/la) carpenter

**carrera** (la) career, major, race

**carrera de carros** (la) car race

**carretera** (la) road

**carro** (el), **coche** (el) car

**carro automático** (el) automatic car

**carro eléctrico** (el) electric car

**carro híbrido** (el) hybrid car

**carro mecánico** (el) standard shift car

**carta** (la) menu

**cartera** (la) purse, wallet

**casa** (la) house

**casado(a)** married

**casi** almost

**casualidad: por ~** by chance; **¡Qué casualidad!** What a coincidence!

**catarro** (el) catarrh

**catedrático(a)** (el/la) university professor

**CDT (Certificado de Depósito a Término)** (el) CD

**cebolla** (la) onion

cebolleta (la) scallion, spring onion

cejas (las) eyebrows

celebración (la) celebration

celebrar to celebrate

celular, móvil (el) cell phone

cena (la) dinner, supper

cenar to have dinner (supper)

centavo (el) cent

centenial (el/la) centennial (Generation Z)

centro (el) center, downtown

centro de salud (el) clinic

cepillarse to brush

cepillo (el) brush

    de dientes toothbrush

    para el pelo hairbrush

cerca close to, near to

cercano(a) close

cerdo (el) pork, pig

    chuleta de cerdo (la) pork chop

cereal (el) cereal

cerebro (el) brain

cerrar (ie) to close

    cerrar sesión to log out

certificado bancario (el) bank certificate

cerveza (la) beer

césped (el), pasto (el) grass

cesta (la) basket

champiñón (el), hongo (el), seta (la) mushroom

champú (el) shampoo

chao/chau (good)bye

chatear to chat

cheque (el) check

    chequera (la), talonario (el) checkbook

chica (la) girl

chico (el) boy

chimenea (la) fireplace

chistoso(a) funny

chocar to collide, to crash; to shock

chocolate (el) chocolate

chofer (el/la) driver

choque (el) crash

ciclismo (el) cycling

ciencias (las) sciences

    de la salud (las) health sciences

    políticas (las) political sciences

    sociales (las) social sciences

científico(a) (el/la) scientist

ciento: por ~ percent

cintura (la) waist

cinturón (de seguridad) (el) seat belt

cirugía (la) surgery, surgical operation

cirujano(a) (el/la) surgeon

cita (la) appointment, romantic date

ciudad (la) city, town

ciudadano(a) (el/la) citizen

claro(a) clear

clase (la) class

    clase económica economy class

    clase ejecutiva business class

    primera clase first class

clase virtual (la) online class

clave (la), contraseña (la) password

clima (el) climate, weather

clínica (la) clinic

closet (el) closet

cobrar to charge, to get paid

coche (el) car, coach

cocina (la) kitchen

    cocina integral (la) full kitchen

cocinar to cook

cocinero(a) (el/la) chef, cook

codo (el) elbow

cojear to limp

colegio (el) school (elementary, middle, high school)

colonia (la) neighborhood

color (el) color

comedor (el) dining room

comenzar (ie) to start

comer to eat

comida (la) dinner, food, meal

comida de mar (la) seafood

como as. . .as, like

cómodo(a) comfortable

compañero(a) (el/la) fellow student, schoolmate

compañero(a) de trabajo coworker, colleague

compañía (la) company

compartimiento superior overhead compartment

competencia (la) competition

competir to compete

complejo turístico (el)/ resort (el) resort

completar to complete

complicado(a) complicated

comprador(a) (el/la) buyer

comprar to buy

comprender to understand

compulsivo(a) compulsive

computador(a) (el/la) computer

comunicación (la) communication

comunidad (la) community

concesionario (el) car dealer, car dealership

concluir to conclude

condimentado(a) seasoned

condimentar to season

condimentos (los) condiments, seasoning

conducir to drive, to conduct

conductor(a) (el/la) conductor, driver

conexión (la) connection

conferencia (la) conference

confirmar to confirm

confusión (la) confusion

congelador (el) freezer

congelar to freeze

congestionado(a) congested

conjunto residencial (el) residential complex

conmemorar commemorate

conocer to know, to meet

conseguir (i) to get, to obtain

consejero(a) (el/la) advisor

considerar to consider

construir to build

consulta de doctor (la) medical consultation

consultar to consult

consultorio (el) doctor's office

consumidor(a) (el/la) consumer

consumir to consume

contado (al) cash

contador(a) (el/la) accountant

contaduría (la) accounting

contar to count, to tell

contento(a) happy

contestar to answer

contraseña (la)/clave (la) password

contratar to hire

control de crucero (el) cruise control

convencer to convince

convenir (ie) to suit

conversación (la) conversation

conversar to chat, to converse

convertir (ie, i) to convert

copa (la) glass

corazón (el) heart

cordero (el) lamb

coro (el) choir

correo electrónico (el) email

correr to run, jogging, running

corresponder to correspond

correspondiente corresponding

cortar el pelo to cut hair

cortinas (las) curtains

corto(a) short

coser to sew

cosmetología (la) cosmetology

cosmetólogo(a) (el/la) cosmetologist

costar to cost

costoso(a) expensive

creador(a) de contenido (el/la) content creator

crear to create

creativo(a) creative

crecimiento (el) growth

crédito (el) credit

~bancario (el) bank credit

~hipotecario (el) mortgage credit

creer to believe, to think

crema (la) cream

~ de afeitar (la) shaving cream

~ dental (la) toothpaste

criminal (el/la) criminal

cruce (el) intersection

cruzar to cross

cuaderno (el) notebook

cuadra (la) block

cuarto (el) quarter, room

cubiertos (los) cutlery

cubrir to cover

cuello (el) neck

cuenta (la) account, bill

cuenta corriente (la) checking account; cuenta de ahorros (la) savings account

cuerpo (el) body

cuidadoso(a) careful

cuidar(se) to take care of

cultivar to cultivate, to grow

cumpleaños (el) birthday

cumplir to achieve, to fulfill

cumplir años to celebrate his/her birthday

cumplir las leyes to comply with the laws

cuñado(a) (el/la) brother-in-law/sister-in-law

cuota (la) fee

de manejo (la) handling fee

cupo (el) limit

cura (el) priest

cura (la) cure

curar to cure, heal

## D

dañar(se) to damage, to break

dañado(a)/descompuesto(a) broken (not working properly)

**dar** to give

    **dar la bienvenida** to welcome

    **dar regalos** to give gifts

    **dar reversa** to reverse (a car)

**debate (el)** debate

**deber** must, should

**deber dinero** to owe money

**débil** weak

**decano(a) (el/la)** dean

**decidir** to decide

**decir** to say, to tell

    **decir que sí/no** to say yes/no

**decisión (la)** decision

**dedo (el)** finger, toe

**dejar** to leave

    **dejar de** to stop doing something

**delgado(a)** slim, thin

**delicioso(a)** delicious

**demorar** to delay

**dentista (el/la)** dentist

**depender de** to depend on

**deportes (los)** sports

**deportista (el/la)** athlete

**depositar** to deposit

**depósito (el)** deposit

**depresión (la)** depression

**derecho(a)** right, straight

**derecho (el)** law

**dermatólogo(a) (el/la)** dermatologist

**desayunar** to have (eat) breakfast

**desayuno (el)** breakfast

**descansar** to rest

**descargar** to download

**descargar** to die (*the car battery*)

**descontento(a)** unhappy

**describir** to describe

**descubrir** to discover

**desde** from

**desear** to want, wish

**desembarcar** to disembark

**desempeño (el)** performance

**desempleado(a)** unemployed

**deshacer** to undo

**desinflar** to deflate

**desmayarse** to faint

**desocupado(a)** free, vacant, empty

**desordenado(a)** messy

**desordenar** to make a mess

**despacio** slowly

**despedir** to say good-bye (*to someone*), to dismiss, to fire (*from a job*)

**despegar** to take off

**despegue (el)** takeoff

**despertador (el)** alarm clock

**despertarse** to wake up

**despierto(a)** awake, alert

**después (de)** after, afterwards

**destino (el)** destination

**destruido(a)** destroyed

**destruir** to destroy

**detallista** detail-oriented

**detener** to stop, detain (*people*)

**deuda (la)** debt

**deudor(a)** debtor

    **deudor(a) moroso(a)** slow payer

**día (el)** day

    **a mediodía** at noon; **buenos días,** good morning; **por día** per day, daily

    **día festivo (el)** holiday

**diagrama (el)** diagram

**diario(a)** daily

**dibujar** to draw

**diciembre** December

**diente (el)** tooth

**dientes (los)** teeth

**dieta (la)** diet

**difícil** difficult

**digitar la clave** to enter the password

**dinero (el)** money

**dirección (la)** address

**direccionales (las)** turn signals

**director(a) (el/la)** director/manager

    **director(a) ejecutivo(a) (el/la)** CEO

**dirigido(a)** leaded, guided

**dirigir** to lead

**disciplina (la)** discipline

**diseñador(a) (el/la)** designer

**diseñar** to design

**diseño (el)** design

**disfrazado(a)** disguised

**disfrazarse** to disguise as, to dress up as, to wear costumes

**disfrutar de** to enjoy

**disponible** available

**disponibilidad (la)** availability

**divertido(a)** fun

**divertirse (ie, i)** to have fun

**divisa (la)** foreign money, currency

**divorciado(a)** divorced

**doblar** to turn, bend

**doble** double

**doctor(a) (el/la)** doctor

**documento** document

**doler (ue, u)** to ache, to hurt

**dolor (el)** pain

**domicilio (el)** address, home

**domingo (el)** Sunday

dormir (ue, u) to sleep

dormirse to go to sleep, to fall sleep

dormitorio (el) bedroom

droguería (la) drugstore

ducha (la) shower

ducharse to shower, to take a shower

dulce sweet

durar to last

durazno (el)/melocotón (el) (Spain) peach

## E

echar de menos, extrañar to miss

edad (la) age

edificio (el) building

    edificio de apartamentos (el) apartment building

educación (la) education

efectivo(a) effective; efectivo in cash (*with cash*)

ejercicio (el) activity, exercise

    hacer ejercicio to exercise

eléctrico(a) electric

electrodomésticos (los) electrical appliances

elegante elegant

embarazada pregnant

embotellamiento (el)/ atasco (el)/trancón (el) traffic jam

emergencia (la) emergency

empacar to pack

empezar to begin, to start

empleado(a) (el/la) employee

empresa (la) business, company

enamorado(a) in love

    estar ~ to be in love

enamorarse to fall in love

encantado(a) pleased

encantar to charm, like a lot

encargarse de to be in charge, to take charge of,

encender (ie) to light

encestar to score a basket

encontrar (ue) to find

encontrarse to meet, find

enero January

enfermarse to get sick

enfermedad (la) sickness, illness

enfermero(a) (el/la) nurse

enfermo(a) ill, sick person, patient

engordarse to gain weigh

enojarse con to get angry with

escritor(a) (el/la) writer

espejo (el) mirror

ensalada (la) salad

enseguida, en seguida right away

enseñar to teach

ensuciar (se) to get (something or someone) dirty

entender (ie) to understand

entero(a) all, entire

entonces then

entornos (los) surroundings

entrar a (en) to enter

entrada (la) entrance

entrada (la)/los entremeses appetizers

entregar to deliver

entremés (el) appetizer

entrenador(a) (el/la) coach, trainer

entrenamiento (el) training

entrenar to coach, to train

entretenido(a) amusing

enyesar to put in a plaster cast

época (la) season, epoch

equipaje (el) baggage, luggage

    equipaje de mano (el) carry-on baggage

equipo (el) team

escala (la) stop, stopover

escalar to climb, climbing

escalera (la) ladder, staircase, stairs

escalofríos (los) feverish chill, shivering

escoba (la) broom

escribir to write

escritor(a) (el/la) writer

escritorio (el) desk

escuchar to listen

escuela (la) elementary school

esfero (el) pen (*Colombia*)

eso: por ~ because of that

espacio (el) space

    espacio funcional (el) functional space

espalda (la) back (*of a person*)

espárragos (los) asparagus

especializar (se) to specialize

espectacular spectacular

espejo (el) mirror

    espejo retrovisor (el) rear-view mirror

espontáneo(a) spontaneous

esposo(a) (el/la) spouse

esposa (la) wife

esposo (el) husband

esquí (el) ski

estación (la) season, station

    estación de buses (la) bus station

estación de gasolina, gasolinera, bomba de gasolina (la) gas station

estación de trenes (la) train station

estacionamiento (el) parking

estacionar, parquear to park

estadio (el) stadium

estado (el) state

estado de ánimo (el) mood

esta noche tonight

estante (el) bookshelf, bookcase

estar to be

estar al día to be up to date; estar a dieta to be on a diet; estar asegurado(a) to be insured; estar enfermo(a) to be sick; estar estresado(a) to be stressed; estar de vacaciones to be on vacation; estar nublado to be cloudy

este (*m.*) this

estilista (el/la) stylist

estomacal related to the stomach

estómago (el) stomach

estornudar to sneeze

estratega (el/la) strategist

estrecho(a) narrow

estrellada (la) crash

estrellado(a) crashed (car), starry (sky)

estrellar(se) to crash

estreñido(a) constipated

estreñimiento (el) constipation

estrés (el) mental stress

estresado(a) stressed

estresante stressful

estresarse to stress

estricto(a) strict, severe

estudiante (el/la) student

estudiar to study

estudios (los) studies

estudio (el)/cuarto de estudio (el) study, office

estufa (la) stove

estupendo(a) fantastic, terrific

examen médico (el) medical examination

examinar to examine/to test

excelente excellent

excursión excursión, hike

éxito (el) success

experimentar, hacer experimentos to experiment

exquisito(a) exquisite

extendida(o) extended

extenuado(a), exhausto(a) exhausted

extracto bancario (el) bank statement

**F**

fábrica (la) factory

fácil easy

factura (la) bill, invoice

facturar to check in

falta: sin ~ without fail

faltar to miss, to be lacking, to lack

familia (la) family

fantástico(a) fantastic

farmacia (la) pharmacy

faro (el) headlight

fascinante fascinating

fatiga (la) fatigue

febrero February

fecha (la) date (calendar)

fecha de nacimiento (la) birthdate

felicidad (la) happiness

felicidades, felicitaciones (las) congratulations

felicitar to congratulate

feliz happy

feo(a) ugly

festejar to feast, to celebrate

festival (el) festival

festivo(a) festive

fiebre (la) fever

fiesta (la) party

fiesta de cumpleaños (la) birthday party

filete (el), bisté (el) steak, filet

finalista (el/la) finalist

financiero(a) financial

finanzas (las) finances

fin: en ~, por ~ in short, finally

fin de semana (el) weekend

firma (la) signature

firmar to sign

flor (la) flower

forma (la) way

fortalecer to strengthen

fracturarse to break, to fracture

fracturado(a) broken

fraternidad (la) fraternity

freír/fritar to fry

frenar to brake

freno (el) brake

freno de emergencia (el) emergency brake

freno de mano (el) handbrake

frente (la) forehead

fresco(a) fresh, cool

frijol (el) bean

frío(a) cold

fruta (la) fruit

fuegos (juegos) artificiales (los) fireworks

fuerte strong

fumar to smoke

funcionar to function, to work properly

fútbol (el) football, soccer

fútbol americano (el) American football

futuro(a) future

## G

galletas (las) cookies

galón (el) gallon

ganancias (las) earnings, profits

ganar to earn, to win

ganga (la) bargain

garaje (el) garage

garbanzo (el) chickpea

garganta (la) throat

dolor de ~ (el) sore throat

gasolina (la) gasoline

gasolinera (la) gas station

gastado(a) worn-out

gastar to spend

gasto (el) expense

gato(a) (el/la) cat

gemelo(a) (el/la) twin brother/ twin sister

generación (la) generation

gentil elegant

gerente (el/la) manager

gerente general (el/la) CEO/ general manager

gerente de recursos humanos (el/la) human resources manager

gestionar to arrange

gimnasia (la) gymnastics

gimnasio (el) gym

gimnasta (el/la) gymnast

girar/voltear to turn

giro internacional (el) international money order

giro (postal) (el) money order, postal order

golf (el) golf

golfista (el/la) golf player

gordo(a) fat

gracias thank you

gracioso(a) funny

grande large, big

grasa (la) grease, fat

grasoso(a) greased, fat

gratis free, free of charge

grave grave, serious

gripe/gripa (la) flu

gris (el) gray

guantera (la) glove compartment

guapo(a) handsome

guardar to save (a file in the computer)

guardar cama to stay in bed

guiar to guide

guisante (el) green pea

guitarra (la) guitar

gustar to like

gusto (el) taste

gusto: con mucho ~ it's a pleasure

## H

haber to have

habitación (la) room

hablar to speak

hace + tiempo ago (*hace una hora= an hour ago*)

hacer to do, make, to be (*weather*)

hacer buen tiempo, hacer bueno to have good weather; hacer calentamiento to warm up; hacer calor to be hot; hacer caso to pay attention; hacer desorden to make mess; hacer ejercicios to workout; hacer estiramiento to stretch; hacer fresco to be cool; hacer fila to stand in line; hacer frío to be cold; hacer la boca agua to make one's mouth water; hacer la cama to make the bed; hacer la maleta to pack the suitcase; hacer mal tiempo, hacer mal to have bad weather; hacer quehaceres domésticos to do household chores; hacer sol to be sunny; hacer viento to be windy; ¿Qué tiempo hace? What's the weather like?

hágame el favor please, do me a favor

hambre (*f.*) (el) hunger

hamburguesa (la) hamburger

hasta until, to

hay que (+ verb) it's necessary to (+ verb)

helado (el) ice cream

hermano(a) (el/la) brother, sister

medio hermano (el) half-brother

media hermana (la) half-sister

hermanastro(a) (el/la) stepbrother/stepsister

hervir to boil

híbrido(a) hybrid

hidratarse to hydrate

hielo (el) ice

hierba (la) grass

hijastro(a) (el/la) stepson/
stepdaughter

hijo(a) (el/la) son, daughter

hipoteca (la) mortgage

hoja de vida (la), currículo
(el) resume, curriculum vitae

¡Hola! Hi!

hombre (el) man

hombro (el) shoulder

hora (la) hour, time

horario (el) schedule

hornear to bake

horno (el) oven

horno microondas (el)
microwave

hospital (el) hospital

hotel (el) hotel

hoy today

huella (la) fingerprint
~digital (la) digital fingerprint

hueso (el) bone

huésped (el/la) guest

huevo (el) egg

huir to flee

**I**

ida (la) one-way ticket
ida y vuelta (la) round-trip

idea (la) idea

idioma (el) language

iglesia (la) church

imaginar to imagine

importante important

importar to matter, to be
important, to import

imprevisto(a) unexpected

impuesto (el) tax

incluir (y) to include

increíble incredible

incremento (el) increase,
increment

indigestión (la) indigestion

inflar to inflate

influyente (el/la) influencer

informar to inform

informática (la), ciencias de
computadores (las)
computer science

ingeniería (la) engineering

ingeniero(a) (el/la) engineer

ingenioso(a) resourceful

ingresar to enter

inhalar to inhale

iniciar sesión to login

inmediato(a) immediate

inmobiliaria (la) real state
agency
agente inmobiliario (el/la)
realtor, estate agent

inmueble (el) property

inodoro (el) toilet

inoxidable stainless

inspeccionar to inspect

Instagram (el) Instagram

instituto (el) institute, secondary
or high school

inteligencia artificial (la)
artificial intelligence

inteligente intelligent

interés (el) interest

interesante interesting

interesar to interest

internacional international

Internet (el/la) Internet

intersección (la) intersection

inversión (la) investment

invertir to invest

invierno (el) winter

invitación (la) invitation

invitar to invite

inyección (la) shot,
injection

ir to go
ir de compras to go
shopping

irse to go away, to leave

irritación (la) irritation

itinerario (el) itinerary

**J**

jabón (el) soap

jamón (el) ham

jarabe (el) syrup

jardín (el) garden, yard

jefe(a) (el/la) boss

joven young

joven (el/la) young person

juegos (los) games

jueves (el) Thursday

jugador(a) (el/la) player

jugar (ue) to play

jugo (el), zumo (Spain) (el)
juice

junio June

junto: ~ a close to, near

julio July

**K**

kilómetro (el) kilometer

kiubo (¿qué hubo?)
what's up?

**L**

labio (el) lip

laboratorio (el) laboratory

lámpara (la) lamp

langosta (la) lobster

lanzar to throw

lápiz (el) pencil

largo(a) long

lastimarse to get hurt

lavadora (la) washing machine

lavamanos (el)/lavabo (el) sink

lavaplatos (el) dishwasher

lavar(se) to wash

lección (la) lesson

leche (la) milk

    leche de almendras (la) almond milk

    leche descremada (la) fat free (*skimmed*) milk

    leche deslactosada (la) lactose free milk

    leche de soya (la) soy milk

lechuga (la) lettuce

leer to read

legumbres (las) legumes

lejos far away

lengua (la) tongue, language

lenguas (las) languages

lento(a) slow

levantamiento de pesas (el) weightlifting

levantar pesas to lift weights

levantarse to get up

leyes (las) laws

librería (la) bookstore

libro (el) book

licencia de conducir (la) driver's license

licenciatura (la) degree

limonada (la) lemonade

limón (el) lemon

limpiaparabrisas (el) windshield wiper

limpiar to clean

    limpiar el polvo to dust

limpio(a) clean

lindo(a) pretty

lingüística (la) linguistics

listo(a) ready, smart

literatura (la) literature

llamar to call

llamarse to be called

llanta (la) tire

    llanta de respuesto (la) spare tire

llave (la) key

llave del carro (la) car key

llave/tarjeta (la) key, key card

llegada (la) arrival

llegar to arrive

llenar to fill

    llenar el tanque to fill the tank

    llenar una receta to fill a prescription

lleno(a) full

llover (ue) to rain

lluvia (la) rain

locutor(a) (el/la) announcer

luces (las) lights

    luces altas (las) high lights

    luces delanteras (las) headlights

luego then

luego: hasta ~ so long

lugar (el), sitio (el) place

lujoso(a) luxurious

lunes (el) Monday

luz (la) light, electricity

    luz roja (la) red light, traffic light

## M

madrastra (la) stepmother

madre (la) mother

maestría (la) master's degree

maestro(a) (el/la) elementary or primary school teacher

maíz (el) corn

maleta (la) suitcase

maletero (el) porter, trunk (*of a car*)

maletín (el) briefcase

malo(a) bad, sick

mamá (la) mom

mandar to send, order

mandarina (la) mandarin, tangerine

manejar to drive

    manejar el presupuesto to manage the budget

mango (el) mango

mano (la) hand

mantequilla (la) butter

manzana (la) apple

mañana (la) morning

mañana tomorrow

    hasta mañana see you tomorrow

mapa (el) map

maqueta (la) project model

maquillaje (el) makeup

maquillarse to put on makeup

máquina (la) machine

    máquina de afeitar (la) shaver

mar (el) sea

maratón (la) marathon

    media maratón (la) half-marathon

maratonista (el/la) marathon runner

marca (la) trademark, car make, brand

marearse to get dizzy

mareo (el) dizziness, nausea

margarina (la) margarine

marisco (el) seafood, shellfish

marrón brown

martes (el) Tuesday

marzo March

más more

    más: ~ o menos more or less

matemáticas (las) mathematics

materno(a) maternal

matrícula (la) license plate,
    university or school tuition

mayo May

mayonesa (la) mayonnaise

mayor older

mayoría (la) majority, most

mecánico(a) (el/la)
    mechanic

mecánico(a) mechanical

medicamento (el) medication

medicina (la) medicine

médico(a) (el/la) physician,
    doctor

médico(a) medical

medio(a) half

    en medio de in the
        middle of

mejilla (la) cheek

mejor better,

el mejor the best

mejorar to improve

mellizo(a) (el/la) twin

melón (el) melon

memoria (la) memory

menor younger

menos less

mensaje (el) message

    mensaje de texto (el)
        text message

mensual monthly

menú (el) menu

menudo: a ~ frequently, often

mercadeo (el) marketing

mercadeo digital (el)
    digital marketing

mercado (el) market

mercadotecnia (la)
    marketing (*major*)

merecer to deserve

merendar (ie) to snack

merengue (el) merengue
    dance

merienda (la) snack

mes (el) month

    mes pasado (el) last
        month

mesa (la) table

mesero(a) (el/la) waiter,
    waitress

meter to put into

meteorología (la)
    meteorology

meteorólogo(a) (el/la)
    meteorologist

método (el) method

    métodos de pago (los)
        payment methods

metódico(a) methodical

mi, mis my

mientras while

miércoles (el) Wednesday

milla (la) mile

ministro (a) (el/la) minister

mirador (el) the viewpoint

mirar to look at, to watch

mochila (la) backpack

modelo (el) model

moderno(a) modern

modo: ¡ni ~! no way!

molestar to bother, annoy

moneda (la) currency, coin

monetario(a) monetary

morado(a) purple

morir (ue) to die

mostrar (ue) to show

mostrador de la aerolínea (el)
    airline counter

motivo (el) motive, reason

motor (el) engine

móvil (el) cell phone (*Spain*)

mucho(a) much, a lot

mueble (el) furniture

mujer (la) woman

    mujer de negocios (la)
        business woman

    mujer policía (la)
        policewoman

muleta (la) crutch

multa (la) fine

mundo (el) world

muñeca (la) wrist, doll

músculo (el) muscle

música (la) music

músico(a) (el/la) musician

muy very

## N

nacer to be born

nadar to swim

naranja (la) orange

nariz (la) nose

natación (la) swimming

náusea (la) nausea

navegador GPS/Waze (el)
    GPS

Navidad (la) Christmas

necesario(a) necessary

necesidad (la) need

necesitar to need

negro(a) black

nervios (los) nerves

nervioso(a) nervous

    estar ~ to be nervous

neumático (el) tire

nevar (ie) to snow

nevera (la) refrigerator

nieto(a) (el/la) grandson/
  granddaughter
nieve (la) snow
niño(a) (el/la) boy/girl
noche (la) night
  buenas noches good
    evening.
Nochebuena (la) Christmas
  Eve
nómada (el/la) nomad
nómada nomadic
nombre (el) name
no: ¡cómo ~! of course!
nota (la)/calificación (la)
  grade
novela (la) novel
noviembre November
novio(a) (el/la) boyfriend,
  girlfriend/fiancé, fiancée/
  bridegroom, bride
nube (la) cloud
nublado(a) cloudy
nuera (la) daughter-in-law
nuevo(a) new
número (el) number
  ~ de la clave (contraseña)
    (el) pin number

**O**

o or
obeso(a) obese
obsesionado(a) obsessed
ocasión (la) occasion
octubre October
ocupado(a) busy, occupied
ocupar to occupy
ocuparse to look after
ocurrir to happen
odontólogo(a) (el/la) dentist
oficina (la) office

oficina de admisiones (la)
  admissions office
ofrecer to offer
oído (el) hearing
oír to hear
ojo (el) eye
oler (hue) to smell
  olerle mal a uno to smell fishy
olfato (el) smell
olvidar(se) to forget
opción (la) option, choice
optómetra (el/la) optometrist
ordenar to arrange, to order
ordenado(a) organized, tidy
ordenador(a) (el/la)
  computer (*Spain*)
oreja (la) (outer) ear
organizado(a) organized, tidy
oro (el) gold
oscuro(a) dark
otoño (el) autumn, fall
otorgado(a) awarded, granted
otorgar to award, to grant

**P**

paciencia (la) patience
paciente (el/la) patient
padecer to suffer
padre (el) father
padres (los), papas (los)
  parents
pagar to pay
pagos (los) payments
país (el) country
paisaje (el) landscape, scenery
pájaro (el) bird
palabra (la) word
pálido(a) pale
palos de golf (los) golf clubs
pan (el) bread

panadería (la) bakery
panadero(a) (el/la) baker
pantalla (la) screen, lamp
papá (el) father, dad
papás, patatas (las) potatoes
  papas fritas (las) French
    fries
papaya (la) papaya
papel (el) paper
paquete (el) package
par (el) couple (*things*)
  un par de a couple of
    (*things*), a few
para to, in order to; for
parabrisas (el) windshield
parachoques (el) bumper,
  fender
parada (la) stop
paraguas (el) umbrella
parapente (el) paragliding
parar(se), detenerse to stop
parecer to seem
pared (la) wall
pareja (la) couple, pair
parientes (los) relatives
párpado (el) eyelid
parque (el) park
parqueadero (el) parking
parquear(se) to park
participar to participate
partida (la) departure
partido (el)/juego (el) game
pasabordo/pase de
  abordar (el) boarding
  pass
pasaje (el) ticket (bus,
  train, airplane)
pasajero(a) (el/la) passenger
pasantía (la) internship
pasaporte (el) passport

**pasar** to happen, to pass

    **pasar la aspiradora** to vacuum

    **pasarlo(la) bien** to have a good time

    **pasar tiempo** to spend time

**Pascua (la)** Easter

**pasillo (el)** aisle (*in a plane*), hallway (*in a house*)

**pasta (la)** pasta

**pasta (crema) dental (la)** toothpaste

**pastel (el)** pastry, cake, pie

**pastelería (la)** pastry shop

**pastilla (la)** pill, tablet

**patata (la)** potato

**patear** to kick

**paterno(a)** paternal

**patinaje (el)** skating

    **patinaje sobre el hielo (el)** ice skating

**patines (los)** skates

    **patines para el hielo (los)** ice skates

**patio (el)** patio, back yard

**patrimonio histórico de la humanidad (el)** world heritage site

**pavo (el)** turkey

**peaje (el)** toll

**pecho (el)** breast

**pediatra (el/la)** pediatrician

**pedir (i)** to ask for

    **pedir prestado** to borrow

**peinar (se)** to comb

**peine (el)** comb

**peinilla (la)** comb

**película (la)** movie

**peligro (el)** danger

**peligroso(a)** dangerous

**pelo (el), cabello (el)** hair

**pelota (la)** ball

**peluquero(a) (el/la)** hairdresser

**pensar (ie)** to think

**pepino cohombro (el)** cucumber

**pequeño(a)** small

**pera (la)** pear

**perder(se) (ie)** to lose, miss

    **perder el tiempo** to waste time;
    **perder peso** to lose weight

**pérdidas (las)** losses

**perdonar** to pardon

**perfume (el)** perfume

**periódico (el)** newspaper

**periodismo (el)** journalism

**periodista (el/la)** journalist

**permitir** to allow

**pero** but

**perro(a) (el/la)** dog

    **perro caliente (el)** hot dog

**personal de administración de seguridad (el)** security administration agents

**pesas (las)** weights

**pescado (el)** fish (*to eat*)

**pesebre (el)** crib, manger, nativity scene

**peso (el)** peso, weight

**pestañas (las)** eyelashes

**pez (el)** fish (alive)

**picante** hot, spicy

**pickleball (el)** pickleball

**pie (el)** foot

**pies (los)** feet

**pierna (la)** leg

**píldora (la)** pill

**piloto (el/la)** pilot

**pimentón (el)** pepper

**pimienta (la)** black pepper

**pintarse** to paint

**pintor(a) (el/la)** painter

**pincharse** to get a flat tire

**piña (la)** pineapple

**pirámide (la)** pyramid

**piscina (la), alberca (la)** pool

**piso (el)** floor, storey, *apartment* (*Spain*)

**pista de atletismo (la)** athletics track

**pista de carreras (la)** race track

**pista de patinaje (la)** skating rink

**pitar** to sound the horn

**pito (el)** horn

**placa (la)** license plate

**planta baja (la)** ground floor

**plan turístico (el)** plan for the tour

**plata (la)** silver, money (*Colombia*)

**plateado(a)** silver (*color*)

**plato (el)** dish, plate

    **plato principal (el)** main dish

**playa (la)** beach

**plaza (la)** square

**plazo: a ~s** in installments

**plomero(a) (el/la)** plumber

**pluma (la)** pen

**pobre** poor

**poco(a)** little

**poder (ue)** to be able to

**policía (el/la)** police officer

**policía (la)** police department

**política (la)** politics

**políticas (las)** policies

**político(a) (el/la)** politician

**póliza (la)** policy

pollo (el) chicken

    pollo asado (el) roasted chicken

poner to put

    poner las direccionales to put on the turn signals

    poner la mesa to set the table

    ponerse to put on

    ponerse (+ adjective) to turn (+ adjective); ponerse a (+ verb) to begin (+ verb)

ponqué (el) cake

por: a ... millas por hora at ... miles per hour; por ser usted for being you

porcentaje (el) percentage

porque because

por qué why

portátil (el) laptop

postre (el) dessert

práctica (la) practice

practicar to practice

precio (el) price

predecir to predict

preferible preferable

preferir (ie, i) to prefer

preguntar to ask questions

preguntarse to wonder

prender to start, to turn on

preocupado(a) preoccupied, worried

preocuparse (por) to worry (about)

preparado(a) prepared, ready

preparar(se) to prepare

prepararse to get ready

presentador(a) (el/la) presenter

    presentador(a) de noticias (el/la) news anchor

presentar to present

presidente (el/la) president

presión (tensión) arterial (la) blood pressure

préstamo (el) loan

prestar to lend

    prestar (poner) atención to pay attention

presupuesto (el) budget

primavera (la) spring

primero(a) first

primeros auxilios (los) first aid

primo(a) (el/la) cousin

probar to taste, to try

probarse to try on

problema (el) problem

producir to produce

profesional (el/la) professional

profesor(a) (el/la) professor, secondary/high school/faculty

profesorado (el) university faculty

programa (el) program

prohibir to forbid

promedio (el) average

prometer to promise

prometido(a) (el/la) fiancé/fiancée

pronosticar el tiempo to predict the weather

pronunciar to pronounce

propina (la) gratuity, tip

propósito: a ~ by the way

proyecto (el) project

próximo(a) coming, next

prueba (la) exam, test

prudente prudent

psicología (la) psychology

psicólogo(a) (el/la) psychologist

pública(o) public

publicidad (la) advertising (*career*)

publicista (el/la) publicist

puente (el) bridge

puerco (el) pig, pork

puerta (de embarque) (la) door, gate

puesto de trabajo (el) job position

pulmonar related to lungs

pulmones (los) lungs

punto: en~ sharp (*exact time*)

puntual punctual

## Q

que that

quebrado(a) broken

quedarse to stay

quedársele to leave behind

quejarse to complain

querer (ie) to wish, want

queso (el) cheese

química (la) chemistry

quitar to take away, remove

quitarse to move away, stay away, to take off

## R

radio (la) radio station, set

radio (el) radius

radiografía (la) X-ray

radiología (la) radiology

radiólogo(a) (el/la) radiologist

rapidez (la) speed

rápido(a) fast, quick

raqueta (la) racket

rascacielos (el) skyscraper

rato (el) a while

razón (la) reason

razonable reasonable

recado (el) message, errand

recámara (la) bedroom

recepción (la) front desk

recepcionista (la/el) receptionist

receta (la)/fórmula (la) prescription; recipe

recetar/formular to prescribe

recibir to receive

reciclaje (el) recycling

reciclar to recycle

reciente recent

reclamación de equipaje (la) baggage claim

recomendar (ie) to recommend

reconocer to recognize

reconocimiento (el) recognition

~facial (el) face recognition

~de voz (el) voice recognition

recordar (ue) to remember

recorrer to tour

recorrido (el) tour, itinerary

recto(a) straight

rector(a) (el/la) principal, provost, vice-chancellor

recursivo(a) recursive

red (la) network

redes sociales (las) media, social networks

reducir to reduce

refresco (el) cold drink, soft drink, refreshment (*non-alcoholic*)

refrigerador (el), nevera (la) refrigerator

regalo (el) gift

registrarse to register

religioso(a) religious

reloj (el) clock, watch

reloj inteligente (el) smart watch

remedio (el) remedy

remoto(a) remotely, remote

requerir to require

requisito (el) requirement

reservación (la) reservation

reservar to reserve

resfriado (el) common cold

residencia (la) residence

resort (el), complejo turístico (el) resort

respirar to breathe

responsable responsible

responsable de contenidos (el/la) content curator

retirar, sacar dinero to withdraw

retiro (el) withdrawal/retirement (*from a job*)

reunión (la) gathering, meeting, reunion

revisar to check, to review

revisión (la) review, revision

revisión mecánica (la) mechanical inspection

rico(a) rich (wealthy)/tasty, delicious

riesgo (el) risk

robótica (la) robotics

rodilla (la) knee

rojo(a) red

romántico(a) romantic

romper(se) to break

rosado(a) pink, rosé wine

rostro (el) face

roto(a) broken (*in pieces*), torn

rueda (la) wheel

ruinas (las) ruins

rutina (la) routine

## S

sábado (el) Saturday

saber to know (*facts, information, skill*)

saber a to taste like

sabor (el) taste, flavor

sabroso(a) tasty, delicious

sacar to take out

sacar la basura to take out the trash

sal (la) salt

sala (la) living room

sala de embarque (la) departure lounge

salado(a) salty

salario (el) salary

salchicha (la) sausage

salida (la) departure, exit

salir to leave, go out

salir de + (lugar) to leave (*a place*)

salir negativa (*la prueba*) to come out negative

salir positiva (*la prueba*) to come out positive

salmón (el) salmon

salsa (la) sauce, salsa dance

saltar to jump

salud (la) health

saludable healthy

saludar to greet someone

sánduche, bocadillo (*Spain*), emparedado (el) sandwich

sangre (la) blood

sano(a) healthy

sastre (el/la) tailor

secadora (la) dryer machine

secador de pelo (el) hair dryer

secar(se) to dry

seco(a) dry

sede principal (la) headquarters, main office

sedentario(a) sedentary

seguir (i) to follow

seguridad (la) safety

    caja de seguridad (la) safe deposit box

seguro(a) safe

seguro (el) insurance

    de viajes travel insurance

    médico (el) health insurance

semana (la) week

    semana pasada (la) last week

    Semana Santa (la) Holy Week

semanal weekly

sencillo(a) single (*room*), one-way (*ticket*); simple

senderismo (el) hiking

    hacer ~ to hike

sensor (el) sensor

sentarse (ie) to sit down

sentidos (los) senses

sentirse (ie) to feel

señal de pare (la) stop sign

señales de tráfico (las) traffic signs

señor Sir

señora Madam

señorita Miss

separado(a) separated

septiembre September

ser to be

serio(a) serious

    en serio seriously

servicio (el) service

    ~ a los cuartos (el) room service

    ~ al cliente (el) customer service

servir (i) to serve, help

signo (el) sign

    signos vitales (los) vital signs

silla (la) chair

sillón (el) armchair

simpático(a) nice, pleasant

síntoma (el) symptom

sintomático(a) symptomatic

sistema (el) system

    sistema inmunológico (el) immune system

    sistema de seguridad avanzado (el) advanced security system

sobrar to be left (*over*)

sobre about, above

    sobre todo above all

sobrino(a) (el/la) nephew/niece

sobrio(a) sober

sociología (la) sociology

sociólogo(a) (el/la) sociologist

soda (la), gaseosa (la) soft drink

sofá (el) sofa

sol (el) sun

    hacer ~ to be sunny

solamente only

solicitar to request, to apply for

solicitud (la) application, request

solo(a) alone

solo, solamente only

sopa (la) soup

soltero(a) single

sonar (ue) to ring, sound

soñar (ue) to dream

sopa (la) soup

sorprendido(a) surprised

sótano (el) basement

stop (el), alto (el) stop (sign)

su, sus his/her (*s. & pl.*)

subir to go up, climb

subirse a to get on (a bus, car, etc.)

sucio(a) dirty

sucursal (la) branch

    bancaria (la) bank branch

    virtual del banco (la) virtual bank branch

suegro(a) (el/la) father-in-law, mother-in-law

sueldo (el) salary

sueño (el) dream, sleep

sufrir to suffer

supuesto: por ~ of course

sur (el) south

**T**

tableta (la) tablet

tablero de mandos (el) dashboard

tacto (el) touch

talento (el) talent

talentoso(a) talented

taller mecánico (el) mechanic's workshop, garage

también also, too

tampoco neither, either

tanque (el) tank

taquilla (la) ticket window

taquillero(a) (el/la) ticket agent, clerk

tardar to be long, last

tarde (la) afternoon

    buenas tardes good afternoon

tarde late

   más tarde later

tarea (la) homework, assignment

tarifa (la) tariff, fee

tarjeta (la) card

   tarjeta de crédito
      (la) credit card

   débito (la) debit card

   tarjeta de embarque
      (la) boarding pass

taxi (el) taxi

taxista (el/la) taxi driver

té (el) tea

   té helado (el) iced tea

tecnología (la) technology

tejado (el) roof

teléfono (el) telephone

   teléfono inteligente (el)
      smartphone

televisión (la) television
   (*programs*)

televisor (el) television (*set*)

tema (el) theme

temperatura (la) temperatura

temporada (la) season (*sports and
   activities*)

   temporada baja/alta (la)
      low/high vacation
      season

temprano early

   más temprano earlier

tener to have

   no tener remedio to have no
      solution; tener
      ansias de, tener ganas
      de to feel like, want
      to; tener . . . años to
      be . . . years old; tener
      buena pinta to look good;
      tener calor to feel hot;
      tener control to have
      control; tener éxito to be

successful; tener frío to
feel cold; tener hambre to
be hungry; tener mala
suerte to be unlucky; tener
mareos to be dizzy; tener
que + (infinitivo) to have to
+ (infinitive); tener razón to
be right; tener sed to be
thirsty; tener sueño to
be sleepy; tener suerte to
be lucky; tener tos to
have a cough

tenis (el) tennis

   tenis de mesa (el) ping
      pong

tenista (el/la) tennis player

tensión (presión) (la)
   pressure

teología (la) theology

tercero(a) third

terminado(a) finished

terminal (el/la) terminal

termómetro (el) thermometer

terraza (la) terrace

terreno (el) terrain

terrible terrible

tiempo (el) time, weather

   a tiempo on time

tiempo compartido (el)
   timeshare

tienda (la) store

tierno(a) soft, tender

TikTok (el) TikTok

tinto (el) red (*wine*), small
   cup of coffee
   (*Colombia*)

tío(a) (el/la) uncle/aunt

típico(a) typical

toalla (la) towel

tobillo (el) ankle

tocar to play, touch

   tocar la bocina to
      sound the horn

tocar un instrumento to play
   an instrument

todavía still, yet

todo(a) all

tomado(a) drunk, taken

tomar(se) to take, drink

   tomar apuntes to take
      notes

   tomar asiento to take
      a seat

   tomar el pelo to pull one's leg

   tomar el sol to sunbathe

tomate (el) tomato

torcer (se) (ue) to twist,
   sprain

torcido(a) twisted, bent

torneo (el) tournament

torta (la) cake

tortilla (la) omelette

tos (la) cough

toser to cough

trabajador(a) (el/la) worker

trabajar to work

trabajo (el) job, work

traducir to translate

traductor(a) translator

traer to bring

tráfico (el) traffic

trámites (los) procedures

   digitales (los) digital
      procedures

transacción (la) transaction

transferencia de dinero (la)
   money transfer

transmisión manual, de cambios
   (la) standard transmisión

transmitir to broadcast,
   to transmit

tratamiento (el) treatment

tratar de to try to

tren (el) train

triste  sad

tu, tus  your

turismo (el)  tourism

turista (el/la)  tourist

turístico/a  tourist

**U**

úlcera (la)  ulcer

último(a)  last

único(a)  only, unique

universidad (la)  college, university

uña (la)  nail

    uñas de las manos
        (las)  fingernails

    uñas de los pies (las)
        toenails

usado(a)  used

usar  to use

uvas (las)  grapes

**V**

vaca (la)  cow

vacaciones (las)  vacation

    vacaciones de invierno (las)
        winter break

    vacaciones de primavera
        (las)  spring break

vacío(a)  empty, vacant

vacuna (la)  vaccine

valer  to be worth

    valer la pena  to be worthwhile

valioso(a)  valuable

valor (el)  value, stock

valorizarse  to increase
    the value

varado(a)  stranded

vararse/quedarse varado(a)  to
    be stranded

variedad (la)  variety

varios(as)  several, various

vaso (el)  (*drinking*) glass

vegetales (los)  vegetables

velocidad (la)  speed

velocímetro (el)  speedometer

vejez (la)  old age

vehículo deportivo
    utilitario (el)  SUV

vencer  to defeat

venda (la)/curita (la), esparadrapo
    (el)  bandage, sticking plaster

vender  to sell

venir  to come

ventajas (las)  advantages

ventana (la)  window

ventanilla (la)  small window

ver  to see, look at

verano (el)  summer

verdad (la)  truth

verde  green

verdura (la)  green vegetable

vestirse  to get dressed

veterinaria (la)  veterinary
    science

veterinario(a) (el/la)
    veterinarian

vez (la)  time (*in a series*)

vía (la)  road, railroad track

viajar  to travel

viaje (el)  journey, trip

viajero(a) (el/la)  traveler

victorioso(a)  victorious

vida (la)  life

video (el)  video

    video conferencia (la)  video
        conference

    videojuegos (los)  videogames

viejo(a)  old

viernes (el)  Friday

vigente  current

vigilar  to watch over,
    to guard

vinagre (el)  vinegar

vino (el)  wine

vino blanco (el)  white wine

vino espumoso
    (el)  sparkling wine

vino tinto (el)  red wine

visa (la)  visa

visión (la)  sight

visitar  to visit

vista (la)  sight, view

vista panorámica (la)
    panoramic view

vitamina (la)  vitamin

viudo/viuda (el/la)
    widower/widow

vivienda (la)  housing

vivir  to live

volante, timón (el)  steering wheel

volar (ue)  to fly

volver (ue)  to come back, return

vuelo (el)  flight

vuelta (la)  change, ride, return

**W**

Wifi (el)  WiFi

**Y**

y  and

ya  already

yerno (el)  son-in-law

yeso (el)  plaster cast

**Z**

zanahoria (la)  carrot

zona de trabajo compartido
    (la)  coworking space,
    shared work area

zona de recoger equipaje/maletas,
    recogida de equipaje  baggage
    claim

Zoom (el)  Zoom

zumo (el)  juice (*Spain*)

# English–Spanish Vocabulary

## A

**able: to be ~ to** poder (ue)

**about** sobre

**above all** sobre todo

**accelerator** acelerador (el)

**accept (to)** aceptar

**accompany (to)** acompañar

**accommodations** alojamiento (el)

**account** cuenta (la)

    **checking account** cuenta corriente (la)

    **savings account** cuenta de ahorros (la)

**accountant** contador(a) (el/la)

**accounting** contaduría (la)

**ache (to)** doler

**achieve (to)** cumplir

**act (to)** actuar

**acting** actuación (la)

**action** acción (la)

**active** activo(a)

**actor** actor (el)

**actress** actriz (la)

**address, home** dirección (la), domicilio (el)

**administer (to)** administrar

**administration** administración (la)

**advantage** ventaja (la)

**advertisement, ad** anuncio (el), aviso (el)

**advertising** publicidad (la)

**advise (to)** aconsejar

**advisor** asesor(a) (el/la), consejero(a) (el/la)

**after, afterwards** después (de)

**afternoon** tarde (la)

    **good ~** buenas tardes.

**age** edad (la)

    **old~** vejez (la)

**agent** agente (el/la)

    **travel agent** agente de viajes (el/la)

**agriculture** agricultura (la)

**airbags** bolsas de aire (las)

**air conditioning** aire acondicionado (el)

**airline** aerolínea (la)

    **airline check-in counter** mostrador de la aerolínea (el)

**airplane** avión (el)

    **airplane cabin** cabina del avión (la)

**airport** aeropuerto (el)

**aisle** pasillo (el)

**alarm** alarma (la)

    **alarm clock** despertador (el)

**alert** alerta (la)

**all, entire** todo(a)

**allergy** alergia (la)

**allergic** alérgico(a)

    **be ~ (to)** ser alérgico(a)

**allow (to)** permitir

**almost** casi

**alone** solo(a)

**already** ya

**also** también

**although** aunque

**amusing** entretenido(a)

**analyst** analista (el/la)

**analyze (to)** analizar

**anchor (news)** presentador(a) de noticias (el/la)

**ancient, former** antiguo(a)

**animal** animal (el)

**ankle** tobillo (el)

**announcer** locutor(a) (el/la)

**annoy (to)** molestar

**answer (to)** contestar, responder

**antibiotic** antibiótico (el)

**anthropology** antropología (la)

**apartment** apartamento (el), piso (el) (*Spain*)

**aperitif** aperitivo (el)

**app (the)** aplicación (la), aplicativo (el)

appear (to) aparecer

appetizer entremés (el)

apple manzana (la)

appliances (electric) electrodomésticos (los)

application solicitud (la)

apply (to) aplicar (crema, conocimiento, teorías)

appointment cita (la)

appreciate (to) apreciar

April abril

architect arquitecto(a) (el/la)

architecture arquitectura (la)

arm brazo (el)

armchair sillón (el)

arrange (to) arreglar, gestionar

arrival llegada (la)

arrive (to) llegar

art arte (el)

artist artista (el/la)

as . . . as como

asparagus espárragos (los)

assign (to) asignar

assistant asistente (el/la)

ask for (to) pedir

ask questions (to) preguntar

asthma asma (el)

ATM (the) cajero automático (el)

atheist ateo(a) (el/la)

athlete deportista (el/la), atleta (el/la)

athletics atletismo (el) ~track pista de atletismo (la)

attend (a class, event, meeting) asistir a

attend (to someone) atender a (alguien)

attentive atento(a)

audio audio (el)

August agosto

aunt tía (la)

author autor(a) (el/la)

authoritarian autoritario(a)

authorization autorización (la)

auto automóvil (el)

automatic automático(a)

autumn otoño (el)

availability disponibilidad (la)

available disponible

average promedio (el)

avocado aguacate (el), palta (la)

awake, alert despierto(a)

award (to) otorgar

## B

back (person) espalda (la)

backpack mochila (la)

backyard patio (trasero) (el), jardín (el)

bad, sick malo(a)

baggage equipaje (el) carry-on baggage equipaje de mano (el) baggage claim zona de reclamación/recojida de equipaje (la)

bake (to) hornear

baker panadero(a) (el/la)

bakery panadería (la)

balance (to) balancear

balance (bank account) saldo (el), balance (el)

balcony balcón (el)

ball balón (el), pelota (la)

banana banana (la), banano (el), plátano (el)

bandage curita (la), esparadrapo (el), vendita (la)

bank banco (el) bank branch sucursal bancaria (la); virtual bank branch sucursal virtual del banco (la) bank certificate certificado bancario (el) bank credit crédito bancario (el)

banking bancario(a) online banking banca en línea (la)

bargain ganga (la)

baseball béisbol (el)

basement sótano (el)

basket cesta (la) (in basketball), cesto (el) (for shopping or to put the trash in)

basketball baloncesto (el)

bat bate (el)

bat (to) batear

bathe (to) bañarse take a bath (to) bañarse

bathroom baño (el)

battery batería (la) (of a car), pila (la) (of a device)

be (to) estar, ser be happy (to) alegrarse, estar (ser) feliz (alegre) be hungry (to) tener hambre be lucky (unlucky) (to) tener suerte/tener mala suerte be right (to) tener razón be sleepy (to) tener sueño be successful (to) tener éxito be wrong (to) no tener razón/ estar equivocado(a) be . . . years old (to) tener . . . años

beach playa (la)

bean frijol (el)

**beautiful** bonito(a)

**because** porque

    **because of that** por eso

**bed** cama (la)

    **queen size bed** cama doble (la)

    **twin bed** cama sencilla (la)

**bedroom** dormitorio (el), alcoba (la), habitación (la), recámara (la)

**beef, livestock** res (la), carne de res (la)

**beefsteak** bisté (el), bistec (el)

**beer** cerveza (la)

**beforehand, before** antes (de)

**begin (to)** comenzar, empezar, iniciar

    **begin (+ verb) (to)** ponerse a (+ verb)

**believe (to)** creer

**bellboy** botones (el), mozo (el)

**belt** cinturón (el)

    **seat belt** cinturón de seguridad (el)

**bent** torcido(a)

**besides** además

**better, best** major, el mejor

**beverage** bebida (la)

**bicycle** bicicleta (la)

**big** grande

**bill, invoice** factura (la), cuenta (la); **bill, ticket** billete (el), tiquete (el)

**biologist** biólogo(a) (el/la)

**biology** biología (la)

**bird** ave (el), pájaro (el)

**birth** nacimiento (el)

    **birthdate** fecha de nacimiento (la)

**birthday** cumpleaños (el)

    **to celebrate his/her birthday** cumplir años

**black** negro(a)

**block** cuadra (la)

**blog** blog (el)

**blogger** bloguero(a) (el/la)

**blond** rubio(a)

**blood** sangre (la)

    **blood pressure** presión (tensión) arterial (la)

**blue** azul

**board (to)** abordar

**boarding pass** pasabordo (el), pase de abordar (el), tarjeta de embarque (la)

**body** cuerpo (el)

**boil (to)** hervir

**bone** hueso (el)

**book** libro (el)

    **bookcase, bookshelve** estante (el)

**bookstore** librería (la)

**bomb** bomba (la)

**boring, bored** aburrido(a)

**born: to be ~** nacer

**borrow (to)** pedir prestado

**boss** jefe(a) (el/la)

**bossy** autoritario(a)

**bother (to)** molestar

**bottle** botella (la)

**bowling** boliche (el), bolos (los)

**boy, son** niño (el), chico (el)

**boyfriend** novio (el)

**brain** cerebro (el)

**brake** freno (el)

    **emergency brake** freno de emergencia (el), **handbreak** freno de mano (el)

**brake (to)** frenar

**branch** sucursal (la)

**brand** marca (la)

**bread** pan (el)

**break (to)** dañar(se), fracturar(se), quebrar(se), romper(se)

**breakdown** avería (la), daño (el)

**breakfast** desayuno (el)

    **have ~ (to)** desayunar

**breast** pecho (el)

**breath (to)** respirar

**bridge** puente (el)

**brief** breve, corto(a)

**briefcase** maletín (el)

**bright** brillante

**brilliant** brillante

**bring (to)** traer

**broadcast (to)** transmitir

**broccoli** brócoli (el)

**broken, torn** fracturado(a), roto(a), dañado(a), descompuesto(a)

**broom** escoba (la)

**brother** hermano (el)

    **half-brother** medio hermano (el)

    **stepbrother** hermanastro (el)

    **twin brother** gemelo (el), mellizo (el)

**brother-in-law** cuñado (el)

**brown** marrón

**brush** cepillo (el)

    **hairbrush** cepillo para el pelo (el)

    **toothbrush** cepillo de dientes (el)

**brush (to)** cepillar(se)

**budget** presupuesto (el)

**build (to)** construir

**building** edificio (el)

    **apartment building** edificio de apartamentos (el)

**bumper** parachoques (el)

**bus** autobús (el), bus (el), *camión (el) (Mexico)*

**business** compañía (la), empresa (la), negocio (el)

**busy** ocupado(a)

**but** pero

**butter** mantequilla (la)

**button** botón (el)

**buy (to)** comprar

**buyer** comprador (el), compradora (la)


C

**cake** pastel (el), ponqué (el), torta (la)

**call (to)** llamar

    **be called (to)** llamarse

**calm (down) (to)** calmar(se)

**calm** calma (la)

**calm** calmado(a)

**calorie** caloría (la)

**camera** cámara (la)

    **back-up, rear-view camera** cámara de visión trasera (la)

    **digital camera** cámara digital (la)

**can** lata (la)

**candidate** candidato(a) (el/la)

**car** auto (automóvil) (el), carro (el), coche (el)

    **automatic ~** carro automático (el)

    **electric ~** carro eléctrico (el)

    **hybrid ~** carro híbrido (el)

**car dealer, car dealership** concesionario (el)

**car rental** alquiler de carros (el)

**card** tarjeta (la)

    **credit ~** tarjeta de crédito (la)

    **debit ~** tarjeta débito (la)

**cardiologist** cardiólogo(a) (el/la)

**cardiology** cardiología (la)

**career (major)** carrera (la)

**careful** cuidadoso(a)

**carnival** carnaval (el)

**carpenter** carpintero(a) (el/la)

**carpet, rug** alfombra (la)

**carrot** zanahoria (la)

**cash (*to pay*)** al contado, en efectivo

**cashier** cajero(a) (el/la)

**cash register** caja (registradora) (la)

**cast (*plaster*)** yeso (el)

**cat** gato(a) (el/la)

**catarrh** catarro (el)

**CD (the)** certificado de depósito a término
CDT (el)

**celebrate (to)** celebrar

**celebration** celebración (la)

**cellular** celular (el), móvil (el) (*Spain*)

**cent** centavo (el), céntimo (el)

**centennial (Generation Z)** generación Z (la), centenial (el/la)

**center** centro (el)

**cereal** cereal (el)

**chair** silla (la)

**champion** campeón (el), campeona (la)

**championship** campeonato (el)

**chance: by ~** por casualidad

**change** vuelta (la), cambio (el)

**change (to)** cambiar

**characteristic** característica (la)

**charge (to) (*a device*)** cargar

**charge, get paid (to)** cobrar

**charger** cargador (el)

**charm, like (to)** encantar

**charming** encantador(a)

**chat (to)** chatear, conversar

**cheap** barato(a)

**check** cheque (el)

    **checkbook** chequera (la), talonario (el)

**check (to)** revisar

**check in (to)** facturar, registrarse

**cheek** mejilla (la)

**cheerful** alegre

**cheese** queso (el)

**chef** cocinero(a) (el/la)

**chemistry** química (la)

**chicken** pollo (el)

**chickpeas** garbanzos (los)

**chills** escalofríos (los)

**chin** barbilla (la), mentón (el)

**chocolate** chocolate (el)

**choice** opción (la)

**choir** coro (el)

**Christmas** Navidad (la)

**church** iglesia (la)

**citizen** ciudadano/a (el/la)

**city** ciudad (la)

**class** clase (la)

    **business class** clase ejecutiva (la)

    **economy class** clase económica (la)

    **first class** primera clase (la)

    **online class** clase en línea (la)

**classmate** compañero/a de clase (el/la)

**clean** limpio(a)

**clean (to)** limpiar

**clear** claro(a)

**climate** clima (el)

**climb (to)** escalar

**clinic** clínica (la), centro de salud (el)

clock, watch reloj (el)

    alarm clock despertador (el)

close cercano(a), unido(a) (close family)

close (to) cerrar (ie)

close (to a place or a person), near cerca a, junto a

closet closet (el)

cloud nube (la)

cloudy nublado(a)

    be ~ (to) estar nublado

coach entrenador(a) (el/la)

coincidence: what a coincidence! ¡qué casualidad!

coffee café (el)

coffee maker cafetera (la)

coffee shop cafetería (la), café (el)

cold frío(a)

    be cold (to) (weather) hacer frío, be cold (to) (feeling) tener frío

cold (common) resfrío (el) estar resfriado(a)

college, university universidad (la)

collide (to) chocar

color color (el)

comb peine (el), peinilla (la)

comb (to) peinar(se)

come (to) venir

    come back (to) volver (ue)

    come in (to) entrar a (en)

    come out negative/positive (to) (test) salir negativo(a)/ positivo(a)

comfortable cómodo(a)

commemorate (to) conmemorar

company compañía (la)

compartment compartimiento (el)

    overhead compartment/locker (in an airplane) compartimiento superior (el)

compete (to) competir

competition competencia (la)

complain (to) quejarse

complete (to) completar

complicated complicado(a)

compulsive compulsivo(a)

computer computador(a) (el/la), ordenador(a) (el/la) (Spain)

communication comunicación (la)

community comunidad (la)

comply with the law (to) cumplir las leyes

conclude (to) concluir

condiments condimentos (los)

conduct (to) conducir

conductor conductor(a) (el/la), director (music)

conference conferencia (la), congreso (el)

confirm (to) confirmar

confusion confusión (la)

congested congestionado(a)

congratulate (to) felicitar

congratulation: ~s felicidades (las), felicitaciones (las)

connection conexión (la)

consider (to) considerar

constipation estreñimiento (el)

    constipated estreñido(a)

consult (to) consultar

consultation consulta (la)

consume (to) consumir

consumer consumidor(a) (el/la)

contain (to) contener

content creator creador(a) de contenidos (el/la)

conversation conversación (la)

converse (to) conversar

convert (to) convertir(ie, i)

convince (to) convencer

cook (to) cocinar

cook cocinero(a) (el/la), chef (el/la)

cookies galletas (las)

cool fresco(a)

    be ~ (to) hacer fresco

corn maíz (el)

correspond (to) corresponder

corresponding correspondiente

cosmetologist cosmetólogo(a) (el/la)

cosmetology cosmetología (la)

cost (to) costar(ue)

cost costo (el)

costume, disguise disfraz (el)

cough tos (la)

cough (to) toser

count (to) contar

country país (el)

countryside campo (el)

couple par (things), pareja (la) (people)

    a couple of (things), a few un par de

course: of ~ ¡cómo no!, por supuesto

cousin primo(a) (el/la)

cover (to) cubrir

cow vaca (la)

coworker compañero(a) de trabajo (el/la)

cramp calambre (el)

crash choque (el), estrellada (la)

crash (to) chocar(se), estrellar(se)

cream crema (la)

    shaving ~ crema de afeitar (la)

create (to) crear

creative creativo(a)

credit crédito (el)

    **bank ~** crédito bancario (el)

    **mortgage ~** crédito hipotecario (el)

**criminal** criminal (el/la)

**cross (to)** cruzar

**cruise control** control de crucero (el)

**crutch** muleta (la)

**cucumber** pepino (el)

**cultivate (to)** cultivar

**cure** cura (la)

**cure, heal (to)** curar

**currency, coin** moneda (la)

**current** actual

**curriculum vitae** currículo (el), hoja de vida (la)

**curtains** cortinas (las)

**customs** aduana (la)

**cutlery** cubiertos (los)

**cut (to)** cortar

    **cut hair (to)** cortar el pelo (*el cabello*)

**cycling** ciclismo (el)

## D

**daily** diario(a)

**damage (to)** dañar

**dance (to)** bailar

**dancer** bailarín (el), bailarina (la)

**danger** peligro (el)

**dangerous** peligroso(a)

**dark** oscuro(a)

**dashboard** tablero de mandos (el)

**date (calendar)** fecha (la); **(romantic)** cita (la)

    **be up to ~ (to)** estar al día

**daughter** hija (la)

    **daughter-in-law** nuera (la)

    **stepdaughter** hijastra (la)

**day** día (el)

    **at noon** a mediodía

    **per day** por día

    **day before yesterday** anteayer

**dean** decano(a) (el/la)

**debate** debate (el)

**debt** deuda (la)

**debtor** deudor(a) (el/la)

**December** diciembre

**decide (to)** decidir

**decision** decisión (la)

**defeat (to)** vencer

**deflate (to)** desinflar

**degree** grado (el), licenciatura (la)

    **master's degree** maestría (la)

**delay (to)** demorar, atrasar

**delayed** atrasado(a)

    **be ~ (to)** estar atrasado(a)

**delicious** delicioso(a)

**deliver (to)** entregar

**dentist** dentista (el/la), odontólogo(a) (el/la)

**departure, exit** salida (la)

    **departure lounge** sala de embarque (la)

**depend on (to)** depender de

**deposit** depósito (el)

**deposit (to)** depositar

**depression** depresión (la)

**dermatologist** dermatólogo(a) (el/la)

**describe (to)** describir

**desk** escritorio (el)

    **front desk** recepción (la)

**desert** desierto (el)

**deserve (to)** merecer

**design (to)** diseñar

**design** diseño (el)

**designer** diseñador(a) (el/la)

**dessert** postre (el)

**destination** destino (el)

**destroy (to)** destruir

**destroyed** destruido(a)

**detail-oriented** detallista

**detain people (to)** detener

**diagram** diagrama (el)

**die (to)** morir (ue)

**diet** dieta (la), alimentación (la)

    **be on a ~ (to)** estar a dieta

**difficult** difícil

**dining room** comedor (el)

**dinner** cena (la), comida (la)

    **have ~ (to)** cenar, comer

**director** director(a) (el/la)

**dirty** sucio(a)

**disaster** desastre (el)

**discipline** disciplina (la)

**discover (to)** descubrir

**disembark (to)** desembarcar

**disguise as, wear costumes (to)** disfrazarse

**disguised** disfrazado(a)

**dish, plate** plato (el)

**dishwasher** lavaplatos (el)

**dismiss (to)** despedir del trabajo

**dive (to), diving** bucear

**divorce** divorcio (el)

**divorced** divorciado(a)

**dizziness** mareo (el)

    **dizzy: to be ~** tener mareos; **to get ~** marearse

**do, make (to)** hacer

**doctor** doctor(a) (el/la)

**document** documento (el)

**dog** perro(a) (el/la)

    **hot dog** perro caliente (el)

**doll** muñeca (la)

**door, gate** puerta (la)

**double** doble

**download (to)** descargar, bajar

**down there** (allá) abajo

**downtown** centro (el)

**draw (to)** dibujar

**dream, sleep** sueño (el)

**dream (to)** soñar (ue)

**dress** vestido (el)

    **to get dressed** vestirse

**dressing (salad)** aderezo (el)

**drink** bebida (la)

    **energy drink** bebida energizante (la)

**drink (to)** beber, tomar

**drive (to)** conducir, manejar

**driver** chofer (el/la), conductor(a) (el/la)

**drugstore** droguería (la)

**drunk** bebido(a), borracho(a), tomado(a)

**dry** seco(a)

**dry (to)** secar

**dryer (machine)** secadora (la)

    **hair dryer** secador de pelo (cabello) (el)

**dust (to)** limpiar (sacudir) el polvo

**E**

**ear (outer)** oreja (la)

**early** temprano

**earn (to)** ganar

**earnings** ganancias (las)

**Easter** Pascua (la)

**easy** fácil

**eat (to)** comer

**economic** económico(a)

**economics** economía (la) (discipline)

**economist** economista (el/la)

**economy** economía (la)

**education** educación (la)

**effective** efectivo(a)

**egg** huevo (el)

**elbow** codo (el)

**electric** eléctrico(a)

    **electricity** electricidad (la)

**elegant** elegante, gentil

**elevator** ascensor (el)

**email** correo electrónico (el)

**emergency** emergencia (la)

**employee** empleado(a) (el/la)

**empty** vacío (a), desocupado(a)

**end: by the ~ of** a finales de

**energy** energía (la)

**engine** motor (el)

**engineer** ingeniero(a) (el/la)

**engineering** ingeniería (la)

**enjoy (to)** disfrutar de

**enough** bastante, suficiente

**enter (to)** entrar, ingresar

    **enter the password** digitar (entrar) la contraseña (clave)

**entrance** entrada (la)

**erase (to)** borrar

**eraser** borrador (el)

**espectacular** spectacular

**evening** noche (la), tarde (la)

    **evening: good ~** buenas noches

**exam** examen (el), prueba (la)

**examine (to)** examinar

**excellent** excelente

**excursion** excursión (la)

**exercise** ejercicio (el)

    **exercise (to)** hacer ejercicios

**exhausted** exhausto(a), extenuado(a)

**exit** salida (la)

**expense** gasto (el)

**expensive** caro(a), costoso(a)

**experiment** experimento (el)

**experiment (to)** experimentar, hacer experimentos

**export (goods) (to)** exportar

**exquisite** exquisito(a)

**extended** extendido(a)

**extinct** extinto(a), extinguido(a)

**eye** ojo (el)

**eyebrow** ceja (la)

**eyelash** pestaña (la)

**F**

**face** cara (la), rostro (el)

**factory** fábrica (la)

**fail: without ~** sin falta

**faint (to)** desmayarse

**fall** caída (la), otoño (el) (season)

**fall (to)** caer(se)

**family** familia (la)

**fantastic** estupendo(a), fantástico(a)

**far away** lejos

**farmer** agricultor(a) (el/la), campesino(a) (el/la)

**fascinating** fascinante

**fast, quick** rápido(a)

**fasten (to)** abrochar (se)

**fat** gordo(a), grueso(a)

**father** padre (el)

    **father, dad** papá (el)

    **grandfather** abuelo (el)

    **great-grandfather** bisabuelo (el)

    **stepfather** padrastro (el)

**father-in-law** suegro (el)

**fatigue** fatiga (la)

**favor: please, do me a ~** hágame el favor

**feast (to)** festejar

**February** febrero

**fee** cuota (la)

    **handling fee** cuota de manejo (la)

**feed (to)** alimentar

**feel like, want to (to)** tener ganas (*ansias*) de

**festival** festival (el)

**festive** festivo(a)

**fever** fiebre (la)

    **have ~ (to)** tener fiebre

**few** algunos(as), pocos(as)

**fiancé** novio (el), prometido (el)

**fiancée** novia (la), prometida (la)

**field** campo (el)

**fill (to)** llenar

    **fill a prescription (to)** llenar una receta

**finalist** finalista (el/la)

**finally** por fin

**finances** finanzas (las)

**financial** financiero(a)

    **financial advisor** asesor(a) financiero(a)

**find (to)** encontrar (ue)

**fine** multa (la)

**finger, toe** dedo (el)

**fingerprint** huella (la)

    **digital ~** huella digital (la)

**fire** fuego (el), incendio (el)

**firefighter** bombero(a) (el/la)

**fireplace** chimenea (la)

**fireworks** juegos (*fuegos*) artificiales (los)

**first** primero(a)

**fish** pescado (el), pez (el)

**fish (to)** pescar

**fix (to)** arreglar, reparar

**flat** piso (el)

**flavor** sabor (el)

**flee (to)** huir

**flight** vuelo (el)

**flight attendant** auxiliar (*asistente*) de vuelo (el/la)

**fly (to)** volar

**food** alimentación (la), alimento (el), comida (la)

    **sea food** comida de mar (la)

**floor, story** piso (el)

    **ground floor** planta baja (la)

**flower** flor (la)

**flu** gripa (la), gripe (la)

**fly (to)** volar (ue)

**follow (to)** seguir (i)

**food** alimento (el)

**food, meal** comida (la)

**foot** pie (el)

    **feet** pies (los)

**for: just ~ you** por ser usted, por ti

**forbid (to)** prohibir

**forehead** frente (la)

**foreign money** divisa (la)

**forget (to)** olvidar

**former** antiguo(a)

**fracture** fractura (la)

**fracture (to)** fracturar, romper

**fraternity** fraternidad (la)

**free, free of charge** gratis

    **free, vacant** desocupado(a), vacío(a)

**freeze (to)** congelar

**freezer** congelador (el)

**French fries** papas fritas (las)

**frequently, often a** menudo

**fresh, cool** fresco(a)

**Friday** viernes (el)

**friend** amigo(a) (el/la)

**friendship** amistad (la)

**from** desde

**front desk** recepción (la)

**fruit** fruta (la)

**fry (to)** freír, fritar

**fulfill (to)** cumplir

**full** lleno(a)

**fun** divertido(a)

    **have ~ (to)** divertirse

**function (to)** funcionar

**funny** chistoso(a), gracioso(a)

**furnish (to)** amueblar

**furnished** amueblado(a)

**furniture** mueble (el)

**future** futuro(a)


**G**

**gallon** galón (el)

**game** juego (el), partido (el)

**garage** garaje (el)

**garden** jardín (el)

**garlic** ajo (el)

**gasoline** gasolina (la)

**gas pump** bomba de gasoline (la)

**gate** puerta de embarque (*salida*) (la)

**generation** generación (la)

**get, obtain (to)** conseguir (i)

    **get dirty (to)** ensuciarse

    **get a flat tire (to)** pincharse

    **get hurt (to)** lastimarse

    **get a tan** broncearse

    **get off, go down (to)** bajar(se) (de);

    **get on (to)** subir a (*car, train, etc.*)

    **get ready (to)** alistarse, arreglarse, prepararse

    **get relief (to)** aliviarse

    **get sick (to)** enfermarse

    **get a tan (to)** broncearse

    **get up (to)** levantarse

    **get used to (to)** acostumbrarse

**gift** regalo (el)

**girl** chica (la), niña (la)

**give (to)** dar

    **give gifts (to)** dar regalos, regalar

    **give reverse (to)** dar reversa

**glass** copa (la), vaso (el), vidrio (el)

**glove compartment** guantera (la)

**go (to)** ir

    **go to bed (to)** acostarse

    **go to sleep (to)** dormirse

    **go down (to)** bajar

    **go up, climb (to)** subir

**gold** oro (el)

**golf** golf (el)

    **golf clubs** palos de golf (los)

    **golf player** golfista (el/la)

**good** bueno(a)

**good-bye** adiós, chao/chau

**GPS/Waze** navegador de GPS/Waze (el)

**grade** calificación (la), nota (la)

**granddaughter** nieta (la)

**grandfather** abuelo (el)

**grandmother** abuela (la)

**grandparents** abuelos (los)

**grandson** nieto (el)

**grant (to)** otorgar

**grapes** uvas (las)

**grass** césped (el), hierba (la), pasto (el)

**gray** gris

**grease** grasa (la)

**greased** grasoso(a)

**great-grandfather** bisabuelo (el)

**great-grandmother** bisabuela (la)

**great-grandparents** bisabuelos (los)

**green** verde

**green pea** guisante (el), arveja (la)

**greens, green vegetable**(s) verdura(s) (la[s])

**greet (to)** saludar

**grill** asador (el)

**grooming** arreglo personal (el)

**grow (to)** cultivar (*plants*), crecer (*people*)

**growth** crecimiento (el)

**guest** huésped (el/la)

**guide (to)** guiar

**guitar** guitarra (la)

**gym** gimnasio (el)

**gymnast** gimnasta (el/la)

**gymnastics** gimnasia (la)

## H

**hair** pelo (el), cabello (el)

**hairdresser's** peluquería (la)

**half** medio(a)

**ham** jamón (el)

**hamburger** hamburguesa (la)

**hand** mano (la)

**handsome** guapo(a)

**happen (to)** ocurrir, pasar

**happiness** felicidad (la), la alegría

**happy** alegre, feliz, contento(a)

    **be ~ (to)** alegrarse, estar alegre, estar contento(a), estar feliz

**have (to)** tener, haber

    **have a cough (to)** tener tos;

    **have fun (to)** divertirse (ie); **have just . . . (to)** acabar de (+ verb); **have no solution (to)** no tener remedio; **have to + (infinitive) (to)** tener que + (infinitivo)

**head** cabeza (la)

**headlight** faro (el), luces delanteras (las)

**heal (to)** curar

**health** salud (la)

**healthy** saludable, sano(a)

**hear (to)** oír

**heart** corazón (el)

**heat** calor (el)

**heat (to)** calentar

**heating** calefacción (la)

**hello!** ¡aló!, dígame, hola

**help** ayuda (la)

**help (to)** ayudar

**here** aquí, acá

**Hi!** ¡Hola!

**high, tall** alto(a)

**highway** autopista (la)

**hike (to)** hacer senderismo

**hiking** senderismo (el)

**hip** cadera (la)

**his/her** (*s. & pl.*) su, sus

**holiday** (día) festivo (el)

**hood** capó (el)

**horn** bocina (la), pito (el)

**hose** manguera (la)

**hospital** hospital (el)

**hot** caliente, picante (spicy)

    **be hot (to)** hacer calor (*weather*), **be hot (to)** (*feeling*) tener calor

**hotel** hotel (el)

**hour** hora (la)

**house** casa (la)

**housing** vivienda (la)

**hunger** hambre (*f.*) (el)

**hungry: to be ~** tener hambre

**hurt, ache (to)** doler (ue)

**husband** esposo (el), marido (el)

**hybrid** híbrido(a)

**hydrate (to)** hidratarse

## I

**ice** hielo (el)

**ice cream** helado (el)

**idea** idea (la)

ill, sick enfermo(a)
    be ~ (to) estar enfermo(a)
illness enfermedad (la)
imagine (to) imaginar
immediate inmediato(a)
import (goods) (to) importar
important importante; to be ~
    importar
include (to) incluir (y)
increase aumento (el)
    incremento (el)
increase (to) aumentar,
    incrementar
incredible increíble
indigestion indigestión (la)
inflate (to) inflar
influencer influyente (el/la)
inform (to) informar, avisar
injection inyección (la)
inquiry averiguación (la)
inside adentro
inspect (to) inspeccionar
Instagram Instagram (el)
installment: in ~s a plazos
institute instituto (el), colegio de
    secundaria (Spain)
insurance seguro (el)
    health insurance seguro
        médico (el)
    travel insurance seguro de
        viajes (el)
insured asegurado(a)
    be ~ (to) estar asegurado(a)
intelligence inteligencia (la)
    artificial intelligence
        inteligencia
        artificial (la)
intelligent inteligente
interest interés (el)
interest (to) interesar
interesting interesante
international internacional

international money order
    giro internacional (el)
Internet Internet (el)
internship pasantía (la)
intersection intersección (la),
    cruce (el)
itinerary itinerario (el)
invest (to) invertir
investment inversión (la)
invitation invitación (la)
invite (to) invitar
irritation irritación (la)
it's necessary to (+ verb) hay
    que (+ verb)

**J**

January enero
job trabajo (el)
jog (to), jogging
    correr, trotar
journalism periodismo (el)
journalist periodista (el/la)
joy alegría (la), felicidad (la)
juice jugo (el), zumo (el)
July julio
June junio
jump (to) saltar
just justo(a)

**K**

key llave (la)
    key card tarjeta (la)
kilometer kilómetro (el)
kind, nice amable
kiss beso (el)
kiss (to) besar
kitchen cocina (la)
    full kitchen cocina
        integral (la)
knee rodilla (la)

know (to) saber (*facts,
    information, skills*), conocer
    (*to meet for the first time, be
    familiar with*)

**L**

laboratory laboratorio (el)
lack (to) faltar
ladder escalera (la)
lamb cordero (el)
lamp lámpara (la), pantalla (la)
land (to) aterrizar
landing aterrizaje (el)
landscape paisaje (el)
language idioma (el), lengua (la),
    lenguaje (el)
laptop portátil (el)
large, big grande
last último(a) (el/la)
last (to) durar
late atrasado(a); tarde
later más tarde
law derecho (el) (*career*)
laws leyes (las)
lead (to) dirigir, guiar
learn (to) aprender
lease alquiler (el), arriendo (el),
    renta (la)
leave (to) salir, dejar
    leave (a person) (to) dejar a
        + (persona)
    leave (a place) (to) salir de +
        (lugar), irse de
    leave behind (to) quedarse atrás
left: be ~ over (to) sobrar
leg pierna (la)
legumes legumbres (las)
lemon limón (el)
lemonade limonada (la)
lend (to) prestar
lesson lección (la)

**lettuce** lechuga (la)

**librarian** bibliotecario(a) (el/la)

**library** biblioteca (la)

**license** carné (el), licencia (la)

**license plate** matrícula (la), placa (la)

**lift weights (to)** levantar pesas

**light** luz (la)

   **traffic light** semáforo (el); **light (to)** encender (ie)

**light, quick** ligero(a)

**like** como

**like, please (to)** encantar, gustar

**limit** cupo (el), límite (el)

**limp (to)** cojear

**linguistics** lingüística (la)

**lip** labio (el)

**listen (to)** escuchar

**literature** literatura (la)

**little** poco(a)

**live (to)** vivir

**lively** animado(a)

**load, charge (to)** cargar

**loan** préstamo (el)

**lobster** langosta (la)

**lodging** alojamiento (el)

**log in (to)** iniciar sesión

**log out (to)** cerrar sesión, salir de la sesión

**long** largo(a)

   **be long, last (to)** tardar; **so long** hasta luego.

**look after (to)** ocuparse

**look at (to)** mirar

**look for (to)** buscar

**look good (to)** tener buena pinta

**lose, miss (to)** perder(se) (ie)

   **lose weight (to)** adelgazar, bajar de peso, perder peso

**losses** pérdidas (las)

**love** amor (el)

**to be in ~** estar enamorado(a)

**to fall in ~** enamorarse

**low, short** bajo(a)

**lubricate (to)** engrasar

**lucky: to be ~** tener suerte

**luggage** equipaje (el)

**lunch** almuerzo (el)

**lung** pulmón (el)

**luxurious** lujoso(a)

## M

**Madam** señora

**main** principal

**major** carrera (la), especialidad (la) (*university program*)

**majority, most** mayoría (la)

**make (to)** hacer

**make a mess (to)** desordenar, desorganizar

**make one's mouth water (to)** hacer agua la boca

**makeup** maquillaje (el)

   **put on ~ (to)** maquillarse

**man** hombre (el)

**map** mapa (el)

**manage (to)** administrar, manejar

   **manage the budget (to)** manejar el presupuesto

**management** administración (la)

**manager** administrador(a) (el/la), gerente (el/la), jefe(a) (el/la)

   **general manager, CEO** gerente general (el/la)

   **human resources manager** gerente de recursos humanos (el/la)

**mango** mango (el)

**marathon** maratón (la)

**half-marathon** media maratón (la)

**marathon runner** maratonista (el/la)

**March** marzo

**margarine** margarina (la)

**marinate (to)** adobar

**market** mercado (el)

   **stock market** bolsa de valores (la)

**marketing** mercadotecnia (la), mercadeo (el)

**married** casado(a)

**maternal** materno(a)

**mathematics** matemáticas (las)

**matter (to)** importar

**May** mayo

**meal** comida (la)

**meat** carne (la)

**mechanic** mecánico(a)

**mechanical** mecánico(a)

**mechanic's workshop** taller de mecánica (el)

**medical** médico(a)

**medication** medicamento (el)

**medicine** medicina (la)

**meet, find (to)** encontrarse

**melt (to)** deshacer(se)

**memory** memoria (la)

**mental stress** estrés (el)

**menu** menú (el), carta (la)

**message, errand** recado (el)

   **text message** mensaje de texto (el)

**messy** desordenado(a), desorganizado(a)

**meteorologist** meteorólogo(a) (el/la)

**meteorology** meteorología (la)

**method** método (el)

**methodical** metódico(a)

**microwave** horno microondas (el)

**middle: in the ~ of** en medio de

**mile** milla (la)

**milk** leche (la)

    **almond ~** leche de almendras (la)

    **fat free (skimmed) ~** leche descremada (la)

    **lactose free ~** leche deslactosada (la)

    **soy ~** leche de soya (la)

**minister** ministro(a) (el/la)

**minutes** minutos (los), acta (el) (*meeting*)

**mirror** espejo (el)

    **rear-view mirror** espejo retrovisor (el)

**miss (someone or something) (to)** echar de menos, extrañar, faltar

**miss (a flight) (to)** perder

**Miss** señorita

**model** modelo (el)

    **project model** maqueta (la)

**modern** moderno(a)

**mom** mamá (la)

**Monday** lunes (el)

**monetary** monetario(a)

**money** dinero (el), plata (la) (*Colombia*)

    **foreign money** divisa (la)

    **money order** giro (*postal*) (el)

**month** mes (el)

**monthly** mensual

**more** más

**more: ~ or less** más o menos

**morning** mañana (la)

    **good ~** buenos días

**mortgage** hipoteca (la)

**mother** madre (la)

**stepmother** madrastra (la)

**mother-in-law** suegra (la)

**motive** motivo (el)

**mouth** boca (la)

**move away (to)** quitarse

**much, a lot** mucho(a)

**muscle** músculo (el)

**mushroom** champiñón (el), seta (la) (*Spain*), hongo (el)

**music** música (la)

**musician** músico(a) (el/la)

**must, should** deber

**my** mi, mis

## N

**name** nombre (el)

**narrow** estrecho(a)

**nativity scene** pesebre (el) nacimiento (el)

**nausea** náusea (la), mareo (el)

**near** cerca

**necessary** necesario(a)

**neck** cuello (el)

**need** necesidad (la)

**need (to)** necesitar

**neighbor** vecino(a) (el/la)

**neighborhood** barrio (el), colonia (la)

**neither** tampoco

**nephew** sobrino (el)

**nerves** nervios (los)

**nervous** nervioso(a)

    **be ~ (to)** estar nervioso(a)

**new** nuevo(a)

**news** noticias (las)

    **news anchor** presentador(a) de noticias (el/la)

**next, coming** próximo(a)

**nice, pleasant** (*people*) amable, simpático(a)

    **how nice!** ¡qué lindo!

**niece** sobrina (la)

**night** noche (la)

    **good night** buenas noches

    **last night** anoche

**nomad** nómada (el/la)

**nomadic** nómada, nomádico(a)

**noon** mediodía (el)

    **noon: at ~** a mediodía

**nose** nariz (la)

**notebook** cuaderno (el)

**notes** apuntes (los)

**notice** aviso (el)

**November** noviembre

**novel** novela (la)

**now** ahora

**number** número (el)

    **pin ~** clave (la), contraseña (la)

**nurse** enfermero(a) (el/la)

## O

**obese** obeso(a)

**obsessed** obsesionado(a)

**obsession** obsesión (la)

**obtain (to)** conseguir, obtener

**occupied** ocupado(a)

**occupy (to)** ocupar

**October** octubre

**of course** por supuesto

**offer (to)** ofrecer

**office** oficina (la)

    **admissions office** oficina de admisiones (la)

    **doctor's office** consultorio (el)

**oil** aceite (el), petróleo (el)

**old** viejo(a)

**olives** aceitunas (las)

    **olive oil** aceite de oliva (el)

omelette tortilla (la)

onion cebolla (la)

    scallion, spring
        onion cebolleta (la)

online en línea, virtual

    online access acceso en
        línea (el)

only solo, solamente, único(a)

open (to) abrir

opened abierto(a)

opportunity oportunidad (la)

option opción (la)

optometrist optómetra
    (el/la)

or o

orange naranja (la)

order pedido (el), orden (la),
    ración (la)

order (to) ordenar, pedir

organized ordenado(a),
    organizado(a)

outside afuera

outskirts afueras (las)

oven horno (el)

owe money (to) deber (*dinero*)

**P**

package paquete (el)

pack (to) empacar

    pack the suitcase (to)
        empacar (*hacer*) la maleta

pain dolor (el)

painkiller calmante (el)

paint (to) pintar

painter pintor(a) (el/la)

painting cuadro (el), pintura (la)

pair par (el), pareja (la)

pale pálido(a)

papaya papaya (la)

paper papel (el)

paragliding parapente (el)

pardon (to) perdonar

parents padres (los), papás (los)

park (to) estacionar,
    parquear, aparcar

parking estacionamiento (el),
    parqueadero (el)

participate (to) participar

party fiesta (la)

pass (to) pasar

passenger pasajero(a) (el/la)

passport pasaporte (el)

pasta pasta (la)

pastry, cake pastel (el)

    pastry shop pastelería (la)

password contraseña (la), clave (la)

paternal paterno(a)

patience paciencia (la)

patient paciente (el/la)

patio patio (el)

pay (to) pagar

    pay attention (to) hacer caso,
        poner (*prestar*) atención

payment pago (el)

peach durazno (el), melocotón (el)

pear pera (la)

pediatrician pediatra (el/la)

pen pluma (la), bolígrafo (el),
    esfero (el)

pencil lápiz (el)

pepper pimentón (el)

    black pepper pimienta (la)

percent por ciento

percentage porcentaje (el)

per: at . . . miles ~ hour
    a . . . millas por hora;
    ~ day por día

perfume perfume (el)

perhaps a lo mejor

peso peso (el)

pharmacy farmacia (la)

piano piano (el)

pickleball pickleball (el)

pie pastel (el)

pig, pork cerdo (el), carne de cerdo
    (el)/chancho (el)/puerco (el)

pill pastilla (la), píldora (la)

pilot piloto (el/la)

pineapple piña (la)

pink, rosé (wine) rosado(a)

place lugar (el), sitio (el)

plan plan (el)

plaque placa (la)

plate placa (la) (*license plate*),
    plato (el) (*dish*)

play (to) jugar (ue)

    play an instrument (to) tocar
        un instrumento

pleasant agradable

please por favor

please (to) agradar

pleased encantado(a)

pleasure: it's a pleasure con
    mucho gusto

plumber plomero(a) (el/la)

police department
    policía (la)

police officer oficial de
    policía (el/la)

policies políticas (las)

policy póliza (la)

polite atento(a), educado(a)

politician político (a) (el/la)

politics política (la)

pool piscina (la); alberca
    (la) (*Mexico*)

poor pobre

position posición (la), puesto (el)

positive positivo(a)

potato papa (la), patata (la)

practice práctica (la)

practice (to) practicar

**predict (to)** predecir, pronosticar

**prefer (to)** preferir (ie)

**preferable** preferible

**preoccupied** preocupado(a)

**prepare (to)** preparar(se)

**prepared** preparado(a), listo(a)

**prescribe (to)** formular, recetar

**prescription** fórmula (la),
    receta (la), prescripción (la)

**present** actual, presente (el)

**present (to)** presentar

**presenter** presentador(a) (el/la)

**president** presidente (el/la)

**pressure** presión (la), tensión (la)

**pretty** bonito(a), lindo(a)

**price** precio (el)

**priest** cura (el), sacerdote (el)

**problem** problema (el)

**procedure** procedimiento
    (el), trámite (el)

**produce (to)** producir

**product** producto (el)

**professional** profesional (el/la)

**professor** catedrático(a)
    (el/la), profesor(a) (el/la)

**program** programa (el)

**project** proyecto (el)

**promise** promesa (la)

**promise (to)** prometer

**pronounce (to)** pronunciar

**property** propiedad (la)

**prudent** prudente

**public** público(a), público (el)

**publicist** publicista (el/la)

**pull one's leg (to)** tomar el pelo

**pump** surtidor (el)

**punctual** puntual

**purple** morado(a), púrpura

**purse** bolso (el), bolsa (la),
    cartera (la)

**put (to)** poner

**put in a plaster cast
    (to)** enyesar

**put into (to)** meter

**put on (to)** ponerse

**pyramid** pirámide (la)

## Q

**qualify (to)** calificar

**quarter** cuarto de un dólar (el)

**queen** reina (la)

**question** pregunta (la)

    **ask a ~ (to)** hacer una
        pregunta, preguntar

**to question** preguntar(se)

**quiz** prueba (la)

## R

**race** carrera (la), raza (la) (*physical
    appearance*)

    **car race** carrera de carros (la)

**racket** raqueta (la)

**radio device** radio (el)

**radio station** radio (la)

**radiologist** radiólogo(a) (el/la)

**radiology** radiología (la)

**railroad** ferrocarril (el)

**rain** lluvia (la)

**rain (to)** llover (ue)

**read (to)** leer

**reading** lectura (la)

**ready, smart** listo(a)

**real estate** bienes raíces (los)

    **real estate agency**
        inmobiliaria (la)

    **real estate agent, realtor**
        agente inmobiliario (el/
        la), corredor(a) de bienes
        raíces (el/la)

**reason** razón (la)

**reasonable** razonable

**receive (to)** recibir

**recent** reciente

**receptionist** recepcionista (el/la)

**recipe** receta (la)

**recognition** reconocimiento (el)

    **face ~** reconocimiento de
        rostro (el)

    **voice ~** reconocimiento
        de voz (el)

**recognize (to)** reconocer

**recommend (to)** recomendar (ie)

**recommendation**
    recomendación (la)

**recursive** recursivo(a)

**red** rojo(a)

**reduce (to)** reducir

**refreshment, cold drink
    (*non-alcoholic*)** refresco (el)

**refrigerator** nevera (la),
    refrigerador (el)

**register (to)** registrarse

**relative** pariente (el)

**relax (to)** descansar

**relieve (to)** aliviar

**religious** religioso(a)

**remedy** remedio (el)

**remember (to)** recordar (ue),
    acordarse de

**remote, remotely** remoto(a)

**remove (to)** quitar

**rent, lease** alquiler (el), arriendo (el)

**rent (to)** alquilar, arrendar

**repair (to)** arreglar, reparar

**require (to)** exigir, requerir

**requirement** requisito (el)

**reservation** reservación (la)

**reserve (to)** reservar

**residence** residencia (la)

**residencial complex** conjunto
    residencial (el)

resort  complejo turístico (el), resort (el)

resourceful  ingenioso(a)

responsible  responsable

rest (to)  descansar

return, change  cambio (el), vuelta (la)

reunion  reunión (la)

review (to)  revisar

revision, review  revisión (la)

rice  arroz (el)

rich  rico(a)

right, straight  derecho(a)

    be right (to)  tener (la) razón

right away  enseguida, en seguida

ring  anillo (el), sortija (la)

    wedding ring  allianza

ring, sound (to)  sonar (ue)

risk: at all ~  a todo riesgo

road  carretera (la)

road, way  camino (el), carretera (la)

roast (to)  asar

roasted  asado(a)

robotics  robótica (la)

romantic  romántico(a)

roof  tejado (el)

room  cuarto (el), habitación (la)

    room service  servicio a los cuartos (el)

routine  rutina (la)

ruins  ruinas (las)

run (to), running  correr

    ~ out of (to)  acabarse


S

sad  triste

safe  seguro(a)

    ~ deposit box  caja de seguridad (la)

safety  seguridad (la)

salad  ensalada (la)

salary  salario (el), sueldo (el)

salmon  salmón (el)

salsa  salsa (la)

salt  sal (la)

salty  salado(a)

sandwich  bocadillo (el), sánduche (el), emparedado (el)

Saturday  sábado (el)

sauce  salsa (la)

sausage  salchicha (la)

save (to)  ahorrar

    save the document (in the computer) (to)  guardar el documento

savings  ahorros (los)

    savings account  cuenta de ahorros (la)

say, tell (to)  decir

    say yes/no (to)  decir que sí/no

    say good-bye (to)  despedirse

scare (to)  asustar

schedule  horario (el)

scholarship  beca (la)

school  escuela (la) (elementary); colegio (el) (middle, high school)

schoolmate, fellow student  compañero(a) (el/la)

science  ciencias (las)

scientist  científico(a)

score (to)  anotar, marcar

    score a basket (to)  encestar

sea  mar (el)

    seafood  comida de mar (la), marisco (el)

season, epoch  época (la), estación (la) (*of the year*), temporada (la)

season (food) (to)  condimentar, sazonar

seasoned  condimentado/a

seat  asiento (el)

    seat belt  cinturón de seguridad (el)

sedative  calmante (el)

sedentary  sedentario(a)

see, look at (to)  ver

seem (to)  parecer

self-esteem  autoestima (la)

self-service  autoservicio (el)

sell (to)  vender

seller  vendedor(a) (el/la)

send (to)  enviar, mandar

senses  sentidos (los)

sensor  sensor (el)

separated  separado(a)

September  septiembre

serious  serio(a)

    seriously  en serio

serve, help (to)  servir (i)

service  servicio (el)

several, various  varios(as)

shampoo  champú (el)

sharp (*exact time*)  en punto

shirt  camisa (la)

shopping: to go ~  ir de compras

short  corto(a)

    short, brief  breve

    in short  en fin, por fin

shot  inyección (la)

should  deber

shoulder  hombro (el)

show (to)  mostrar (ue)

shower  ducha (la)

shower (to)  ducharse

shrimp  camarón (el)

sick, ill  enfermo(a)

    get sick (to)  enfermarse

sickness  enfermedad (la)

sidewalk  andén (el)

sight, view vista (la)

sign señal (la), signo (el)

sign (to) firmar

signature firma (la)

silver plata (la), plateado(a) (color)

sing (to) cantar

singer cantante (el/la)

single soltero(a) (person)

    single; simple sencillo(a);

    single (room), one-way
      (ticket) sencillo(a)

sir señor

sister hermana (la)

    fraternal sister melliza (la)

    half-sister media hermana (la)

    stepsister hermanastra (la)

    twin sister gemela (la)

sister-in-law cuñada (la)

sit down (to) sentarse (ie)

skate (to), skating patinar

    ice skating patinaje en el
      hielo (el)

skates patines (los)

skating rink pista de patinaje (la)

ski (to) esquiar

skyscraper rascacielos (el)

sleep (to) dormir (ue)

    fall sleep (to) dormirse

    sleepy: to be ~ tener sueño

slim delgado(a)

slow lento(a)

    slowly despacio

slow down (to) bajar la velocidad

slow payer deudor(a)
    moroso(a) (el/la)

small pequeño(a)

smell (to) oler (hue)

smile (to) sonreír

smoke (to) fumar

sneeze (to) estornudar

snow nieve (la)

snow (to) nevar (ie)

so así que

soap jabón (el)

sober sobrio (a)

soccer fútbol (el)

sociologist sociólogo(a) (el/la)

sociology sociología (la)

sofa sofá (el)

soft suave

some algunos(as)

someone alguien

something algo

sometimes a veces

son hijo (el)

    stepson hijastro (el)

son-in-law yerno (el)

song canción (la)

sound sonido (el)

sound the horn (to) sonar (tocar)
    la bocina, pitar

soup sopa (la)

south sur (el)

space espacio (el)

    coworking space zona
      de trabajo
      compartido (la)

spacious amplio(a)

speak (to) hablar

specialize (to) especializar(se)

speech discurso (el)

speed rapidez (la), velocidad (la)

speedometer velocímetro (el)

spend (to) gastar

spontaneous espontáneo(a)

sports deportes (los)

    sports court cancha (la)

    sports field campo (el)

spouse esposo(a) (el/la)

spring primavera (la)

square plaza (la)

stadium estadio (el)

stainless inoxidable

stairs, staircase escalera (la)

start (to) comenzar (ie),
    empezar (ie)

start, root (to) arrancar

starter arranque (el)

state estado (el)

station; season estación (la)

    bus station estación de
      buses (la)

    train station estación de
      trenes (la)

stay (to) quedarse

    stay away (to) quitarse

    stay in bed (to) guardar cama

steak, fillet filete (el), bisté (el)

steering wheel timón (el),
    volante (el)

still, yet todavía

stocks acciones (las)

    stock market bolsa de
      valores (la)

stomach estómago (el)

stop parada (la), paradero (el)

    stop (sign) stop (el), alto (el);
      señal de pare (la)

    stop (to) dejar, dejar de,
      parar, pararse; stop, detain
      (people) (to) detener

    stop doing something (to) dejar
      de + infinitive

    stopover escala (la)

store tienda (la)

stove estufa (la)

straight derecho(a), recto(a)

straighten up (to) arreglar

street calle (la)

stress estrés (el)

stress (to) estresarse

stressed estresado(a)

stressful estresante

strict, severe estricto(a)

**strong** fuerte

**student** estudiante (el/la)

**studies** estudios (los)

**studio** apartaestudio (el), estudio (el)

**study (to)** estudiar

**suburbs** afueras (las), suburbios (los)

**success** éxito (el)

    **be ~ (to)** tener éxito

**suffer (to)** padecer (c), sufrir

**sugar** azúcar (el/la)

**suit (to)** convenir (ie)

**suitcase** maleta (la)

**summer** verano (el)

**sun** sol (el)

    **sunny: to be ~** hacer sol

**Sunday** domingo (el)

**supper** cena (la)

**surgeon** cirujano/a (el/la)

**surgery** cirugía (la)

**surprise** sorpresa (la)

**surprise (to)** sorprender

**surprised** sorprendido(a)

**surroundings** alrededores (los)

**sweep (to)** barrer

**sweet** dulce

**swim (to)** nadar

**symptom** síntoma (el)

**symptomatic** sintomático(a)

**system** sistema (el)

    **immune system** sistema inmunológico (el)

**syrup** jarabe (el)


**T**

**table** mesa (la)

**tablet** tableta (la)

**tailor** sastre(a) (el/la)

**take, drink (to)** tomar

    **take a seat (to)** sentarse, tomar asiento;

    **take away (to)** quitar; **take care (to)** cuidar, ocuparse;

    **take charge of (to)** encargarse de; **take off (to)** despegar (*plane*), quitarse (*clothes*) **take out (to)** sacar

**talent** talent (el)

**talented** talentoso(a)

**tan (to)** broncearse

**tanned** bronceado(a)

**tank** tanque (el)

**takeoff** despegue (el)

**takeoff (to)** despegar

**tariff, fee** tarifa (la), arancel (el)

**taste, flavor** sabor (el)

**taste like (to)** saber a

**tasty, delicious** sabroso(a)

**tax** impuesto (el)

**taxi** taxi (el)

**taxi driver** taxista (el/la)

**tea** té (el)

    **iced tea** té helado (el)

**teach (to)** enseñar

**teacher** maestro(a), profesor(a) (el/la)

**team** equipo (el)

**technology** tecnología (la)

**teeth** dientes (los)

**telephone** teléfono (el)

    **smartphone** teléfono inteligente (el)

**television** televisión (la), televisor (el) (*device*)

**tell (to)** decir, contar

**temperature** temperatura (la)

**tender, soft** blando(a), tierno(a)

**tennis** tenis (el)

**tennis player** tenista (el/la)

**terminal** terminal (el)

**terrace** terraza (la)

**terrain** terreno (el)

**terrible** terrible

**terrific** estupendo(a)

**thanks** gracias (las)

**thank (to)** agradecer

**thankful** agradecido(a)

**that** que, ese (*m.*), esa (*f.*)

**theme** tema (el)

**then** entonces, luego

**theology** teología (la)

**there, over there** allí, ahí, allá

    **up ~** arriba

**thin, skinny** delgado(a), flaco(a)

**think (to)** pensar (ie), creer

**third** tercero(a)

**thirst** sed (la)

    **thirsty: to be ~** tener sed

**this** este (*m.*), esta (*f.*)

**throat** garganta (la)

    **sore throat** dolor de garganta (el)

**throw (to)** lanzar

**Thursday** jueves (el)

**ticket** billete (el), pasaje (el), boleto (el)

    **one-way ticket** ida (la);

    **round-trip** ida y vuelta (la);

    **ticket agent, clerk** taquillero(a) (el/la); **ticket window** taquilla (la)

**time** tiempo (el), hora (la)

    **time** (*in a series*) *vez* (la);

    **ahead of time** con anticipación; **on time** a tiempo

**timeshare** tiempo compartido (el)

**Tik ToK** Tik Tok (el)

**tip, gratuity** propina (la)

tire llanta (la), neumático (el)

    spare tire llanta de respuesto (la)

tired cansado(a)

    get ~ (to) cansarse

to, in order to; for para

today hoy

toe dedo del pie (el)

    toenails uñas de los pies (las)

toilet inodoro (el)

toll peaje (el)

tomato tomate (el)

tomorrow mañana

    see you ~ hasta mañana

tongue lengua (la)

tonight esta noche

too también

tooth diente (el)

    toothbrush cepillo de dientes (el)

    toothpaste crema dental (la)

touch tacto (el) (*sense*)

touch (to) tocar

tour recorrido (el), tour (el)

tour (to) recorrer

tourism turismo (el)

tourist turista (el/la)

tourist turístico(a)

tournament torneo (el)

towel toalla (la)

town pueblo (el)

townhome casa (la)

trademark marca (la)

traffic tráfico (el)

    traffic light semáforo (el)

    traffic signs señales de tráfico (las)

train tren (el)

train (to) entrenar

trainer entrenador(a) (el/la)

training entrenamiento (el)

transaction transacción (la)

transfer (to) transferir

    money transfer transferencia de dinero (la)

translate (to) traducir

translator traductor(a) (el/la)

transmit (to) transmitir

travel, trip viaje (el)

travel (to) viajar

    travel agency agencia de viajes (la)

traveler viajero(a) (el/la)

treatment tratamiento (el)

tree árbol (el)

truck camioneta (la), camión (el)

    semi-truck camión articulado (el), tractomula (la)

trunk baúl (el), cajuela (la), maletero (el)

truth verdad (la)

try to (to) tratar de

Tuesday martes (el)

tuna atún (el)

turkey pavo (el)

turn, bend (to) doblar

    turn (+ adjective) (to) ponerse (+ adjective); to

    turn down the volume bajar el volume; to

    turn off apagar

turn (to) girar, voltear

    turn signals direccionales (las)

twist, sprain (to) torcer (ue)

twisted, bent torcido(a)

two dos

typical típico(a)

U

ugly feo(a)

ulcer úlcera (la)

umbrella paraguas (el), sombrilla (la)

unaware, unconscious inconsciente

uncertain incierto(a)

uncle tío (el)

unconditional incondicional

under bajo

underline (to) subrayar

undershirt camiseta (la)

understand (to) comprender, entender (ie)

understanding entendimiento (el), comprensión (la)

undo, melt (to) deshacer

unexpected imprevisto(a)

unhappy descontento(a)

uniform uniforme (el)

unique único(a)

unit unidad (la)

universal universal

universe universo (el)

university, college universidad (la)

unlucky: to be ~ tener mala suerte

unpack the suitcase (to) deshacer la maleta

unpleasant (*people*) antipático(a)

until, to hasta

up there arriba

urgent urgente

use (to) usar

used usado(a)

useful útil

useless inútil

V

vacation vacaciones (las)

be on vacation (to) estar de vacaciones

vaccine vacuna (la)

vacuum cleaner aspiradora (la)

valuable valioso(a)

value, stock valor (el)

van camioneta (la)

variety variedad (la)

various varios(as)

vegetable verdura (la), vegetal (el)

veterinarian veterinario(a) (el/la)

veterinary veterinaria (la)

victorious victorioso(a)

video video (el)

video conference video conferencia (la)

videogames videojuegos (los)

view vista (la)

viewpoint mirador (el)

vinegar vinagre (el)

virtual assistant asistente virtual (el/la)

visa visa (la)

visit (to) visitar

vitamin vitamina (la)

W

waist cintura (la)

wait on (to) atender (ie)

waiter, waitress camarero(a) (el/la), mesero(a) (el/la)

wake up (to) despertarse

walk (to), walking andar, caminar

wall pared (la)

wallet, purse billetera (la), cartera (la)

digital wallet billetera digital (la)

want, wish (to) desear

warm (to) calentar

warn, inform (to) avisar

warning aviso (el)

tornado warning aviso de tornado (el)

wash (to) lavar

washing machine lavadora (la)

waste time (to) perder el tiempo

watch reloj (el)

watch (to) mirar

watch over (to) vigilar

water agua (*f.*) (el)

mineral water agua mineral (el)

wave ola (la)

way camino (el), forma (la)

way: by the ~ a proposito; no ~! ¡ni modo!

weak débil

wealthy adinerado/a

weather clima (el), tiempo (el)

weather: what's the ~? ¿qué tiempo hace?

wedding boda (la), matrimonio (el)

Wednesday miércoles (el)

week semana (la)

weekly seminal

weight peso (el)

weights pesas (las)

weightlifting levantamiento de pesas (el)

welcome bienvenida (la)

welcome (to) dar la bienvenida

well-being bienestar (el)

wheel rueda (la)

while rato (el)

white blanco(a)

why por qué

wide ancho(a)

widow viuda (la)

widower viudo (el)

wife esposa (la)

Wifi Wifi (el)

win, earn (to) ganar

wind viento (el)

windy: to be ~ hacer viento

window ventana (la)

small window ventanilla (la)

windshield parabrisas (el)

windshield wiper limpiaparabrisas (el)

wine vino (el)

red wine vino tinto

winter invierno (el)

wish, want (to) querer (ie)

withdraw (to) retirar, sacar

withdrawal retiro (el)

without sin

woman mujer (la)

wonder (to) preguntarse

wool lana (la)

word palabra (la)

work (to) funcionar, trabajar

world mundo (el)

world heritage site patrimonio histórico de la humanidad (el)

worn-out gastado(a)

worry (to) preocuparse
worried preocupado(a)
   be ~ (to) estar preocupado(a)
worth: to be ~ valer
worthwhile: to be ~ valer la pena
wrist, doll muñeca (la)
write (to) escribir
writer escritor(a) (el/la)

X

X-ray radiografía (la)

Y

year año (el)
   last year año passado (el)
yearly anual

yellow amarillo(a)
yesterday ayer
young joven
your tu, tus

Z

Zoom Zoom (el)
Zucchini, courgette calabacín (el)

Printed and bound by CPI Group (UK) Ltd, Croydon, CR0 4YY

07/12/2025

14785991-0003